The REAL DEAL

MY LIFE in BUSINESS and PHILANTHROPY

SANDY WEILL

and Judah S. Kraushaar

WARNER
BUSINESS
BOOKS™

NEW YORK   BOSTON

Warner Business Books

Hachette Book Group USA
1271 Avenue of the Americas
New York, NY 10020

Visit our Web site at www.HachetteBookGroupUSA.com.

Warner Business Books is an imprint of Warner Books, Inc.
Warner Business Books is a trademark of Time Warner Inc. or an affiliated company.
Used under license by Hachette Book Group USA, which is not affiliated with
Time Warner Inc.

Printed in the United States of America

First Edition: October 2006

10   9   8   7   6   5   4   3   2   1

Library of Congress Cataloging-in-Publication Data
Weill, Sandy.
   The real deal : my life in business and philanthropy / Sandy Weill and
Judah S. Kraushaar.—1st ed.
          p.   cm.
      Includes index.
      "Memoir of American businessman and financial dealmaker Sanford I.
   Weill, chronicling his forty-year career from his days at American Express
   to his creation and chairmanship of Citigroup"—Provided by the publisher.
      ISBN-13: 978-0-446-57814-1
      ISBN-10: 0-446-57814-2
      1. Weill, Sandy.   2. Bankers—United States—Biography.   3. Citigroup
   (Firm)—Biography. 4. Financial services industry—United States.
   I. Kraushaar, Judah S. II. Title.

   HG2463 .W45 .W45   2006
   332.1092—dc22

                                                          2006008612

Book design by SDDesigns, Inc.

To Joanie—
our fifty-one years together have been quite a trip.
Without you there never would have been a book.
I look forward to many more chapters together.

To Arthur Zankel—
you are a great friend and were always there to help.
You are never far away and always in my thoughts.

Contents

A Collaborator's Story

first saw Sandy Weill on a momentous day in April 1998 when I worked as the lead financial services analyst for Merrill Lynch. Led by Weill, Travelers Corporation had just announced its $150 billion mega-merger with Citicorp. The deal represented the biggest combination in U.S. corporate history at that time and promised to create a global powerhouse with an unparalleled array of products and distribution. According to the buzz, Sandy Weill had dreamed up the deal, and I felt awed that one person could have conceived of something so bold and have had the guts to reshape an entire industry overnight.

Attending the historic meeting for analysts and investors where Weill and his new partner from Citicorp, John Reed, would explain the merger, I observed with interest the scene unfolding around me in the large auditorium. There were throngs of cameras in the back of the room. Small groups of journalists, investors, and analysts spoke excitedly in the aisles among themselves. Periodically, some of the attendees would interact with management representatives who surely were out in the crowd to talk up the merger. I had attended plenty of merger announcements, but none rivaled the drama and sense of importance evoked by the new Citigroup.

Finally, the lights dimmed and, out from the shadows, Sandy Weill and John Reed appeared entering stage left and taking seats beside one another at a rectangular table. I looked closely at Sandy Weill, who all at once seemed shorter of stature and more rotund, but also friendlier, than I had expected. The reality didn't exactly fit his reputation as a shrewd builder of companies and steward of shareholder value. Here was a man whose press clippings could fill a small library, yet Weill exuded an overwhelming youthfulness as he gushed about the merits of his merger coup. All the while, I kept thinking that before me was a man who had incredible longevity in an industry famous for eating its young. I wanted to know more. I wanted to have the chance to engage him and figure out what made him tick. I wanted to decide for myself whether Weill was really as good as his myriad of admirers in the investment community had argued over the years.

A month later, I met Sandy in person for the first time. The venue was a lunch hosted by Merrill Lynch at the Metropolitan Club in Chicago's Sears Tower. The meeting had been arranged months earlier by my research colleague who had covered Travelers before the merger. Wall Street analysts frequently arranged sessions like this one as a means of taking care of their best investor clients. A meeting with a top CEO typically could influence millions of dollars in trading-related income to the sponsoring firm.

The intimate group of investors eagerly awaited Sandy's arrival, and I remember the group parting deferentially when Weill strode into the room. There was plenty of adulation in the air even as I thought to myself cynically that no one can be *that good* and that the reputation was probably more myth than reality. For me, a healthy skepticism was something taught to me at an early age and a quality I always had sought to protect in my work as an analyst.

Yet all cynicism aside, I, too, was excited to meet Sandy in this more personal setting and see for myself whether he was as impressive as so many others had claimed. After his trademark thrust of the hand and declaration "Hi, I'm Sandy Weill," we chatted briefly about the merger, my plans to follow Citigroup's stock, and my eagerness to set up a private meeting. We then sat down, and the presentation commenced. Sandy was relaxed and spoke off the cuff in a surprisingly broad manner before turning the microphone over to his chief financial officer to fill in the details. I was struck by Sandy's informality and focus on the big picture. I'd learn only later that he loathed making formal presentations and usually left it to his lieutenants to communicate financial details.

I worked hard that spring to get to know Weill, his management team, and the Citigroup behemoth. In July, I published an extensive report on the new company entitled "A New Model for the Millennium" and had the distinction to be the first analyst out of the gate with a detailed analysis. The report carefully weighed Citigroup's pluses and minuses. I mused about the challenge of managing such a large company, the chance for culture clashes between investment and commercial bankers, and the need to integrate risk controls. Nevertheless, the huge opportunities for cost efficiencies and new revenues steered me to a positive overall conclusion. When the report hit their desks, most of my clients applauded my new buy recommendation.

As part of my initial research, I had a couple of opportunities to visit one-on-one with Sandy. In both cases, I was taken aback by his apparent aloofness and what seemed to me a detachment from the specific issues facing the company. One of these sessions directly followed a meeting I had with Citigroup's president-to-be, Jamie Dimon, who was widely known as Sandy's protégé. In the session with Dimon, I heard one version of events within the company. Weill, on the other hand, kept asking defensively, "Who told you that?" while going on to say something almost completely contradictory. Little did I realize that I was witnessing firsthand the endgame in the disintegration of their fifteen-year relationship (Sandy later confessed that Dimon was keeping him out of the loop on information during this period, an exclusion which infuriated him).

In November 1999, Sandy agreed for me to host him in a series of investor meetings in the Midwest. This trip was important for my career, as I was determined to be the dominant analyst—"the ax" in Wall Street parlance—in Citigroup's stock. Sponsoring Sandy Weill before major investors represented an outstanding opportunity to get to know him better and to gain prestige in my clients' eyes. For these two days of meetings, I was invited to fly with Sandy. It was a great chance to probe Weill's thought process, but it also meant a lot of time together and I felt an obligation to deepen my credibility with him.

On balance, the trip proved successful; it allowed me to witness Sandy's intensity firsthand and to see how he could become engaged in details. Still, I couldn't help but notice that Sandy would tighten up when I would ask about cultural differences between the old Citicorp and Travelers organizations. He also spoke surprisingly little about his relationship with John Reed. Once again, I had stumbled unwittingly onto the brewing problems in an important partnership. Three months after this trip, in February 2000, Citigroup's directors held a decisive meeting in which it was announced that Sandy would become sole chairman and CEO while John Reed would retire. A year later, Sandy confided that most of his time spent as Reed's partner had been among the worst of his life and that he felt relief to have resolved his difficult issues with Reed.

Sandy nearly always solicited my views in these meetings and others which followed. This was a disarming practice; it intrigued me that someone with his perspective and accomplishments would be interested in what I had to say. I saw Sandy take the same approach with investors, and it struck me that he was always on the prowl for how he could make his business better. It seemed that Sandy would listen to anyone if he thought the advice might help.

Over the first five years of Citigroup's existence, I believe I came to understand Citigroup better than any other analyst on Wall Street. I had accomplished my aim of being the ax in the stock. Even as I had gotten to know Sandy Weill over this period, I still felt I had seen only a small portion of what lay behind his accomplishments, and I barely grasped the full history of this man's life. In short, Sandy Weill remained for me a fascinating but enigmatic success story.

In early 2003, I decided to retire from Merrill Lynch. I was ready for a professional change and was eager to find a new vocation that would challenge my creative and entrepreneurial instincts. Ironically, the restructuring of Wall Street research—a change heavily influenced by Citigroup's Salomon Smith Barney unit and its alleged conflicts of interest—played a role in my decision to hang up my spurs as an analyst. The job suddenly had narrowed uncomfortably and became too bureaucratic for my taste.

Yet the end of this stage of my career did not represent the final chapter in my association with Sandy Weill. To the contrary, upon learning of my pending departure from the business and my plans to write a book, Sandy approached me to collaborate with him on his autobiography (a very different project than what I had been planning). At first, I expressed appreciation for his interest but steadfastly argued that he would be better served by a professional business writer. However, in his inimitable way, Sandy refused to take no for an answer. He insisted that only a successful analyst who understood the business could challenge and draw him out in the manner he wanted.

After his fifth entreaty, I decided to take a serious look at working on a book together. I reviewed years' worth of newspaper and magazine articles and spent considerable time interviewing Sandy on his motivation for wishing to write a book and exploring whether he was prepared to open up and confront honestly all his important life experiences and relationships. I probed in detail his relationships with executives such as Jamie Dimon, Peter Cohen, and John Reed. I asked him tough questions regarding his feelings about New York attorney general Eliot Spitzer, including whether he'd candidly give his side of the story on the regulatory issues that followed the great bull market of the 1990s. We reviewed his business triumphs, but I pushed harder to learn about his mistakes.

The more I read and the more we spoke, I realized that Sandy Weill possessed an intensely powerful life story and that he was committed to opening up and would not whitewash the challenges and setbacks he faced over his career. He promised that I'd have free rein to interview anyone I wished including those who might speak critically. Throughout our conversations, he consistently portrayed business in intensely personal terms and demonstrated his emotional nature. He spoke in an intimate and plainspoken way on the history of the financial services business, his major business challenges and successes, and his insights into relationships with important business and world leaders. In telling his life's story, Sandy couldn't have invented a more compelling narrative.

Any student of business would be fascinated with Weill's life. In my opinion, he has been the single most important figure in the financial services industry over the past half century. Throughout his long career, he consistently stayed ahead of the curve and built two leading companies essentially from scratch. As important, he pursued more transformational acquisitions, built more shareholder value, and enjoyed more respect from his peers than any other contemporary. Indeed, his success transcended financial services—it's hard to think of many other businesspeople who built so much shareholder value over such a long span of time. Anyone interested in learning about business history and what makes for managerial success should view Sandy Weill's life story as a rich case study.

Sandy Weill's story is compelling for a variety of reasons. His tale intersects completely with a long period of exceptional dynamism in financial services, a history he in large measure helped shape. His story began in an age when partnerships on Wall Street were dominant and extended through the rise of the modern corporate form of ownership; it spanned vastly different eras in regulation and in the appetite for investors to take risk; it mirrored the rise and empowerment of the individual in making financial decisions; and it followed closely the globalization of an entire industry.

His account also addresses gaps and misperceptions in the public record. For instance, Sandy tells of the mergers that almost happened, how he worked with figures who went on to illustrious careers of their own in public life, what really happened between him and various regulators after the market crash in 2002, and what was behind the disintegration in the industry's more storied mentor-protégé relationships, those between himself and Jamie Dimon and Peter Cohen.

Sandy Weill also has been the consummate entrepreneur. Starting with $30,000 of borrowed capital in 1960, Sandy turned himself into a billionaire. He built two companies from scratch and showed prowess in a variety of environments and businesses. He also proved his tenacity in the face of exceptional reversals, be it with a misguided sale of his company to American Express, an unanticipated set of problems with his partner, John Reed, after forming Citigroup, or his 2002 run-in with regulators, who at times, it seemed to outsiders, were intent on destroying his career. His retirement announcement conveyed a determination, unusual for a self-made man, to hand off his business to a team that would stick together and sustain success.

There also are important lessons one can learn from Weill's experience. His success at growing via acquisition has been legendary, while his formula for managing a large organization successfully through periods of change demands closer study. Sandy mastered the art of seeing the big picture but also staying focused on the details. In addition, he and his wife, Joan, have demonstrated over many years a commitment to philanthropy in causes tied together by a focus on education, the arts, and health care. The manner in which Weill has integrated his business skills with his philanthropic work offers an excellent lesson for us all.

Finally, for those interested in studying management techniques, his career includes a series of paradoxes. For example, Weill for the most part engendered great loyalty among his managers, yet a few of his closest relationships deteriorated to the point where the back-and-forth squabbling at times resembled an intense family feud. He also drove his companies relentlessly forward, but he had a tendency to overreach on occasion and created his own set of issues as a result. For instance, in teaming up with American Express in 1981, he underestimated the intensely political environment of that organization. Similarly, Weill had more experience and perspective in the securities business than almost anyone, yet market insight failed him during the epic bull market of the late 1990s when he might have reined in some of the practices which later came to haunt Citigroup after the market crashed. He amassed hundreds, if not thousands, of business relationships over his career, but he still showed himself given to naïveté on occasion in dealing with people.

Weill's approach to risk management seems a study in contrasts. Over the years, he studiously avoided the risk that comes with excessive balance sheet leverage but still pursued with ease one acquisition after another in which integration issues easily could have threatened. Late in his career, too, he had to deal with a harsh regulatory climate which focused him on the critical importance of managing reputation risk. How Weill came to terms with these issues makes for compelling reading.

Ultimately, Sandy Weill's successes and shortcomings take on a typically human dimension. Throughout his career, he was adept at seeing industry trends well before they became apparent to competitors and acting boldly on those insights. His drive to succeed, meanwhile, often reflected a focus on outdoing others, and he typically enjoyed the trappings of wealth and prestige. On occasion, he probably could have been accused of giving in to arrogance, and he certainly made mistakes. But, through it all, Sandy Weill still comes across as a kid from Brooklyn, filled with passion, who can't believe his good fortune. In the pages that follow, Sandy tells all, intimately recounting the highs and lows of his career, debunking myths, and offering a variety of life lessons. I hope the reader will enjoy it all.

Judah S. Kraushaar
April 2006

Prologue

I wasn't sure what to expect as I arrived at my seventieth birthday party. The development director at Carnegie Hall, along with my wife, Joanie, had planned the March 2003 celebration to raise money for a new music education endowment I had encouraged as Carnegie Hall's chairman. Normally, I would have been excited about a gala in my honor. Recent events, though, weighed on me, and I hadn't felt like myself in months. The bears had come out on Wall Street at the start of the new millennium, and the mood across the financial industry had been ugly for the past three years.

As the chairman and CEO of Citigroup—the largest financial institution in the world—I had been thrown into the ensuing maelstrom by those seeking scapegoats for the losses experienced by countless investors. Citigroup's past standards had been no worse than average, yet, sadly, the attention of investors, regulators, and the press managed to stick on our company. For several months during 2002, regulators questioned our company's practices and made my life extraordinarily difficult.

At its worst, I felt as though Citigroup and I were being tried in the press and worried that the facts would be lost upon the regulators. I had seen a lot over the years, but those weeks represented some of the worst of my career.

Fortunately, the investigation ran its course with Citigroup and the other major Wall Street firms settling the regulatory issues at the end of 2002. I wasn't charged with any wrongdoing, and I insisted that Citigroup lead the industry in implementing reforms. My colleagues and I got back to business. Still, the crisis had taken its toll. The weeks of seeing my reputation—my most important asset—dragged through the mud wore me down and hurt deeply.

In the period leading up to my birthday, the gloom had lifted a bit; however, I couldn't help but worry whether my reputation and legacy had been permanently scarred. That's why I was nervous about my party at Carnegie Hall and also why it proved so cathartic. Striding into Carnegie Hall's great auditorium that evening, I almost didn't recognize the place. The staff had arranged for a makeshift floor to cover the seats and allow the stage to extend out over the entire auditorium. Countless tables adorned with red tablecloths and flowers beckoned from the enlarged stage while warmly glowing candles offset the dimmed chandelier.

The hundred-year-old edifice, whose walls had played host to countless great maestros, never looked better, and I couldn't help but reflect for a moment on how Carnegie Hall had revitalized itself over the dozen years in which I had served as its chairman. More poignantly, I experienced a rush as I realized that a massive crowd of seven hundred guests had turned out in my honor.

And these were no ordinary guests. I saw that my life would flash before me that evening as family and old friends joined past and present business colleagues, public officials, and even a few competitors to celebrate with me. Walter Cronkite emceed the evening, and I loved it as he introduced one friend after another who toasted my professional accomplishments and my contributions to Carnegie Hall and other philanthropies. Prominent state and local leaders took to the stage including Governor George Pataki, Senator Charles Schumer, and Mayor Michael Bloomberg. Even former President Bill Clinton wished me well.

I've always enjoyed a good party, but that birthday celebration, coming after the stress and uncertainty that had accompanied the regulatory investigation, buoyed my mood like none other. The worries over what people thought of me dissipated. That so many prominent and respected friends didn't think twice about coming out in my honor moved me deeply. Suddenly, I recognized that my reputation as an honest, successful, and civic-minded business leader had survived after all. What's more, Carnegie Hall raised $60 million that evening, a record for a single philanthropic event.

I couldn't help but reflect during that fantastic evening on how far I had come. In 1960, at age twenty-seven, I had formed a securities broker dealer on a shoestring budget along with three partners. During the 1970s, our company went public, overcame extraordinarily difficult industry conditions, and—then under my leadership—pursued a string of daring acquisitions which transformed us into Shearson Loeb Rhoades, one of the country's leading securities firms.

We sold our company to American Express in 1981 for $1 billion, and I became president of Amex for a time. That experience, however, proved disillusioning, and I resigned after four years with the company. A brief "midlife crisis" ensued in which I was out of work for a year, but in 1986, I talked my way into becoming CEO of a troubled small finance company known as Commercial Credit and quickly took it public, restoring its balance sheet integrity in the process. From that modest second beginning, and with the help of many able colleagues, I strove once more to create a truly great company.

Over the following seventeen years, we turned that little consumer credit company into Citigroup, the premier financial institution in the world with a market value exceeding $200 billion.

The business accomplishments were many, but on the night of my party, I felt equally good about how I had contributed to the not-for-profit world. In addition to helping rejuvenate Carnegie Hall, I founded the National Academy Foundation, a progressive force in secondary education, and became chairman of the Weill Cornell Medical College. Gazing at Carnegie Hall's majestic surroundings that evening, I marveled how I had gone from a mediocre bass drummer in my high school marching band to the chairmanship of Carnegie Hall, one of the world's great music institutions.

Where else but in America?

More than helping me overcome my reputation-related fears, my birthday spurred me to decide upon my retirement and succession, two of the most important decisions I had ever made. I first had begun to consider retiring in 2001, three years following the merger which created Citigroup. At that time, investors were beginning to zero in on Citigroup's awesome potential and were avidly snapping up its shares.

I loved watching our surging stock price and interpreted the gains as a vote of confidence in my leadership. I understood that creating Citigroup amounted to the deal of a lifetime. It represented the culmination of nearly fifty years of hard work and personal sacrifice. The company resembled no other financial institution in the world with its global reach, extensive products, and diversified distribution capabilities. We had broken every mold in conceiving this great company. Knocking off one integration challenge after another, I realized that there might be no better time to retire, since leaving on a high note meant a great deal to me. Nonetheless, any thought of retiring had to be set aside as the regulatory events soon took center stage.

Fortunately, our regulatory travails didn't last forever, and Citigroup's earnings came through the bear market remarkably well—for instance, even with unusual charges, earnings grew 8 percent during 2002. The resilient earnings countered the hits to our firm's reputation, and the firm's growth improved sharply entering 2003. Between the afterglow from my seventieth birthday party and the improving earnings prospects, I soon decided that I once more faced the opportunity to go out as a winner. That spring, I found myself thinking increasingly about spending more time with Joanie and the rest of my family, especially my grandchildren. I couldn't remember the last time I had taken a real vacation. I always looked for commonsense answers in life, and logic suggested it was time to change my priorities.

I announced my retirement four months after my birthday in July 2003. The decision caught my colleagues off guard, but I knew the timing was right. We had put our regulatory house in order, and Citigroup's earnings were on their way to their third consecutive quarterly record. I moved fast to name my succession team and took pains to avoid the sort of damaging competition experienced by so many companies when CEOs telegraph their retirement plans far in advance. In making Chuck Prince CEO, I tapped a colleague with whom I had worked for years and trusted.

Stepping down, I felt the wistfulness of giving up the prestige to which I had grown accustomed, and I looked upon the idea of a slower lifestyle with a healthy dose of nervousness. Still, I felt good about my legacy. The businesses that I had run had faced all sorts of challenges but still thrived over five decades of remarkable change for the financial services industry. I managed to stay one step ahead of the industry's evolution, and more than once, I played the key role in instigating changes of my own.

I'm also proud that I had the opportunity to prove my business skill two times over, first with Shearson Loeb Rhoades and then with Citigroup. I've seen many competitors come and go over the years, but my company always managed to survive and prosper. I'm thrilled how Citigroup and its predecessor companies under my leadership outperformed other blue chip companies like General Electric, American International Group (AIG), and even Warren Buffett's Berkshire Hathaway.*

How did this success and shareholder value creation come about? Some might contend I enjoyed more than my fair share of luck, and that certainly would be true. But, over the years, I adhered to a number of disciplines that contributed immeasurably to my success. This book brings these business lessons alive by recounting the challenges and opportunities I faced over my career. In brief, here's my list of ten lessons for leadership and success in business:

---

*From the initial public offering of Commercial Credit in 1986 to the date of my retirement as CEO in October 2003, Citigroup's share price grew 2,644 percent. In contrast, over the same period, Berkshire Hathaway appreciated 2,583 percent; AIG advanced 1,081 percent; and GE rose 813 percent. The performance of all of these companies far exceeded that of the S&P 500 Index, which grew 331 percent over the period, but Citigroup outshone them all.

1. **Win when others lose.** From my early working years, I equated change with opportunity and wanted my company to be flexible and resilient during times of industry stress. It's good to be contrarian. A strong balance sheet and highly efficient operations are the keys to taking advantage of adverse industry cycles. If a company can't keep growing, it will atrophy or die. Thinking that way encourages decisive action, even when times are tough.

To illustrate, my first company emerged from obscurity and grew to become an industry leader over a short four-year period between 1970 and 1974. Those years proved some of the toughest on record for the securities business owing to operational difficulties, the uncertainty that accompanied the Watergate crisis, and the worst recession in decades.

Yet, we were prepared while many of our competitors had entered the new decade fat and happy in the wake of a bull market that had run through much of the 1960s. Sensing the good times would not last forever, we had been among the first firms to surrender our partnership in favor of a public ownership model, a move that gave us a far more stable financial structure and better access to capital. We also assembled a first-class back office with efficient systems and excess processing capacity.

These investments paid off as one competitor after another was overwhelmed by a shortage of capital and processing-related difficulties in the early 1970s. Our first large deal, the acquisition of the old-line firm Hayden Stone, gave us name recognition and transformed our company into a national player overnight. We then speedily moved on two other large acquisitions which further quadrupled our size in only two years. We used competitors' distress to our advantage and made a name for ourselves in the process.

I learned a great deal from these early acquisitions, especially the value of a conservative balance sheet, flexibility, and strong operations. These lessons later gave me the fortitude to merge with countless companies including icons like Travelers and Citicorp.

2. **Learn together and fight together.** As our company grew during the 1970s, I learned the importance of building a team-oriented culture. Awarding stock to employees and insisting on retention of that ownership interest proved a valuable technique for bringing executives together and fostering cooperation. I also insisted upon an informal decision-making style, which encouraged my team to raise issues in a forthright and often intensely passionate manner.

Over time, my colleagues and I perfected a number of management disciplines. We implemented the Capital Accumulation Plan and "blood oath" which forced equity ownership deep into our employee base and required our top executives to hold most of their stock until retirement. The plan discouraged the sort of short-term thinking that afflicts many companies.

We also encouraged spousal participation in off-site meetings, reasoning that it's critical for spouses to understand the demands placed on their working partners and to offer support at home. We built a culture where executives would own issues that they surfaced and take accountability for problem solving. Similarly, I pushed for consistent operating and financial results. Some might contend that too much focus on each quarter's results could lead to short-term thinking, but I felt good executives could manage that risk and that it represented a powerful discipline.

The disillusioning sale of my company to American Express in 1981 showed me a very different management culture that suffered deeply from an absence of teamwork. I misgauged Amex's CEO, Jim Robinson, and unfortunately learned too late that I had joined with someone who seemed incapable of making tough decisions. Instead, Jim allowed strong-willed executives too much autonomy and condoned instances where personal fiefdoms were allowed to undercut the corporation. I learned a number of valuable lessons in the few years I spent there, but the insights into the pitfalls of bureaucracy and corporate infighting were among the most valuable.

3. **Let your insecurities work for you.** I always worried about my business and never felt I could ease up on thinking about potential risks. Indeed, I had many sleepless nights, some of which I even spent at the office. My team understood the special importance I placed on surfacing problems early. Certain principles helped me steer the right course. I've long prized a diverse business mix and a reliable base of core earnings that enables a company to selectively layer on higher risk/higher return activities. I also limited the risk to our company's balance sheet and preferred to take operational risk rather than assume too much financial leverage. Having proved our operational execution skills early gave us the fortitude to aggressively pursue acquisitions. Never betting the balance sheet, we could live with the consequences of an occasional operational mistake. Moreover, I routinely emphasized driving down our costs, knowing that efficient companies enjoy more staying power during industry downturns.

In 1993, our company undertook two high-profile acquisitions in short order when we acquired Travelers Insurance and bought Shearson back from American Express. Overnight, these transactions made our company a major force in the insurance, retail brokerage, and asset management businesses. Under prior management, these companies had run afoul of the risk management principles I espoused: They each allowed large credit-related issues to fester; they suffered from inadequate capital; and they lost control of their costs. In contrast, our company's financial and managerial strengths allowed us to aggressively go after both nearly simultaneously. Once we took over each firm, we moved quickly to extract the tremendous value inherent in each franchise.

4. **The past is not perfect—let it go.** I've learned, sometimes the hard way, that it's a big mistake to take too many things for granted in business. Sometimes executives need to completely reassess the environment in order to protect their company. When faced with an external disruption, it's often critical not to get stuck in a rut defending past practices. Resistance to change can easily undermine one's reputation. The intense bear market of 2000–2002 and its aftermath etched in my brain this lesson once and for all. For many years leading up to that market break, competitive pressures encouraged a gradual loosening in acceptable industry practices. The shifts came slowly enough that it was easy to miss the industry's growing vulnerability to a regulatory backlash.

   The bear market finally provoked that change in the regulatory climate, and the rules facing financial firms changed nearly overnight. That Citigroup and I personally both got caught up in the difficult regulatory investigations which followed caused enormous stress and reputation damage. Even so, I decided relatively early on that it would be folly for our company to resist the regulators and instead elected to dramatically overhaul Citigroup's practices and get out in front of the sweeping changes required of the industry. I learned from this experience that managing reputation risk is every bit as important as dealing with other more conventional business risks.

5. **There's nothing wrong with brand envy.** Companies need to look constantly for ways to improve how they meet the needs of their customers. Over most of my career, I've pursued selling more products to existing customers and ensuring a low enough cost structure so that our company would enjoy a price advantage over its competitors. Acquisitions

certainly helped us gain an efficiency edge, but I typically spent much of my time thinking about what deals might get us to a new level in the minds of our customers. Indeed, I've had a penchant for buying companies with top-quality brands and rarely minded adopting a more prestigious name for our company. Our corporate identity changed many times over the years as we "rented" one moniker after another before latching on to the next superior brand.

In the 1970s, this meant we went from being known as CBWL to Hayden Stone to Shearson Hayden Stone to Shearson Loeb Rhoades. Later, what began as Commercial Credit became Primerica and Travelers before we got to Citigroup. Maybe I suffer from a subconscious need to buy the best labels, but my accumulation of brands over the years opened doors for our professionals, served our clients better, and built a more powerful enterprise.

6. **Gut instincts are made; they're not inborn.** Some observers have suggested that I've managed with a highly intuitive, almost opportunistic, style over the course of my career. That may be true; I was never a believer in grand strategic schemes. But it's a mistake to conclude that I approached decisions without a clear and reasoned plan.

Leaders who amass data, process information efficiently, and have the guts to move quickly gain competitive advantage. I'm not sure it's possible to teach good intuition, but constantly seeking information and insight is vital. Over the years, I relentlessly read, sought the advice of employees, and networked with other leaders in the public and private sectors. My informal decision-making approach allowed my colleagues and me to act quickly when we saw opportunities, often as our competitors dithered.

I also have to give credit to Joanie. My wife never interfered with how I ran the company, but she provided a reassuring sounding board for big decisions. I'd often get squeamish just prior to making an important commitment, and her eleventh-hour feedback typically calmed my nerves. Were it not for her reassurance, I might have gotten cold feet on many deals, including my most important one, the creation of Citigroup.

7. **Be brave but vulnerable.** I've sweated more mergers and other important decisions than I'd care to admit, but having a sense of vulnerability helped tremendously in successfully executing decisions. I'd always encourage my colleagues to shoot holes in our assumptions and discuss issues intensively. Having the conviction on an idea and the buy-in of my management team ensured that my nervousness would push us forward rather than become a source of paralysis. I wanted us to shine and not end up as Humpty Dumpty. It all goes back to developing strong self-confidence, a capable team, and good business instincts.

8. **Losing can be a good thing.** I've had plenty of failed merger negotiations and have made my share of mistakes over the years, but there's one thing I learned early: Don't dwell on defeat. Usually, a better deal has a way of coming along. In 1997, I negotiated extensively for our company to merge with J. P. Morgan. At the time, I was getting increasingly nervous over our firm's failure to globalize, and I relished the idea of tapping into J. P. Morgan's international franchise and its preeminent brand. However, the talks foundered when the company's chairman insisted on an unreasonable management structure. I felt deeply disappointed by our inability to conclude a deal, yet less than a year from the end of those talks, we bought Salomon Brothers and created Citigroup via our merger with Citicorp.

   We ended up with a global powerhouse that far exceeded anything we might have hoped for had we combined with J. P. Morgan.

9. **Be a pragmatic dreamer.** My wife has labeled me a pragmatic dreamer because I looked at the big picture and aimed to build a great and lasting company, recognizing all the

while that success comes one step at a time. Sometimes, it took time for investors to appreciate what we were building, yet I always worked hard for our shareholders. For instance, it took nearly seven years after we took our company public in 1971 for our share price to match the original offering value. In those years, a tough economy was our nemesis. When market conditions improved, our market value surged and made our investors happy. Similarly, after we bought Primerica, our stock price languished for a time as investors were unsure whether we could turn around that company. Once again, it paid handsomely to stay focused on the ultimate payoff.

10. **Not-for-profit institutions offer a great personal return on investment.** Successful business leaders ought to give back to society and share business and organizational skills with not-for-profit institutions which serve the public. Many successful executives contribute financially to favorite institutions, but it's important to go beyond monetary support and share one's time, skills, and relationships. Executives can set an example for their employees and encourage others to give of themselves. I didn't think much about involving myself with the not-for-profit world until the late 1970s when I hit upon the idea of creating the National Academy Foundation, a program for inner city high school students to teach them about careers in the financial industry. The idea then may have been self-serving because we needed more well-trained applicants, but getting involved in educating others opened my eyes to how knowledge can empower people. Likewise, in sharing my business skills as the chairman of Carnegie Hall and the Weill Cornell Medical College, I have experienced personal satisfaction every bit as strong as being CEO of Citigroup. I now see that you can run a better private business if you help run philanthropic enterprises.

Beyond the lessons I've learned over my fifty years in business, other perspectives run through the pages which follow. The business world and the financial services industry have undergone massive changes in recent decades. I've ridden the rapids: the globalization of commerce and finance, the revolution in technology, the empowerment of the consumer, and the waves of consolidation across many industries, to name just a few of the dramatic changes which form the backdrop to my narrative.

For better or worse, my story has had plenty of drama. I've made mistakes along the way and recognize that I have my share of personal inadequacies. This book doesn't mask these shortcomings. While I genuinely enjoy being around people, some of my toughest recollections relate to problems I had dealing with others. Sometimes, I misjudged individuals; and on other occasions, I gave in to hotheadedness. Undoubtedly, I could have done better in confronting errant colleagues and regret in particular that my relationships with two well-known protégés, Peter Cohen and Jamie Dimon, didn't work out better. I also wish I had done a better job protecting Citigroup against reputation risk in the wake of the bust that followed the boom of the 1990s.

Fortunately, my success and good fortune far outweighed the occasional disappointments. I've been blessed with a wonderful family and accomplishments that I never would have anticipated in my early years. I'm proud that I built two extraordinarily successful companies in very different competitive eras. Most people would have been happy to have had just one such accomplishment. It's especially fulfilling to look at Citigroup, the culmination of my career, and see that the company remains unique in its scale and scope years after its creation. I also take great pride in having had the chance to lead three remarkable philanthropies and for having helped in the education and empowerment of others.

In my corporate and philanthropic worlds, I've been lucky to have worked with many able and loyal partners. My partnership with my wife, though, towers above all the rest. For more than fifty years, Joanie has stood by me offering her support and guidance at all the important junctures of my adult life. I've loved and admired her every step of the way. When I'm called upon to speak of the virtues of teamwork and partnering, I need only think of Joanie for my inspiration.

All in all, it's been a wonderful ride, and I hope the reader will enjoy it as much as I have.

1

Separation

S omehow, I entered into many of my biggest deals over the years in May. The cycle seemed as regular as the seasons: another year, another deal. My colleagues insisted I'd purposely announce an acquisition by Memorial Day simply to wreck their summer vacation plans and demand that we roll up our sleeves with yet another big merger. Looking back on my very first deal, though, I barely could have imagined possessing that sort of sway over other people's lives.

For four years, my friend Arthur Carter and I dreamed of starting our own company. Arthur was a fledgling investment banker at Lehman Brothers while I had made my way from Bear Stearns to Burnham & Company as a young stockbroker. Commuting into Manhattan each morning to our respective jobs, we talked incessantly of pooling our resources and opening our own business. It was the late 1950s; I was in my mid-twenties; and the Space Age was upon us. American industry was benefiting from an explosion of new technologies, and prosperity was in the air. The promise of a new decade was at hand, and the stock market was surging. We had a limited perspective on the securities business, but we were young, optimistic, and infused with self-confidence.

As we imagined our new business, we looked to Allen & Company, the prestigious merchant bank. Charles Allen had made a fortune investing in start-up companies and profiting as the companies in which his firm had ownership stakes sold out to the public. We were drawn to that sort of enterprise but knew we didn't want to stop there. I had experience selling securities to individuals and figured a brokerage business alongside a merchant bank would cover our day-to-day operating costs.

How to produce sufficient cash flow to have enough left over to feed our families soon became our major challenge. Before long, we effectively solved that problem by bringing in two additional partners, Roger Berlind and Peter Potoma. Like me, Roger and Peter were brokers who could be relied upon to generate a steady stream of business while we'd hunt for the episodic and lucrative investment banking deal.

Opening day for Carter, Berlind, Potoma & Weill was thrilling. It was May 2, 1960. We had found a small no-frills office with an address that oozed respectability within sight of the New York Stock Exchange: 37 Wall Street. Along with a newly hired secretary, the four of us spent our first day in cramped quarters opening boxes, getting our phone lines working, and calling as many clients as we could to announce our new venture. Conscious of our young age—we were all in our twenties—Peter Potoma had suggested that we buy hats and black umbrellas so that we might appear older. After all, with our own money on the line, credibility and bringing in new accounts would be more important than ever.

Shortly after we set up shop, the four of us and our wives convened at Arthur's home on Long Island to celebrate. It was a festive occasion, and we all openly shared our aspirations. To this day, I remember the others stressing over and over their desire to become wealthy. Given that Joanie and I were raising two toddlers and lived nearly hand to mouth, the talk was certainly seductive. Still, what I remember most from that dinner was my declaration that the money should be secondary—what mattered more to me was to build a great firm: one that would lead the industry, employ lots of people, endure over many years, and importantly, command respect.

Over the next forty-three years, I never altered my priorities.

I don't recall how my partners reacted to my idealism that evening. It was probably a good thing that none had known me in my younger years. Had they been more familiar with my up-and-down experiences growing up and my family background, I'm sure they would have snickered at my outburst and accused me of hubris. In truth, setting off with my new partners amounted to a genuine coming-of-age. Being my own boss was empowering and nerve-wracking all at the same time. It allowed me to dream, but it also instilled discipline, self-confidence, and a work ethic the likes of which I had never consistently mustered before.

I'm still amazed I was able to summon the confidence to start my own business. I was shy as a child and through all my years of schooling was at best an uneven student. My parents never enjoyed a close relationship, and neither represented a particularly good role model. And I lacked the family connections that gave many of my college classmates and early colleagues that certain swagger as they approached their first jobs.

I was born on March 16, 1933, and lived in a modest three-story home in the Bensonhurst section of Brooklyn until I was ten. My mother's parents owned the home and lived on the first floor with my Aunt Rose, while my family lived in two bedrooms on the second level. The third floor was reserved for tenants. Since I was meek and introverted, I depended heavily on an Irish nanny, Miss Heally, with whom I shared a room and who doted on me so much that I almost looked to her as my real mother. Our neighborhood was filled with Italian, Jewish, and Irish kids, but I never went out of my way to make friends. Between my shyness and reliance on my nanny, I must have been sort of a sissy. It was always easier to talk to Miss Heally or play with my younger sister, Helen.

Summers were special, as we spent them in Peekskill, New York, then a largely agricultural community on the Hudson River. My mother's father originally had owned a hotel there; by the time I was born, he had sold it and bought a farm. It was a terrific escape from the noise and hubbub of Brooklyn. The farm was a gathering point for my extended family, which included my mother's four siblings and their spouses and children. While my mother would move up for the full summer, dad commuted from his city job on weekends. Helen and I had a great time at that farm swimming in the pond, learning to milk cows, fishing, and racing down a sweeping hill in our matching red wagons.

By the time I knew them, my maternal grandparents were already well on in years. In his prime, though, my grandfather, Philip Kalika, must have been a risk taker with good business sense. He had grown up in what is now Poland but then was part of Russia. Though he had been engaged to someone from his hometown, he met my grandmother, Riwe Schwartz, while serving in the Russian army. Falling in love, my grandfather never returned home and instead married my grandmother and settled in a village northwest of Warsaw. Before long, with three of their five children born, including my three-year-old mother, they emigrated to the United States, entering through Ellis Island in 1908.

I don't know the story of how my grandfather went from being a penniless newcomer to his later prosperity; by 1919, he had bought his first home in Brooklyn (the house in which I grew up) and by 1926 opened his own business mass-producing black mourning dresses. Somehow, the company thrived through the Depression years to the point where my grandfather was investing in hotels and farmland and giving his children trips abroad for high school graduation presents.

My grandmother played the role of supportive wife—she was a tiny lady and very old-world in her ways. However, she knew how to juggle the household and raise her kids with a strong hand. I never had the chance to understand what lay behind my grandfather's business success since he was in failing health by the time I knew him. All I recall is an old man suffering from consumption and spitting constantly into an oatmeal box.

My grandparents' children followed fairly predictable routes. My uncles joined the family business while my mother and aunts stayed close to home. My mother, Etta, was an old-fashioned Jewish mother—she cooked and cleaned and was always loving. Her family meant everything. Like her mother, she physically was short of stature and unsophisticated in her ways. Shy to the point of being socially awkward, she never liked going out and was given to housedresses and hairnets. She never learned to drive and was a penny-pincher by nature, often walking ten blocks if she could buy something for a few cents cheaper. Until the day she died in 1994, she never used a credit card.

My mother was no great intellect, yet she had a terrific head for numbers and always was concerned that Helen and I should have a good education. Maybe it was because of her basic frugality, but my mother had an unbelievable knack for memorizing and calculating figures, and she taught me at a very early age about arithmetic before it was called modern math. To this day, I can manipulate numbers in my head with ease.

As a child, I certainly didn't appreciate the mismatch, but my father and mother were worlds apart. I see now that theirs had to have been an arranged marriage of some sort. In fact, it wouldn't surprise me if my father was attracted to my mother because of her family's money. After their wedding in 1932, Max "Mac" Weill went to work with my maternal grandfather in the dressmaking business—accommodating his new son-in-law, my grandfather changed the company name to Kalika & Weill.

Over the years, my relationship with my father would change dramatically, and I'd come to resent him in many ways. As a child, though, I adored him. He was tall and athletic and enjoyed the gift of an ebullient personality. I marveled at his gregarious nature, his terrific sense of humor, and his ease with people. Like my mother, he had been born in Poland and came to America as a child—insisting he hailed from more aristocratic stock, he used to contend (I assume tongue in cheek) that his family had migrated to Poland from Alsace.

Unlike my mother's family, my paternal grandparents remain largely a mystery. My grandmother died at a young age, and we didn't have much to do with my grandfather since my mother didn't enjoy his company. I know that my grandfather was a religious man with little money. After the death of his second wife, he apparently married again, this time to a disabled cousin as a *mitzvah*. I don't know much beyond those few facts.

By the outbreak of the Second World War, my father had split off from my grandfather and had established his own dressmaking business. For a while, his business thrived. I admired his work ethic and took note that he seemed more prosperous than anyone else in the family. Sadly, though, disaster suddenly struck. To the eyes of a ten-year-old, little made sense. By my early twenties, though, I pieced together what happened in this period. In the early 1940s, my father had taken advantage of wartime price controls for personal profit. He was caught by the Office of Price Administration for buying raw materials at controlled prices and then selling the goods on the black market at an inflated price rather than producing dresses for a fixed price as the rules dictated. He was convicted and given a probationary sentence.

My parents did their best to protect Helen and me from those difficult events. In 1943, for instance, we learned abruptly that the family was moving to Miami Beach. Our parents told us only that we had to move there for business reasons. In truth, my father sought to gain physical distance from his legal troubles and probably felt it was too risky to stay in business for himself. I learned much later that he secretly maintained a stake in the garment business in New York by having others front for him.

I had mixed feelings about our move to Miami. Emotionally, I was uprooted from my comfortable surroundings and experienced a sense of loss at being told I would no longer have Miss Healy taking care of me. I was devastated as though I had lost a parent. Joanie contends this forced separation from my surrogate mother had a deep psychological impact on me for the rest of my life. She often reminds me how I consistently attached great importance to personal loyalty, both in business and in my personal life. While I don't know if in fact there was a lasting impact, my world certainly was turned upside down.

Arriving in Florida, we settled into a house on Royal Palm Avenue five blocks from the ocean. My parents insisted that I drop back a year in school but that did little to improve my academic performance. Over the three years we spent in Florida, I was a terrible student. On the other hand, I enjoyed the sunshine and was constantly outside riding my bike or playing basketball with my next-door neighbor, Frankie. All of the physical activity helped me realize that I had natural athletic abilities. Within a year, I took on my first job, delivering newspapers, and used to pay Helen a penny a paper to act as my assistant and roll each paper. I proved good at sales and making on-time deliveries and soon began winning contests for new subscriptions.

As I reached my teens, I became conscious of my father's boisterous personality. He dominated our household, always forcing my mother to take a back seat. He'd often embarrass me in front of my friends by telling lewd jokes or pointing out my inadequacies. In restaurants, he'd flirt with pretty waitresses and extravagantly grab the check when we ate with friends. These were little things that were harbingers of a gradually diminishing reverence I'd have for him over the next several years. The louder he became, the more I shrank back in shyness and passivity.

In 1947, my father surprised us again by announcing that we were heading back to New York. He had decided to start a new business with a partner importing steel. In the years following the war, New York suffered one of its periodic housing shortages, and we struggled to find a place to live. Reluctantly, my father moved the family into his father's house in Brooklyn for a year. One of my great-aunts already shared the house with my grandfather and his second wife, and quarters would be tight. At the same time, I was still doing poorly in school—in fact, my freshman high school grades in Florida were horrible. To ease the housing crunch and also acknowledge my scholastic difficulties, my parents decided I should go to boarding school upon our return.

From our summers spent in Peekskill, my parents were familiar with the Peekskill Military Academy. With little time to research alternatives and my parents' sense that I might benefit from a disciplined environment, I was enrolled as a lowly plebe. As had been the case when we moved to Florida, I was put back a year, while my more academically inclined sister was skipped forward. We might have been three years apart in age, yet grade-wise she was steadily catching up on me.

Originally, I was supposed to go to PMA only for a year until my parents found more permanent living accommodations, but I really took to the school and insisted on staying the full four years even after my family found a home of their own in the Flatbush section of Brooklyn. Military school was fantastic for me. There was plenty of hazing my first year, and I learned how to take criticism before dishing it out, a skill with lifelong value. The attractive campus with its ivy-covered redbrick buildings did little to detract from the administration's insistence on tight discipline and hard work. We attended classes six days a week, and there were strictly enforced curfews. The discipline was exactly what I needed.

Early on, I had the good fortune to develop a close relationship with Clare Frantz, who was my Latin teacher and tennis coach. Tall and lean, the Germanic Frantz took an active interest in me and motivated me to improve my study habits. He worked with me both in the classroom and on the tennis court and tremendously boosted my self-confidence. Unlike my father, who always seemed immersed in business, Clare and I related well to one another.

He had an attractive wife, and the two would often invite me to their on-campus house for dinner. It didn't take long for rumors to fly that I was having an affair with Clare's wife, but the gossip simply reflected the fantasies of my classmates. By my second semester, my academic performance had begun to improve visibly. By the third term, I really took off, and my grades consistently ranked in the top two or three out of a class of thirty-five for the rest of my years at PMA. One year, I ranked top in my class and earned high honors.

PMA also allowed me to experiment with a variety of extracurricular activities. For a time, I worked for the school newspaper, *The Reveille,* but I wasn't much of a reporter. Being a bass drummer in the marching band was much more to my liking. I still remember marching in a Columbus Day parade down the main street in Peekskill with my large bass drum hoisted from my shoulders—a German shepherd leapt from the curb and began nipping at my heels before sinking its teeth into my leg. Undeterred, I insisted on finishing the parade before attending to my wound.

With Frantz's steady encouragement, I worked at my tennis game with passion and soon excelled. I loved representing the school in various competitions. By my senior year, I won the Westchester County singles tournament for private and parochial school teenage boys and was invited to join the Junior Davis Cup team from New York, which gave me the opportunity to practice in the professional stadium in Forest Hills with Pancho Segura, then one of the sport's great professionals. The thrill of those tennis experiences represented a high point of my high school years.

I matured tremendously during my teenage years at Peekskill Military Academy. My teachers and peers liked me and gave me two nicknames: "Duck" (because they claimed I waddled) and "Mr. Five O'Clock Shadow." By my junior year I was appointed an officer with the rank of first lieutenant. Being on the battalion staff accorded me certain privileges such as officer's quarters (still awfully spartan), later curfews, and opportunities to head into Peekskill on weekends.

I also discovered girls while at PMA. My first experience came the summer after my sophomore year when I worked as a lifeguard at a hotel near my grandparents' farm. There I met a college-aged girl who took more than a casual interest in me. The relationship was brief, but she gave a terrific boost to my self-esteem at a time when I was figuring out my place in the world. Later, I had my first real girlfriend when I met Marian Rogers. Neighbors of my parents were friends with Marian's folks and made the introduction. For the next two years, Marian and I saw one another steadily—she'd come up to PMA on weekends to attend dances and other social functions.

Marian's father owned a pipe and tobacco store in Manhattan. He taught me the art of breaking in a pipe and how to distinguish good tobacco. Soon I became his unofficial distributor in Peekskill. I was the only one with this special blend of tobacco, and it was 100 percent legal! I still have a black-and-white photo of me wearing a sweater and leaning back in a comfortable chair with crossed legs, confidently clutching my pipe. Whatever serenity that picture may have shown, I never felt it once I headed off into the real world.

During my years at PMA, my parents were regular visitors. Sometimes they'd arrive together, while on other occasions my father would drive up alone. Either way, my father never failed to make his presence known to all and always eclipsed my mother when they came together. Chomping on a big cigar, he'd typically beckon my friends and regale them with stories and jokes. I was embarrassed and proud all at the same time.

By now, my father was engaged in his steel importing business operating under the name the American Steel Company. To outward appearances, the business seemed hugely successful as my father lived extravagantly. He drove expensive cars, owned tons of clothes, and took a haircut and manicure weekly. I learned later, though, that all was not as it seemed. The business was highly cyclical and did well only during steel industry strikes, which pushed up prices and profit margins for my father's company. Also, working at the company one summer, I noticed my father and his partner seemed constantly to be in a competition on who could run up the largest expense account. I thought such a practice represented a bad culture for building a business, and it troubled me that the company was absorbing personal expenditures.

These were observations that would only hit home in later life as I reflected on my father's business practices. For the most part, I respected my father greatly in those years and felt he could offer me important life lessons. Indeed, during another summer, he arranged a job for me in a pocketbook factory doing piecework installing metal fasteners. All my co-workers were hardworking and friendly minorities who I realized were locked into their menial jobs. My father made a point to tell me, "If you don't do well in school, this is the type of job that will be available to you. If you want more, you have to apply yourself." On another occasion driving back to New York from a stay in Florida, he put us up at the fancy Mayflower Hotel in Washington. Seeing how I enjoyed the hotel's luxurious appointments, my father stressed that "as an adult, you'll only get to enjoy such nice things if you're willing to work very hard." These were simple statements, but somehow the words hit home.

———————————

By early 1951, my days at Peekskill Military Academy were quickly drawing to a close, and I knew it was time to think about my future. After a weak start, I finished nearly at the top of my class, which taught me a valuable lesson in the importance of self-discipline. My hard work paid off, for I was accepted at both Harvard and Cornell. I felt my aptitude lay in math and science, as I particularly excelled in those subjects at PMA, and I was also interested in metallurgy thinking that I might eventually join my father in his business. Accordingly, I enrolled in Cornell's well-regarded Engineering School. As a graduation gift, my ever extravagant father presented me with a yellow Plymouth convertible in which I drove off to find my destiny.

My high school years were terrific, but they conveyed a false sense of security. In fact, the following four years were turbulent to say the least. Yes, I'd meet and fall in love with Joanie, but I'd also recognize that I was not cut out for my chosen field of study, and more important, face the crushing news of the disintegration of my parents' marriage. I quickly came to realize that I could never take the future for granted and that attaining one's goals only comes from hard work and self-reliance.

My first experiences at Cornell were deceptively enjoyable. Freed from the rigid restraints of life in military school, I settled into the freewheeling social scene and enjoyed dating and drinking with friends. Cornell had an extensive fraternity system, and I quickly decided to pledge Alpha Epsilon Pi. In the 1950s, fraternities were almost entirely segregated. All I cared about was feeling at home with the members who happened to be Jewish and predominantly from the New York area. I was a skillful Ping-Pong player, which helped boost my popularity with the older brothers. I integrated in no time into the fraternity's social scene, which included great weekend parties with sister sororities. With my yellow convertible and my father's credit card, I found it easy to impress my dates, and I soon learned the joys of weekend road trips with friends to neighboring schools.

The freedom was seductive, but it didn't take long for the reality to set in that Cornell was a place of academic rigor. In my orientation to the metallurgy program, I recall the department head asking us to "look to your left and right because most of you won't be here at graduation." It was an early lesson in how not to motivate people. Before long, I realized firsthand that his admonition was no joke. I may have done well in math and science at PMA but I now was thrown in with truly exceptional students, and I began to struggle.

Things got progressively worse. I'll never forget my physics midterm in which we had to determine where a cannonball would land in relation to a group of hills. Though I wasn't cheating, I happened to notice my neighbor was drawing a landing spot across his piece of paper on a far hill whereas the best I could figure the shell would barely hit the nearest hill. Stumped, I decided to write on my paper that I couldn't answer the question because "my cannon was malfunctioning." When the graded paper came back, I received a zero alongside a sarcastic comment from the professor.

By November, I was doing so poorly that I decided to drop out. I went home for Thanksgiving and told my parents I'd transfer to NYU, an idea they acceded to so long as I'd commit to finishing college. Within weeks, however, Cornell sent me a letter saying that the school had set up a special probationary program for eleven students that would allow me to switch to a liberal arts program to which I might be better suited. I took the opportunity and subsequently went to summer school at the University of Wisconsin and Cornell to make up for my lost semester. Fortunately, the switch was just what I needed. I ended up avoiding science classes and instead focused on economics and government. My grades improved, and I eventually spent my final year taking courses from the graduate business school.

With a more manageable academic load, I began to enjoy college life once more. I took a two-bedroom apartment with three of my fraternity brothers my junior year where we had never-ending bridge tournaments. I figured out how to study just hard enough to get by without sacrificing my active social schedule while my weekend road trips became more regular and far-reaching. By now, Helen was studying at Smith College and had begun dating my roommate Lenny Zucker. He and I often would snag one of our other friends and head off to Massachusetts in search of a good time.

My days of playing the field soon ended abruptly. While I was home for spring recess, my aunt told me of an attractive nineteen-year-old named Joan Mosher whose family had just moved to the neighborhood from California. My solicitous relative suggested I call her for a date. Having just broken up with a girlfriend, I eagerly called Joan to ask her out. I was disappointed when I heard her say, "I have a party that night and won't be able to meet you, but I have a friend who you might like . . ." Undeterred, I replied firmly, "There's no way I'm going out with a blind date set up by a blind date . . . I'll call again."

My steadfastness paid off, and we soon arranged to meet on April Fool's Day 1954. That evening, I was greeted by Joanie's mother, who carefully looked me up and down so she could report to her daughter, who was strategically waiting in her room—the big issue at that moment was to determine my height so Joanie could decide whether she should wear heels. In a flash, I saw an energetic and very beautiful girl in flat-soled shoes come bounding down the hall. On the way to drinks at the White Cannon Inn in Freeport, Joanie ribbed that I was nothing like the fair-haired boys she knew in California and joked that at least I didn't have a New York accent.

From the first moment, I was drawn in completely. I felt relaxed and comfortable around her. I had done my share of dating, but no one attracted me like Joanie. She was beautiful and vivacious, confident, full of easy conversation, and quick with a joke. The entire evening proved exciting and intoxicating. Neither of us wanted it to end; at nearly 3:00 A.M., we reluctantly agreed it was time to go home.

Joanie and I were eager to see each other again. Unfortunately, she had another date for the following evening. I couldn't bear the thought of her seeing someone else, so I decided to cruise by her house with my car's top down to check out her date that night as he picked her up. Joanie probably didn't appreciate the gesture, but I wanted her to know I would not be deterred.

We saw a lot of each other over the next several weeks. Joanie was finishing her junior year at Brooklyn College so we were limited to weekends. She'd either come up to Cornell for one of our bacchanalian fraternity parties or I'd drive to her house. Yet time seemed in short supply. I was receiving reserve officer training (ROTC) during college with the notion that I'd receive an officer's commission in the air force upon my graduation. That summer I was due to report for training in South Carolina. We dated a lot right up to the day I left. We proved to be avid letter writers that summer—each time I'd receive a note from Joanie, she'd enclose my last letter complete with corrections to all my misspelled words. I should have realized then and there that Joanie would make me a better person!

Shortly after my return from boot camp in August, we became engaged and planned for a wedding the following June after my graduation. However, Joanie's parents were not thrilled by their daughter's plans. Her parents were snobbish and never felt I was good enough for their daughter. Their disapproval began with our very first date, as they were upset at my dropping off Joanie in the middle of the night, and I learned later that they kept telling Joanie of their preference for one of her earlier boyfriends. Her folks saw me as someone who came from an uncultured background who hadn't graduated on time and—though brash—didn't seem to have much direction when it came to thinking about the future.

Unfortunately, my parents did little to counter the impression. Around the beginning of 1955, my parents invited the Moshers to their home for dinner. I wasn't there, but Joanie told me it was a dreadful evening. At first my father grew angry at my mother for burning the roast lamb. He then talked about his recent retirement from the steel business and bragged incessantly about the extravagant lifestyle he could afford. He announced he'd give us a car as a wedding present and suggested to Joanie's father that he should give us $3,000. The idea must have struck a nerve as my normally reserved future father-in-law bellowed, "My daughter is not for sale!" From that time forth, I felt nothing I could do would ever redeem me in Joanie's parents' eyes.

———————

It was right after this ill-fated dinner that my world suddenly turned upside down. I was preparing for midterm exams when word came from a family friend that my father had left my mother and had disappeared. The news came like a bolt from the blue. Maybe I should have realized over the years that my parents barely had a relationship, but I took for granted that their marriage was normal. My first instincts were to protect my mother and also to find my father and reason with him why he needed to return home. With the help of a private investigator, I found out that he was in Washington, D.C. Disregarding my two remaining exams, I raced to pick up Helen at Smith, and we drove all night to talk sense into our father. I was mostly shaken up while Helen was clearly resentful.

When we confronted him, we heard his convoluted side of the story. "I haven't been happy for a long time," he declared. "You are now old enough to deal with the change, and it's time for me to think about myself. The reason I left the way I did was that it was the best way not to upset your mother with a bad scene." As if we were not shocked enough, our father went on to confess that he had been seeing another woman for two years, a Hungarian lady named Marian. In an admission that especially incensed me, he let on that he had once arranged secretly for her to sit next to us at the theater so that she could check us out. We argued and cajoled for two days before giving up and deciding we needed to return to New York to console our mother.

My mother hadn't even called to tell me about what had happened out of concern for upsetting me during my exams—that was her way of trying to protect me. When we finally sat down, she did her best to put on a brave face. "Go back to school," my mother implored. I could not fathom how my father could have been so self-centered and cruel to my mother—I was seared by the act of disloyalty and abandonment. I eventually returned to Cornell, but my final semester was a blur as I tried my best to finish my studies while helping my mother with her divorce settlement.

As if my father's abandonment were not enough, I found his stinginess in how he proposed to settle with my mother especially distasteful. He had some wealth at that point but initially offered my mother only the house in Brooklyn. Incredibly, he claimed my mother lived frugally and didn't need much to live on. Eventually, my mother accepted a settlement whereby she received the house and $50,000. She remained in that house for many years. The experience with my father embittered her, and she never remarried.

In subsequent years, I'd alternate between feelings of disdain and guilt in how I'd relate to my father. From the day he left my mother, his shortcomings, if not outright failure, had become glaringly obvious. I was repelled by his lack of commitment and loyalty and his self-centered approach to life. I could no longer count on joining him in his steel importing business let alone on asking him for financial support. And as an adult, I understood how his unethical practices had killed his first business while his free-spending ways undermined his second company. My father may have taught me the value of working hard, and he may have given me part of his outgoing personality, but ultimately, he became mostly a negative role model—more than anything, I learned firsthand the importance of loyalty and being ethically upright in one's business and personal life.

My life's disruption didn't end with my parents' divorce. Joanie and I had planned our wedding for the week following graduation, but toward the end of the school year, I received more unexpected news. Everyone was receiving their diploma in an envelope ahead of the actual ceremony. When I opened mine, it was empty except for a note claiming I couldn't graduate because of an incomplete in my cost accounting course. I had missed the final exam in order to console my mother after my father's departure. The irony looking back is striking. At the time, however, it was no laughing matter. My advisor had incorrectly assured me that I had sufficient credits to graduate, so the news was devastating. Without my diploma, I wouldn't be eligible to receive my air force commission as planned, and the inability to graduate only lowered me further in the eyes of my prospective in-laws.

As it happened, I was able to make up the missed exam the day after graduation and had to wait until September for my degree to be official. Forty-nine years later, in another ironic twist, I'd receive an original diploma in person from Cornell's president as a gesture of appreciation for my leadership in supporting the university. In accepting the gift, I made sure to remark that Cornell had taught me a powerful lesson about the pitfalls of bureaucracies. I also joked that the diploma "was a little late" and that "I'd carry it home since it seemed to have gotten lost in the mail the last time."

With my future still very much undecided, Joanie and I married in June. Our wedding and honeymoon were terrific. The elegant ceremony, held at the Essex House, was small—about fifty people and mostly family. My college roommate Lenny was the best man while Helen was Joanie's maid of honor. In typical fashion, my father failed to show as he had decided to go to Mexico in order to remarry speedily. He got married to Marian a day after us but sent a photographer so that he could have his own photos of our ceremony. It was for the best since I'm sure his presence would have ruined the day for my mother.

Despite the tussle with my dad earlier that year, Joanie's father told us he'd be willing to spend $5,000 on our wedding and gift and gave us the option on how the sum should be split. We ended up receiving $3,500 in cash. My father-in-law insisted on investing it for us since he didn't respect my judgment on financial matters. In absentia, my father made good on his original promise of giving us a car, a Mercury convertible with defective gears that allowed it only to drive forward. We spent our wedding night at the Essex House before heading to the Concord Hotel in the Catskills where Joanie had won a free week for appearing on a game show.

After our week in the mountains, we headed to Florida for a leisurely two-month vacation where we traveled the length and breadth of the state. Early on, we had an embarrassing incident. I had deposited the cash we received from our wedding in a savings account in New York and thought that the checks I had been writing drew from that account. Much to our surprise, we learned that we had been paying for one motel after another with bouncing checks. I'll never forget arriving at the Jack Tar Motel in Marathon Key and being accused of check fraud. Fortunately, we convinced the authorities of our naïveté and arranged to repay our debts. It was far from an auspicious omen for a future banker!

Returning from our extended honeymoon that August, Joanie and I lived with our parents. We stayed with my mother during the week since her Flatbush home was more convenient to Brooklyn College where Joanie was still finishing her degree. On weekends, we'd shift to Joanie's old bedroom in her parents' home. I had another month before I'd receive my college degree after which I still planned to join the air force.

Living with Joanie's parents was awful. My relationship with them remained strained, as it clearly bothered them that their new son-in-law lacked a job, had a problem graduating from college, and came from a broken home. They didn't think I deserved their daughter and barely masked their feelings. Making matters worse, Joanie's bed was on wheels—there was no carpet, and I always felt like her dad had a stethoscope pressed to the wall. I took a commission job selling *The Greater New York Industrial Directory* and hated it. After selling only one book in ten days, I quit. With nothing better to do, I'd play arcade games in my free time. I recall making up stories each day about how I had passed the time so I wouldn't lower myself even further in the eyes of Joanie's parents.

One day I passed a Bache & Company office and peered in. The sputtering ticker tape and buzz of activity looked interesting, and I ended up asking my father what he thought about the business. His wife, Marian, soon introduced me to a friend who happened to be a broker at Bear Stearns. Suddenly, I had a job as a runner earning $150 a month. Most of the people with whom I initially worked were on Social Security, and I knew I could do better. I quickly graduated to margin clerk.

The brokerage business was fascinating. I used to spend my lunch break taking in the scene in the "board room," a large bullpen where the brokers worked. There was a two-sided glass partition. On one side were salespeople and traders while on the other stood the firm's legendary leader, Cy Lewis, a big man oozing with power who constantly barked out instructions to his traders. Alongside Cy sat a young Ace Greenberg, who one day would earn his own reputation as Bear's CEO. Being a margin clerk taught me a great deal about how the business operated and instilled a lifelong appreciation regarding the importance of a good back office. As a margin clerk, I received calls from brokers asking how much money their clients had to invest. These were the days before computers, and I had to perform all the calculations by hand, matching securities and figuring borrowing capacity based on margin rates.

I was just getting my feet wet working when I received a notice from the air force that it was time to report for duty. Since more than a year had now passed since my last physical, I was told to go first to Mitchell AFB on Long Island for the required checkup. Unexpectedly, I failed the exam because of a cavity that required root canal work. By the fall of 1955, the administration of Dwight Eisenhower was beginning to reduce the military's manpower requirements, and before I knew it, I was given the option to change my mind on my service obligation.

Ever since I crashed a T-33 flight simulator during my summer boot camp experience a year earlier, I had begun to have second thoughts about becoming a pilot, and now my positive experience at Bear Stearns encouraged me to think about a different career. I ended up asking my boss whether he thought I could make it in the brokerage business. With his encouraging reply, I decided to turn in my air force bars. It's funny how events had conspired to change my destiny: First, my parents' divorce forced me to graduate late, thus delaying my service obligation, and now, a simple physical exam steered me in an entirely different direction.

During late 1955 and early 1956, I plugged away at my job while studying for my broker's license at night. By June, I passed the required exam. Bear Stearns moved me to the brokerage office at One Wall Street. I was excited by my rapid progress and the move to the heart of the financial world. It felt great receiving the license and having the chance to run what felt like my own business. I worked hard as a young broker. Since I was still given to shyness, Joanie helped me immensely. She'd push me to make cold calls and to touch base with my clients each day. Her words still ring clearly: "Did you call So-and-So today? Be sure to follow up!"

I never had a sophisticated calling program; rather, I took every referral I could get, first concentrating on family friends and then soliciting waiters and maître d's in the restaurants I frequented. Early on, probably a fifth of my clients worked in restaurants. Once in a while, there were some pleasant surprises as when the maître d' of Jimmy's Lagrange Restaurant gave me an account which included $100,000 worth of AT&T stock.

My first year had its ups and downs. I vividly remember losing sleep because I had made some bad stock calls and lost money for my clients. For a while, I was afraid to go out to eat since I knew I'd have to confront my waiter clients. Still, working hard to master the firm's investment research, I soon began to excel. By September 1956, I was doing well enough that Joanie and I could afford to take an apartment of our own and thankfully get out from under the discomfort of living with her parents. Our new apartment in East Rockaway cost $135 a month in rent, or half my income, but the independence was well worth it. Just as we were set to move, Joanie gave birth to our son, Marc. I loved being a new father, though the sense of responsibility now pushed me all the more to excel at work.

I continued to increase my production and generated $25,000 in gross commissions in 1957, which meant I was bringing home $7,500. I was doing well enough, but 1957 was a difficult year for the market. President Eisenhower's heart attack reversed investors' prior surge in confidence, and the Dow Jones Average dropped nearly 13 precent that year as trading volume flattened. I was still nervous at the start of 1958, and one of my uncles encouraged me to consider moving to a small brokerage operation named after its owner, Frank LaGrange. This was only a three-person firm, but what appealed to me was the offer for a guaranteed $7,500 in base pay plus profit sharing. Conservatively, I believed the pay structure would insulate me against the risk of a poor market.

Working for LaGrange was generally unpleasant. My boss had a love affair with railroad and sugar stocks (this was pre-Castro), while I was drawn to start-up and technology-oriented companies. I used to hang out at lunch with analyst-brokers from neighboring Unterberg Towbin and share stock ideas. Tommy Unterberg and I soon became good friends—he'd often sleep on the sofa in my apartment so that we could get an early start the next day going out to research companies in the area. Frank LaGrange didn't approve of my hanging out with technology analyst friends and insisted that I should concentrate instead on more staid companies. Not helping matters any, he hated my smoking and constantly harped that his wife didn't like the smell of tobacco on his shirts. Before I knew it, I felt whipsawed as the market recovered vigorously in 1958. It surged 34 percent for the year and had undermined my original reason for leaving Bear Stearns. Thinking I'd receive a healthy bonus, I felt entirely misled at year end when LaGrange announced there were no profits to share.

Fortunately, I saw a way out. For weeks, the sales manager at Burnham & Company had been calling trying to get me to jump ship. He'd play on everything I didn't like about LaGrange by advertising Burnham's family-like culture, its emphasis on a wide range of stocks, and its paternalistic founder. The sales manager assured me that with my skills and Burnham's support "you'll triple your production, I guarantee it." Usually words like that should make anyone suspicious, but I took the bait and, sure enough, my commissions zoomed to the point where I brought home $25,000 in 1959. Of course, those were years when commissions were regulated and actually maintained at very rich levels. For instance, commissions then approximated 7 percent of clients' assets, or ten times the rate typically earned forty years later. However I earned it, my pay put me in the elite of all retail brokers at the time.

Burnham & Company was a terrific place most of all because of its founder, I. W. "Tubby" Burnham. Tubby was one of the most down-to-earth and nicest men I have ever known. The grandson of the distiller I. W. Harper, Tubby had earned his nickname as a child when he was forced to gain fifty pounds as part of the cure for typhoid fever. He opened the firm's doors in 1935—I was impressed that someone could build a firm that could stand such a test of time. Tubby was the perfect mentor: He was a consummate retail broker and always enjoyed working with young employees with whom he shared his accumulated wisdom. He'd constantly walk around the fifty-person firm and ask employees for their ideas. He demonstrated his humanity by treating his employees as though they were family and imparted to each the sense that they were all equally important. It was a style so lacking elsewhere on Wall Street. Tubby may not have been a rocket scientist, but he taught me the importance of focusing on the basics in running a business, especially the need to respect and value one's employees.

Mirroring my professional growth, our family and lifestyle were also maturing. My success at Burnham gave Joanie and me the means to afford a larger two-bedroom apartment in our building. The expansion came just in time for the birth of our daughter, Jessica. We were proud parents but followed traditional roles with Joanie staying home to take care of Marc and Jessica while I was the breadwinner. Unlike most of our friends, we didn't benefit from a wealthy parental support system, a fact which I resented since I never asked for a lot. Without any extra financial help, it felt like we were in a titanic struggle to make a place for ourselves. In hindsight, I wish I had been able to spend more time with my kids in those years, but I felt that the majority of my time and energy had to go toward building my business. It was a matter of basic survival.

In early 1959, Burnham & Company celebrated its twenty-fifth anniversary, an event which had a profound impact on me. With my father's businesses, I had never seen such longevity, and the notion of building something which would be bigger than any one person seemed awesome. By this point, Arthur Carter and I already were thinking of starting our own firm, and that celebration spurred us on. I even figured

Tubby might back us if I appealed to him and used his story as an example of what we wanted to accomplish.

We had already spent nearly four years fantasizing about opening our own business. Our ruminations had begun shortly after we first met as across-the-hall neighbors in our East Rockaway apartment. Arthur and his wife, Linda, had moved in a month before us and also had a newborn child. Arthur and I used to talk about the stock market at every chance we could get. We had plenty in common and quickly became good friends. We'd rarely allow much time to go by without cooking dinner for one another, and as time went on, we vacationed together as well.

Arthur was a year and a half older than I and clearly brilliant. The son of an IRS agent father and a mother who was a French teacher, he had grown up in Woodmere and graduated from Brown where he had studied French and music. His father once had him tested to determine what sort of career would most suit him, and the results showed a remarkable breadth of aptitude. He considered a career as a classical pianist before aiming his sights on becoming an investment banker. As I'd see more in later years, his multiple talents imparted an impatient nature and an eagerness to experiment with new things.

Commuting together into Manhattan each morning, Arthur and I compared notes on our companies, the brokerage industry, and stocks we liked. We were not sophisticated, but that didn't stop us from thinking otherwise. We were both young and idealistic, and we soon began to dream about what we might create if we were to start our own business. It was fun thinking out loud together, but our planning was premature, as Arthur soon decided to quit Lehman and enroll at Dartmouth for his MBA. While he was there, I managed his investment account. I'd come up with stocks to buy; and, just as often, Arthur would tell me what he liked, and I'd go off and research the idea and determine whether we'd buy it. It was a great collaboration and all the more fired our ambitions to team up one day.

Upon obtaining his degree, Arthur went to work for an investment bank other than Lehman but realized the job wasn't for him. It was now late 1959, and the stock market was enjoying a terrific year. I was thriving at Burnham and gaining self-confidence. Arthur and I were commuting together once more, and we redoubled our talk about starting our own firm. We quickly settled on our business plan, which would take the best of Allen & Company and its investment banking focus and combine it with retail brokerage services which might cover our overhead. We each felt we weren't good at big-company politics and believed we could make a decent living with our newly conceived business model. I reasoned that if we took the plunge and it didn't work out I could always go back to working for Tubby.

Filled with enthusiasm, we decided to run our idea past Arthur's father-in-law, Peter Schweitzer, who was a successful and wealthy entrepreneur making cigarette paper. Schweitzer did not discourage us, but he made us realize that we lacked enough customers to make a viable venture and recommended we bring in additional partners. Arthur suggested we approach his childhood friend Roger Berlind. Roger had a passion for songwriting. An unsuccessful attempt at writing for a career had brought him to the Wall Street firm Eastman Dillon as a broker instead.

Perhaps Roger had already been thinking of going off on his own as he quickly warmed to the idea of joining us. However, he insisted we also bring along his friend and Eastman colleague Peter Potoma, who was the son-in-law of publishing magnate George Delacorte. We accepted the idea as we figured Peter's family connection might come in handy. As I got to know Roger, I realized he hid his being Jewish well, and Arthur and I assumed he wanted Potoma to be included so that we wouldn't be seen to the outside world as a Jewish firm. After all, in the 1950s, Wall Street firms were clearly classified by their ethnicities. In that regard at least our new firm would surely break the mold.

Coming together, the four of us must have sounded awfully arrogant for our young ages. We all agreed there was little good investment research around and that we could do much better by pooling our collective intelligence. The Dow Jones Industrial Average had surged over 50 percent in 1958–59 all the way to 680. No doubt those robust market conditions made us all feel particularly smart even if we knew the old adage on the Street never to confuse brains with a bull market.

The group assembled, Arthur went back to his father-in-law and asked him to help us buy a seat on the New York Stock Exchange in order to get our business up and running. In addition, each of us agreed to kick in what we could out of our own savings. For Joanie and me, that meant contributing $30,000, which was virtually all we had—we only held back $1,000 in case of an emergency.

Schweitzer initially responded positively to our request for help in buying the seat, and we soon signed a contract that gave us two weeks to come up with the $160,000 purchase price. Suddenly, though, Arthur's father-in-law changed course and declined to give us the financial support he had promised. By early 1960, the market had turned soft and so, too, had Mr. Schweitzer.

It was a terrible quandary as, by now, we had all given notice to our employers, and we felt on the hook legally with our contractual commitment. I got especially cold feet and even offered at one point that we should sell the seat, take a loss, and wait a couple of years before trying again. Yet our luck turned when Peter's wife's family and Roger's mother and mine pitched in and committed to help us pay for the seat.

As a Delacorte, Peter's wife came from substantial means and helped him step up his initial contribution. I didn't have wealthy family connections on which to draw, but unbelievably, my mother gave us $30,000, which was fully 60 percent of all she owned following her divorce. It was an act of complete selflessness. In contrast to Peter Schweitzer, who was probably worth $50 million and gave us nothing, my mother, with her $50,000 net worth, went to the mat for her son.

Altogether, we raised $250,000, which was enough to pay for the seat on the exchange and still have enough left over to defray the cost of our office space and our other operating costs. Each of the four partners actually had contributed different amounts, but we decided we'd still each have an equal ownership share as we knew we were all pulling together. We decided to pay ourselves $12,500 apiece in our first year, which helped us have something left over after our other costs to reinvest in the business.

That payout amounted to a 50 percent cut from what I had been earning at Burnham, but the drop didn't bother me as I felt proud to be

in business on my own. Joanie was also incredibly supportive and willing to pinch pennies and sacrifice. While many of our friends were then
buying their first homes in fancy North Shore neighborhoods on Long
Island, we plowed our savings into the business and moved into a garden apartment rental in Baldwin, a middle-class neighborhood on the
South Shore.

As we got closer to setting up shop, the market downturn of early
1960 intensified. Everyone we knew began to question whether we
really wanted to take on such a risk. People like Arthur's father-in-law
asked, "Who are you guys to think you can do this successfully?" In
fact, we could only point to two similarly oriented firms which had successfully started up in the 1950s, Donaldson Lufkin Jenrette and Faulkner
Dawkins.

Nonetheless, none of us would countenance backing out now. After
all, we knew what our costs would be and the commissions we'd need
to be profitable. Given our past production, we felt it wasn't as big a risk
as everyone seemed to think. We were also reassured by Tubby Burnham's willingness to have Burnham & Company settle our trades, which
we all took as a vote of confidence. In the end, we figured we had plenty
of room to cover our costs even factoring in the risk of a sharp falloff
in commissions.

As I look back on that period now, I marvel at our naïveté and our
inherent optimism. We were young and infused with energy and had
gained our first business experience during the mostly dynamic 1950s.
There surely were economic fluctuations in those years, but for the most
part it was a time of rising prosperity, healthy economic growth, and
empowerment for American investors. The end of the Korean War initially unleashed the country's potential, and the economy grew steadily
through most of the decade.

By the 1957 launch of Sputnik, the Space Age burst onto the scene
and spawned a slew of new companies built on technological innovation. Between rising personal incomes and the explosion in innovation,
the fundamentals underpinning the stock market were very positive
indeed. Between 1955 and the end of 1959, the Dow Index surged 40
percent to nearly 700 while trading volumes jumped 25 percent to three

million shares a day, a whopping number at the time even if it's laughable by today's billion-share standard. Equally important, individuals were coming to realize how they might diversify their savings by investing in stocks and bonds. As we opened our doors, there were about fifteen million individuals in the United States actively buying stocks—that number was less than 10 percent of the country's population but was up sharply from only about five million at the start of the 1950s.

We may have started Carter, Berlind, Potoma & Weill with uncomfortably small quarters and little more than our collective optimism, yet we instinctively felt that we were in a business full of promise. From the start, we worked incredibly hard to build our new company, and looking back, it was a tremendously exciting time in my life. I loved going out and visiting companies I thought might represent good investments and then pitching the ideas to our clients.

Each day, we'd listen to the sound of the ticker tape for a sign of the markets' direction—a loud tape meant stronger trading volumes and typically higher prices while a quiet tape meant we had to redouble our client-calling efforts to generate business. And all of us tried as hard as we could to build relationships with companies, which we hoped might lead to an eventual payday from an investment banking transaction. We rarely thought too much about the big picture, but in our hearts we felt as though the capital markets were wide open and poised for tremendous growth.

In retrospect, I didn't know the half of it!

2

Building the Business

Politics trumped economics in 1960. Business conditions were stable that year, but stocks reacted to the heightened uncertainty of the close presidential contest and fell sharply in the months leading up to the election. When we opened our doors in May, the Dow Jones Average stood at 600, more than 10 percent lower than at the start of the year. The market briefly rallied and nearly returned to start-of-year levels by early June. This upturn, though, proved to be a tease, and the Dow then plunged all the way to 572 by late October. The drop didn't meet the test of being labeled a bear market—for that, stocks have to fall 20 percent—yet it was disconcerting nonetheless.

The stock market usually discounts information rapidly, and the uncertainty surrounding the election peaked two weeks before the vote. With the victory of John F. Kennedy, fear soon gave way to hope that our new young president would usher in an era of activist government that would propel the country forward. In later years, investors would come to fear activist government as a recipe for budget deficits and higher interest rates, but with the approach of the Kennedy administration, investors embraced the country's growing idealism. By the end of 1960, the market rebounded 7 percent from its low; by March, it added another 8 percent; and by the end of 1961, the Dow surged all the way to 725, a new high and 27 percent above the low point just before the election.

As optimism spread, investors committed more of their savings to buy stocks, and companies—both established and start-ups—came to the market to raise capital. For Carter, Berlind, Potoma & Weill, the wind was soon at our back. By early 1961, our monthly revenues had jumped to $34,000, more than double the $14,000 we averaged in our first seven months. Monthly profits before partners' salaries rose nearly threefold to $28,000—that was $336,000 annualized—and gave us confidence to step up our annual take-home pay to $18,600. We also added our first junior partners.

Each of us instinctively knew what we needed to do. For Arthur, that meant searching for companies interested in raising capital or needing advice with acquisitions. On the other hand, Roger, Peter, and I tended to our retail clients. I had 150 to 200 clients at the time. Roger and Peter could tap into family connections, while my clients were just average people I had found by cold-calling or word of mouth. I learned early never to turn anyone down since you never knew where a relationship might lead. A lot of my best accounts came from referrals from small customers.

Tubby Burnham had taught me the importance of developing a feel for the market, and I soon gained a reputation as a fanatical tape watcher incessantly punching ticker symbols into my quote machine to check on prices. When I wasn't watching the tape or calling customers, I oversaw our over-the-counter trading and researched new investment ideas. I never liked having to write up my ideas, though I enjoyed searching for moneymaking stocks. Some of my most exciting finds were private companies that were ready to go public. I was happy to develop any relationship that would lead to business for our firm.

I recall being enamored with cosmetic companies at one point and finding a company called Tip Top Products which I felt was undervalued. Somehow I rationalized that its business of manufacturing hair curlers was close enough to cosmetics. The company rewarded my enthusiasm by offering our firm the chance to underwrite a stock offering which ended up being a big success. Similarly, I originated offerings for Spencer Gifts and Famous Artists Schools. My track record was decent but far from perfect. At one point, I decided that Smith Corona would give Xerox a run for its money in the photocopying business and pushed the stock avidly. In Wall Street terminology, I became the "ax in the stock," meaning investors respected my views on the company more than others' and tended to come to me first for information. Unfortunately, on this occasion, my ax turned out to be broken.

Life with my partners was all at once raucous, intellectually stimulating, and, at times, downright intimidating. From the start, Arthur Carter was our de facto leader. Always out to prove himself, Arthur benefited from a dominant personality and great mind. I felt very close to Arthur and normally deferred to his judgment. The four of us sat around a common desk, and there was never a moment of privacy—everything we did was open to group scrutiny or kibitzing as though we were in a college fraternity. Occasionally, I'd have a fight with Joan over the phone and would pretend to have a conversation long after she had hung up simply to avoid one zinger or another from my partners.

Even as we were competing with more established firms, we'd vie among ourselves and constantly needle one another about not working hard enough. Weekly dinners soon became ritual, and more often than not, we headed uptown to a private room at the Christ Cella steakhouse. For an appetizer, Arthur and I typically would order a raw sirloin steak, split it in half, and season it with salt and pepper in our own version of steak tartare before we'd move on to our lobster entrée. The red meat worked wonders stoking our aggressiveness, and soon we'd have a free-for-all critiquing one another and pushing ourselves on ways to do more business. An outsider would have thought us an unruly bunch, but we collectively honed our business skills and injected one another with enormous passion for succeeding.

Carter, Berlind, Potoma & Weill prospered for nearly two years, and Joanie and I were finally in a position to afford a home on Long Island's upscale North Shore. Just as we were growing accustomed to our emerging prosperity, though, storm clouds appeared. Kennedy's honeymoon with Wall Street had begun to fray in late 1961 as his administration proposed tax reforms designed to limit deductions on business expenses and impose withholding taxes on dividends and certain types of interest income. Yet it was not until April 1962 when he opposed the steel industry's attempt to raise prices that the business community realized that the new president was going to follow a far different route than his predecessor.

Rumors began to circulate that the administration would be less aggressive in restraining union wage demands, and businesspeople openly worried about a new hostile climate for corporate profits. During the spring and early summer stocks plunged, and on a day of unmitigated panic in late May, the market experienced its largest one-day point drop since 1929. Volume surged to 9.4 million shares, the fifth highest daily total ever and the most since 1933. The sharp drop happened to take place on the very day we moved into our new home, which of course was particularly unsettling given the step-up in our carrying costs. During the first five months of 1962, the bottom fell out of the stock market as the Dow cascaded down 23 percent.

Now, this was a real bear market!

The market sustained another 4 percent drop during June before touching bottom, but the damage had been done. Investors were shell-shocked and cautious, while corporations stopped coming to market. Our partnership's financial results mirrored the market as commissions fell sharply and investment banking deals dried up. We learned some painful lessons, too, about holding inventories of stocks during bear markets and how trading liquidity can dry up in an instant. Still, we had done a good job keeping our costs and trading risks in check, and our business model from the start had a built-in capacity to absorb a more difficult market climate. We managed to muddle through.

The market, though, took a long while to recover. June 1962 marked the low point for the major averages, as stocks meandered for the next eighteen months. Following the market rout, investor fear gave way to apathy—trading volumes remained depressed as investors stuck to the sidelines.

That summer proved nerve-wracking. We had made a large financial commitment in buying a new home just as the market began its swoon, and our firm's cash flow was deteriorating thanks to the inactivity of our customers. As much out of boredom as a wish to save money, I often left work early that summer so that I could act as groundskeeper at our new home. I'd buy plants at a nursery named Cheap Sam's and tend to our garden. The physical labor of planting trees or mowing the lawn helped release some of the tension, but I still drove Joanie nuts with my pleas to cut back on our spending.

"Joanie, we're going to get through this and be fine," I said, "but let's not extend ourselves for a while. Please hold off on shopping unless it's absolutely necessary, and turn out the lights when we're not home." Joanie went along, though she reminded me often that I hadn't given a second thought to buying our expensive new home only weeks before. When I think back over my life, however, I've typically found it easier to accept a one-time large expense rather than to get used to a stepped-up level of ongoing overhead.

Perversely, the stock market didn't improve meaningfully until President Kennedy's assassination. Like most Americans, I reacted emotionally to the astounding news—it shocked me that this sort of thing could happen in a country as great as the United States, and I was amazed someone could do something so disruptive to a free society.

When the news of the president's death arrived, a huge selling surge hit the market. Normally during market routs, the exchange's specialists are supposed to step in and buy shares in order to inject liquidity. Sadly, many of these professionals ceded their responsibilities that day. The New York Stock Exchange closed at 1:00 P.M., but the hopelessly delayed ticker didn't stop running until after 6:00 P.M. because of the enormous trading volume. All the while, market professionals feared what might happen over the next few days as brokers sent clients an enormous number of margin calls. We all worried whether investors who had borrowed to finance stock purchases would be forced to sell their holdings to cover their margin obligations and cause a second wave of panic selling.

Fortunately, when trading resumed the following day our worst fears did not materialize. The hasty swearing-in of Lyndon Johnson as president reassured the public, and soon professional investors came swooping into the stock market to snap up shares at bargain prices. Stock prices rebounded, and we avoided the dreaded surge in margin calls. Over the following six months, the Dow Index rose 15 percent as investors settled down—the market was back on track.

In hindsight, the 1962–63 bear market turned out to be an event limited to the financial markets as the economy never slowed materially. The market may often discount future economic trends, but this rule certainly is not etched in stone. In this case, the tumble looked more like a case where stock valuations simply had gotten too euphoric and needed to adjust. After all, new investors had been streaming into the stock market for a decade with ever-growing confidence. The typical stock in the Dow Index had a price twenty-three times its earnings as this downturn began, compared to a multiple of only ten times in the early 1950s.

Amid this gut-wrenching market, our partnership faced a crisis of its own unconnected to the market's seizure. In early 1962, we were stunned to learn that Peter Potoma was being investigated by the SEC regarding liberties he had taken trading his wife's account. We had known for some time that Potoma was a risk, but we never imagined it would lead to potential regulatory issues. We were more concerned with Peter's erratic behavior. On more than one occasion, he had disappeared inexplicably only to resurface several days later. Once, he arrived at the office roughed up and sporting a black eye. We surmised he drank too much and warned him to straighten out, but his unpredictable actions persisted.

The SEC investigation was like a cold shower that taught an important business lesson on the need for picking good partners and focusing on reputation risk. As we learned more about the investigation, Arthur became nervous and insisted that we remove Potoma from the firm's name—the last thing we wanted was a stain on our young firm's reputation in the event of an adverse judgment. Peter went before the regulators early in the fall and chose to strike an arrogant pose rather than plead contrition. At that point, we knew events were heading toward a bad end and insisted he leave the firm. His departure came just in time to avoid tainting the rest of us. In October he was suspended from the business for a year for improperly handling discretionary accounts and violating margin rules.

Potoma's departure couldn't have come at a worse time. We severed our relationship as news of the Cuban missile crisis was pummeling stocks some six months into the horrid bear market. Peter had been our single biggest capital contributor and generator of commissions—he accounted for about a third of our recurring revenues. However we looked at it, his departure was a big loss, yet we understood we had no alternative.

As a postscript, we lost track of Peter until Arthur and I were approached by his attorney years later asking for help in raising bail money. Apparently, Potoma had been arrested for shooting a woman he was seeing after divorcing his wife and was now desperately turning to his former partners. While we ignored the entreaty, Arthur and I worried Potoma might come after us out of resentment upon his release from prison. It turned out, though, that he died shortly thereafter.

With Potoma's departure, we tried our best to hold on to his customers but were not particularly successful. Fortunately, Arthur's father-in-law passed along the name of a young salesman specializing in tax shelters whom he recommended highly. Soon, we all met Arthur Levitt Jr. and immediately liked him—he lacked experience selling securities, but we figured if he could sell cattle as tax shelters, he'd have no problem selling stocks and bonds. Even more impressively, his father was a one-man institution in New York, having served as state comptroller for more than twenty years. Arthur was comfortable around moneyed people and had great connections and sales skills. It took him about six months to pass his securities license at which point we made him a junior partner in our firm with a 5 percent equity stake. In a short time, he was leveraging his connections and bringing municipal bond underwriting assignments and retail orders our way.

As the bear market finally ended, we realized we needed to broaden our business model to avoid being too dependent on a single producer or one type of business. We also believed the flow of investment banking deals would recover only slowly; as it turned out, we did not execute a single banking transaction in 1963 or 1964. While our options to diversify were limited, one area seemed natural: the institutional business.

In those days, stocks of most large companies were traded on the New York Stock Exchange, which set minimum commission rates at relatively high levels. The appeal of selling thousand-share blocks to large institutions was overwhelming from a profitability standpoint. At the same time, the institutional market was growing sharply. In the early 1950s, individuals and corporate pension plans largely had avoided investing in stocks given fears about their safety, but after a decade of generally advancing stock prices, market participants stopped being so risk-averse. Consequently, money poured into the stock market and especially into the hands of a rapidly expanding industry of professional money managers. By the early 1960s, institutions controlled more than $100 billion in equities, and volumes were growing geometrically.

Setting our sights on the institutional business, we decided to hire salespeople and build a professional investment research department that would generate high-quality research that would hopefully steer commission dollars our way. After all, the model had worked well for a couple of our upstart competitors such as Donaldson Lufkin Jenrette and Faulkner Dawkins. Though the bear market was barely a memory, we took the risk of building our staff. By 1965, we had about thirty employees including roughly fifteen salespeople and half a dozen analysts. Along the way, our office needs were exploding. We first moved around the corner to 60 Broad Street where our partners, salesmen, and traders shared a common room while our research staff literally worked out of a hallway. A second move next door to 55 Broad a little more than a year later alleviated some of the overcrowding, but our quarters always seemed tight even to the point where our syndicate manager had to use a closet for his office.

We hired some terrific people in the early and mid-1960s. Brean Murray, who'd later go on to start his own firm, ran institutional sales; Ed Netter oddly enough came to us as our decorator but soon asked to join our research department where he proved better at picking insurance stocks than matching fabrics; and Carl Fredericks, a bit of a madman when it came to the intensity of his work habits, trained a cadre of young research analysts in his role as our first director of research. We also hired

Marshall Cogan, who soon flourished as an incredible salesman. While we were expanding rapidly, we did our best to control our cost structure—Arthur Carter was especially tough at deflecting requests for raises, and we avoided paying straight salaries, focusing instead on variable bonuses.

We insisted that our analysts go beyond writing research reports and sell their ideas, and we based their incentive pay accordingly. We also innovated with our organizational structure, as we were among the first brokerage firms to incorporate. Concerns about how our rapid growth might impact our personal liability represented an important consideration, yet we recognized, too, that the traditional partnership model tended to encourage excessively large partner payouts at the expense of capital formation. As fast as we were growing, we needed to do all that we could to promote a conservative capital structure.

During 1965, our investment in the institutional business began to pay off as market volumes grew and as corporations began to return to the capital markets to raise funds. We were pleasantly surprised by the amount of business we were doing with large institutions as commissions and trading large blocks of stock grew sharply, all the while proving that the market was underserved and hungry for rigorous idea-oriented research. We found, too, that the quality of our investment banking deals improved immeasurably from the types of business we had done at the start of the decade. It was a virtuous circle: Our reputation for hot deals and quality research improved our standing with large investors, which in turn helped us win better issuers as clients.

In these years, we began to think about diversifying into the fast-growing money management business, an area which we figured would offer a stream of recurring revenues. Between 1960 and 1965, mutual fund industry assets had doubled to $35 billion. By today's standard in which mutual fund assets exceed $7 trillion, this number seems laughable, but we were intent on pursuing every reasonable opportunity to grow and even out the fluctuations in our earnings. In 1967, we finally found what we were looking for when Arthur Levitt introduced us to Peter Bernstein, an economist and second-generation owner of the small but well-regarded Bernstein-Macaulay Company, one of the pioneers in the business of managing money for individuals. We offered Peter stock in our company and soon completed our first acquisition of this high-margin business, enabling us to brag that we were now a full-fledged money manager.

Later in my career, people would identify me as a champion of the retail brokerage business, but our original business plan envisioned the retail business primarily as a means to an end for supporting our investment banking business. As institutional and asset management businesses complemented our investment banking strategy, retail continued to play a supporting role—it helped us distribute deals and cover our overhead. Nonetheless, we remained fiercely competitive at growing our retail commissions.

More than just targeting new businesses, we looked for talented people who would help our firm grow. Unlike the established broker dealers who typically had ethnic or religious criteria for hiring new employees, we had an unbiased approach. We didn't consciously set out to make a statement, but I'm proud looking back that we hired the first African-American partner on Wall Street, Clarence Jones. A lawyer and speechwriter for Dr. Martin Luther King Jr., Clarence approached us to underwrite a new minority-oriented life insurance company in 1964. Initially, we had given him a commitment but exercised our option to withdraw during a temporary bout of market weakness. Clarence ended up hiring his own marketing staff and registered with the SEC to do his own offering. Proudly, he marched into our offices one day to tell us what a mistake we had made by not backing him. Arthur Levitt ceremoniously bowed low in Clarence's honor while I confessed, "I didn't know how smart you really were—you're obviously in the wrong business." It took Clarence a couple of years more to join our firm, but we recognized his sales skills and the entrée he'd provide to clients we'd never see otherwise. Although we hired him largely out of self-interest, the story illustrates how we placed a premium on being flexible and pursuing almost any reasonable growth opportunity.

As the institutional business continued to grow, the hiring of Marshall Cogan proved to be especially adroit. A young Harvard Business School graduate, Marshall initially joined as an analyst covering automotive and auto parts stocks but quickly demonstrated a remarkable skill at selling his ideas. Within three months, he began writing huge tickets. He was unbelievable. Friendly with Ned Johnson of Fidelity and a half dozen other prominent Boston money managers, Marshall was never afraid to ask for the order and soon turned our firm upside down with gigantic volumes of new business.

By 1966, the stock market was really humming after having enjoyed three consecutive years of double-digit percentage gains since the now faded 1962 bear market. Average daily trading volume was approaching seven million shares with increasing institutional activity playing an important role. Indeed, in just five years, institutional ownership of equities had doubled. Growth stocks rapidly were becoming the rage in this bull market, and prices for the market leaders commonly reached forty and fifty times a year's worth of earnings, giving rise to the "Nifty Fifty" label. Conglomerates especially were coming into fashion as investors warmed to the notion that valuations might benefit from less volatile earnings coming from highly diversified businesses.

It was a market made for Marshall Cogan, and clients avidly lapped up his well-crafted sales pitches. He soon developed close ties to some of the leading conglomerateurs of the day such as Charlie Bluhdorn of Gulf & Western, Meshulam Riklis of Rapid-American, and Jimmy Ling of LTV Corporation, which enabled Carter, Berlind & Weill to tap into highly sought after securities offerings. In no time, we had a busy calendar of initial public offerings and merger advisory assignments and were trading huge blocks of stock with increasing frequency.

At times, we'd all marvel at Marshall's selling skills. He used to write messages to himself in large print and stick the notes on the wall so he could refer to them as a means for inciting himself as he spoke with clients in feverish tones. One day, we heard Marshall relentlessly pushing one of his clients to reposition her automotive holdings. Suddenly, Marshall's assistant strolled into our main room and instructed our trader to sell twenty thousand shares of Ford. In unison, everyone looked up in recognition of the large order. A few minutes later a new order came in to buy thirty thousand shares of Chrysler. Worrying whether we were taking too much trading risk, I pinned the young employee and demanded, "Who the hell are you talking to?" and then instructed him to check to be sure he had the order right. I worried that Marshall was forcing us to take on excessive risk, yet he was adept at quickly finding large buyers for inventory we were eager to turn over.

Marshall's success came so fast we didn't quite know what to do with him; it was clear that he was driving our still new institutional business to a new level. Within a year, we rewarded him with a junior equity interest in the company. All of us felt thrilled that we had found such a supersalesman who could help us reach our potential with large institutional accounts.

Mirroring the growth of Carter, Berlind & Weill, my perspective and the quality of my clients also matured in this period. In 1964, five years after meeting my first mentor, Tubby Burnham, I had the good fortune to meet Sonny Werblin, another outsized personality who would teach me important lessons and build my self-confidence. Sonny had enjoyed success as a top executive and celebrity promoter at MCA before going off on his own to start the American Football League and buy the New York Titans, the forerunner to the New York Jets. I met Sonny through my continued involvement with Peekskill Military Academy where, by happenstance, the Jets used the athletic fields for training.

Not that long after meeting, Sonny and I shared an experience that drew us together. We were both serving on my alma mater's board of trustees when the school fell onto hard times and had to file bankruptcy and, sadly, face liquidation. It troubled Sonny and me greatly that the school had failed to meet its payroll and that the teachers' back pay was at risk. The other trustees all lived out of town and quickly dispersed, leaving the school to the mercy of the judicial system. Sonny and I, however, worried about the teachers and the potential legal and reputation risks that the board might face, and we decided to step up and personally cover the amount owed to the teaching staff. My share was in the neighborhood of $35,000, an amount I eventually recovered once the bankruptcy was sorted out. While it was a small incident, Sonny and I knew that bailing out the teachers was the right thing to do; the shared experience laid a foundation of mutual respect.

Nearly twenty years my senior, Sonny soon became almost a father figure, and he was a great client. He introduced me to a wide array of his celebrity friends—it was a whole new world. Until then, I was relatively introverted and unexposed to a sophisticated clientele. Before I knew it, I was hanging around with the likes of Johnny Carson and Bobby Sarnoff, not to mention a slew of professional athletes and team owners. Sonny lived large, had enormous energy, and was gifted at dealing with people. He also had a close relationship with his wife, something I especially admired. We enjoyed many evenings together when, between drinking and staying up late, he taught me many important lessons. "Think creatively and dream big," he'd say, "and don't be afraid to take risks." Sonny deserves credit for drawing me out of my shell and for allowing me to see the big leagues.

He certainly introduced me to an entirely different clientele far removed from the waiter and maître d' clients I had begun with just a few years earlier. I'm a sucker for associating with well-known figures, and thanks to Sonny, I had some terrific client relationships during the 1960s. Johnny Carson and his wife lived in Sonny's building and soon became clients. Offstage, Carson was tremendously funny, quick-witted, and easy to work with, at least until he split up with his first wife. Howard Cosell and Muhammad Ali also gave us business. Once the two came to our office together—immediately, everyone stopped dead in their tracks. Cosell marched Ali over to Clarence Jones and reported to the great boxer that Clarence was the only black partner on Wall Street "and he's smart, too." Never one to be upstaged, Ali looked Clarence in the eye and declared, "Well, you're not as smart as me. You can't box and let me see your poetry!" The room erupted in laughter.

I had relationships with a variety of other sports figures including Jets running back Billy Mathis, whom I met on the training field one summer. I counseled him to start thinking about a second career for when his football days would end; sure enough, he came to work for us a few years later. In turn, he introduced personalities like Bill Bradley, Joe Namath, Tucker Fredrickson, and Rod Gilbert to our firm. At one point, we tried to entice Namath to come to work for us, too; however, he was intent on starting his Broadway Joe restaurant chain instead.

All these relationships enhanced my self-confidence, and I tried to emulate Sonny Werblin's people skills and judgment. Yet I still regret not taking advantage of a golden opportunity he once offered. In 1967, Sonny asked if I'd like to buy out his partner, Leon Hess, for a 50 percent ownership interest in the Jets. I obviously had little appreciation for the business and failed the test of thinking large because all I could focus on was the money the team lost. Not grasping that cable and television networks one day would offer vast sums to team owners for broadcasting rights, I turned him down cold. With twenty-twenty hindsight, the offer was a steal, as it would have cost me less than $4 million in contrast to the hundreds of millions of dollars teams have sold for in recent years.

Similarly, another lesson taught me to think outside the box. Our analyst, Ed Netter, came to the conclusion that the staid insurance industry was filled with excess capital and that many stocks were incredible bargains when considering the potential for possible acquirers to better deploy these funds. Detailing his insight, he wrote a major report which our sales force aggressively marketed to our clients. Arthur Carter soon hooked Saul Steinberg, CEO of an acquisitive computer leasing company named Leasco, on the appeal of buying Reliance Insurance, an old-line Philadelphia insurer gushing with spare capital. Steinberg realized that he could use Reliance's resources as an inexpensive way to fund the continuing rapid growth of his leasing business.

When we announced the bid, skeptics questioned the deal's feasibility let alone why Steinberg had chosen the backing of little known Carter, Berlind & Weill. Yet, Steinberg's tenacity paid off, and he soon prevailed in the landmark transaction. Our firm ended up receiving a $750,000 advisory fee, a considerable amount of money in those days. Suddenly, that large fee made me realize how small our company's fees were in relation to the value that our clients could build by growing their firms effectively and illustrated how smart managers could drive huge payoffs for their shareholders. While I feared making any abrupt changes in my career, I began to think about shifting my focus one day toward managing and pursuing acquisitions of our own.

Although the firm and I matured during the 1960s, one thing remained constant: Arthur Carter's dominance. We might have joined together technically as equal partners, yet, in practice, Arthur drove our firm's decision making with an iron fist. At our weekly dinners, he'd lead the conversation and finger who was lagging in production that week. With his steely blue eyes, he had a knack for making us sweat. Even our desk layout spoke to his centrality as he sat at its head flanked by Roger and me.

With his great intelligence, natural impatience, and legendary temper, Arthur overshadowed everyone, and he was widely feared. He'd have his secretary in tears at least once a day, and watching younger employees ask for a raise soon became a spectator sport. On these occasions, Arthur might explosively react with protestations of unworthiness or suggest the petitioner should be prepared to leave the firm. One of our analysts earning $12,000 a year once asked Arthur to approve his hiring an assistant for $5,000 in annual pay. After making the analyst grovel, Arthur surprisingly approved the request; yet, as the employee turned to leave, Arthur yelled out, "You have your assistant, but you now earn $7,000 a year!"

Arthur's ferocious competitiveness often made life unpleasant, but through our first several years together, I respected him greatly as someone with tremendous business acumen who through the force of his personality would drive all of us to success. We had been friends for a number of years, and I felt we had a special relationship. Since Arthur frequently asked for my advice, I rationalized I could veto any important decision.

The pressurized environment led us all to focus intensively on generating revenues. Never hesitant to ask questions, Arthur Levitt soon mastered the basics of the securities business. He had a natural ability to schmooze people into believing in him and, before long, built a nice book of business with wealthy investors. Within two years of joining the firm, he was generating commissions on a par with Roger and me, and we equalized his ownership share. In contrast, Roger approached the business in a low-key, almost diffident manner reflecting a faux WASPishness learned at Princeton and Eastman Dillon. He never had the same ego as the rest of us and probably secretly yearned to return to his first love of songwriting. Still, Roger built a solid book of retail, institutional, and family business.

As for me, I was obsessed with writing transaction tickets and servicing my clients. As the firm's institutional business grew, I eagerly added accounts which complemented my retail-oriented client base. When I'd see a good investment idea or read an insightful piece of research, I'd take the lead in championing the opportunity both inside our firm and with our customers. I also contributed my share to managing the firm especially as it related to overseeing our trading risks and the quality of our research and sales efforts; however, in truth, I feared taking on too much responsibility and in practice remained content to defer to Arthur on the overall direction of the firm.

Sadly, our firm's success fed Arthur's already outsized ego, and tensions gradually mounted as Arthur increasingly bullied the rest of us. Our long-standing friendship and mutual respect gave way to a very different relationship, one in which Arthur increasingly flexed his power and sought to intimidate me—along with my other partners—into a subservient role. "Get off your asses and pull your weight," he'd frequently bellow, and more often than not, he'd rail that Roger's commissions were particularly weak. At the same time, I felt Arthur was intentionally divisive as he schemed with a couple of our lesser shareholders on important decisions. In one instance, Arthur brought in a friend named Kenny Rosen to work on investment banking deals; as much as anything, the relationship seemed geared to shifting the firm's political balance. Soon, nothing I did seemed good enough for him, and I hardly felt like a founding partner. It was a terrible time for me emotionally: My stomach was constantly churning, and I dreaded coming to the office.

Events began to come to a head by early 1968. In February, Arthur suddenly called me aside and proposed that we reduce Roger's ownership share and split his stake among ourselves. I was flabbergasted. No matter how much I saw our firm as a meritocracy, cutting a founding partner's stake seemed ruthless and, until that point, unimaginable. I felt Arthur was being disingenuous, as it seemed more like a grab for personal gain than a justifiable business decision. More than anything, it gnawed at me that if Arthur could do this to Roger, what would stop him from coming after me? I realized that once you start playing around with a firm's equilibrium, you set a process in motion with totally unpredictable results.

I told Arthur that I wouldn't agree to his plan and prayed that it would be the end of the matter. I feared Arthur would never let go of the idea and wondered if he'd penalize me for opposing him. Summer came, and Arthur spent a great deal of time out at his beach house on eastern Long Island. Just as I started to breathe a bit easier, my worst fears came to pass when in August Arthur Levitt and his wife, Marilyn, invited Joanie and me to dinner. Meeting on a Saturday night at a restaurant on City Island, Arthur confided that Carter had proposed to him a plan similar to that which he had discussed with me earlier in the year. However, this time, there was one critical change: Instead of cutting only Roger's stake, Arthur Carter was now proposing to cut my ownership share as well!

When I heard this stunning news, my heart sank. I realized that everything I had achieved over eight years was completely at risk, and it unnerved me that someone with whom I had shared such a close personal relationship for so many years was now stabbing me in the back.

Fortunately, Arthur Levitt wasn't passing along this news just to scare me. He never had gotten along with Arthur Carter, and I'm sure he worried that he could be next if he were to go along with the plan. Even if he were to survive, Arthur Levitt had to appreciate that working with Carter as his sole senior partner would be nearly unbearable. In short, he, too, planned to turn down Carter. Through dinner and a two-hour walk afterward, we and our spouses collectively thought through our options.

We realized that Carter had gone too far and that a simple rejection of his proposal wouldn't resolve the issue—it was now him or us. And beyond Carter, we also had to deal with a couple of his cronies, like

Ken Rosen. We needed legal advice and on Monday scurried to find a competent advisor. We turned to Ken Bialkin from Willkie, Farr & Gallagher, who had impressed us representing Saul Steinberg in the Reliance transaction. Kenny Bialkin would become a lifelong friend, but it was all deadly serious business at that point. Arthur Levitt arranged to meet with Bialkin on a warm Friday afternoon and explained our predicament. Kenny quickly explained that this was no simple legal matter as there was little precedent for a New York Stock Exchange member firm forcing out its president.

Researching the matter over the weekend, Kenny informed us that our articles of incorporation conferred upon the board the power to fire members and redeem their shares at book value so long as a majority concurred. Curiously, Roger still was completely out of the loop regarding how his stake had been hanging in the balance all year long. We hadn't yet informed him of the fast-moving events but took for granted that we'd have the votes to successfully confront Arthur.

Kenny proceeded to advise us on tactics, which called for us to present our own ultimatum for Carter to resign. Upon hearing the plan, Levitt incredulously blurted, "I can do that?" He then started to suggest that we should take time to think things through more carefully but was immediately shut down by Kenny. "If you want to do this, you have to do it the right way, and that means acting swiftly and decisively. You need to be resolute and know there's no turning back." To his great credit, the normally deliberative Levitt signed on to lead the charge.

That very morning, Levitt called a special board meeting and announced Carter's proposal. Arthur Carter was stunned to realize that Levitt was not going along with his plan. At once, Levitt called for the decisive vote rejecting Carter's bid for control. Following Kenny's carefully devised game plan, Levitt then called for a recess until 3:00 P.M. When we reconvened, an unusually authoritative Arthur Levitt dropped our bombshell on Carter: "We want your resignation in hand by 6:00 P.M. If you comply, we'll allow you to write your own press release; otherwise, we plan to put out a release announcing that we fired you." The timing was especially crafty and was designed to exert maximum pressure since we knew this would give Carter exactly an hour to get his version of his departure to the press before the evening deadline for the next day's papers. Carter was flabbergasted but somehow managed to respond with the equanimity only a true egotist could muster, "I'll have to think about it."

He purposely took his time, but in the end Arthur Carter had no other option but to fold. The following morning—September 10, 1968—a half-column story was buried in *The Wall Street Journal* reporting his departure. In a triumph for public relations, the story declared "it was an amicable parting." Carter got to say that he decided to leave in order to start his own publicly owned merchant bank and that he already was lining up investors. Meanwhile, we announced our new lineup, which avoided naming a president and now included Marshall Cogan as senior vice president. I took the chairman of the board title; Roger became chairman of the executive committee; and Arthur Levitt was made executive vice president.

Arthur Carter went off and soon formed his new company, The Carter Group. Before announcing a single transaction, he sold shares to the public, pitching that he'd operate a successful merchant bank boutique. On the strength of his reputation alone, money flowed to him in a remarkably large offering for the time. With funding in hand, Arthur went on to invest in a series of manufacturing, publishing, real estate, and utility ventures and eventually bought out his public investors. After we parted, he must have owned a hundred different companies. Our relationship has had its up and down cycles over four decades with the determining factor often being the friendliness of the editorials that he'd publish about me in *The New York Observer* or one of the other newspapers he owned. Finally, in 2003 after I announced my retirement, the *Observer* ran an especially complimentary editorial, and I saw immediately that it was Arthur's way of reaching out to reconcile once and for all. We've both worked to become good friends again and put to rest our long unresolved relationship.

———

The rapidly unfolding events during the summer of 1968 never gave us the chance to consider how things would change without Arthur's strong presence. We soon had to strike a new balance in how we'd run the firm. Arthur's departure initially provoked in me a tremendous sense of relief, but I realized that this was far from the end of our political jockeying. A couple of issues demanded immediate attention, especially the need to resolve how we'd change the firm's name and how we'd adjust ownership stakes and titles.

We urgently needed to convince Marshall Cogan to stay. Everyone could see Marshall's value as our largest producer, not the least Arthur Carter, who immediately tried to woo Marshall to join The Carter Group. Though Marshall may have been torn at first, he knew he'd play a far more important role by staying with us. Of course, his strength as a producer emboldened him to make his own set of demands. While he initially pressed to be made head of the firm, we compromised by granting him a full equity stake and changing our firm's moniker to prominently incorporate his name. At the same time, Arthur Levitt asked to be rewarded for his decisive actions in standing up to Carter—he had already enjoyed a full ownership share for three years, but we moved to step up his visibility in our corporate identity as well. We consequently cast our new name as Cogan, Berlind, Weill & Levitt. Abbreviated CBWL, a few wags—to my dismay—started referring to us as "Corned Beef With Lettuce," yet the label was a small price to pay in return for keeping everyone happy.

Rearranging names and ownership, however, failed to resolve how we'd actually manage the firm. Although Marshall may have wanted to assume Carter's leadership position, we all could see that he lacked management skill. Marshall was first and foremost a great salesman, nothing more and nothing less. In contrast, I had an underlying fear of taking responsibility for running the firm—I simply hadn't reached the maturity necessary to take on the risk of making mistakes, and I was comfortable playing the role of second-guessing with veto power. Meanwhile, Arthur and Roger had their own drawbacks—Levitt was a good salesman but was weak at understanding financial details; Roger was mild-mannered and lacked the personality to manage the firm decisively.

We spent many of our weekly dinners debating what we should do as directly and confrontationally as ever. One evening, Marshall turned to Kenny Bialkin, who was now advising us regularly, and offered: "You're a good neutral choice; why don't you leave Willkie Farr and come run our firm?" Kenny, however, was far too smart to trade his position of prominence at his prestigious law firm to work full-time with such an unruly bunch. The debating continued. In another instance, Levitt turned to Cogan and declared, "Marshall, you can't be selected since you have a bad reputation. Too many people think you're slick and don't trust you." Not missing a beat, Marshall shot back, "Arthur, you're so smooth. If you had any brains, you'd be dangerous." We were at an impasse, but we still needed to select someone to sign legal documents as our CEO. At last, we decided to make Roger our titular CEO. We concluded that mild-mannered Roger would pose the least threat to the rest of us and that we could each have a good measure of influence over him.

Shortly after settling the CEO issue, we were faced with a very different management challenge when one of our top managers, Don Shagrin, tipped me off that he and three other important executives were contemplating resigning en masse in order to buy into a small brokerage firm. I don't think their intention was to hold us up, though the group was clearly restive for an equity stake. Had Don not warned me of the impending departure, we might have lost the heads of our research and investment banking departments and two senior sales executives all at once.

I placed great weight on personal loyalty, so the news wounded and angered me. Still, circumstances demanded pragmatism as we could hardly sit idly by and let four important producers walk out the door. Swallowing my hurt, I went along with a plan to allow each to buy a 5 percent ownership stake in our company, which probably doubled the ownership share our secondary equity holders held in the firm. In total, a group of roughly twenty-five executives below the top level now owned 40–50 percent of the firm.

Fortunately, business conditions remained good while we sorted out these issues. The Dow briefly touched the 1,000 mark for the first time in 1966, and while 1967 was an off year, stocks came roaring back all through 1968. Somehow, the market was willing to disregard the increasing turmoil in our society relating to the Vietnam War, including incipient signs of inflation relating to financing the war effort and Johnson's Great Society programs. We'd soon realize it was only a temporary calm, but the continuing healthy market backdrop allowed our financial results to absorb our changes without making us feel impoverished.

Apart from the work-related stresses, Joanie and I faced a different set of issues in our personal life. Candidly, most of the 1960s were difficult years. In 1963, we took a skiing vacation with Arthur and Marilyn Levitt during which Joanie fell off a ski lift and seriously hurt her back. The doctors first misdiagnosed what turned out to be a ruptured herniated disk—she underwent an operation to fuse her vertebrae and then spent months in the hospital with a full body cast.

For the next three years, she was in and out of hospitals all the while suffering guilt at not being home for our children. At one point, Joanie lost a dangerous amount of weight, dropping to eighty-five pounds as the depression from being incapacitated overwhelmed her. Joanie demanded that I stay at home more to tend to the kids, and in hindsight I should have been more sensitive; however, I had difficulty disengaging from work, given we were working at full tilt to build the business. I felt my primary responsibility was to earn a proper living for my family. It also frustrated me that my wife's ailment was so out of my control.

Gradually, Joanie regained her strength, though she has had to contend with periodic back problems ever since. All the social turmoil in the 1960s—especially the nascent feminist movement—presented other challenges in our relationship. Having married and started a family at a young age, we had fallen into typical roles early in our marriage. Soon Joanie began to question whether we had the right balance in our lives. Many of her friends were going back to college or pursuing careers of their own, and they influenced Joanie to reassess her place in life.

Moving residences added additional stress into our lives. Given my long hours, I hated the commute from Long Island and pressed to buy an apartment in Manhattan. We thought we had a deal and sold our home only to find that the cooperative's board would not act on our application in a reasonable time. Hurriedly, we settled on buying another house on Long Island in Kings Point, which was a letdown for both of us. I still had to contend with a long commute while Joanie complained about the school system and our nouveau riche neighbors.

With all our frustrations, life at home frequently was contentious, which perversely led me to throw myself into my work all the more. Nonetheless, I always shared what was going on at the office, and I continued to ask for Joanie's advice especially on people issues as we were hiring new employees at a rapid pace. While Joanie appreciated my interest in her opinions, that was far from a solution to the tension in our marriage. Despite our challenges, we never stopped pulling together and obviously never gave up on one another.

––––––––

Despite bumps along the way, our company had thrived in its first eight years, and our maturing business model reassured us that we increasingly could take on the industry's giants and at least hold our own. Yet our growth forced us to confront challenges in the part of the business not readily seen by clients, our financial structure and our operations. We had moved away from a partnership model as early as 1965 recognizing that a corporate form of ownership would promote reinvestment of capital (thanks to tax considerations) and insulation from personal liability. At the same time, we presciently wondered whether the New York Stock Exchange's prohibition against public ownership for securities firms would change one day and wanted to be prepared.

The wisdom of incorporating soon became obvious as the size and complexity of our new securities offerings and trading positions posed significant new risks and need for capital support. In his exuberance promoting our business, Marshall had taken the lead in getting behind riskier investment banking clients and pushing our trading desk to accept positions in less liquid securities. Marshall may have emphasized closing the sale, though we all accepted underwriting assignments from companies with complicated balance sheets and business propositions.

It was only a matter of time before our risk profile grabbed the attention of Burnham & Company, our clearing agent. Over the years, Tubby and his firm had played a valuable role in standing behind our growth; however, by the late 1960s, our transaction volumes were swiftly overtaking Burnham's. In fact, across the entire industry, trading volumes had grown so much during the bull market that many firms were beginning to encounter difficulty processing the mountains of customer orders. Clearing firms legally stand behind each trade, so Tubby and his partners understood that their operational risks were growing sharply. Around the beginning of 1969, Tubby came to see me and explained that his partners were growing uncomfortable with the relationship. He described how his firm now faced the need to step up its fixed costs and allocate more capital to support our growth, and pointed out how much our two firms' trading risks overlapped.

Although he didn't say it, I suspected that he also harbored concerns about the quality of some of our deals, which in a few cases were the subject of SEC reviews. Tubby did his best to play the good cop and lay the issues at the feet of his partners; still, I understood that we had outgrown our business relationship. Not wishing to compromise our friendship, I chose not to argue and simply asked Tubby to grant us a year to find another solution.

We were one of the largest brokerages to rely on a third party for clearing services at that point and recognized that being kicked out of Burnham really meant we'd have an impossible time finding another firm to do our clearing. To clear for ourselves, we either had to buy or build a full-fledged back office, which certainly would be a major undertaking.

Lacking the managerial resources, we began to look for an executive with the requisite skill to help us solve our dilemma. Happily, an acquaintance at the accounting firm Haskins & Sells referred us to Frank Zarb, the second-ranking operations officer at Goodbody & Company, a very large brokerage firm in those days. We met Frank in a hastily arranged meeting and took to one another right away. Frank appreciated the opportunity to head an operational unit of his own, while we were impressed by his credentials of managing a business that was far larger than that which we planned to establish.

Frank quickly demonstrated that he was an able administrator. He was an intensely determined individual—one of those people with a blue-collar family background intent on proving themselves as professionals. I never met anyone so organized and with such a specific plan for where he wanted to be two, five, and ten years into the future. Upon his arrival, we first assessed whether we might acquire another firm with an existing back office, but nothing seemed reasonable. Setting that option aside, we took on the task of designing and building our own operational unit. Frank immediately leveraged his contacts and began hiring a team.

Building a new back office required financial resources, and with Arthur Levitt leading the way, we raised $3 million from two private placements, the first outside capital we had sought since we went into business. We then opened a storefront office on Madison Avenue for recruiting purposes and quickly hired a small army of data processing people and accountants. Having no existing computer systems, we hired a unit of RCA to provide software while we took space on two floors at 100 Wall Street for our new computers and a vault for our securities.

Soon our new team was humming with activity getting our systems ready to accommodate our deadline of early 1970 for the handoff from Burnham. Frank had begun Monday morning meetings for his management team, and I eagerly attended on a regular basis. I had some basis for understanding operational issues from my early work experience as a margin clerk at Bear Stearns, and I wanted to be absolutely sure we were going to handle this high-risk investment without a hitch. Those Monday morning meetings proved invaluable as I learned for myself the nuances of the back office.

While most other Wall Street executives took their operations people for granted, I came to respect the enormous challenges these folks faced in handling large numbers of transactions with minimal errors and in reconciling our firm's books during each night so we could safely begin to trade again with each new day. On occasion, I'd even spend the night in the back office. Those experiences enabled me to see how we actually settled transactions, and by demonstrating my sincere interest, my presence motivated our staff. Knowing that strong operations represented the critical key to success, I invested more time than any of my partners in order to learn the ins and outs of the back office. Computers were just being introduced on Wall Street in a major way, and the experience proved exceptionally valuable.

By the end of 1969, we had completed our testing and were ready to go live with our new state-of-the-art back office. We pulled the switch, and thankfully everything ran smoothly. We were relieved to have finished this demanding project, but we realized our success still came with a price as our fixed costs had now grown meaningfully. Our new system had substantial excess processing capacity, as it could handle three times our normal daily trading volumes, and our challenge soon became finding ways to more fully utilize our new systems. For a short time, we considered clearing for other firms, but we worried about taking on others' risks, especially as nightmarish stories of settlement problems across the industry were beginning to become more frequent. I also felt we should devote our carefully built systems exclusively to the benefit of our own clients. Instead of clearing for others, we began to consider acquisitions.

A massive wave of industry consolidation was just beginning. The seeds of the shakeout had been sown during the headiest days of the bull market. The industry's top executives generally were ill prepared for the surge in trading volumes, and with most having backgrounds in marketing, they lacked appreciation for how to adapt to new computer technology. As early as 1967, the problem in Wall Street firms' back offices had become painfully obvious as the industry was overwhelmed by a deluge of orders.

Normally, brokerage firms strive to match their prior day's orders overnight so as to begin the new trading day with a minimum of unreconciled orders. During this period, volumes were so heavy that many firms were unable to keep up with their orders. Because these firms lacked the luxury to place a moratorium on new business, unmatched orders mounted rapidly, and conditions on the Street became increasingly chaotic. Horror stories began to emerge about mountains of unclaimed securities piling up in brokerage vaults and even Mafia involvement in a rising wave of securities thefts. In 1968, market "fails"—those orders not being properly settled within a normal four-day span—rapidly accelerated as trading volumes by this time had more than doubled from only three years earlier. By year end, the industry was staring at over $4 billion in unmatched orders, implying huge potential losses.

Everyone recognized the growing risk. Mounting losses impaired capital adequacy at many firms, while the prevailing system of subordinated debt—where investors or lenders would provide their brokers with cash or stock that counted as capital—added to the stress as nervous investors withdrew their funding support. Regulatory requirements mandated that firms' indebtedness could not exceed twenty times capital. When capital shortages surfaced, individual firms were compelled by both prudence and the securities regulators to rein in their growth. One after another, firms began to come up short on capital, and the New York Stock Exchange took increasingly visible action. For example, it mandated a cessation of trading on Wednesdays to help sort out processing backlogs and limited the activities of scores of firms. Nevertheless, there was no easy fix.

By early 1970, Wall Street's difficulties were sapping market confidence. Stocks hit a three-year low in January after plunging 15 percent during the prior year. Major firms were being forced to merge or liquidate amid record losses.

While the climate was horrible, CBWL remained above the fray, as we had solid capital and a new back office untouched by the industry's processing issues. We were in the midst of considering how to fill our spare processing capacity, and we immediately started to consider whether we might take advantage of the industry's turmoil. An opportunity arose when the small but well-regarded McDonnell & Company, a firm connected to the wife of Henry Ford, was forced into liquidation. We ended up acquiring McDonnell's Beverly Hills office, which would act as an experiment in running a branch outside of New York. This small acquisition proved problematic in many ways, not the least because of its distance and the aggressive mind-set of its brokers, but it still was a valuable exercise that sensitized us to many of the challenges in building a branch system.

By April 1970, the industry's crisis was gathering new legs. A brief rally in February and March gave way to a new market slide as the Dow hit 724 at the end of April, 10 percent below where it began the year. In early May, stocks had their single worst day in seven years—the market was moving lower now on increasingly light volumes as a funk was settling over investors. With summer came more depressing news: The United States invaded Cambodia; protesters were killed at Kent State; and Penn Central declared bankruptcy. Perversely, the awful political and economic news was at last solving the industry's volume crunch, but nothing, it seemed, could arrest the slide in Wall Street's profits. And yet, out of these dark days, CBWL was about to benefit from a truly gargantuan opportunity.

Hayden Stone had been one of the leading names in the securities industry with a reputation for serving an upscale clientele. In the mid-1960s, the firm boasted more than eighty retail brokerage offices across the country and advised on countless investment banking transactions. It earned an impressive $100 million in 1968. Like many other firms, though, Hayden Stone's prestige did little to insulate it from the industry's operational turmoil. Its leadership chased new business with ease but was inept at handling the firm's growth.

Its profits turning on a dime, Hayden reported an $11 million loss for 1969.

Unfortunately for Hayden, matters continued to deteriorate as the market resumed its downward course. Securities that Hayden had counted for capital were declining in value and gradually impaired the firm's capital adequacy. By June, the situation erupted into a full-fledged crisis as a surprise audit revealed Hayden's precarious financial position. By July, the New York Stock Exchange injected $5 million in emergency funding, but it was clear a buyer was needed.

Financial experts agreed that a failure of Hayden Stone potentially posed catastrophic risks for the financial system and the economy at large given the firm's prominence and its web of relationships with banks and other brokers. While confidence deteriorated, partners and other creditors rushed to withdraw capital, feeling that Hayden surely was in a death spiral.

This was the opportunity we had been waiting for. We realized that both Hayden and the New York Stock Exchange were on the defensive—Hayden's downside risk had become obvious while the exchange's leadership had to worry that its stabilization fund might run out of resources if Hayden were to fail. Roger knew a number of people at Hayden and approached its CEO, Don Stroben. Roger pointed out CBWL had the capital, the back office, and the know-how to be part of the solution. With nowhere else to turn, Hayden began negotiating a deal with us. Roger took the lead in the negotiations while I focused on the financial and operational challenges.

Almost immediately, the New York Stock Exchange and Hayden's key creditors largely took over the negotiations. Although our firm enjoyed a healthy balance sheet, these parties saw that our swallowing Hayden Stone would be difficult. Accordingly, we settled on a plan where, instead of a full-blown merger, CBWL would be allowed to buy selected assets. Luckily, we were able to get the pick of Hayden Stone's assets and quickly identified twenty-eight choice retail branches and key staff in the institutional and investment banking franchise.

In structuring the deal, we convinced the New York Stock Exchange to kick in $7.5 million in funding support and to relieve CBWL of the bulk of Hayden Stone's liabilities. I calculated that we already had in place the $6 million in spare capital needed to handle the transaction. With our deal done, a competing firm named Walston agreed to buy Hayden's other offices. Still, there was no hiding the fact that we had cherry-picked Hayden's choicest assets.

To complete the transaction, we needed to surmount one last hurdle, namely to convince Hayden Stone's more than one hundred creditors to approve the transaction. It was critical to the deal's viability that these creditors keep their capital committed. On September 3, Hayden called a meeting at the New York Racquet Club on Park Avenue where we hoped to convince the firm's full array of creditors of the deal's wisdom. On the eve of that meeting, in an instance of unbelievably bad timing, we were stunned to learn that the Chicago Board of Trade unilaterally had determined that Hayden Stone was insolvent and was prepared to go public with trading-related sanctions. The news of course added great drama to an incredibly tense situation.

That night, the president of the New York Stock Exchange, Robert Haack, and crisis committee head Felix Rohatyn rushed to Chicago and successfully urged a week's delay in the pronouncement. Still, we were now working against a tight deadline. At the next day's meeting with the creditors, CEO Don Stroben underscored that the transaction was absolutely essential if the lenders were to salvage their investment. He then spoke eloquently about CBWL and had Roger join him in telling the assembled group how CBWL was the perfect solution to Hayden Stone's woes.

That session went reasonably well, and over the next few days, we scurried to be sure we had the support of the creditors. Importantly, we claimed that we needed unanimous support for the transaction to be viable and that the alternative would mean a forced liquidation of Hayden Stone, a financial panic, and a complete loss on the creditors' funds.

In truth, we would have been willing to close the transaction so long as the bulk of the creditors participated, but it was important to keep up pressure to the final moment. The team, comprised of executives from the New York Stock Exchange, Hayden Stone, and CBWL, made good progress winning the needed support until we realized we had one last and very vociferous holdout, a creditor from Oklahoma named Jack Golsen.

Golsen felt badly cheated by Hayden Stone and contended the firm had purposely misled him and a few fellow Oklahomans just a few months before in order to secure funding. He was by now intent on teaching the "city boys from New York" a lesson and determined to oppose the transaction on principle. Phone call upon phone call failed to dislodge him from his moral high ground. With a declaration of insolvency looming, many on Wall Street worried what would happen to the stock market and the soundness of the American financial system if a firm as important as Hayden Stone were to be forced into liquidation.

With time growing desperately short, Roger Berlind, Marshall Cogan, and a few others decided to charter a Learjet and fly to Oklahoma City to negotiate with Golsen personally. I stayed back in Willkie Farr's offices with Kenny Bialkin and Hayden's retail head, George Murray, in order to keep planning the deal's implementation assuming we would in fact reach an agreement. Ratcheting up the drama, severe weather prevented our emissaries' plane from taking off until the middle of the night.

Finally, in the wee hours of the morning, the team got off the ground. Landing in Oklahoma at 4:30 A.M., Roger and the others roused Golsen from bed and forced him to meet in his basement office. For the next four hours they argued with him, begging and cajoling him to change his mind. At one point, the team felt compelled to put the chairman of the New York Stock Exchange, Bunny Lasker, on the phone to weigh in. Lasker, a close friend of President Richard Nixon, reminded Golsen of the economic stakes and threatened to have the president call directly to make the point.

Back in New York, the tension was palpable. At the exchange, the Hayden Stone floor trader supposedly was pacing nervously with a fistful of customer orders not knowing if the firm would remain solvent so that he could place them. George Murray came over to me in Willkie Farr's offices and declared, "If this deal doesn't go through, I'm jumping out the window." What finally tipped the balance remains unclear, though with only minutes to spare, Golsen finally capitulated.

The popular theory had the threat of a call from Nixon the pivotal event, but Roger Berlind reported that the decisive argument was far more mundane, namely that Golsen feared being permanently ostracized in the local community for contributing to a national economic crisis. At 9:50 A.M., with ten minutes to go before the market's opening, word hit the tape that we had a deal. Understanding that he could now place his orders under a new CBWL–Hayden Stone name, Hayden's nervous floor trader passed out on the floor from the release of tension.

While I had little time to enjoy our coup at that moment, I knew one thing for sure: We had just increased the scale of our business by a factor of thirty times. A minnow had swallowed a whale.

Even as acquiring the bulk of Hayden Stone transformed CBWL, my partners and I didn't dwell on the deal's risks. I might have been naive, but I felt we had plenty of capital and an edge running our back office "factory." Thanks to the funding supplied by Hayden's creditors and the financial support committed by the New York Stock Exchange, we enjoyed a solid balance sheet coming out of the transaction. Yes, we'd have to learn how to operate a national distribution system, and we'd have to realign Hayden Stone's cost structure to ensure profitability, but had we not moved on this deal, I believed that CBWL would be at risk of suffering a slow death from heavy overhead and a shortfall in revenues as the market weakened.

As we rolled up our sleeves to integrate our greatly enlarged company, we tried not to become mesmerized from going from two offices to thirty and from 5,800 to 51,000 customer accounts. After all, CBWL–Hayden Stone still accounted for less than 1 percent of all shares traded on the New York Stock Exchange. I had taken the lead among my partners in thinking through the financial and operational requirements of how to properly absorb our new business.

In an exercise I'd repeat often in later transactions, I first made assumptions for what a difficult operating climate would mean for revenues and, from that estimate, calculated an appropriate expense base that would allow for continued profitability. This meant we needed to cut Hayden Stone's expenses in half. I determined George Murray should communicate the rationalization plan to his team and immediately directed him to target $1.5 million for monthly expenses split nearly evenly among branches, operations, and administration.

Similarly, our operations staff needed to work overtime to ensure a smooth transition. We never had run a thirty-office network, and we all learned on the job. Of course, Hayden's back office was a mess—after all, that had been the genesis of its problems—and we needed to take care not to foul up customer accounts as we converted them onto our system. Fortunately, the New York Stock Exchange gave us needed breathing room in the pace at which we'd move accounts; on occasion, though, exchange officials tried to strong-arm Frank Zarb and our operations people into moving faster. More than once, I had to protect our interests by stepping in and playing hardball with one of the exchange's senior people. Looking back, it was an excellent lesson in how to negotiate successfully.

Unfortunately, we suffered high turnover among many of our front-line producers, especially our brokers and investment bankers. Many of Hayden Stone's best people questioned whether we'd be able to run the business successfully and whether we had enough stature to compete with the industry's leaders. After all, we were still a no-name company. With Wall Street firms failing left and right, who could blame many of these people for jumping ship at the first attractive offer? And jump they did. We experienced nearly 30 percent turnover in brokers following the acquisition.

Eager to stem the attrition, I began attending broker recognition events and soon came to develop an array of close personal relationships similar to those I had created a couple of years earlier with our operations staff. At many of these events, I'd be called upon to speak before a crowd, which always made me nervous since I hated speaking before a large group. Gradually, I found a device that worked well: I'd simply state, "You've heard enough speeches—what questions do you have for me?" The sales force liked the informality of that approach and not being lectured at. It proved a good tactic for getting me past my stage fright and ingratiating me with our new distribution force.

The better part of a year would pass before we worked out the most important challenges that came with the merger, yet overall, the Hayden Stone acquisition went surprisingly well. The transaction capped ten years of phenomenal growth: By 1970, we employed more than 1,500 people and were generating nearly $12 million in revenues, a long way from the $400,000 run-rate we began with in 1960. We had experienced a number of setbacks along the way; still, our overall success illustrated that taking risks could pay so long as a disciplined and inherently conservative set of assumptions underpinned one's thought process.

Throughout this period, I worked harder than ever, yet I remained fearful about stepping in front of my partners and assuming the burden of leadership. Instead, I concentrated on mastering the financial and operational details of the business. I may have lacked the maturity to assume greater responsibility, but I was amassing insights that would prove invaluable in later years. In particular, I appreciated our early move to incorporate and realized the importance of building a permanent source of capital as many of the industry's great firms succumbed to financial pressures during the latter part of the decade.

Vast changes were overtaking the securities business—consolidation, rapidly expanding client service demands, increasing volatility—all of which meant a higher cost of doing business and the beginning of the end for the traditional partnership model. These trends forced me to consider how we might build competitive advantage from operations. The great Prussian general Clausewitz used to talk about "defending the heartland," which I saw as an apt metaphor for the back office. I had learned firsthand how first-rate operations could confer a low cost structure and flexibility, two exceptionally powerful advantages.

Finally, I began to consider how our firm might take advantage of future acquisitions. Hayden Stone put us on the map as a credible acquirer and demonstrated the potential of buying a very large firm at nearly no cost—we paid no premium, and others provided the bulk of the capital. I might have considered the Hayden deal a unique event at the time, but it broadened my imagination in thinking about other potential combinations. I began to think more about our business model as well. For a decade, I had looked at our business primarily in terms of investment banking and institutional business—retail brokerage was mostly a means to an end.

My thought process didn't change overnight, but the Hayden Stone transaction provoked interesting questions, especially as we now owned a meaningful retail network and for years had seen individual investors stepping up their appetite to "own a share in America." Should we stay on the path of primarily serving large institutions, a business which required low capital investment but entailed high earnings volatility? Or would we be better off pursuing a more investment-heavy retail model where enduring customer relationships plausibly could generate a steadier stream of profits?

As with so many of our prior important decisions, outside circumstances soon would help us decide.

3

The Rise to Prominence

A rhythm rules Wall Street: Healthy markets invariably alternate with lean years; product innovation typically comes in waves; and regulatory oversight shifts between tides of stringency and laxity.

The petering out of the bull market in 1969 at first seemed just one more cycle, but before we knew it, cataclysmic events, notably the Street's operational crisis, grabbed the markets and portended that the 1970s would be a decade of massive change. As the rising tide of forced mergers proclaimed that a revolution was at hand, DLJ, a small but highly regarded institutional firm, dropped its own bombshell when it filed with the SEC to sell shares to the public. Securities professionals for years had debated the industry's need to address the limitations of partnerships and find permanent sources of capital, yet the May 1969 announcement startled everyone because the New York Stock Exchange had continued to expressly forbid public ownership for securities firms. Although DLJ faced the possibility that it would lose its exchange membership privileges, its need for fresh capital outweighed this concern. Suddenly, a firm only eleven years old—and one whose institutionally oriented model CBWL emulated—had dared to take on the establishment.

Before 1970, the New York Stock Exchange existed as a protective club. It exercised monopolistic power by fixing commissions at high levels and carefully limiting who could become a member. DLJ's announcement threatened the status quo, and in shooting back, the exchange's leadership employed a scare tactic by stating that public ownership of member firms would lead to institutional investors dominating the market.

The convoluted logic assumed that the brokers' clients would take control of these firms and attack the lucrative fixed commission structure. Nevertheless, the genie was now out of the bottle, and DLJ's action focused everyone on the need to reassess the market's structure. The small firm had seen public ownership as a way to better finance its growth and for its partners to partially cash out, a logic which certainly appealed to many other firms.

DLJ didn't fire the only salvo at the New York Stock Exchange. A year earlier, the Department of Justice had begun to question the exchange's competitive practices, especially the structure of fixed commissions. The SEC immediately picked up on the issue and began crusading for commission deregulation. Technological advances, too, threatened the status quo as the computerization of Wall Street gave way to the formation of the Nasdaq market. This new electronic meeting place cut out layers of middlemen and satisfied institutions' hunger to trade at lower cost. Nasdaq put the Big Board's monopoly at risk. The exchange understood the threat and responded by announcing flexible commissions for large order sizes, the first of many cuts in pricing that would follow over the next three decades.

As with most Wall Street executives, I was gripped with nervous anticipation as the 1970s began. In two short years, the limits of the partnership model had been exposed. Prestigious companies were being pushed into a wave of desperation mergers, and the pricing umbrella that had protected the industry's profits had been pierced with holes. The entire industry was riding a tiger. I for one had little idea where the ride would end but readily could see that our company couldn't afford to remain passive. I knew Hayden Stone represented only the start of a journey, though I barely could have dreamed that the decade would end with our firm challenging Merrill Lynch for leadership of the industry.

DLJ won its game of chicken with the New York Stock Exchange as it completed its $12 million sale of shares to the public in 1970 without losing its exchange membership. The need to shore up the industry's capital had become overwhelming, and within a year the Big Board finally changed its rules allowing others to go public. Merrill Lynch led the way in the spring of 1971 by filing a four-million-share offering which sought to raise $100 million. Our decision a few years earlier to incorporate and receive professional audits now paid off as our unique structure enabled us to respond with remarkable speed for a small firm. Less than a week after Merrill filed its deal, we presented our own offering to the SEC. Merrill's shares opened for public trading in June, and the stock promptly soared. The successful Merrill offering only lit a fire under us to complete CBWL–Hayden Stone's initial public offering without delay.

We had chosen to offer one million shares, which represented nearly a 40 percent interest in our company. CBWL–Hayden Stone ranked as a junior player on the Street, but it enjoyed a cachet in the wake of the Hayden Stone acquisition. As carefully as we had financed that transaction, I recommended that we use the offering to reduce our borrowings, especially volatile subordinated debt, to satisfy my long-held preference for managing a conservative balance sheet.

My partners and I also determined that we would sell some of our personal shares in the offering, a feature which differed notably from Merrill's transaction. Many of our top executives were personally highly leveraged since they had most of their equity tied up in the firm, and they were eager to pay down debt. Ever the optimistic salesman, Marshall especially lived large and had borrowed greatly to finance his lifestyle. Meanwhile, Joanie and I had finally made our move into Manhattan and had spent more than $500,000 to buy and renovate an apartment on Fifth Avenue—the purchase gave me a personal incentive to raise some cash.

None of the established investment banks were willing to underwrite our offering since they saw us as a competitor, but we took advantage of a rule change that allowed us to self-market our transaction so long as we could get two independent parties to attest to the fairness of our value. In July, we heavily promoted our offering to investors while we awaited the SEC's go-ahead to complete the transaction. We stressed our strong growth record, our national network of brokerage offices, and the opportunity to leverage our profits from the Hayden Stone deal. Our prospectus proclaimed how our revenues had surged from $4 million to $45 million between 1967 and 1971 while our profits had grown from $338,000 to $3 million.

Our pitch yielded interest from retail investors, though it was far from a hot deal with institutions, which saw as distinct drawbacks our limited track record and the numerous uncertainties then facing the securities industry. In those days, investment banking clients freely bought into brokerage offerings—it's interesting to consider whether regulators would allow such a practice today. I still remember our firm's close friend Jimmy Ling, of conglomerate LTV fame, taking a stake in our offering.

Everything seemed on track until the SEC hit us with a few curveballs in August. Our friends in Washington compelled us to insert in our offering document a disclosure that our firm's investment strategist was negative on the market outlook—this issue was relatively minor, but I felt the SEC was needlessly nitpicking. With far greater import, the SEC staff then informed us that it had decided that Bache, one of our rivals, would get to offer shares before us even though we had filed our deal first. The securities regulator was concerned with Bache's far weaker financial condition and appeared eager to see it raise capital while market conditions were favorable. Of course, we wanted the same opportunity and worried that a weak reception for Bache's shares would hurt investor confidence for our deal. Bache came to market in early September. The deal boosted Bache's capital and then, living up to our fears, soon proved a bust for investors as the stock price subsequently slid.

Worse still, a few days later the SEC suddenly dictated that it would not approve our plan to offer secondary shares, the stock which our partners had planned to sell. My partners and I were apoplectic at this news since each of us had already counted on an infusion of cash. It seemed patently unfair that the SEC was now changing the rules of the game. No doubt, the securities regulator feared investors would panic at the sight of brokerage managements cashing out, especially after all the adverse industry turmoil in the years that preceded the new offerings.

The SEC's bombshell had come during the Jewish High Holy Days, and many of us prayed our hearts out that we'd successfully change the SEC's mind. Soon, we were given a chance to make our case at the end of September. As Roger and our attorneys were about to head to Washington to address the commission, we learned that SEC head Bill Casey was in meetings at the New York Stock Exchange and did not plan to attend the session in D.C. Arthur Levitt and I promptly headed to the exchange where we waited outside the chairman's office for an hour before Casey emerged.

Casey must have been stunned to be accosted so unexpectedly, but we pressed for a chance to explain our point of view. "I have a luncheon speech to give on Long Island, and I don't have time for this right now," he demurred. Unwilling to take no for an answer, we offered to give him a ride to his meeting in order to make our case. "Do you have a car?" he asked, to which we unthinkingly answered, "Yes, it's downstairs."

When we reached the curb, we surprised Casey by hailing a cab. Pressed tightly together in the back seat, we put on the hard sell. I began: "This is September; we filed early this year, and we've spent a lot of money. It's not right that you change the rules of the game. I can't argue whether the rules are right or wrong, but those were the rules."

Notwithstanding my logic, Casey defended the commission's decision: "The SEC has already decided not to allow selling shareholders to cash out." We went back and forth for the entire cab ride. As Casey departed, all he could say was that he appreciated our sense of not having been fairly treated. Arthur and I dissected the conversation during the ride back to the city. At least, the cabdriver had a positive word: "If you didn't win *that* argument, you'll never win any!" We were far from reassured, although Arthur and I felt that we had given it our best shot.

That afternoon, a Friday, the other half of our lobbying team made our case in Washington. With far more eloquence, Ken Bialkin reiterated our fairness argument in a marathon afternoon meeting. Happily, the SEC gave in and allowed us to proceed with our offering as originally planned. As it turned out, Casey had phoned in the decisive vote. We received word in New York at 4:45 P.M., and in a completely unorthodox move, we scrambled to complete the deal on a Friday night.

It remained touch-and-go whether we had enough orders to complete the offering. Indeed, we first concluded that we were 150,000 shares short of our one-million-share goal. Pressing our sales force to leave no stone unturned, we finally discovered Dreyfus would come in and buy the remaining block of stock. We priced the offering at $12.50 per share, or at just over two times our book value, implying our company was worth about $30 million. It felt like a big number at the time, but I can't help but marvel how small it looks in hindsight.

———

Needless to say, we were thrilled by the success of our initial offering. On paper my partners and I were now millionaires, but more important, we had proven that we could be in the forefront of industry change. We quickly decided to shorten our company name to Hayden Stone as our success with the acquisition rebuilt the status that traditionally had gone with the name. Prestige aside, being publicly owned entailed new demands. Hayden Stone now faced the pressure to report earnings growth, and I was especially eager to broaden our shareholder base. I was disappointed that employees dominated our first annual meeting—as hard as we had worked to generate interest for our initial public offering, the newness of publicly traded brokerage stocks still put off most investors.

Almost everything we did was opportunistic and centered upon practical ways to generate revenues. Forget about any sort of formal strategic thinking! We also lacked sophistication in our approach to management, and in most respects still operated day to day as though we were a partnership. Roger officially served as our CEO, but the title remained a formality as we essentially ran the company by committee. Looking back, it's hard to understand how we ever interested new investors with such an ad hoc approach.

The timing of our stock offering turned out to be better for company insiders who sold stock than for our new shareholders, as the market for financial stocks began to sour almost immediately after our deal. Our price rose exactly ⅛ of a point before setting off on a three-year dive. The broad market performed well through the first week of 1973 with the Dow closing above 1,000 for the first time, but that didn't stop investors in brokerage stocks from fretting about the consequences of rising inflation, large budget deficits, and a sinking dollar. Indeed, these issues roiled the financial markets in 1971–72 as President Nixon took the United States off the gold standard, devalued the dollar, and instituted wage and price controls. In part owing to the cost of financing the Vietnam War, the country was living beyond its means—steps taken such as devaluing our country's currency only delayed the day of reckoning as many industries were beginning a decade-long slide in competitiveness.

As 1973 unfolded, things turned ugly. Inflation and interest rates were gaining momentum; the Watergate scandal broke; and the Yom Kippur War quickly led the OPEC cartel to flex its power over energy supplies and prices. The ensuing energy crisis soon precipitated a punishing economic recession and loss of investor confidence. The Dow dropped 17 percent in 1973, and at year end, with no relief in sight, Wall Street suffered: Trading volumes evaporated; the flow of investment banking deals stopped; and bonds were marked down in value.

Even more painful, brokerage stocks skidded dangerously. By the end of the year, Hayden Stone was struggling to turn even a modest profit while our share price had fallen below $2 per share. It was a horrible time for everyone in the securities business to the point where our Hayden Stone 1973 annual report grumbled, "The brokerage community has not been a happy place." Our only solace came from our continued strong capital position, which exceeded regulatory requirements by $16 million.

We didn't waste time responding as the market turned south. Other companies may have rationalized that the downturn was temporary and feared managing in an overly reactive manner, but I have never been comfortable taking such an actuarial approach. Instead, I felt as though we needed to make a more immediate judgment call and pressed to bring down our costs in order to remain no worse than cash flow neutral.

In a decision I regret to this day, I forced all our employees, including myself, to accept cuts in pay. While the percentage reduction was greater for higher-paid staff, everyone suffered: from secretaries who lived paycheck to paycheck up to our senior executives, many of whom relied upon their pay to cover interest on borrowings that had been used to purchase shares in our company. Over two consecutive years, some staff (including me) suffered a 40–50 percent drop in pay. It was a brute-force way to manage, which only undermined morale. I would have been far wiser to have fired our poorer-performing staff and redistributed their pay to deserving employees. Apart from this lesson, I realized the importance of keeping costs under control during the good times in order to build a profit cushion to defend against periods of adversity.

Deteriorating market conditions also made the risk to our reputation a more active concern. As business initially eroded, many firms, including Hayden Stone, saw a weakening in the quality of the deals brought to market. Moreover, regulators began to focus on certain aggressive industry practices. Hayden Stone's actions typically were no better or worse than those of the average firm—on occasion, we could have acted more responsibly, but we understood the importance of keeping our customers' trust. My partners and I each had our share of deals which had been duds, but these usually were overshadowed by more successful transactions. Yet, with our greatly expanded retail franchise, I began to more actively worry about our reputation and legal exposure.

Since the beginning of the 1970s, we had been sourcing larger and more complex deals that demanded a great deal of investor sophistication. Marshall typically led the charge thanks to his array of contacts with high-profile and often complex conglomerates. I came to appreciate, however, that some of our transactions weren't always appropriate for a retail sales force that often lacked the wherewithal to judge a deal's quality. As field complaints mounted, I argued that we should view our retail brokers as a natural check and balance on the quality of our product. Unfortunately, Marshall had difficulty accepting this idea and insisted we couldn't afford to let up on growing our business. Our disagreement festered as none of us was prepared yet to make the tough decision to alter our practices.

It would be unfair to single out Marshall as the only source of controversial deals. I suffered my share of poor judgments, and none was worse than my experience with the Topper Toy Company. Beginning in the late 1960s, I thought I had uncovered a gem of a company when I spotted Topper. It sported a history of growth and was led by a seemingly impressive CEO named Henry Orenstein. I soon cultivated a relationship with Orenstein, and Hayden Stone brought the company public. In those days, we'd commonly ask for an ownership stake and board representation from companies we underwrote, and Topper readily agreed to make Roger Berlind and me directors.

For three years, everything went smoothly, and we handled additional secondary stock offerings. Then, in December 1971, Roger and I were called away from our company's Christmas party for a hastily arranged special board meeting. Aghast, we were told that Orenstein had been making side agreements with distributors to buy back unsold merchandise after the Christmas holidays. The side letters meant that sales were being overstated. Overnight, Topper went bust, and investor lawsuits started to fly.

For the next two years, private investors filed numerous suits against our company while the SEC investigated our actions and, all the while, Roger and I sweated over the damage to our reputation. We learned how tough it is to defend oneself against fraud allegations and that litigants will always come after those with deep pockets. Finally, the SEC ended its investigation, and the lawsuits ran their course, but

I was angered that we as board members had been kept in the dark and also by the money I had lost for myself and our clients.

I refused to serve on a public company board for the next twenty-five years.

With the Topper mess and the unfolding bear market, life became exceptionally stressful in the early 1970s. I smoked more heavily, and my temper flared regularly both at home and at work. I asked my family to make plenty of sacrifices even if I refused to acknowledge these at the time.

Our recent move into Manhattan was a good example. I liked the idea of moving into a cavernous apartment in a swank building and thought it was great that we'd have the likes of Harold Geneen, Charles Allen, and Leonard Lauder as neighbors. The prestige meant little to Joanie as she focused on the building's snobbishness and the absence of young families with children. Our meeting with the cooperative's staid board was especially memorable. In those days, Joanie often wore miniskirts, and our real estate broker insisted in advance that it might be best if she not take off her overcoat during our interview. Joanie ended up wearing a below-the-knees dress she usually reserved for funerals. It didn't matter since no one ever asked us even to sit down. Once we were approved, Joanie pleaded for us not to move, but I was adamant. On moving day, she was busy unloading boxes in the building's basement when a resident stopped to ask if she was a new neighbor. Self-conscious to be seen in moving clothes, Joanie memorably pretended to be the domestic help and stated, "Oh, no. Madam is upstairs." Suffice it to say, Joanie never felt comfortable there.

Our kids also paid a price. I had been wrapped up in my work for years by this time, and Marc and Jessica were now old enough where they would have benefited from more attention. Marc especially struggled at school. Even before we moved to the city, Joanie and I elected to send him away to the Milton Academy boarding school in Massachusetts, which we thought would strengthen his sense of independence and self-discipline. Unfortunately, he struggled there both academically and socially, yet I insisted he stick it out in order not to be labeled a quitter. Marc never forgave me for that. Jessica, meanwhile, stayed closer to home, but with work demands intruding on most nights and weekends, I spent all too little time with her as well. Looking back, it would have been nice to have spent more time at home. In truth, though, I'm not sure I had it within my power to act any other way.

My intensity and increasingly public profile, not to mention our move into the city, isolated Joanie. I often insisted that she join me on business trips where her presence would be useful, which only made her feel guilty for being away from Jessica and added to the demands on her life. An outgoing person, she had to be careful what she told her friends for fear of giving others inside information on our newly public company. At the same time, her feminist friends kept nudging her to consider a career for herself or some other way to build her sense of identity. Joanie ended up seeking the help of a therapist during these years to help her deal with the conflicting pressures.

It took many years for her to sort through her issues, although she gradually came to see the rewards of pursuing more education as a means for helping others. In 1972, at age thirty-eight, she enrolled at the New School to study social work and soon began volunteering to help the homeless at Bellevue Hospital in the psychiatric ward. More than once, we walked down the street outside our Fifth Avenue apartment and would run into one of Joanie's homeless friends. That was always quite an experience! Later, she attended the Bank Street College for master's level courses in counseling, and eventually became involved with her first major philanthropic effort, the Citymeals-on-Wheels program, which delivers food to the elderly. These pursuits gave Joanie perspective and the ability to relate to all sorts of people—they also gave her a long-sought sense of personal identity.

After about three years, Joanie finally got her wish to move from our stuffy building thanks to the increasingly horrid economy. In 1974, Hayden Stone's business, along with our peers', was in the tank, and we concluded we could no longer afford our expensive home. We put the apartment on the block at the worst possible time as New York City was on the verge of filing bankruptcy and real estate prices were sinking fast.

Unloading the apartment wasn't easy, but we eventually found a buyer. We moved into the Stanhope Hotel with our two children, a dog, and a cat while we looked for a new place with more reasonable carrying costs. We finally found a new home on 79th Street, which we virtually stole for $30,000 in back maintenance. We used a portion of the savings to buy a second home in Greenwich, Connecticut. Six years later, we sold the apartment for over $1 million. As with my business, I was rapidly developing a nose for value.

Managing our firm by committee worked reasonably well for a time, but disputes between our top executives occurred with more frequency in the months following our initial public offering. Marshall and I especially butted heads as our visions for the company had sharply diverged. He never liked the retail business and insisted we should remain primarily a merchant bank. By nature, Marshall was comfortable taking large financial risks—he thought nothing about committing the firm's capital to risky trading positions and typically argued that we were being overly conservative in the way we managed our capital. As business conditions deteriorated in early 1973, he even suggested we should buy out our public shareholders and return to private ownership.

I had always placed a premium on limiting our financial risks and never wanted to put my net worth on the line. My ideas for the business may have been relatively static when it came to risk, but I began to look on the retail business far more favorably during this period. Politically and economically, the world was growing more volatile in the early 1970s, and I calculated that retail earnings would prove comparably stable. I sensed, too, that we'd find other retail-oriented firms to acquire, which would allow us to build value.

In April 1973, opportunity knocked once more. H. Hentz & Company, an old-line securities and commodities firm once run by Bernard

Baruch, was on the ropes. Operational problems and excessive reliance on short-term funding had buffeted the firm for some time, and its CEO, Alvin Schonfeld, had counted on a prospective sale to an insurance company to bail out his company. Unfortunately for Hentz, an untimely accounting fraud unexpectedly sidelined the acquisition. The deal had gotten so close that there was no time for Schonfeld to cancel a planned celebratory party at his home to which I was invited. The house was filled with champagne and orchids, and I'll never forget Schonfeld telling me that the demise of the merger was like life support being pulled on his firm. In a fit of gallows humor, Schonfeld then proclaimed, "At least we can use all these flowers to cover my body in my coffin!" At once, I knew we had found another opportunity to buy on our terms and resurrect a wounded franchise.

We reached a preliminary deal in mid-April and began to prepare for a June closing. With its thirty-five offices, including several overseas catering to wealthy individuals, Hentz would double our retail distribution system and increase our revenues by 50 percent. As I toured its franchise with Schonfeld, I quickly realized we had an opportunity to inject the firm with stronger management.

The firm had an office network which nicely complemented ours and a substantial commodities operation which would provide a hedge against inflation. In Europe, Hentz had relationships with aviation pioneer Marcel Dassault and billionaire J. Paul Getty. Memorably, one of Hentz's executives took me to Getty's estate outside London one evening for dinner. A wild lion roamed the property as though it were a guard dog. Once we arrived, we had to wait an hour for Getty to appear, as he was upstairs watching his favorite TV program, the safari series *Daktari*.

As we prepared to complete the merger, our operations people suddenly alerted me to the unexpectedly chaotic scene in Hentz's back office where systems were antiquated. The firm still used a Morse code device to confirm European orders—it had to be the last one in commercial use. With only a weekend left, we were confronting massive difficulty reconciling accounts. One of our senior operations people, flushed with panic, argued we needed to pull out of the deal. In so many other instances over the years, I had refused to take on responsibility for the really big decisions for our firm, but now everything changed. I had become the senior executive responsible for financial and operations matters, and in this instance practically the future of our firm rested on my shoulders.

Could it be that we had bitten off more than we could chew?

I understood by then that we had miscalculated in assessing the transaction's risk, but I also felt we had a strong operations team and hated the idea of giving up on the merger. Ensconced in our operations center into the wee hours of the morning, I finally turned to Tony Fedele, our co-head of operations whose sense I trusted most. "It's not pretty, but give me Hentz's back office, and we'll get it done," he confidently asserted.

Having worked so closely and successfully with Tony and our operations people for four years, I was sure their can-do attitude was no bluff. I stood and announced simply, "Let's go for it." With that, I strode down the hall to inform Schonfeld that we'd only complete the merger if he agreed to delay the closing but give us an immediate carte blanche to run his back office. He had no other options, and at 5:00 A.M., our team marched in and took over Hentz's operations center.

We ended up changing the closing date of the deal and, as with Hayden Stone, acquired Hentz without having to pay a premium over the book value of its assets. The deal closed in late August. This time we received no assistance from the New York Stock Exchange—consequently, the deal had greater risk; by now, though, we had learned valuable lessons in how to encourage Hentz's creditors to transfer their commitments and recognized that strong capital would give us time to sort out the operational challenges.

Even before Hentz, the friction among our management team had become intolerable, and the acquisition alerted everyone that management by committee no longer worked. It had slowed our capacity to make fast decisions, blurred whether we operated with a consistent philosophy, and confused employees. We were now making a big commitment that our future lay primarily with the retail business, and we no longer could tolerate dissension at the top. Marshall seemed passive as I negotiated the Hentz acquisition. Once we finalized the terms, however, Marshall objected strenuously only to realize that he was largely isolated from the rest of our executive team. Our whole company was preoccupied with closing Hentz during the summer of 1973. Incredibly, at precisely the same time, we had to solve our management problem once and for all.

Executive changes often come when a company or industry falters, and we were no exception. The balance of power among our top executives had eroded for two years, and the tough climate made none of us eager to compromise any longer. It was easy to tolerate Marshall during the good years since he was so instrumental in generating revenues. With the unfolding bear market and our expanding retail business, we no longer could ignore the conflicts in both vision and tactics. Increasingly, our retail brokers would complain about being compelled to sell Marshall's complicated deals, while his erratic behavior further upset the retail group.

One memorable transaction illustrated our dilemma. Though the popularity of conglomerates came to an end with the close of the 1960s, Marshall remained friendly with many of these companies' CEOs. In 1971, Marshall announced that his friend Jimmy Ling would be making a splashy comeback with his new company, Omega-Alpha, and that we had been selected to underwrite the new issue. Ling's venture employed the catchphrase "the end is the beginning," but several of us suggested that perhaps "the end should be the end" would be more fitting.

We felt Ling's new venture suffered from hopeless complexity and surely would be a very tough sell, but Marshall refused to be deterred. The offering provoked a lot of rancor within our sales force and finally came at a price of $5 per share after being marked down several times. With the deal done, the price promptly plunged to $1 per share; Omega-Alpha eventually went bust, adding insult to injury for our firm's reputation.

The quality of our deal flow eroded during this time, and Omega-Alpha represented just one example. As business continued to weaken, I worried about Marshall's judgment and began to watch our trading risks more carefully. I'd frequently nose around the sales and trading floor, which usually provoked Marshall to snap that I was "invading his domain." He acted as though he was smarter than everyone. As business became more stressful, his personality became more toxic, and he wore his disdain for our retail business on his sleeve.

By the summer of 1973, our dysfunctional management was becoming obvious to our senior people. Marshall barked at one executive committee meeting that he wanted half of our branch managers fired since business was off so sharply. The diatribe was enough to convince George Murray—who then headed our retail brokerage force—that it was time to head for greener pastures.

By August, we were about to double the size of our retail business with Hentz, and the last thing we needed was a drain of talent from our pool of retail executives. Arthur Levitt and Frank Zarb came to me, and we spoke at length about our predicament. I soon gained their support to be named CEO. Each of us recognized that the future of our company depended on repairing our leadership vacuum. Perhaps Arthur would have liked the top job, but his strength rested primarily in his polished salesmanship, and I guess he understood that he lacked the financial and operational skills necessary to run our business.

For thirteen years, I had been happy to duck taking ultimate responsibility for the business, yet I finally had amassed the self-confidence to step out in front and lead. Each of my partners had limitations, and I felt I could do a better job than any of them. Building our back office, helping structure the Hayden Stone transaction, and leading the charge on Hentz were all powerful experiences that made me sure of myself.

And, of course, Joanie's encouragement didn't hurt either.

I was prepared to become CEO though not if it meant simply becoming a figurehead lacking authority. I felt strongly that I'd never be able to control Marshall and that as long as he remained, we'd never have a cohesive company. It was time for a bit of hardball: I'd only accept so long as Marshall would agree to leave. Cumulatively, Arthur, Frank, and I had the votes to prevail, and we called our executive committee together. Roger was miffed that we hadn't consulted him earlier. However, we all were under a lot of pressure and knew we didn't have time for sentimentality. With the shakeup, Roger became vice chairman and Arthur became president. As we presented our plan, Marshall fortunately understood his isolation and in agreeing voluntarily to resign avoided a needlessly messy separation. As we ended the meeting, I felt both proud and anxious. I had a pretty good idea of where I wanted to lead our company, but I was now unambiguously responsible for its success or failure.

I breathed only a very shallow sigh of relief.

Marshall ended up running one of Jimmy Ling's companies and later pursued a variety of merchant banking ventures. True to form, he pushed his businesses aggressively and eventually suffered a financial meltdown. He grew bitter and took the jaded view that he was responsible for all the successes I enjoyed over my career. Marshall undoubtedly was a phenomenal salesman who contributed greatly to our firm. As is true of many stars, though, his strengths were not those of an effective manager. Just as I had learned a decade earlier with Peter Potoma, Marshall showed the importance of choosing trustworthy and like-minded partners.

Now that I had become CEO, I knew I needed to be well organized and fully master all facets of our business—I urgently needed to find a competent assistant. Luckily, the solution stood in plain sight. At twenty-six, Peter Cohen had worked in our company for two years as a research analyst under Marshall in a role that challenged him to make sense out of very complicated underwriting transactions. During the Omega-Alpha deal, Peter literally took an apartment in Jimmy Ling's Texas home in order to learn the ins and outs of a company no one other than Ling seemed to understand. Short of stature with a dark complexion, Peter radiated talent: He was detail- and numbers-oriented, very smart, and an amazingly hard worker. Never one to fear hiring bright people, I saw at once that Peter represented the ideal candidate to serve as my assistant, and within two days of Marshall's departure, I sought to take him under my wing.

By that time, we had moved our office uptown to the General

Motors Building. I asked Peter to join me for lunch at my favorite dining spot, the Harmonie Club, an old-line place that traditionally catered to German-Jewish financiers. I wasted no time and suggested that he take his career in a new direction. My pitch was simple: "Peter, I don't know enough about the details of our business and need to learn an awful lot very quickly. You are very analytical and can help me figure things out."

Pausing to judge the reaction, I watched Peter smile nervously. He then blurted out, "I thought you invited me here to fire me since I worked so closely with Marshall!" I reassured him that I looked forward to working closely together and that he'd enjoy a great career with the company. Peter seemed relieved but asked for time to consider my offer. After a brief walk around the block, he met me back in my office to sign on for his new job.

Peter began by shadowing me virtually everywhere I went. We were busily integrating Hentz at that time, and Peter and I carefully studied our financial trends. We also sat in on the weekly meetings of our operations staff where we pressed for updates on the merger. Peter needed little downtime—he'd work late each evening studying the business and highlighting issues I needed to address. On weekends, he'd typically spend Saturday in our downtown accounting department collecting numbers which we'd jointly review at my home that Sunday. The gathering bear market already had constricted our profits. Together, Peter and I learned how we might enhance our results. We came to see that most Wall Street firms essentially chewed up their commissions with operating costs and that profits as a rule came from interest earned on customers' idle cash balances. That insight led us to think of ways to better leverage our fixed costs and maximize our interest-related revenues.

The more he learned, the more Peter gained confidence to stick his nose into all aspects of the business, and I immediately appreciated his inquisitiveness and lack of shyness. In those days, my temper often boiled over. Peter had the strength of character to face my tirades, remain composed, and speak out when he disagreed. Some of our staff at first might have been afraid to approach me during my "moments," so Peter played a valuable role as a go-between until my anger cooled. My management team soon learned that my temper would blow over and that upon reflection I'd embrace legitimate ideas. By his example in arguing back at me, Peter helped us develop a culture where managers learned to speak their minds. It had taken remarkably little time for Peter and me to forge a very close relationship.

I settled into the CEO role quickly. Marshall's departure undoubtedly eased the adjustment. My senior colleagues and I all had plenty on our plates, and we appreciated the end of the squabbling that had marked our prior management by committee approach. Unfortunately, there was plenty going on around us that kept us on our toes, as the economy and business conditions continued to grow more worrisome.

4

Against the Grain

nflationary pressures had been gathering momentum for some time, and by the middle of 1973, the Federal Reserve finally felt compelled to raise interest rates. From May to October, the prime rate jumped from 7 percent to over 10 percent. At first, the stock market disregarded the news. In the closing weeks of the year, the Watergate scandal began to grab headlines, and the Arab oil embargo created new and massive inflationary pressures. With the triple whammy of higher interest rates, energy shortages, and dimming consumer confidence, the economy and the stock market began a synchronized swoon, one that would send shivers down the spine of anyone in the securities industry. The opening act of the bear market came in November when in two short weeks the Dow plummeted 13 percent to about 860. Stocks then settled into a plateau until the following summer, while politics and interest rates remained deeply unsettled. Congress began debating Nixon's impeachment in August just as interest rates surged once more, hitting a peak of 12 percent. Meanwhile, stocks headed into free fall as investors anticipated the coming of a deep recession.

The Dow would bottom at 587 by the end of 1974, a nightmarish drop of almost 45 percent over two years.

As bad as the market became in this period, Hayden Stone benefited from its conservatively managed balance sheet and the intensity of its operations staff. Through the opening months of the bear market, we pressed on to finish integrating Hentz, and by the spring of 1974, we had resolved the bulk of the merger's issues. While we had successfully slashed the fixed costs, our profits remained elusive owing to rapidly deteriorating market conditions.

By early 1974, Hayden Stone had experienced a year of going back and forth between reporting small operating losses and equally small profits. We hadn't lost as much money as many of our peers had, and in fact our cash flow had remained consistently positive, but that didn't make me feel better. I constantly worried about the risk of mounting losses. No one at that moment dared imagine how low the market might go, and the regulators continued to discuss ways to further limit brokers' ability to charge fixed commissions.

Standing still seemed like a sure recipe for atrophy, and I resolved that we should keep looking for other ways to acquire more scale in order to better absorb our fixed costs. Acquiring Hayden Stone and Hentz had not been easy, yet we had gained valuable expertise, and I was confident we had enough capital to take advantage of other firms in distress.

With my new CEO title, I took it upon myself to seek out other potential partners. I approached St. Louis–based A. G. Edwards, a firm with which we had at one time come close to a deal, but its CEO, Ben Edwards, somehow felt we had destroyed our desirability as a partner following our purchase of Hentz. With that rejection, I began to think in bigger terms and soon became intrigued with Shearson Hamill, a large national firm with a highly productive sales force, a decent investment bank, and the resources for us to amass the needed scale to take on the industry's largest firms.

Shearson seemed like a dream deal in every way . . . except for the low probability of its ever coming to pass.

Industry conditions were so bad in 1974 that soon nothing seemed impossible. Shearson hadn't faced the operational problems that others had experienced, but the firm had maintained an overly leveraged balance sheet during the good years only to see its capital steadily erode as business volumes evaporated. I unsuccessfully had put feelers out to Shearson's CEO, Alger "Duke" Chapman, months earlier, and in April 1974 Duke called to say he was ready to talk.

Meeting in a remote restaurant in Little Italy—a place reputed to attract Mafia bosses—Duke and I felt each other out. Shearson's franchise remained solid in most respects but its shortage of capital had begun to squeeze the company. Several months earlier, it had successfully appealed to Cincinnati financier Carl Lindner to commit $7 million in fresh capital, but the firm's subsequent trading losses stopped Shearson's supposed benefactor from delivering more than half the promised funds. The New York Stock Exchange and Shearson's primary lender, Citibank, also worried about its financial exposure and began to press Duke to find a merger partner. I'm sure Duke and his partners would have preferred to remain independent. Once again, though, one of the industry's major firms had found itself in a corner with all too few options.

Through April and May, we hammered out the terms of the deal while often meeting in my apartment to preserve secrecy. Duke usually came with his head of investment banking and his retail head, Fred Joseph (who'd later become CEO of Drexel Burnham), while I led our team, which primarily included Peter Cohen and Arthur Levitt.

During our talks, New York Stock Exchange trading volumes had dried up and were averaging a meager 11.5 million shares per day, 30 percent lower than prior highs, and we needed to establish how we would make money at the low level of customer activity. We worked in tandem to scrutinize each firm's business mix and soon identified the ruthless personnel cuts that the harsh climate demanded. We also settled the company's name and other matters relatively painlessly.

I decided to change our name to Shearson Hayden Stone given Shearson's excellent reputation. My friend Bob Greenhill at Morgan Stanley also influenced the decision on our new name when he informed us that we'd have a much better chance of being included in Morgan-led deals if our name alphabetically followed Morgan's in the tombstone ads that are published after deals close.

Valuing Shearson wasn't a big issue either. We gave in a little during our negotiations but were careful to stay true to an approach that would advance the interests of our shareholders. Peter and I had assembled a framework for projecting earnings and then demanded that we needed to earn a return on investment at twice the rate Hayden Stone had typically targeted. This requirement ensured we'd be properly compensated for the risks we were assuming. In any case, most of the consideration we offered came in the form of an incentive plan—our low-priced stock and warrants whose worth would only become meaningful once Shearson had exceeded a certain profit threshold.

We announced our newest deal in late May 1974 (always May!) and immediately heard a chorus of skeptical voices. Even as we had more than doubled our revenues to nearly $150 million and put together a 1,500-person national broker network, certain journalists couldn't grasp what we had accomplished. Alan Abelson, the writer of *Barron's* "Up and Down Wall Street" column, even compared our new firm to the *Titanic* and suggested we were just "rearranging the deck chairs." Undeterred, I marveled that we had positioned ourselves to seize a big opportunity as others were paralyzed.

We had doubled in size not once but twice in the space of a year. Yes, we gave away 250,000 shares of stock to purchase Shearson, but the price of our shares neared its low of $1⅜ right before we closed the deal, so the shares implied little immediate reward to its recipients. We had granted warrants, too, but these allowed the recipients to buy stock only at a price far above where our shares were trading at the time.

Integrating Shearson proved far less painful than our earlier acquisitions for a few important reasons. Unlike Hentz or Hayden Stone, our latest target had a reasonably well-functioning back office, and we had learned a great deal from our past mistakes. Early in the process, I had made Peter Cohen responsible for operations, and he rose to the occasion by keeping everyone on track. Shearson's customers owned securities worth $1.5 billion, yet at the end of our integration, we only had trouble reconciling an infinitesimally small $12,000.

By the time our merger actually closed in September, we had already achieved our targets for cutting our back office costs by two-thirds and our overall costs by $20 million per year.

My only major frustration came with the elevated turnover among Shearson's brokers. I was now investing considerable time visiting our retail sales offices, yet we still lost close to 30 percent of our new brokers. Surprised by the exodus, I reached out to George Murray to come back and help run our national network. Marshall Cogan's departure had resolved the management disarray that had originally driven George away, and he readily returned and offered his enthusiastic Irish charisma to staunch the broker outflow.

Shearson proved to be a watershed for our company's reputation. Within weeks of closing the deal, the market and investor confidence began a tentative recovery. By the end of March 1975, our stock price had risen to nearly $5 per share while the Dow had jumped 20 percent from its lows the prior fall. The newly combined Shearson Hayden Stone never lost money, and the relative ease of the integration proved we could make our formula work on a grand scale. By quadrupling in size during one of the harshest bear markets in memory, we had demonstrated our competence.

We had become a force to be reckoned with.

Buying Shearson also shaped my reputation as a manager. I had spent enough time enmeshing myself in the details of our company that I began to develop healthy instincts regarding what we might accomplish. I'd invest a lot of time roaming the company's halls and asking probing questions of our employees to learn how they felt and how we might do things better.

As I approached our employees, I learned a great deal and developed an intuitive feel for what was going on in our company. By constantly probing, I frequently surfaced potential problems faster than had we waited for circumstances to run their course. Each merger also brought large numbers of new and unfamiliar staff. Making the rounds gave me a good feel for those among my new colleagues who were really talented. All the roaming made me far better at making important personnel-related decisions.

I specifically made an effort to develop strong rapport with our operations people and our brokers. I often stayed at work well into the night to understand the nuances of our operations. My improved feel for the business empowered me to pursue later opportunities faster than many of my competitors. Speed of action proved to be a great competitive asset.

Our management culture at Shearson Hayden Stone soon became distinctive as well. My style evolved intuitively. I placed a premium on what I considered best practices: high aspirations, intensity, pride, teamwork, and sacrificing for the company's common good. I still suffered from a volatile temper and hated to be surprised, but I compensated for my shortcomings by setting the example of bringing passion to the job and digging for the facts behind the business. I asserted repeatedly that doing "okay" was not enough and that we couldn't afford to stand still lest we lose our competitive edge. If we were going to build an exceptional company, we'd never get there by following the lead of other companies or by excusing our shortcomings by blaming industry conditions.

If my temper inhibited people, it was hard to see. Our top executives—Arthur Levitt, Duke Chapman, Frank Zarb, Peter Cohen, and many others—always opened up and expressed their views. My team saw that my blowups usually passed quickly and that they were reserved for those about whom I cared. Moreover, I made sure that my colleagues understood that the last thing I wanted was a group of yes-men.

Our collective intensity had come from our rapid string of acquisitions which brought out everyone's competitive juices and revved up our decision making to operate at 110 miles per hour. I insisted on a very personal management style, and low turnover among top management proved that we enjoyed a remarkable collegial spirit. Along the way, we had taken plenty of operating risk, yet I insisted that we never leverage the balance sheet excessively in order to protect our margin for error.

In June 1975, tragedy struck within our ranks. Roger Berlind's wife and three of his four children were returning from New Orleans on the ill-fated Eastern Flight 66 when something went horribly wrong during a storm on their approach to Kennedy Airport. The plane crashed, killing all aboard. Left only with his two-year-old son, Roger barely functioned for months. Once he collected himself, Roger informed me he wanted to withdraw from an active role with the firm. I acceded to his wishes, given his deep anguish. Roger always had been the kindest and most soft-spoken of my original partners—he usually wasn't the most passionate, yet I was still proud to have counted him as my partner. For the next couple of years, Roger maintained an office with us, but he gradually turned his interest to what had always been his first love: writing music and producing Broadway shows. Over the past three decades, he has amassed an impressive list of hits, and he's still going strong.

Roger's departure came at another important juncture for our company. Only a month earlier, the SEC at long last mandated the complete elimination of fixed commissions. Since the late 1960s, pressure had been building to remove this effective profit subsidy. The growth of the Nasdaq market illustrated that transaction costs were falling sharply, and large institutional investors—who increasingly dominated the market—now demanded the ability to trade for less. The SEC had granted these large institutions the power to negotiate commissions on very large orders as early as 1971, but now the regulator set May 1, 1975, as the date on which all commissions would be deregulated. The Street collectively held its breath as May Day approached. No one had any idea how fast and far commission income might fall, but everyone took for granted that negotiated rates meant lower profits.

I worried a great deal about the change that spring, but I also took heart that our aggressive string of acquisitions might have given us an edge over our competition. After all, we had successfully cut our fixed costs and shifted our mix decisively in favor of retail business, which I hoped might not be as vulnerable to discounting as the institutional side. With the arrival of May 1, we immediately dropped our pricing on all retail accounts by 5 percent while capping the maximum reduction at 20 percent. In this way, we could stamp on order confirmation slips that clients "received a preferred rate" while we sought to limit the damage to our retail revenues. The strategy ended up working, as most of our competitors held the line on what they charged for retail orders. Unfortunately, the same did not hold true on institutional trades where commissions plummeted 40 percent in the first weeks under the new system.

Many firms struggled during this period, but we performed relatively well. More than 75 percent of our commissions related to retail, and our commodities business grew vigorously. The stock market bounced back smartly in 1975, which didn't hurt either. Our revenues advanced at a healthy 28 percent clip in the first full year after commissions were deregulated. Meanwhile, we continued to scout for more acquisitions though our torrid growth over the prior couple of years demanded that we give our company some time to settle down before seeking another large deal.

Our success through the turbulence of deregulation gave us a chance to set new objectives, and I set my sights on overtaking E. F. Hutton, the country's second largest broker. While we waited a couple of years to do anything significant, the chance to upgrade our institutional franchise presented itself in August 1977 when Faulkner Dawkins approached us.

During our early years in business, we had modeled our company after Faulkner and DLJ, two firms which built strong institutional franchises around industry-leading research. Our shift toward retail in the 1970s meant we no longer emulated these companies, but I convinced myself that an acquisition of Faulkner would broadcast loudly that Shearson Hayden Stone intended to be a major player in the institutional business. For the first time, I paid a premium to book value, offering all of $7 million to buy the firm. Once the deal was completed, we advertised Shearson Hayden Stone as "the house that research built." Unfortunately, we experienced a lot of turnover following the acquisition, and Faulkner failed to give us the extra traction for which we had hoped.

Around the same time, we found a far more compelling partner and came within a hairbreadth of announcing what would have been a blockbuster combination if only it were not for a destructive leak. Kuhn Loeb was as prestigious as they come, part of the famous "Our Crowd" German-Jewish Wall Street establishment and a leading investment bank. Tipped off that the influential Schiff family was pushing for a sale of the firm, Frank Zarb arranged for me to meet Kuhn Loeb's CEO, Harvey Krueger, and negotiations soon followed.

Unfortunately, Krueger couldn't control his troops, and a rebellious partner who ran Kuhn Loeb's international department spoke out loudly against the deal, arguing that the company would be better off combining with the far more international Lehman Brothers. With only a weekend left to settle final details, the dissident partner apparently leaked our pregnant deal to the press and immediately used the publicity to claim that Kuhn Loeb's international clients were dead set against the combination and threatening to pull their business. In a heartbeat, the tide shifted on our negotiations, and Kuhn Loeb ended up striking a very different deal with Lehman Brothers over that final weekend.

I was incredulous at the turn of events and kicked myself that we hadn't prevailed.

If the disappointment of losing Kuhn Loeb weren't enough, I soon saw three of my top executives jump ship.

The first surprise came in 1978 with a phone call from Arthur Levitt, who told me he was in meetings at the American Stock Exchange and had decided to accept an offer to become its chairman. Arthur's news and the way in which he chose to deliver it floored me. We had enjoyed a close partnership for fifteen years, and I had little idea he was so unhappy that he'd consider leaving. Initially, I was angry that he had sprung his news on me in such a remarkably impersonal manner. The departure of a company's president represents big news, and I'd now have to scramble to explain his departure and fill the senior retail position.

Wasting no time, however, I called Duke Chapman and secured his agreement to run the retail system even before Arthur had time to return to the office. Once I got past the shock of his news, it occurred to me that Arthur must have felt overshadowed for some time, and I appreciated that he probably saw the semi-governmental American Stock Exchange position as a means for following in the footsteps of his public-service-minded father. My relationship with Arthur alternatively turned warm and cold over subsequent years—he should be proud of his public service, yet, as with Marshall Cogan, I've detected a tinge of resentment that somehow he feels I didn't appreciate his contributions to the success of our company.

No sooner had Arthur left than Frank Zarb gave notice that he planned to leave as well. Frank ran our investment bank at that time, and he rationalized that the Kuhn Loeb talks signaled it would be a matter of time before we'd merge with another large investment bank and put his job at risk. I understood his logic and appreciated that he had put the interests of the company above his own when he introduced the Kuhn Loeb opportunity. Over the years, Frank had left and returned to our company on three other occasions for stints in government (as assistant labor secretary and later director of the Office of Management and Budget under Richard Nixon and then as energy czar under Gerald Ford), so his announcement came as something less than a total shock.

I held Frank in high regard and attempted to keep him. I floated the idea of making him president now that Arthur had vacated the role, but this roiled some of my other executives. Peter Cohen especially bridled at my idea, arguing that Frank hadn't done much to bring in investment banking business and suggested alternatively that if we were to have a new president, it should be he. I chose not to press the issue and watched Frank move to become a partner at Lazard Frères.

Peter continued to press for the president's title, and I considered the idea seriously, yet the notion went over poorly with most of our executive committee. After five years of working intimately with me, Peter had learned a great deal about finance, operations, and human resources while his personality perhaps had become more like mine. He was brash, outspoken, and occasionally rude. Those traits may not have been problematic for me, but many members of my team had spotty relationships with Peter and undoubtedly would not have liked reporting to him. At last, I made it clear that the president position would remain unfilled.

Soon thereafter, in April 1978, Peter let me in on a surprise of his own: He was leaving to become president of Republic National Bank where he'd work with billionaire Edmond Safra. In this case, I felt utterly betrayed, and inwardly I became livid. One might argue that selfish considerations dominated my reaction as I had come to depend on Peter for so many operational and financial details and especially valued his role in integrating our numerous acquisitions. After all, he had become my number one sounding board and troubleshooter. I can't deny these thoughts colored my thinking, but I also felt deeply wounded that Peter had disregarded my trust and generosity in giving him great responsibility at such a young age. Peter knew I was under the gun with the departure of Arthur and Frank, and his timing seemed especially insensitive. I felt Peter was trading me in for a new mentor relationship with the reclusive Safra, and I couldn't understand what Safra possibly could offer that Peter couldn't find by staying put.

It is human nature to pull back when one feels a sense of hurt, and I reacted coolly as I listened to Peter offer his reasons for leaving, never once trying to talk him out of his decision. I felt it would have shown weakness to have shared my anger openly.

While I had a reasonably deep management bench, I felt overwhelmed by losing my top three people in such a short period. I tried to pick up the pieces and hired two replacement executives, Jim Tozer from Citibank and my friend George Sheinberg from Bulova. Coming out of a staid banking culture, Tozer didn't last long, but we fared somewhat better with Sheinberg. Nonetheless, he plainly lacked Peter's range of talent.

The experience of losing my top three executives in such a short period drove home the value I placed on loyalty. I viewed our company's employees—especially senior executives—as part of my extended family whom I respected, and I wanted to be treated the same way in return. Developing close ties with my colleagues and their spouses had always seemed a good recipe for motivating people and for bringing out the best in our executive team. Corporate loyalty has fallen from fashion over the years; however, I believed throughout my career that companies suffer when employees see their firm simply as a place to work. The more a business leader can personalize the relationships that tie together employees, the better it will be for the company.

As time passed, I realized that Peter had left a hole that would not be easily filled. Two of our capital markets guys, Herb Freiman and Jeff

Lane, remained close to Peter and pushed me to try to woo him back. They told me that Peter had become bored at Republic and that his new job was not all that he had expected. Before long, the two behaved like diplomatic emissaries as they worked both Peter and me into swallowing our pride and accepting that we each wanted to work with one another once more. In 1979, a year after his original departure, Peter and I met at the Oak Room in the Plaza Hotel. We had planned only for a quick drink; instead, we lingered for multiple rounds and then dinner.

By the end of the evening, we agreed it was time for Peter to return.

———

We enjoyed a relatively peaceful period in the year between Peter's departure and his subsequent return. Of note, we moved our head-quarters back downtown, taking over the top six floors of one of the World Trade Center towers. Since its completion in the early 1970s, the World Trade Center had proved a white elephant, but I smelled an opportunity. We soon struck a sweetheart deal for a twenty-year lease that gave us space at an average cost of only $15 per square foot. At the time, Paine Webber had taken space in one of the lower buildings and its CEO, Don Marron, had sought permission to install a fireplace in the executive suite only to be turned down on the pretext that the city's fire code required a chimney that would rise above surrounding buildings. Eager to show up one of our competitors, I negotiated that we be allowed to build a fireplace in our new location as the height of nearby buildings didn't matter given our location on the 106th floor.

Our new fireplace set a record for being the highest in any man-made structure, and we used to joke that we'd send up white smoke to celebrate the end of a good trading day.

Perhaps it was the soaring height of our new offices, but I soon be-gan dreaming once again about bold ways for our company to leapfrog its competitors. During 1978, I devoured press reports which detailed mounting integration and management problems at the newly merged Loeb Rhoades Hornblower & Company. The new firm had sought to blend the very distinct investment banking culture of Loeb Rhoades and the retail-oriented Hornblower Weeks, which itself was the product of prior mergers. Brokerage industry profits recently had improved, yet Loeb Rhoades Hornblower's profits remained depressed thanks to internal strife and the new company's inability to sort out operational issues.

Sensing the disarray might eventually lead to an opening, I sought to get to know Tom Kempner, who was one of the firm's three co-CEOs and nephew to the iconic Our Crowd legend John Loeb Sr. Kempner and I shared an interest in tennis, and we soon began meeting for weekend matches. After a time, I let Kempner know that we'd be seriously interested if his firm were to choose to sell. By then, we had become a credible potential partner: Shearson Hayden Stone was performing well, and its stock, at over $12 per share, had returned to the 1971 initial public offering price at long last.

Kempner politely deflected my initial entreaties, but I refused to give up hope. Then in March 1979, I ran into John Loeb Sr. at a black-tie event at the Waldorf-Astoria Hotel. Loeb seemed unusually friendly, and I took it as a signal that he was warming to a deal. Sure enough, Kempner soon let on that it was time to talk. The idea of merging with Loeb Rhoades filled me with anticipation, as it had been four years since we had completed a large deal.

I sat down with Kempner and one of his two co-CEOs and investment banking head Sherman Lewis in early May, and we discussed broadly how we might merge our companies. I reassured them that Shearson could pull off the transaction, and we soon settled tentatively on terms: We'd pay for the purchase by offering a mix of stock and debt; we'd mesh the Shearson and Loeb Rhoades names; and we'd make Sherman Lewis head of our investment banking business. The session ended on an upbeat note, but we understood that we still needed John Loeb Sr.'s approval followed by his partners' consent.

The meeting with Loeb turned out to be a lovefest, or at least the closest thing one could have with someone of patrician stature. It was readily apparent that the stately old man had become disgusted with trends in his company and lacked confidence in his management team, including his nephew, Tommy Kempner. Sitting before both Kempner and me, Loeb ended our meeting by pulling an envelope out of his breast pocket. "Sandy, Mrs. Loeb and I are going to Europe for an extended vacation," he augustly announced. "This is a letter that explains that I've put my trust in you and that I have confidence that you'll keep things moving ahead while I'm gone." I was taken aback by the gesture and vote of confidence, but I also appreciated that Loeb indirectly was addressing Kempner with a message not to screw up the deal.

The meeting with the Loeb Rhoades partners was far less tidy. On Friday, May 11, we invited the company's principal owners and executives to a session at my home in Greenwich to inform them of the transaction and hammer out management assignments. Soon a multitude of stunned partners arrived, each seemingly accompanied by an attorney. At once, the scene became a circus with all the factions. The sound of heated arguments and slamming doors soon reverberated throughout the house.

The marathon meeting lasted through the weekend and Mother's Day Sunday. At first, I let the factions duke things out. These guys may not have trusted us, but they obviously didn't believe in one another either. Kempner exerted no control, and I soon realized that amid their internecine warfare, the partners were bidding against themselves. By Saturday morning, I stepped in. Being as direct as possible, I announced that Sherman Lewis would assume leadership of our investment banking business, but that's where my magnanimity ended. I then revealed that Shearson executives would take charge of the retail business and operations. My news sent Loeb Rhoades' third co-CEO and retail head, Jack Toolan, into orbit since he only wanted to stay in charge of the brokers. He quit on the spot and stormed out of the house.

Toolan's abrupt departure created a big unexpected problem as he was the only senior executive who knew anything about the large retail business that had come from Hornblower. "What do we do now?" several of us seemed to exclaim in unison. If we were going to have a prayer of successfully integrating the two companies, we needed to find someone fast who understood the business's inner workings. We asked Sherman for his advice, and he referred us to Bob Biggar, a well-regarded regional manager based out of Cleveland, whom we quickly summoned to the meeting.

Biggar arrived the next morning amid a scene of organized chaos. Countless people were scurrying about the house, and phones were ringing off the hook. In the center of it all, Joanie stood in the kitchen preparing chicken salad and urged everyone to remember Mother's Day and call home. I immediately saw that there was friction between Biggar and Kempner. I couldn't afford to see another dispute arise, and I quickly stepped in to calm our important guest. "Bob, I can see you two aren't getting along," I began plaintively, "but this merger is going to happen, and I need your help. Toolan has just quit, and I need your help to make this deal a success." I then promised a promotion in return for his help. Charmed by my personal plea, Biggar committed to supply information and play up the merger with his firm's retail brokers. As the tortuous weekend came to a close, we settled the key management assignments and established a reasonable integration plan.

I finally turned to Joanie and asked whether we should move forward. She quietly hunched her shoulders and nodded.

On Monday, we announced the $85 million deal. Once again, we had entered into a transaction that would double our size—Loeb Rhoades brought 160 offices and 1,800 brokers. This time, however, we knew the integration would be especially tricky. In fact, Peter Cohen argued persuasively that we should manage the risk by integrating the merger in stages. He used the analogy that we should gobble Loeb Rhoades as we would a large steak: Eat only a little at a time. Thus, we set three principal conversion dates over a six-month period and planned to pay for the deal in installments.

Our first conversion began inauspiciously, in large measure thanks to Kempner's arrogance and ignorance about operations. We needed to sign documents in order to get under way. Yet Tommy Kempner inexplicably disappeared on the Friday afternoon before the crucial first weekend conversion. We had already authorized work orders to switch countless office phone lines the following day, and the inability to complete a contract would mean pandemonium on Monday.

Everyone was tense, and I had just returned from a grueling trip to meet Loeb Rhoades' retail brokers. Exhausted and worried that I might screw up the deal due to fatigue, I headed home and left the details to Peter, who later complained that I bailed out on him at a crucial moment. However, I saw that there was little I could add to the process and had confidence that Peter would call if he needed me. I learned later that Kempner finally showed up that evening at Willkie Farr's offices and immediately confronted the harried integration team that had been hard at work for hours. Apparently, Kempner couldn't grasp the outstanding complexities and feigned annoyance that the details hadn't been resolved. He then puffed that he was prepared to back out of the deal. Peter then calmly responded how that would be fine and then proceeded to explain how on Monday none of the phones in Loeb Rhoades' offices would operate any longer. His bluff called, Kempner turned white and promptly changed his tune. Working through the night, the team finally completed the contract.

That first conversion went smoothly. Unfortunately, the same could not be said of the next one, which included transferring a large volume of retail accounts. The data processing demands became overwhelming, and we had to scramble to third-party vendors for support. At one point, a workman's ladder fell on a piece of equipment and knocked out one of our main networks. Because orders had to be processed manually, a mountain of incorrect statements soon piled up. Meanwhile, the SEC was breathing down our neck, warily monitoring our progress and financial position given the deal's large size.

Somehow, we managed past the glitches, but tension and disunity swept my management team during the fall of 1979. For the first time in all of our many deals, I wondered whether my colleagues could keep it together. Wick Simmons, our retail co-head, and Duke Chapman had become especially incensed at Peter, contending he had promised things that he had to have known he couldn't deliver. Wick even pressed me to fire Peter. On the other hand, Peter had worked harder than ever that summer and assured me that we had passed the worst of our problems. I backed him all the way.

I understood that I needed to bring my colleagues together in a place where we could think clearly and get our issues on the table. We headed to West Virginia and the Greenbrier Resort for a weekend of introspection. Figuring it would prove cathartic for everyone to spill their guts, I began the session by calling on my colleagues to speak their minds and lay their issues on the table. Shouting and accusations promptly filled the air.

Finally, George Sheinberg declared, "This has become scary. We could lose everything. Maybe the last conversion is a 'bridge too far' and we should stop now." Somehow George's plea shook everyone and forced us to consider how far we had come and the negative consequences that we'd surely face if we backed out of our commitment. The mood settled, and together we resolved to recommit to see this monumental transaction through to completion. I insisted at the end of our off-site weekend that we all prick our fingers and sign a symbolic blood oath that we'd lay to rest our issues with one another. The meeting proved a success and showed that sometimes it's important for a CEO to accept contentiousness if it allows for a release of tension and ill will.

Just after Thanksgiving, we completed the final transfer of sixty branches in a step that went remarkably smoothly. Peter had been right when he argued at the Greenbrier that things were looking up. Curiously, shortly before the final conversion, Tommy Kempner asked that we alter our original terms and replace the common stock component with a debt-related instrument that somehow would accord his partners preferential tax treatment. We were happy to comply and offered an instrument that promised a fixed share of our profits for a five-year period with a cap on our total outlay. It turned out to be a great deal for us and terrible for Loeb Rhoades' partners, as the new arrangement severely limited the recipients' participation in our earnings growth and capped the economic value we'd ultimately have to give away.

Completing the merger, we once more renamed the company—now to Shearson Loeb Rhoades—and set off to seize the deal's tremendous promise. We delivered on our goal of surpassing number-two-ranked E. F. Hutton and boasted a powerful retail distribution network of 270 offices and 3,500 brokers. This time, we held the line on broker turnover. Most realized Shearson was a credible and strongly managed firm, and the brokers liked how we led the industry in offering equity-based pay. At a broker off-site in Bermuda right after we announced the deal, I was approached by a group of former Hayden Stone and Shearson employees waving white handkerchiefs and promising not to jump ship as they had before.

The stock market behaved well over the following year, and the combination of improving transaction volumes and deep cost cutting provided exceptional juice for Shearson Loeb Rhoades' profits. In 1980, we earned over $55 million, more than five times what we had earned just two years earlier. Our stock price zoomed nearly in tandem—adjusted for stock splits, our share price rocketed from $8½ when we completed the deal to $48 less than eighteen months later. The vigorous earnings growth enabled us to issue new stock on favorable terms and pay off early our final commitments to Loeb Rhoades' partners, thus proving their folly at not accepting our shares. Finally, our success buying Loeb Rhoades at last dissipated the residual remorse I had felt since losing the Kuhn Loeb deal.

I learned once and for all the importance of never giving in to despair. As I'd see many times again, losing out on one acquisition has an uncanny way of leading to even better opportunities.

The 1970s had proved a remarkable decade in which the securities industry and our company were completely transformed. In ten short years, the industry moved from a fragmented amalgam of weakly capitalized partnerships to a cadre of large publicly owned institutions far better positioned to serve clients and absorb market volatility. Meanwhile, CBWL shed its anonymity and confronted the great danger of giving in to complacency. Four transformational mergers and an initial public offering later, our company had moved to a position of leadership and prestige, so much so that former President Ford agreed to join the new Shearson Loeb Rhoades board in 1980. A great deal had changed, but through it all, two things remained constant: my nature to worry perpetually and my reluctance to dwell on past accomplishments.

Accordingly, I entered 1980 nervously looking to the future.

5

Riding a New Wave

S hearson Loeb Rhoades enjoyed better earnings momentum than virtually any other firm on Wall Street in 1980, and our management team's spirits soared. The rancor that we had experienced a year earlier as we came to terms with integrating Loeb Rhoades suddenly seemed like a distant memory. I shared my colleagues' sense of satisfaction, but I also felt we couldn't rest on our laurels. So difficult for most of the prior decade, business conditions didn't seem to be getting any easier.

To the contrary, four presidents had failed to stem the advancing tide of inflation, and prices were spiraling up at an ever faster clip. Unemployment was surging at the same time, which was unusual since traditional economic theory took for granted that there was an inverse relationship between inflation and unemployment. Confused and worried, most businesspeople shared a palpable feeling that the economy was spinning out of control. I didn't despair, but I realized that Wall Street firms had to institutionalize further and improve their access to capital if they hoped to grow through this unsettled period. Something told me that the financial services industry might soon shift direction toward much more powerful forms of amalgamation.

One thrust in this direction had come in 1978 when Merrill Lynch introduced its revolutionary Cash Management Account (CMA). For the first time, a brokerage firm was giving its customers the means of earning a competitive rate of return on their cash and effectively offering banking services such as check writing and credit cards. Before the CMA innovation, retail brokerages would earn lucrative profits from investing customers' idle cash balances. I first thought the CMA idea represented a needless giveaway of these important profits. However, a couple of my executives convinced me that the product could be a powerful means of aggregating customer relationships and could draw money from the commercial banks.

The immediate lesson—and one to be repeated countless times in the future—was that the increased volume of business from a valuable product innovation could overpower reduced profit margins. An even broader message was that financial firms inevitably would find ways to invade each other's turf. I became obsessed that we had to find an innovative approach to remaining in the vanguard of this trend toward financial supermarkets while preparing for considerably more industry consolidation.

On a personal level, I also had begun to feel that I was ready for a new challenge. For ten years, I had spearheaded one acquisition after another. I was good at it. Yet I felt restive and yearned to take on something new. I wanted to apply my business skills in a larger and more interesting business. Shearson had gone from relative obscurity to an industry leader with nearly $60 million in annual profits. We were now in a position to command the attention of the large financial services organizations. In this way, the business and personal imperatives both argued for linking up with a larger partner.

I began challenging my team to think about organizations such as American Express or any one of several large insurance companies. Such firms would bring huge numbers of new customers, broader products, and expanded distribution. Just as important, I calculated that these types of firms would have more secure earnings and stock prices in the face of increasingly uncertain economic conditions. In fact, in late 1979, under the direction of its newly installed chairman, Paul Volcker, the Federal Reserve had begun to tighten short-term rates aggressively in order to combat inflation. We had no idea then that the prime rate would hit an unthinkable peak of 21 percent within two years, but we felt sure that the dislocations in financial markets were far from ending.

Of all the big-name financial services, I particularly envied American Express, which I saw as the embodiment of the U.S. corporate establishment. Their upscale customers seemed most aligned with Shearson's target market. It was a blue chip company with an impressive history, and it offered the security of a big balance sheet. A union with American Express could set the stage for all kinds of cross-selling synergies. Visions of brokers selling credit cards and insurance danced in my head alongside the notion of trolling American Express's vast customer base for new brokerage clients. The idea that we could dramatically step up our brand advertising was compelling. Our brokers would be set apart from rivals with an unparalleled array of products. American Express shares seemed undervalued, which added further to my fixation. I was intrigued by structuring a deal where Shearson Loeb Rhoades might receive a healthy premium in the form of undervalued stock that would then rise in value.

I wasn't the only one thinking about American Express or how the financial services industry might change. In late 1980, I received a breakfast invitation from Sandy Lewis, son of Bear Stearns' legendary Cy Lewis. Sandy Lewis was managing partner in his own investment banking boutique, S. B. Lewis & Company, and he possessed a mercurial personality, to put it mildly. He had his demons, but they didn't stop him from being intensely creative and tenacious in devising and pursuing new business ideas.

Sandy and I met at the New York Stock Exchange Club on a brisk morning in late October. My friend wasted little time getting to the point and reminded me that he was close to American Express CEO Jim Robinson. He proposed that Shearson and American Express discuss a marketing joint venture between the brokerage and credit card businesses. The idea appealed to me immediately, as Shearson had just rolled out its Financial Management Account, our version of Merrill's CMA product. Upgrading Shearson's offering to include the panache of an American Express gold card (rather than our more generic Visa offering) would represent a nice tactic to differentiate our product. Furthermore, we both knew that an initial joint venture relationship would be a practical way to get the companies talking with an eye toward an eventual merger.

Sandy Lewis arranged for me to meet Jim Robinson in early December over breakfast at American Express's headquarters on Broad Street. I was excited and more than a touch nervous as I headed to the early morning meeting. I hadn't met Jim Robinson before, and his background was substantially different from mine. Robinson came from a patrician Atlanta family where his father and grandfather had each served as chairman of the city's leading bank. Harvard-educated, Robinson had joined Morgan Guaranty Bank out of school and later worked at the elite Wall Street firm White Weld.

Jim had joined American Express in the early 1970s and had risen with seeming ease—he became CEO in 1977. His only setback came in 1979 when he was compelled to abort an unfriendly deal to acquire McGraw-Hill. Adverse publicity stung American Express directors on that occasion and led to the dismissal of Robinson's deputy, but Jim managed to keep his job. This incident had made him more careful in considering other deals, at least in the early 1980s.

Jim met me on my arrival and ushered me into a private dining room. To my disappointment, he indicated that we would be joined by one of his executives, Al Way, who recently had joined American Express from General Electric, where he had lost out in that company's CEO succession. I didn't know much about Way, but I was mildly irked that Jim had diluted our chance to establish a rapport by introducing a third party into this "get acquainted" session. I wondered about the power structure at American Express and how someone like Al Way might complicate a potential merger.

Nevertheless, the breakfast meeting went well. Jim and I spoke about the financial services industry's future, and we compared notes on our firms' respective strategies. "I aim to build a broad-based financial services company," Jim declared. "American Express already enjoys a unique blend of credit card, banking, insurance, and payment-related businesses." In return, I highlighted the things that gave Shearson its competitive edge: "We have operational excellence; we tightly manage our overhead; and we don't take excessive trading risks." Moreover, I stressed that I didn't like excessive balance sheet leverage and that I ran Shearson with a hands-on business philosophy. "These are the values that have propelled our growth and that have enabled us to assemble a leading retail brokerage franchise," I concluded.

I immediately liked Jim and felt we had complementary styles. He was polished and at ease in talking about the broader picture of Washington politics and the strategic outlook for financial services, while I spoke more narrowly about operational details and challenges facing my business. We agreed to commission a team to explore the joint venture idea. Each of us left the meeting thinking that we could do business with one another. I'm sure Jim felt as I did: namely, that the joint venture discussions would be a perfect means for our management teams to get to know one another should we elect to consider a full-blown merger down the road.

Jim and I, along with our executives, met several times over the next couple of months. American Express managers raised concerns whether commercial banks would rebel at distributing its traveler's checks and credit cards if American Express were to enter into an exclusive arrangement with Shearson. Many of their executives worried, too, about protecting their exclusive access to their customer relationships. By February, we had found suitable compromises and agreed on a joint marketing program.

Agreement in principle was one thing, but we soon realized that American Express operated at a much slower speed driven by the firm's bureaucratic culture. Efforts to roll out the joint venture plan languished into March.

———

There's nothing like a little fear to instill a sense of urgency in people. On March 18, 1981, Joanie and I were in Hong Kong touring the newly opened Shearson office. We went to show our support and help recruit new employees and customers. I also had arranged to meet former president Ford, who was still new to our board and who happened to be traveling in the region. This was an excellent opportunity to familiarize him with part of our company. We happened to be in the office at about 10:00 P.M. to check on the market opening in New York. Suddenly, I received an urgent phone call from Jeff Lane, then second in command of our capital markets business. Flushed with excitement, Jeff blurted that stunning news had just crossed the newswire: Prudential Insurance was merging with Bache & Company.

Bache's roots on Wall Street dated back to the 1870s, and as recently as 1970, the firm ranked as the second largest brokerage in the country, before losing its competitive edge during the 1970s and drifting back to seventh place. Bache had been severely weakened owing to its exposure to the Hunt brothers' silver speculation in 1979 and efforts to ward off an ensuing hostile takeover attempt. Still, news of the Prudential-Bache merger was powerful. It heralded the dawn of the modern financial services industry where widely differing products would be offered under a single roof.

No sooner had I finished reading the story than I turned to Joanie and declared, "Just wait until we get back to New York. I'm sure this news will lead to Shearson having serious talks with American Express. The Pru-Bache deal will give Jim Robinson the courage to do a deal."

I looked for an empty office and immediately made two important phone calls. I first called Sandy Lewis and told him I planned to call Jim Robinson and propose we get together on my return from Asia. Lewis was ecstatic; he had dreamed of bringing Shearson together with American Express and now there was a clear call to action. Next, I tracked down Peter Cohen, who was visiting Israel and staying at the King David Hotel in Jerusalem, to discuss our plan of attack. "This will change the face of the business," I told him. "We need to do something." I then asked what he thought about the notion of us merging with American Express.

All I can recall was his decisive answer: "A home run!"

Still in Asia a day or so later and having let the news sink in, I placed a call to Jim Robinson. My approach was simple and direct: With Pru buying Bache, there was now a model of a new financial services company, and it would make a heck of a lot of sense to craft our companies using a similar template. It would be the two best partners getting together instead of being forced to go with our second, third, or fourth choices later. Jim concurred with my observations—much to my relief—and we agreed to meet upon my return.

At the end of March, I headed once more to American Express's headquarters, this time to a private meeting with Jim in his office to discuss a full-blown merger. The mating game had begun. Merger talks typically start with each side laying out its vision of the big picture. The key is to establish good chemistry and atmosphere ahead of the hard bargaining. At that moment, I was thrilled to be commencing negotiations and had made up my mind that a merger with American Express would represent a terrific move for Shearson. My main concern was whether Jim Robinson was completely sold.

Jim and I laid out our opening positions. Jim presented his philosophy of having strong business heads that reported directly to him. He talked about Shearson coming into American Express as another leg for the company, joining Fireman's Fund Insurance, Travel Related Services, and the International Bank. He wanted me to commit to staying on top of Shearson. He made it clear he was thinking of an all-stock deal and suggested he'd be comfortable with Shearson having three board seats out of a total of twenty. Lastly, he insisted that any deal could not weaken American Express's earnings even temporarily.

I concurred with the idea of a stock swap and that American Express shouldn't accept any dilution to its earnings per share—I indicated that I was not interested in forcing American Express to pay top dollar. Instead, I insisted that I had proved myself as a strong operator and wanted to come into the combined company with more responsibility than simply continuing to run Shearson. I stressed that I could bring a lot to the table in enhancing his company. Since this was a first meeting, neither of us pressed too hard. We agreed to set up our negotiating teams and to introduce our executives. I left Jim's office that morning feeling good that we were off to a positive start. I had accomplished my primary goal of getting our priority merger partner to focus on Shearson, even if I sensed deep down that we'd still face tough bargaining ahead.

We spent several days getting to know one another better and conducting due diligence. The talks steadily gathered momentum, and in early April, Joanie and I invited Jim and his wife, Bettye, to our home in Greenwich for Sunday brunch. I always liked to meet spouses when doing a deal and especially wanted to get Joanie's input since we were heading toward a major life-changing event. Spring had arrived early that year, and the Robinsons came over on a brilliant morning. We had our housekeeper prepare grits alongside bagels and lox and joked that we were enjoying a real "Shearson American Express breakfast."

Joanie later took Bettye for a tour of the gardens while Jim and I moved to the living room to assess the status of our negotiations. We felt good about the progress our teams had been making and determined we would soon be in a position to have a serious discussion on price and other open issues. We also began to discuss how the board should be set up. I mentioned that I wanted Peter Cohen to be included while Jim indicated that American Express was willing to provide a fourth board seat for President Ford. I then suggested I'd like to include Dan Seymour, the retired chairman of advertising firm J. Walter Thompson. The board composition would soon take on a life of its own, but there was little reason for worry that Sunday.

We talked more about my role in the new company. Jim reiterated that he wanted me to run Shearson as a freestanding company within American Express, and I repeated that I wanted to do something broader than just watch over Shearson. That was an important reason for my wanting to merge in the first place. I told him I was eager to come in as a clear second in command and that I would bring a great deal in terms of my operating skills, having run a publicly owned company for ten years.

I wanted Jim to consider me as a "Mr. Inside" while he would focus on the board and external constituencies. Jim listened carefully, but—in a tactic he would use repeatedly later—he indicated he might have difficulty getting his board to agree to establishing a chief operating officer role or its equivalent. Still, he told me he would think more about the subject and how I might become more engaged on a corporate-wide basis.

As the Robinsons drove away, Joanie and I compared notes and agreed that while the issue of my role remained subject to further negotiations, Jim and I could forge a close partnership. We also both liked Bettye a great deal. In their walk in the garden, Bettye had expressed to Joanie that she'd be happy with the deal and that I could be a positive influence on her husband since my background and perspective were so different from his.

Within a week, our negotiations moved into high gear. The open issues by then revolved around the usual: price, the makeup of the board, and key management assignments. I'd soon have to face gut-wrenching decisions relating to the board and my role in the company, though the question of price seemed the most straightforward.

Settling the board would soon become a focal point in the negotiations. It all started when Jim called to tell me his directors were having difficulty accepting my recommendation of Peter Cohen. He suggested that American Express typically only had its business heads serve as inside directors on its board and, as I would remain CEO of Shearson, the board preferred to exclude my second in command. I initially resisted as I thought it would be helpful to have a close ally on the board; however, Jim managed to convince me that his board was adamant on the point and that there was no alternative.

I knew Peter would take the news badly but felt that it would be a great mistake to turn this into a deal killer. I made a pivotal decision (a mistake in retrospect) not to tell Peter the bad news until we were closer to resolving the deal's other open issues, fearing that his anger might upend our negotiations. I told Robinson that I'd be willing to have Shearson's outside counsel, Ken Bialkin, replace Peter.

More than a week went by with no further commentary on board matters, and I assumed the issue had been settled. I pressed Robinson to define my role after the merger and asserted I needed the equivalent of a chief operating officer position. Jim continued to resist, using his board once again as an excuse. Robinson contended that his directors had never met me and that there were deep-seated concerns whether American Express might be stepping up its earnings volatility by buying a broker dealer. Turning up his Southern charm, Jim reassured me that the board would grow more comfortable once they had gotten to know me and that we could reconsider my specific role later. In the meantime, he encouraged me to think the board might go along with a title like vice chairman. I wasn't happy but, as with Peter's board seat, I felt the deal was so compelling that I couldn't see turning this into a deal killer.

On Thursday, April 16, Jim and I focused on how to value Shearson. Settling this point would allow us to wrap up our negotiations and reach a definitive agreement to merge. This portion of the negotiations went smoothly and relatively fast. We had agreed at the start of our talks that it was important for American Express to avoid any setback to its earnings. Jim initially proposed that American Express exchange about 1.15 of its shares for each outstanding Shearson share; this ratio actually would boost American Express's earnings, but rather than appear greedy, I chose not to dispute the figure.

As our meeting broke up, however, Jim and I ran into Peter Cohen and told him where we were coming out on price. Peter didn't miss a beat and boldly reminded Jim that he could afford to raise his proposed exchange ratio to 1.3 shares and still have an earnings-neutral transaction. At the higher valuation ratio, American Express would be valuing Shearson at over $900 million. If Jim was surprised or put off by Peter's aggressiveness, he hid it well and indicated that he'd be flexible if Peter could convince the American Express team to go up to the higher figure.

Other details continued to fall into place, and we pressed on to reach an agreement on Good Friday. Jim and I met once more early in the afternoon, at which point he informed me he had accepted the higher share exchange ratio suggested by Peter the prior day. We agreed we'd use the weekend to prepare for board meetings on the coming Monday. We came out from closed doors and announced to our weary teams we had reached a tentative agreement. Once Jim left, I told my top executives that we'd have a ten o'clock meeting the following morning at my Greenwich home to give everyone a chance to weigh in on the proposed deal.

At that point, I had one important loose end that I needed to clear up: I had to find a way to tell Peter that he would not be part of the new board. Communicating bad news has never been one of my strengths, and the challenge this time was particularly difficult since Peter was like a son to me after having worked closely building our business for a decade. I fretted over how to bring up the bad news but even so probably ended up informing Peter in the worst way possible. It came at the end of a shared cab ride home that Friday afternoon around four. As I got out of the cab in front of my apartment, I simply blurted out, "There's something I have to tell you: American Express is insisting on only one insider being added to their board—you can't go on the board."

With that, I slammed the door, leaving Peter stunned and fuming.

I realized immediately that I had handled this badly and hadn't treated my colleague with the respect he deserved nor explained the reasoning behind my decision. Good communication among top executives is of course critical, and I made an amateurish mistake on this occasion. Having erred, I now feared a disruptive Peter Cohen could put the deal at risk. I called him at home later that evening. Never afraid to speak his mind, Peter was furious at me for not having stood up for him and for not leveling with him sooner. "This isn't me; it's Jim," I replied. "If you can change his mind, nothing would make me happier." All Peter could say at that point was that he felt hurt and blindsided and that he'd need some time to assess how he'd think about the future. I suggested that Peter come up to my house the next morning a couple of hours ahead of the other executives so that we might talk more in the light of a new day.

Peter in fact knocked on my door at 8:00 A.M., and I was relieved that he seemed calmer than he'd been the prior evening. I explained that it was important that the full executive team endorse the merger and that the others would consider Peter's words carefully. "You have a make-or-break role in influencing the others, and I need you to back me," I said. Peter listened quietly, then indicated, to my great relief: "I will back you since it's the right thing to do, but I am not sure whether I'll remain at Shearson beyond the integration."

Soon the other members of Shearson's management team arrived. Joining them in my living room, I brought them up to date on the specifics of our tentative agreement with American Express. I took pains to reassure them that I would remain responsible for our company even as I likely would be spending considerable time getting involved with American Express at the corporate level. I explained the stock exchange plan, which would substantially benefit our employees, not only the assembled group of top executives, but the rank and file as well, given the depth of equity ownership in our company. From an operations viewpoint, I emphasized that Shearson would continue to be run on an autonomous basis.

Joanie came in around noon and suggested we move outside on the patio for sandwiches. It was another unusually warm spring day, and we formed a semicircle around the outdoor barbecue. I had finished prepping everyone on the deal's specifics so I suggested we go person to person and survey everyone's feelings. On balance, I think we all shared a sense of wistfulness, having worked together for so long and having built something we all felt was great. Nearly everyone—including Peter—projected excitement. Only Wick Simmons, the co-head of our retail franchise, spoke out eloquently against the deal. Wick feared the politics and bureaucracy of a large firm like American Express, and he suggested Shearson had considerable momentum and opportunities to acquire smaller firms. He argued we were selling ourselves short and that our proposed affiliation might prove distracting and limiting.

I give credit to Wick for standing up and speaking from conviction, but I knew it was my role to lead. I felt that it would be a grave mistake to turn back and go it alone. At this point, I asked a simple question: "How would each of you feel if we decided not to do this deal and woke up tomorrow morning to learn that American Express was instead buying E. F. Hutton?" We all agreed this would be our worst nightmare, and the question snuffed out any further dissent. With that, the meeting broke up—everything seemed on course for Monday board meetings and a public announcement of a definitive agreement.

An unspoken issue, of course, hung over the Saturday meeting in Greenwich: Peter Cohen's unhappiness. As promised, Peter remained silent on his personal disappointment. I didn't realize it then, but I soon learned to my dismay that Peter's status was in fact anything but settled at that point.

I can only speculate what may have happened over the next twenty-four hours. All I know is that in a phone conversation the next afternoon, Jim Robinson completely flip-flopped on the composition of the board. "I've been speaking individually with a number of my directors, and there seems to be an emerging consensus that it would be unwise to add an attorney to the board. Many are focusing on the importance of making sure that Shearson remains firmly on course. If you plan to spend a lot of time getting involved at American Express, my directors want to be sure that Peter is committed long term. We may want to add Peter to the board after all."

I was flabbergasted. It would have been one thing had Jim expressed these thoughts originally. Now I looked completely foolish. I was angry, as I felt undermined, and I suspected that Peter had gone around me to make his case directly to Jim. Still, what was my choice? We had come so far; we were about to receive a healthy premium for our shares; and however my exact title would be settled, I knew I'd have a chance to play a prominent role in one of America's iconic companies. I kept my feelings to myself and told Jim I'd go along with the new formula if necessary. That evening I called Ken Bialkin to advise him I might have to shift directions and go with Peter in his stead. Kenny was deeply disappointed—I make it a policy never to renege on a promise, and it pained me greatly to have to make an exception with such a close friend. I elected to await the board's final decision the following day before informing Peter.

How did Jim come to change his mind? His board members may have had some influence, but I suspect Peter made his unhappiness known and that the message probably got across that he likely would not remain with Shearson beyond the initial integration phase. However it happened, Jim's reversal put an extra edge on my emotions coming into Monday, April 20, the day of American Express's final board meeting to vote on our deal.

That Monday was incredibly tense. We notified the New York Stock Exchange of the pending news, and the exchange halted trading in Shearson and American Express shares. I understood the American Express board meeting had begun around midday, but by late afternoon, we had received no word.

The more time that went by, the more I began to wonder whether Jim had been successful in selling his board on the merger. After all, throughout our negotiations, Jim had frequently used "issues" with his board to deflect certain of my entreaties, especially those regarding my future role in the company. Finally, at 6:30 P.M., Jim telephoned and asked if he could come to my office at the World Trade Center.

My heart skipped a beat as I heard, "There are a few minor changes, but everything should be okay." What did "a few minor changes" mean? I suspected Jim was downplaying what might be a meaningful alteration in our agreement, and I told him that I wanted Joan to join us as well. If I was going to have to agree to something new that would affect our lives, I needed to consult my wife.

Sometime after 7:00 P.M., Jim arrived for what would turn out to be a two-hour meeting. Joanie came at about the same time, and the three of us ensconced ourselves in my office. Jim began by dispensing with the board issue once and for all, indicating that his directors wanted Peter to be included on the board. We then focused on my future role at American Express. Jim stated that his board felt obliged to take into consideration how the merger might impact other senior American Express executives, especially Lou Gerstner, head of the important credit card and traveler's check business, and Al Way. The board had decided to give Al Way the president title, while Gerstner would be elevated to vice chairman. Jim said that I would be rewarded by becoming chairman of the executive committee and taking on responsibility for managing American Express's investments and funding in addition to remaining CEO of Shearson.

I listened to the offer and realized that Jim was promoting his other executives in order to buy their support for bringing me into American Express. It was an early warning that Jim was afraid to stand up to his direct reports, a tendency I'd learn too well later. Unlike in our other negotiating sessions, I now chose to push back as forcefully as I could and insisted that I should be made a clear-cut second in command. Jim demurred, saying that his board didn't know me well enough to confer such authority up front.

I argued my position further and realized I was getting nowhere. Jim explained, "The board is not prepared to anoint a successor. It isn't possible at this point." I then shifted to seek some assurance about how my role might evolve in the future. Jim emphasized how I'd be coming in as his partner and as one of American Express's top executives and that he looked forward to relying on me for advice as his "alter ego." He then suggested his board probably would become more forthcoming later. "This is as far as they'll go now. It's not that they don't like or trust you. We'll get there, but this is the way we need to start. Trust me; it'll work out after you prove yourself to the board."

The pivotal question was whether Jim was being sincere or really pressing his advantage at the eleventh hour. It all boiled down to a matter of trust. The toughest choice of my career suddenly lay before me. I turned to Joanie and asked, "Should we trust him?" In retrospect, it put enormous responsibility on my wife's shoulders since I asked the question in front of Jim. Joanie knew I saw this transaction as the culmination of all that I had worked for up to that point and realized I was putting my emotional life, my career, and my reputation on the line.

She also knew how much I wanted to do the deal, so what else could she say but yes?

We sealed the deal, and Jim left to attend to the final details of the next morning's press release. I greeted my executives, who were waiting anxiously in a nearby conference room, and told them we had a deal. It's odd, but I have no recollection of informing Peter Cohen about his inclusion on the board. I have a habit of blocking out distasteful memories, and I'm sure I resented how I had been double-crossed during the decisive moments of closing our deal. Exhausted, we ordered steaks to be sent in from nearby Windows on the World and we quietly celebrated our momentous transaction.

Having built Shearson from scratch and ridden the incredible ups and downs of the securities markets over twenty-one years, I was understandably emotional the next morning. Retail brokerage firms communicate with their field offices and brokers over an internal two-way system colloquially known as the "Hoot 'n' Holler." I announced our transaction over our internal airwaves before the market opened, and began to say how Shearson would benefit and how we'd be leading change in the financial services industry. I stressed how our sales force would benefit from more products and the prestige of being connected with American Express and noted our new advantages in capital, reputation, and access to new markets. Early in my remarks, it hit me how this was all really a venture into the unknown, and I refocused on all the accomplishments of the past two decades. My eyes welled up and my voice began to falter. I regrouped, but my voice broke a few more times before I finally finished my comments.

Various brokers then began to shout out their questions and comments. The reaction uniformly was enthusiastic and reminded me how close I felt to the brokerage force. Toward the end of the call, I suddenly heard the familiar voice of my father. I had long since forgiven him for the way he treated my mother. In his later years, he had been given a back office job in Shearson's Miami branch. He had been working there for about nine years at the time of the merger with American Express. "Sandy, this is your dad talking. I want to congratulate you and tell you I'm very proud of you." With an equal amount of pride, I simply responded, "Thanks, dad." His response gave me a final confirmation that I had done the right thing with this merger.

If anyone had any unvoiced doubts, these would have been dispelled by the market's roar of approval that day and in the following weeks. We had negotiated our deal with about a 20 percent premium to the market, but by the close of trading that Tuesday, Shearson's stock surged to $48 a share, 40 percent over where it had been trading just two weeks earlier. After a single day's trading, our merger now had a value to shareholders in excess of $1 billion. The stock surged 30 percent more to $65 by the time of our shareholder vote in late June.

Other companies soon followed our groundbreaking deal. Sears purchased Dean Witter in early October for $600 million only days after paying $180 million for real estate broker Coldwell Banker. BankAmerica soon announced plans to buy discount broker Charles Schwab while other banks pushed harder to break down regulatory constraints on their approved powers.

———————

Our merger with American Express closed at the end of June, and I spent the next few months getting to know my new colleagues and delving into the company. I realized one thing very quickly: Being chairman of the executive committee meant little. It was a hollow title. That disappointed me, but at least I had responsibility for key financial functions, and Jim reminded me that he wanted me to look over his shoulder and give advice on the company at large. I concentrated on learning as much as possible. There were lots of businesses to which I had little or no previous exposure: credit cards, travel, banking, insurance. Moreover, I needed to understand American Express's approach to capital and funding and how it managed its investments.

The company's managers initially received me politely, sensing I needed to get a lot under my belt. I proved a quick study, however, and soon began asserting myself. I especially pushed for faster reporting of financial results in those early days since I always wanted as much real-time information as possible. I knew this was a key to managing effectively. Jim and I seemed to get along reasonably well, too. I could see immediately how our personalities differed. I was typically emotional while Jim conveyed formality and unflappable composure. I soon realized he ran the company with the same controlled manner in which he handled all his relationships.

Jim was the product of American Express's culture. As I came to know the company's former longtime chairman and CEO, Howard Clark Sr., I realized that the company's Southern roots ran deep. When Jim would refer to issues or constraints with his directors, he obviously was referring to the feelings of Howard Clark Sr., who years after surrendering his executive posts still dominated the board. I always felt a coolness and distance with Clark. There was a barrier that unsettled me in a way I had never felt before. Jim was easier. Despite his formality, he was likable and seemed to deal with people sincerely.

The stiffness of the American Express culture registered in other ways. Right after the merger, Bettye Robinson arranged a lunch for wives of the top managers of Shearson and American Express. A number of Town Cars were ordered to drive the women to the luncheon, and Joanie unwittingly headed to one car to share the ride with other Shearson spouses. Suddenly, Bettye called to her and insisted on reassigning her to a car that had been reserved for the wives of the seniormost executives. In other words, there was a clear hierarchy and protocol even for spouses. Joanie hated the regimentation; it was completely foreign to her after years of informality at Shearson.

In other instances, formality slowed decision making and communication in my new company. I chafed at business review meetings Jim insisted holding before convening board and annual shareholder meetings. Formal staff-driven affairs, these sessions reviewed each business in excruciating detail.

Before each board meeting, Jim required his business heads to assemble a week ahead of time to carefully review everything that would go before the board. The management team—nicknamed "the flying Wallendas"—would jet in from around the world to practice their presentations. As if this weren't overkill, prior to the annual meeting, the staff would produce huge briefing books running over 1,500 pages. Jim then required all his managers to convene in the company auditorium and spend the entire weekend before the shareholder meeting anticipating every conceivable question and scripting carefully considered answers.

I found the first such preparatory meeting useful since I was still learning about my new organization. But after the initial experience, the utility dropped sharply, and I focused more on the incredible amount of time Jim was requiring his managers to spend essentially rehearsing their lines. It seemed to me these study sessions were going over material Jim and the business heads should have been expected to know as a matter of course.

In all my years running my own business, I always wanted my team to think independently and had insisted on an informal management style where people had to think on their feet and express what they truly believed. I couldn't change Jim's regimen, but I told him that these annual meeting reviews were not for me and that I preferred not to attend any longer. My protest irked Jim, but he didn't press the issue.

The differences in culture soon began to show up in important business decisions. Notably, Lou Gerstner resisted efforts to link the credit card business with Shearson almost from day one. Leveraging the card and Shearson's retail product offerings had been one of the key opportunities we had identified as early as our initial joint venture conversations. Yet the more we promoted the idea, the more Gerstner withdrew and found excuses for not cooperating. In fact, right after our merger, we held an introductory dinner for our top executives. My Shearson colleagues were outspoken in asking the Travel Related Services group to supply customer lists for qualified calling leads. Gerstner immediately expressed concern that client relationships might be abused. He continued to be unresponsive. When Jim directed us to work out suitable compromises, Lou initially would pay lip service but subsequently would find issues to derail any cooperation.

Shearson brokers never got access to cardholder names in any meaningful way. American Express was trumpeting its "One-Enterprise" concept of coordinating the company's varied product groups (it even became the central theme of our 1982 annual report), but One-Enterprise soon became largely a myth owing to lack of serious execution. Gerstner must have seen me as competition to taking on a more senior role at American Express. He chose a strategy of focusing his business inward as his preferred method of advancing in American Express's power structure.

Despite our challenges with the Travel Related Services business, the American Express merger still helped Shearson in certain ways. Shearson rolled out its enhanced Financial Management Account in the summer of 1982 and now included an American Express gold card (the tie with the card business was a one-way street since Shearson had not gotten access to cardholder lists). We also changed Shearson's name to Shearson/American Express at my urging, which enhanced our ability to win larger brokerage accounts and attract and retain top brokers. We used American Express's stock and balance sheet strength to fold a couple of regional brokerages and Balcor, a real estate lender, into Shearson's operations. Finally, we enjoyed some success in introducing Fireman's Fund variable annuities to Shearson brokers.

During 1982, I focused my financial skills on American Express's corporate investments. We were then planning to lease space in the new World Financial Center in lower Manhattan. I convinced Jim that we would be better off buying our new building to gain tax benefits. We soon sold American Express's old corporate headquarters to developer Olympia & York for a substantial gain, which we then used to offset losses on sales of underwater municipal securities. We sold tax-free securities that only yielded 1.5 percent and traded into medium-term Treasuries with a far better 11.5 percent return.

As I spent more time exploring opportunities for improvements in American Express's operations, I gradually allowed Peter to enjoy more autonomy at Shearson. I felt we still had a positive, if frayed, relationship at the end of our negotiations to sell Shearson and that I could continue to count on his loyalty. Peter may have felt I never recognized his contributions sufficiently and that I didn't look out for him the way he had expected during the negotiations. Still, it all came out fine for him in the end, and I assumed he'd appreciate my vote of confidence in offering him greater autonomy.

At the end of 1981, I announced that senior Shearson executives would now report through Peter. This was not a popular decision, but I stood behind Peter when Duke Chapman came to me complaining he could not accept the new reporting line. Many of my associates had bridled in the past at the idea of working for Peter, arguing he was too inexperienced. I recognized Peter had issues commanding the respect and loyalty of some of his peers—after all, he was only in his thirties. By now, however, I assumed he and the others could adapt to a different relationship. For the most part, my assumption was correct, but not for Duke, who insisted he would leave Shearson rather than work for Peter. Fortunately, we found a senior role for him in American Express's international bank, which was preferable to losing him altogether.

I thought I had repaired my relationship with Peter, yet I couldn't help but notice a growing tie between him and Jim Robinson. In fact, Jim seemed to waste no time building a rapport with Peter. I worried that the budding relationship might lead to divided loyalties later, something I never had to face professionally. Jim did not hide the growing relationship in the least. Within months, he began to suggest that I should begin preparing Peter to become CEO of Shearson, recognizing my continuing interest in becoming more engaged on corporate-wide issues and the fact that I had relocated my office to American Express's corporate suite immediately following the merger.

I don't criticize Jim for forging a closer bond with Peter. I figured Jim was showing his board that a return on the $1 billion he had paid for Shearson wouldn't be entirely dependent on me. Also, there was plenty of gossip in the press and elsewhere from the first day of the merger that I was after Jim's job and that he needed to watch his back. These stories were pure fantasy, but they may have needled Jim sufficiently to want to hedge his partnership with me. However one might analyze Jim's motives, Peter's receptiveness to Jim's entreaties was a far greater eye-opener. I realized a wedge was slowly opening between Peter and me.

The first hint that this period of relative calm would end came during the summer of 1982 when Jim Robinson commissioned a review of the company's strategy, which prioritized growing its private bank. The American Express International Bank at the time had been a relative backwater business accounting for only about 10 percent of total earnings. The franchise in many respects had been built as an adjunct to the credit card and traveler's check business to accommodate customer transactions in local markets. We had a prestigious name, but the franchise was weak. Shortly after the strategic review, Peter Cohen pitched Jim on the idea of American Express buying the banking assets controlled by Peter's old friend Edmond Safra. The two had remained close despite the brevity of time they had worked together. Apart from a controlling interest in New York–based Republic National Bank, Safra also owned Trade Development Bank, a major Swiss bank.

Jim became enamored with Peter's acquisition idea almost overnight. It didn't seem to matter that Edmond Safra came from a completely alien culture—Edmond was a Syrian-born Sephardic Jew with secretive ways and an imperial personal style. Jim ignored, too, the fact that Edmond's banking franchise might contain lending risks related to underdeveloped countries. Instead, Jim became mesmerized by the idea that Safra's banking business would give him a means of repositioning American Express's languishing International Bank and provide a ticket into an exotic world of dealing with the world's mega-rich.

Peter and Jim negotiated through the fall while keeping me largely on the sidelines. For the first time, Peter was moving on something important without asking for my advice. The venture also stirred up memories of the period in 1978 when Peter had abandoned Shearson to work for Safra. Meanwhile, I couldn't help but notice how he was stoking Jim's enthusiasm for Safra's franchise. Toward the end of the negotiations, Jim asked me to spend time with Edmond to help close the deal, but I never felt any ownership in the transaction.

Inwardly, I harbored serious reservations. I couldn't fathom how Edmond would fit into the American Express culture. American Express had been an adjustment for me, and I knew that Edmond's and Jim's ways were completely alien to one another. Buying out Edmond Safra would make him the company's largest shareholder with about a 3 percent interest—if the relationship faltered, I knew it could become a headache for American Express. I also wondered whether Jim appreciated the potential credit risks embedded in Safra's banking assets. Only a year before, Mexico had defaulted on its sovereign debts and had provoked a serious international banking crisis that was still playing out. I could only wonder whether Edmond's sudden interest in selling had something to do with the risks he perceived in his companies' balance sheets.

Uncharacteristically, I felt awkward speaking my mind on these issues given how Jim plainly had fallen in love with the notion of buying out Safra. The best I could do was to suggest quietly that Jim be careful not to take on too much credit risk and consider focusing on the Swiss bank part of the franchise rather than including Republic Bank as well. As events would have it, purchasing Republic became problematic for another reason: American Express lacked a domestic U.S. banking license, and legally it would have had to find a creative way to include the New York bank in its purchase. American Express in the end elected to cut Republic out of the deal and only pursue the Swiss Trade Development Bank.

With the TDB deal almost completed, unexpected news hit American Express's corporate suite: Al Way announced his resignation as president. Way had been a fish out of water at the company all along and maintained an incredibly low profile, so no one considered his departure a great loss. On the other hand, if I ever had intended to raise more serious objections to the TDB deal, this news stifled me once and for all. The notion of becoming American Express's undisputed second in command was alluring, and I didn't want to shoot myself in the foot politically at that suddenly opportune moment.

I knew Jim would have to make a difficult choice between Lou Gerstner and myself in filling the president's slot. Gerstner moved easily within the company and seemed comfortable with its politics; moreover, he controlled American Express's flagship business. On the other hand, I was older with proven financial and risk management skills as key assets. It's hard to say how much the pending TDB transaction weighed in Jim's decision, but Peter went out of his way to let me know that he had advised Robinson to name me president if he wanted to close the deal with Safra. Peter asserted that Edmond had never met Gerstner and would probably hesitate selling his company if he didn't know the seniormost executives.

Jim in fact offered me the promotion but with one critical proviso: I'd have to surrender being CEO of Shearson if I wanted the new post. Events were unfolding quickly, but I had never imagined having to surrender control over Shearson in order to rise in the American Express hierarchy. This was a painful decision. I was enraptured with the idea of becoming president of the American Express Company, a leading light in America's corporate establishment. Joanie and several of my closest friends, however, counseled against surrendering my power base. I assumed I could continue to count on Peter, but some suggested his loyalty wouldn't last fifteen seconds once I surrendered the CEO position. Naively, I concluded my friends were too harsh and that the title would be more valuable for gaining authority within American Express than my insisting on running Shearson.

On January 17, 1983, American Express issued a dual-headlined press release announcing the $550 million purchase of Trade Development Bank and my elevation to president.

The promotion made me feel great initially. I remember looking at my new business cards emblazoned with "President, The American Express Company" and thinking how I had truly arrived at the pinnacle of the corporate world. I felt a debt of gratitude to Jim for standing up on my behalf. I suspected that Howard Clark Sr. and other tradition-bound board members had not encouraged my elevation and would have preferred the more corporately buttoned-down Gerstner. On this occasion, Jim had demonstrated real leadership with his board.

If it were only true for how Jim dealt with his managers! I realized immediately that Jim was compelled to placate Gerstner and Peter in the wake of my elevation. With my step up to the presidency, Jim insisted that I turn over my chairmanship of the executive committee to Gerstner. Any hope that the president title would translate into a real or de facto chief operating officer role was dashed immediately. Both Lou and Peter had rebuffed Jim when he raised the idea of the two working under my direction.

Gerstner responded to my promotion by turning even further inward into his Travel Related Services organization. He became more resistant than ever to genuine collaboration and must have calculated that building his power base represented his best long-term strategy. Peter, too, seemed to relish his independence. Upon my ceding the CEO office at Shearson, Peter wasted no time moving into my old lair atop the World Trade Center, complete with its working fireplace. Superficially, he offered a token of deference by placing a pair of oversized shoes in front of the fireplace to remind him of my legacy and gave me a gift of a crown and scepter saying I was still the "king." Yet, from that day forward, Peter continued to distance himself from me.

The aura of the president title gradually wore off, and I realized my promotion had been empty. I had received a prestigious title but had paid the price of losing my grip on Shearson. It soon began to sink in that Peter was out to prove his independence once and for all. Moreover, I began to appreciate that I had to share Peter's loyalty with Jim and Edmond. Apart from my feelings toward Peter, I felt ashamed that I held back on expressing reservations on the TDB deal. It bothered me that I had wanted the presidency so much that I compromised my thought process and gave in to political expediency.

———————

I began to feel cut adrift by the spring of 1983. I might have captured my coveted president title, but my responsibilities and authority within the company were fairly nebulous. Except for a group of financial executives, I had relatively few direct reports. I also had too much free time on my hands, to which I was unaccustomed. Seeking ways to apply myself, I found one silver lining in this period: I discovered the pleasure one can draw from working with not-for-profit organizations. In particular, I realized there were tremendous causes to which American Express could contribute financial resources and human capital. One of our board members, former assistant Treasury secretary Bob Roosa, invited me to join the board of Carnegie Hall. The famed concert hall had fallen into disrepair and was desperately trying to raise money to restore its past grandeur. I gladly accepted Roosa's nomination and commenced a relationship that would blossom in coming years and become a major focus of my life.

Around the same time, in 1983, I also concentrated on getting the National Academy Foundation off the ground. For several years, it had struck me how New York City's employment base was not supporting the securities industry. Firms were increasingly moving operations out of the city because there were too few candidates for entry-level back office jobs. Driving through the city one day, I noticed the large number of high-school-aged kids sitting idly on the street corners, and it hit me that New York needed a vocational training program in the public school system that might better allow the city's employment base to match the needs of its hometown companies.

That inspiration pushed me to found the National Academy Foundation. We came up with a curriculum to train high school students for entry-level financial services jobs and then pushed for funding and acceptance in the public school system. At first, teachers unions were stubborn in not getting behind the program as educators bickered over seniority and how teachers would be selected to participate in the program. However, I finally engaged the New York City schools chancellor and got him behind our nascent job training concept.

As a large and civic-minded organization, American Express represented a perfect platform for supporting the National Academy. The program required significant funding in order to train teachers and develop an appropriate curriculum, and I found it relatively easy to line up our company behind the program. For the first time, I felt the enormous pride and satisfaction of focusing on a worthy idea, getting a company to work with the public sector to promote something of value, and offering my business expertise to get an idea off the ground. I may have been facing growing frustrations in my nebulous role at American Express at that time, but the National Academy and soon greater involvement with Carnegie Hall represented real bright spots during this period. Unfortunately, the philanthropic endeavors weren't enough to satisfy my ambitions.

6

The Experiment
That Failed

B eyond my new civic interests, I concentrated on how American Express might improve its operations and kept an eye out for attractive acquisition opportunities. In April 1983, our head of strategic planning, Bob Riley, came to me with the idea that we consider buying Alleghany Corporation, whose crown jewel was Minneapolis-based Investor Diversified Services. Bob had been a candidate to run IDS before joining American Express, and he had gotten to know the organization. With the benefit of Bob's firsthand knowledge and thorough briefing, I immediately became interested in IDS's unique franchise.

IDS was a high-quality firm that suffered from poor systems and weak management owing to the fact that for a number of years it had been run mainly as a financial investment business rather than an operating company. Nonetheless, it had an intriguing franchise, which included a 4,500-person force of independent financial advisors who exclusively sold IDS products to two million loyal retail customers in America's heartland. The company had four product lines—mutual funds, life insurance, banklike certificates of deposits, and annuities—all of which produced steady recurring earnings.

I realized that IDS would complement American Express's business nicely. Whereas American Express had widely promoted the idea

141

that it enjoyed an upscale customer base, I felt the customer base was actually far more aligned with middle America. The IDS insurance and savings products seemed a natural complement for our company's customers, while I believed the new distribution channel would allow us to deepen our penetration in the mass market.

With an introduction from Bob Riley, I soon met in New York with Alleghany's CEO, Fred Kirby. Fred and a number of others in his family owned about 30 percent of Alleghany's shares. We got along fine, but I realized immediately that he was the type that got emotionally attached to his investments, even the mediocre ones. He informed me that IDS was not for sale and that I'd need to make a compelling offer if I had any serious intention of buying his company. He also pointed out that he had a very low tax basis in IDS and that any deal I might propose would have to be structured in a way to be a tax-free transaction.

We had more talks over the following weeks, and I made sure to introduce Fred Kirby to Jim Robinson. I settled on proposing a deal for all of Alleghany, which included IDS as well as a number of smaller businesses, the largest being a steel company. By purchasing the entire company, we could structure a share exchange and account for the transaction in a way to allow the Kirby family and other Alleghany shareholders to avoid paying capital gains tax. I figured we could turn around later and sell off the peripheral businesses.

With Jim's encouragement, we began to discuss price in early July. By this point, Fred Kirby had moved to a summer property he owned in a remote part of the Adirondacks in upstate New York. Unfortunately, his home lacked a normal phone connection, and we were forced to communicate over a nonsecure radiophone. Making matters worse, Fred would only turn on his phone during a limited set of hours each day. Fred's stubbornness and the patchy communications setup made for an incredibly difficult negotiation. I opened by offering around $750 million, but Fred responded that I was far off his required number. For the next couple of days, I had to contend with his inflexibility and the inability to reach him at will.

In the midst of our talks, word of the potential deal leaked. I can only assume we had uninvited company on the radiophone. Exasperated, I realized I'd have to make a serious concession on price if we were going to get the deal done. I ultimately had to raise my price a couple of times in large steps, and we finally agreed on a $1 billion share exchange. We came to a value which was significantly more than I had hoped to pay and at a big premium to Alleghany's market value, but I felt the economics would enable American Express to earn an attractive return. Jim agreed to the deal.

We announced an agreement in principle on July 12 subject to due diligence. Investors initially pushed our stock price down nearly 4 percent based on the substantial market premium, and we were not yet in a position to fully explain the deal. I assumed we would reverse the sentiment once we reached a definitive agreement and could go over specific plans for adding value. As events would turn out, I was on the threshold of an eye-opening experience that would reveal a great deal about several colleagues' characters. Indeed, I would soon learn a lesson in the ugliness of corporate politics, the bounds of personal loyalty, and betrayal.

As we familiarized ourselves with Alleghany's operations, internal dissent soon surfaced. Peter began to question the potential for conflict between the sales forces of IDS and Shearson and raised potential compliance issues with a network of independent salespeople who technically wouldn't be considered full-time employees. He also pointed to weaknesses in IDS's technology. Lou Gerstner, my other nemesis, followed Peter's lead and began to question the potential for confusion with the American Express brand.

Later, I went to Minneapolis with Peter and our treasurer, George Sheinberg. After a day of meetings, we convened for dinner in the local hotel restaurant. I expressed my excitement about IDS only to hear Peter unexpectedly declare that we were overpaying. I told him I couldn't believe he couldn't see the value, while he in turn accused me of seeing only what I wanted. One thing led to another, and we had a full-scale argument with Peter finally declaring he had better things to do than waste his time working on this transaction. Peter had never refrained from arguing matters of principle with me. This time, I sensed something more was at play.

Over the next several days, I felt that Peter's reservations regarding the sales force and systems were manufactured issues and suspected Peter was going out of his way to be critical because IDS wouldn't report to him. Soon Jim began to waffle, which bothered me even more. In all my past deals, I operated on the premise that one's word is one's bond—it troubled me enormously that Jim might consider backing away from a handshake in order to placate his restive managers.

Suddenly, word came from Geneva that Edmond Safra was upset and unhappy that he hadn't been consulted. I don't doubt that Edmond felt slighted in learning about the Alleghany deal via the press—as American Express's largest shareholder, he should have heard from Jim earlier. However, I wondered whether Peter also was encouraging Edmond to object to the deal. All of this was happening only days before our final due diligence review, which would render our verdict on the acquisition. Before I knew it, Peter and Jim flew to Switzerland, ostensibly to consult with Safra.

The following week, our due diligence team convened at headquarters in New York to go over our findings. In typical American Express fashion, we had put a veritable army to work reviewing Alleghany and had nearly fifty people from various teams come together for the final review. I had prepared an extensive presentation that detailed the merits of the transaction and why we should move forward. It quickly became apparent that this would not be a normal rubber-stamping session. Peter made it clear he had a number of reservations and came out publicly for the first time claiming we were overpaying. Suddenly, my supposed friend George Sheinberg blindsided me and jumped on board, questioning my valuation assumptions on the steel company. I was completely unaccustomed to such mutiny and felt betrayed.

The meeting finally broke up, and as I anticipated, Jim soon informed me that he felt uncomfortable moving forward. American Express's stock stood at $45 per share, about 9 percent below its price in the early phase of our negotiations. American Express issued a press release on August 16 stating it was willing to proceed but only on revised terms. It was a clumsy attempt to wriggle out of the deal.

With my parents and
my sister, Helen, around my
twelfth birthday; 1945
(Weill personal photo)

Original 1940 tax
photo taken by the
City of New York of
the house in which I
grew up in Brooklyn
*(Courtesy of
New York City
Municipal Archives)*

6376 - I BK

My Peekskill Military Academy
graduation picture
(Peekskill Military Academy Yearbook)

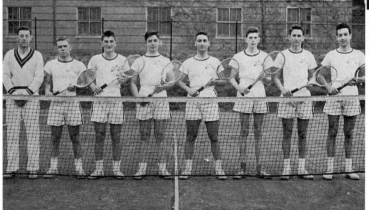

Captain of my
high school
tennis team;
Coach Frantz
was a good
mentor and
helped me
develop self-
confidence
*(Peekskill Military
Academy Yearbook)*

Our engagement picture with both of our families; 1954
(Weill personal photo; taken by Irving Desfor)

Our wedding day, June 19, 1955
(Weill personal photo)

With Joan in the early 1960s
(Weill personal photo)

Our family
with my mother
at Marc's
bar mitzvah
(Weill personal photo)

Our partnership after the departure of Peter Potoma, around 1963
(Courtesy of Citigroup company archives)

Cogan, Berlind, Weill & Levitt thrived in the go-go market during the late 1960s; with Arthur Levitt, Roger Berlind, and Marshall Cogan in *New Breed on Wall Street* by Martin Mayer *(Courtesy of and © Cornell Capa 1969)*

Overseeing the trading floor at Shearson Hayden Stone; 1975
(Courtesy of Citigroup company archives)

My relationship with Jim Robinson was very good as we launched our partnership *(Reprinted from the April 30, 1984, issue of* BusinessWeek *by permission. Copyright 1984 by the McGraw-Hill Companies.)*

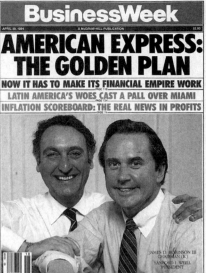

Building the World Financial Center in lower Manhattan with Jim Robinson and Paul Reichmann *(Weill personal photo)*

Receiving presidential advice from Gerald Ford; 1982 *(Courtesy of Citigroup company archives)*

A flawed partnership:
Edmond Safra, me,
and Jim Robinson
(Weill personal photo)

Divided loyalties:
with Jim Robinson
and Peter Cohen
(Weill personal photo)

Taking over Commercial Credit
with an incredibly hard working
team, including Jamie Dimon
(behind me, left), Chuck Prince
(top left), and Bob Lipp
(farthest right)
(Courtesy of and © Bruce Katz 1987)

Our line up for Smith Barney after the Primerica deal: with Frank Zarb and Lew Glucksman
(Courtesy of Michael Mella)

Strong and loyal managers: Bob Lipp, Marge Magner, and Bob Willumstad; 1990
(Courtesy of Citigroup company archives)

Our senior management team with the arrival of Bob Greenhill in 1993— management tensions soon followed; with Bob Greenhill, Jamie Dimon, Frank Zarb, and Bob Lipp
(Courtesy of Citigroup company archives)

My close relationship with Harvey Golub helped win the day when
American Express moved to sell Shearson; with Harvey Golub,
the celebrant, and Josh Golub at Josh's bris
(Courtesy of Harvey Golub)

With Jamie Dimon, having cocktails with Lady Margaret Thatcher
(Courtesy of Harold Hechler Photography)

I was furious. In the weeks that followed, I pushed to have Sheinberg relieved as treasurer. George had stabbed me in the back without warning. I allowed Peter to hire Sheinberg back into Shearson, but it later appeared that the two might have conspired against me. Peter's actions proved that he was no longer reliable or objective. In contrast to the past when we might disagree on a business issue, Peter no longer felt obliged to accept my judgment as final. He obviously was feeling his oats and the need to demonstrate his comfort in opposing me openly. On the other hand, Jim's wavering had mortified me, given that we had shaken hands on the deal.

In early August, the deal might have looked dead, but I refused to accept defeat. I immediately apologized to Fred Kirby and told him I'd do everything in my power to try to find a way to get the deal back on track. I soon approached Jim and said that we would be making a terrible mistake if we made this our final judgment. As I knew by then the influence wielded by consultants on the American Express organization, I proposed and received Jim's acceptance that we commission McKinsey & Company to conduct an independent assessment of Alleghany and IDS. A six-week study ensued during which I explored ways to deflect the contention that we were overpaying.

Ironically, Peter one day came to me and suggested we rebid for only IDS rather than all of Alleghany and offer a mix of cash and shares. He pointed out that financing the cash portion with debt would give certain tax advantages while a fewer number of shares would mitigate the short-term adverse earnings impact for American Express. Exploring our options further with our outside tax counsel, we came up with a strategy whereby IDS could issue a special one-time dividend to its parent in a way that would allow Alleghany to avoid a large capital gains tax on disposition of IDS.

In mid-September, the McKinsey study was nearly complete, and I invited senior partner Harvey Golub to lunch in order to probe how the project was turning out. Harvey tried his best to be circumspect but allowed that we likely would have to replace the IDS CEO were we to have a successful integration. I then began to ask him what he thought about certain candidates I had in mind, at which he declared,

"I can't answer that as I have a conflict." I pressed him on the nature of his conflict, and he confessed he would be interested in running IDS were we to move forward. With that, I declared, "Thank you, Harvey, you just told me what you think of the deal. And, by the way, you're hired!"

With McKinsey's blessing and my thoughts on how to restructure our bid, I went back to Fred Kirby and walked him through my new idea for buying only IDS. Fortunately, Fred was not on vacation, and we were able to settle on the revised terms fairly quickly. Buying only IDS meant we could reduce the stated price for the value of the steel company and various tax carry-forward benefits, and we agreed to a price slightly in excess of $770 million, including about $340 million in cash.

Superficially, the new agreement looked cheaper than the first deal and mollified Peter and Lou Gerstner. On closer inspection, though, I still believe our original deal would have been superior. We had given up nearly $50 million in tax benefits while Alleghany soon sold the steel company for over $225 million. That sale proved decisively how off-base George Sheinberg had been when he had questioned the value I assigned to this unit. Given the pressure in American Express's stock that summer, the value of our original deal would have been less than what we ultimately paid. The moral of this story was to illustrate how politics forced us to surrender value that could have been captured for our shareholders.

As an important postscript, Harvey Golub accepted my offer to run IDS and hit the ground running when we closed the transaction in January 1984. Harvey proved his brilliance as a manager. He quickly sorted out IDS's technology issues, sold noncore assets, refocused the sales force around a core financial planning service, improved investment performance, and overhauled and aligned incentive plans. Before our purchase, IDS's annual profits had been stuck at $50 million. In the first year under our ownership, its earnings grew 15 percent. Harvey remained in charge for about six years during which quarterly profits never faltered. Between 1984 and 2000, IDS's profits grew at more than a 15 percent compound annual rate, a remarkable performance.

It was one of American Express's best acquisitions ever.

————

Despite the tensions over negotiating the IDS deal, Jim Robinson and American Express were riding high going into the fall of 1983. Shearson continued to operate strongly in the two years after its purchase; optimism prevailed that TDB would transform the International Bank into a profit engine; and—despite all the political maneuvering—IDS ended up looking like a triumph. Equally important, everyone expected another year of record earnings, the thirty-sixth in an unbroken streak. If the board had reservations regarding Jim's competency in 1979 following the embarrassing failure of his hostile bid for McGraw-Hill, these issues were now forgotten.

Appearances, though, were deceiving. Disquieting insurance claims began to emerge in the large Fireman's Fund business, which accounted for about 40 percent of total corporate earnings. Fireman's Fund's premium growth had outpaced the industry for more than a year even as the property and casualty business had been in a prolonged pricing slump. Wall Street analysts began to question the acceleration in growth and why reserves were not keeping pace. Nonetheless, Fireman's Fund executives assured everyone—inside and out—that they were carefully managing the risks.

Suddenly, late that summer, insurance claims jumped sharply. The actuaries and Fireman's Fund's top executives resolutely argued nothing was amiss and that the most recent figures simply were an aberration. I listened carefully and felt the process of looking at claims over a twelve-month period seemed logical, but the actuaries were stuck looking through a rearview mirror and seemed in denial regarding a more fundamental shift in the business. During board briefings, I was far from shy in raising questions regarding our pricing and reserve policies.

We elected to make a modest addition to Fireman's Fund's reserves in the September quarter, but it really was a drop in the bucket. Almost immediately, monthly profits fell off a cliff. The debates came to an end: American Express had a serious problem on its hands, and we all knew it.

In November, American Express took its board on a tour of Europe, traveling to Geneva, London, and Paris in order to showcase its newly expanded international activities. In Geneva, we introduced the board to Edmond Safra and Trade Development Bank and also convened to focus on the worsening situation in the insurance business. As we met, we received word that *Fortune* magazine was about to run a story—aptly titled "Fire in the Belly"—that would assert that Fireman's Fund managers had been relying on a variety of financial engineering devices to boost reported profits for some time. Much of the story came from a leaked internal memo written by Fireman's CEO warning that the unit's earnings momentum was nearly out of gas.

The board soon reached a consensus that we needed to change Fireman's management, but internal options seemed limited. Since I had been vocal in the earlier board discussions, the board asked if I'd be willing to go to San Francisco where Fireman's Fund was based in order to clean up the mess. I was flattered by the board's vote of confidence in my operating abilities and frankly was excited by the prospect of finally running a meaningful business. I accepted the assignment on the spot.

A day or two after the board meeting, I recall Jim being upset that I had told others that the board had asked me to take over Fireman's Fund. In fairness to Jim, I should have been more tactful and presented the decision as though it were his as CEO. To dispel the notion of a power play, I offered to turn over my chairman title and reporting line for Shearson. I never expected him to accept the offer, but he did.

Returning from Europe, I prepared to go out to San Francisco immediately after New Year's and lined up Bill McCormick, up until then second in command at Travel Related Services, to be Fireman's Fund's new CEO. With Bill in place, I planned my schedule for at least the coming year: I'd spend three days each week in California and an additional day in Minneapolis on the way home in order to check on IDS.

Before heading west, though, we held one more board meeting to decide on an appropriate reserve action. We convened the board on Sunday, December 11. I argued we needed to take decisive action even as some argued for a more incremental strategy. By now, however, the actuaries and our auditor, Arthur Young, supported my push for sizable charges as the volatility in loss experience from month to month had become so outsized and unpredictable. The following morning, we announced that corporate earnings for 1983 would drop 10 percent owing to a $230 million increase in Fireman's Fund's reserves. That day American Express's stock closed down 8 percent to just over $28, far from its $49 high registered just six months earlier. After thirty-five years, American Express's profits had hit a wall.

On my way to California, I toured several of Fireman's Fund's regional operating centers, stopping in places like Chicago and Kansas City. I came not knowing a great deal about the insurance business, but I quickly received an education and appreciated a number of obvious issues: Claims people and underwriters never spoke to one another; management information systems were in horrendous shape; and operating systems were incredibly inefficient.

In March, I made a presentation to American Express's board of directors on my findings and initial attack plan. This was no typical American Express board presentation with its staff-driven slides and reams of paper. Instead, for forty-five minutes and without the benefit of notes, I rattled off one issue after the next and then pointed to actions that I felt were imperative in order to get the company back on track. Charged with the turnaround assignment, I suddenly felt back in my element of contributing importantly to how American Express was being run.

In the months that followed, we cut costs dramatically and had to fire a lot of people. Fireman's Fund's head count dropped nearly 15 percent as we sorted out back office inefficiencies and cut unproductive agents. Eliminating jobs is never pleasant, but this time the local press made it more uncomfortable than ever as the *San Francisco Chronicle* ran stories and photographs of local executives whom we had let go and savaged me for being a coldhearted and detached executive. I tried my best to ignore the press since I knew that our actions amounted to bitter but necessary medicine.

My taking over Fireman's Fund would prove the beginning of the end of my involvement with American Express. In March 1984, during the peak of my efforts to diagnose and repair the insurance operation, Peter began talks to acquire Lehman Brothers. I might have considered Lehman a choice prize at one time, but in the early 1980s the firm had been torn apart by malicious infighting among its partners.

By this time, Peter Cohen's command of Shearson had become complete, and he never once asked for my advice in pursuing Lehman. Moreover, Peter had been successful at winning over Jim Robinson. With its history as a prominent investment bank, Lehman probably appealed to Jim since it would add to his power and prestige. The era of the hostile takeover was just beginning in the early 1980s, and I suspect Jim might have been enthralled by the idea that Lehman had the power to put firms into play and might give American Express the capacity to shape the world of big corporations on a global scale.

Living in San Francisco and Minneapolis for most of each week, I had been isolated from the details of the negotiations. However, as I learned the shape of the deal in early April, I soon became alarmed. Peter was proposing to pay $360 million, or more than 2.5 times book value, for Lehman Brothers. Superficially, the premium to book value appeared in line with other brokerage companies, but most firms didn't include Lehman's enormous problems. Apart from partners that despised one another, I worried Lehman would bring outsized trading risks, a weak capital base, and the likelihood that its suddenly enriched partners would leave the firm. In short, the deal for Lehman ran against the entire philosophy I had employed over the years at Shearson.

The deal was presented as a fait accompli, so the best I could offer was to recommend that we at least try to lock up the senior partners. We managed to sign employment contracts with all but fifteen of Lehman's seventy-five partners. Yet we were only able to tie up Lehman's seniormost remaining partner, Steve Schwartzman, for a year. As American Express announced the purchase on April 11, I had a sinking feeling about the new risks that Peter and Jim seemed willing to countenance for Shearson and all of American Express. It also wounded me deeply that Peter had come to all but ignore me. The hurtful feeling hit home one day when I called Peter at home on some matter and his young son answered the phone. As I listened to him call for his father, I overheard him say, "Sandy Weill is on the phone—it's the guy you hate."

As American Express was taking on new risks with Lehman, another part of our business began to unravel. Almost from the start of the relationship, Edmond Safra felt slighted at his treatment within American Express. He had reasoned that he'd be joining the leadership of American Express and, since he was its largest shareholder, his voice would matter. However, from the start, Jim did little to make him feel important. I recall Edmond feeling jilted when he first came to New York and realized he had been given an office on the thirty-first floor and not in the executive suite. On that same visit, he asked for a jet to fly him back to Geneva but was informed that the corporate fleet was unavailable.

By the time Fireman's Fund blew up, Edmond must have been wondering why he had been so quick to panic on his bank's developing-country exposure when one of American Express's flagship businesses could do an equivalent job of decimating his personal net worth. He began to talk about buying back TDB (but with American Express keeping the problematic foreign loans), yet Jim rebuffed him completely. Somewhere along the line, I think Edmond's Middle Eastern thought process simply took over: Rather than get mad, he decided to get even.

For more than a year, we had noticed that Republic National Bank—still controlled by Safra—had been taking a lot of business away from TDB. We began to wonder whether Edmond had pocketed his proceeds from selling TDB only to turn around and build up another part of his empire at our expense. As he became more aware of Edmond's unhappiness, Jim probably focused all the more on the business lost to Republic.

By the fall of 1984, Edmond and Jim agreed it would be best for Safra to give up his executive role in the company, and his departure was set for the beginning of 1985. Jim worried that Edmond might try to establish a new bank and pressed Safra to adhere to the noncompete clause of the original purchase agreement. Events eventually would turn ugly, with American Express accusing Safra of violating his contract and Edmond crying foul that American Express was orchestrating a smear campaign against him. Ultimately, Edmond won a high-profile lawsuit against American Express, but I think it's fair to say that by then no one had clean hands.

Around the same time, *The Wall Street Journal* ran a story discussing American Express's problems that probably hit a lot of insiders' hot buttons. The article asserted that too many acquisitions had led to a loss of management control and that management had been stretched too thin. The *Journal* played up the company's internal politics and infighting saying, "On a scale of one to 10, with 10 a Machiavellian jungle, they're at nine and change."* After reading that, I engaged Jim once more in discussions about my role in the company and pressed harder than ever for expanded operating responsibilities.

In hindsight, I stumbled tactically in making my case before Jim. I'm sure I projected a lot of negativity as I came focusing on my fears that the company was taking too much risk. I also began canvassing a number of other executives about our problems and asked for their support as I pushed for a formal overall operating role. American Express's corporate suite was a sieve, and word soon spread that I was campaigning for a new job. Thinking that I might drive home my point, I decided to sell some stock in August in order to send a signal to Jim regarding my fears about the direction of the company. The sale soon became public and must have looked like an ultimatum of sorts.

By October, my concept had evolved into a request to be named officially as chief operating officer. Jim had listened to my arguments for two months, and he now sounded out his top executives. The heads of Fireman's Fund, IDS, and the International Bank—Bill McCormick, Harvey Golub, and Bob Smith—readily agreed to my idea. However, Lou Gerstner and Peter Cohen vehemently refused to work for me. I suppose neither refusal was all that surprising, but learning that Peter

---

*This *Wall Street Journal* article ran on August 15, 1984.

"never wanted to work for me again" became a permanent scar. Time and again, Jim had been unwilling to stand up to his managers—he had always been especially fearful of losing Gerstner. Perhaps at this point, the board was beginning to push Gerstner as Jim's long-term heir. By the end of October, Jim rejected my proposal. For the past three years I had hoped to run American Express's operations; it now sank in that it never would come to pass.

The fall of 1984 represented my darkest time at American Express. I felt that Peter had betrayed me; Jim's earlier promises of a better future role had proved empty; key businesses had imploded or were taking on unconscionable risks; and American Express's stock price had plummeted nearly 50 percent from its high. I felt in limbo: deeply unhappy but with no sense of a logical next step. As my only decisive action, I sold more stock. I normally never would have given up stock in my own company, but I was angry and fearful over how Jim was running American Express and was intent on sending a message. By year end, I had unloaded over 70 percent of my holdings.

For more than a year, I had shared my growing frustrations with my wife. Over much of this time, Joanie counseled me to "give things time to work." But now, seeing my deep unhappiness, she began to change her tune: "Sandy, we have more than enough to be secure financially. If you're so unhappy, why don't you just leave?" I appreciated Joanie's flexibility and that she was encouraging me to see that I had options; however, I worried about quitting and looking as though I were a sore loser.

That January, I learned through back channels that the company had commissioned a study to explore the sale of Fireman's Fund. Having earlier been reassured by Jim that a successful turnaround at Fireman's Fund would keep the unit in the fold (and having stressed this promise to our employees), I was really upset. Once I got past the shock, however, I devised an idea which I thought might allow me to disengage honorably from the company.

I approached Jim in February 1985 with the following proposition: "We should recognize that I'm not happy. I'd like to work to raise money to buy Fireman's Fund. If I'm successful, it would take a problem off

American Express's hands. If not, it would give us a chance to part ways in an honorable manner."

Jim considered my words carefully and didn't disagree. The board met within a month and officially decided to dispose of Fireman's Fund. American Express had hired Salomon Brothers for advice. Jim seemed supportive of my idea to orchestrate a leveraged buyout, but the board also wanted to consider two other options, an initial public offering and a sale to a third party. Following that board meeting, I went off to test whether I could raise the serious money necessary to buy one of the country's largest insurance companies.

My fund-raising efforts were in full gear by early May. We never had made any announcement, but everyone seemed to know of my bid and that my final days at American Express were at hand. Before I would leave the company, though, I had one important anniversary to mark: the twenty-fifth anniversary of starting the company that had become Shearson. Those close to me knew the significance I attached to this milestone. I had never forgotten my feelings watching one of my first employers and mentor, Tubby Burnham, celebrate his firm's quarter-century anniversary—it etched in me awe that one could create a business that might possess such longevity. However events would turn out for Fireman's Fund, no one was going to rob me of the pleasure of celebrating Shearson's birthday.

Mary McDermott had worked for me and been my friend since the mid-1960s, first in research and later as head of public and investor relations. She always has been one of those great people with a remarkable ease in dealing with others combined with boundless energy. Only Mary could have pulled off the anniversary the way she did—given her personal loyalty, she insisted on making it the best celebration in corporate history.

Mary called the party for a Thursday night and rented out Federal Hall, across from the Stock Exchange. Upon entering, one saw a large circular room with tall stone pillars and a high ceiling. Decorated with ten-foot-tall balloons and festooned with orchids (my favorite), the room took on the appearance of a magical fairyland. Mary knew Shearson remained my first love, so she took care to invite only three or four necessary American Express people—instead, the party was filled with salespeople, traders, and operations people who had worked with me for years and with whom we enjoyed a unique family feeling. The surge of emotion lasted the entire evening. Even Arthur Carter and Roger Berlind came to celebrate and were in good spirits.

We reminisced about the old days—the hatchets were buried that night. Between the drinking and the dancing, we let our guard down. Joanie and my kids shared their memories, inspiring great nostalgia. Others spoke in honor of me and the firm. Even Jim Robinson and Peter Cohen offered words of praise, though I remember how the by-then rowdy crowd began to snicker at Jim's formality and long-winded speech, with someone finally yelling jokingly for the "hook." By the end of the evening, eight couples at a time danced in one large circle with arms around one another swaying to the music. The photographer, whom I knew well, whispered to me, "This isn't just a party; it's a love-in!"

How I enjoyed that celebration! Needless to say, few of us made it to work the next day.

With that wonderful party behind me, I concentrated on raising money and preparing my bid for Fireman's Fund. The fund-raising process went surprisingly well, and I was pleased that many seemed willing to back me. Upon an introduction from my friend Art Zankel, I met Warren Buffett and took him through my plan. Buffett was willing to go well beyond my other offers and gave me the good news that he agreed to provide a compelling percentage of the deal's financing.

We devised an attractive bid for American Express to consider. It still would have owned nearly 40 percent of Fireman's Fund—thereby keeping skin in the game if we were to be successful in restoring growth. Warren Buffett's involvement meant he was lending his personal prestige to Fireman's Fund and underscored that we were offering a plan whereby American Express could exit without being embarrassed and in a way where it could benefit along with us. Our single concern, though, related to the fact that an independent Fireman's Fund would lack a sufficiently large balance sheet to stand up to the risk of significant incremental reserving needs. Accordingly, we structured our bid to include a series of indemnifications by American Express on future reserves.

We finalized our bid, and I joined Joanie for our annual June vacation in France. It would have been inappropriate for me as an insider to participate in the presentation, so I left it to Buffett and our investment bankers from Morgan Stanley to present our bid to a special committee of the American Express board.

Basking in the warmth of southern France, I began to suspect a problem when I received a call from my secretary. She had been riding down the elevator during the board presentation and by coincidence happened to overhear two Salomon Brothers investment bankers indiscreetly discussing our proposal. With tears in her voice, she dutifully called to tell me that one said, "I'll be damned if I help two rich guys get richer." It certainly sounded like an oddly anti-capitalist statement for an investment banker to make.

Shortly thereafter, I was paged from my cabana at the Hôtel du Cap for a phone call from Jim Robinson. Joanie and I were relaxing with friends when the call came. To my dismay, Jim informed me that the board did not accept our proposal. He averred that the sticking point had been our request for protection on the reserves and the board's concern with dealing with an insider. I felt the real reason was that the board was paranoid that it would look bad if I proved successful turning Fireman's Fund around. Jim ended the call by saying he had other ideas that he wanted to discuss upon my return.

I returned to the beach cabana. Joanie looked up hesitantly, and I simply declared, "It's over. They rejected our bid. It's time to leave." As I said this, I realized that I had never allowed myself to consider the chance that I'd be left with no alternative but resignation.

Joanie and I realized our life would change. We knew we'd give up a lot of nice perks, but for much of the prior year my wife had pushed me not to be afraid of making a change. She told me once more she'd support whatever action I chose and insisted that it would be preferable to leave than to remain miserable. I had no idea what I'd do next. Never once had I put out a feeler or hint of interest in a position outside American Express.

I returned to New York a few days later and met with Jim. Following up on his "other ideas," he told me the board had settled on an initial public offering for 18–20 percent of Fireman's Fund and that he wanted me to consider staying on as its CEO. He also offered a respectable compensation package including a large number of options. I rejected the idea without a moment's hesitation—the last thing I wanted was to remain part of American Express and subservient to its culture and politics, let alone in a diminished role relative to my past post as president.

I attended one last board meeting on June 24 to announce my resignation. I told the directors I wanted only one thing: to reach a severance deal that night. Accompanied by my two close friends and advisors, attorney Marty Lipton and Morgan Stanley banker Bob Greenhill, I stayed into the small hours of the morning negotiating my departure. It was all anticlimactic. American Express's lawyers seemed most concerned with having me sign a stand-still agreement, suggesting they feared I might somehow try a hostile takeover of the company. It amazed me that a company with $80 billion in assets could be so fearful of one person. In contrast, I only wanted to disengage with honor and on friendly terms. At fifty-two years old, I was mainly concerned about leaving with a reasonable pension.

The following morning, American Express announced my resignation and plans for the initial offering of Fireman's Fund. The $825 million deal ultimately came to market nearly four months later and was the largest U.S. IPO ever at the time. American Express later sold the rest of Fireman's Fund in three separate offerings, and the business eventually was sold to the German insurer Allianz. In retrospect, the deals worked out satisfactorily for American Express, though it's hard to say whether their IPO strategy ended up giving shareholders a better deal than had the board supported my buyout proposal.

I would have loved to have had the chance to run Fireman's Fund but was stoic in being turned down. The effort to gain financial backing had proved that I had kept my good name and reputation and could hope to get others' support in the future. I also felt that my four years at American Express had not been a loss. I had proved myself by building Shearson from a small ragtag company and selling it for $1 billion to one of America's great companies. The value of American Express stock that Shearson's shareholders received in 1981 had more than doubled by the time of my resignation. Also, I felt I had contributed meaningfully to American Express. After all, I had installed much needed financial controls, negotiated the new headquarters, and overhauled the investment portfolio. Moreover, I negotiated the IDS purchase, which proved a huge source of value, set Fireman's Fund on a recovery course, and played a role—however modest—in mitigating some of the risks in the TDB and Lehman transactions.

In the years since my departure, I've come to see that the experience had a positive impact on my subsequent career and that I actually have a lot to thank Jim for despite the frustrations I felt during much of our time working together. To his credit, Jim taught me the value of having an independent board and how to develop a constructive relationship with directors. I also learned the importance of relating to the outside world, especially the global dimension, and that I needed to think more broadly than just focusing on matters internal to my company. Similarly, those years taught me to give back to my community and how corporate leaders can work with their companies to make the world a better place.

American Express failed the test in building a successful integrated financial services company, but my involvement also deepened my conviction that the industry inevitably would move toward a conglomerate model. It struck me during those years that most financial products could be copied easily and that companies that would try to specialize in manufacturing a narrow range of products eventually would face intense pressure on pricing and margins. I came to understand that strong and varied distribution represented the key to overcoming the challenge of product commoditization. When firms control the point of sale and can customize an appropriate group of products to sell to their customers, they create a definite value proposition.

Once we sorted out its operations, IDS proved that a financial services company could integrate and sell multiple products to customers and thereby generate highly profitable and durable relationships. I internalized this lesson while at American Express, and it would dominate my thought process in later years.

As important as anything, I realized that I needed to be my own boss. Jim was a visionary who recognized early that the financial services business would converge and that the industry was poised for vast growth. But his focus on the big picture did him little good. I came to see Jim's flaws as a manager and realized that success could not be garnered with a CEO simply possessing vision and a skill at dealing with external constituencies. My American Express experience told me once and for all that there is no substitute for a powerful and consistent CEO focused on execution, and I felt that I was as good as anyone as an operator.

The years have softened the resentment I once felt toward Jim. In retrospect, I don't regret the deal, and I feel good that I've maintained a very good relationship with my former colleague. It's hard to put my finger on it, but there has always been something about Jim that has made me want to like him. Perhaps it's that he seemed to operate for the most part from his convictions.

It is sad that his management model tolerated independent fiefdoms and never rewarded teamwork. Jim should have set a completely different tone. He should have been more forceful with his directors and insisted that his executives settle their disputes with one another. When I left the company, I only wished he had placed his trust in me as a real partner who could have focused on the inner workings of the company and acted as the point person to make the company's management come together.

Jim's flaws as a manager ultimately came squarely into the open in the late 1980s and early 1990s as the excesses of the junk bond and hostile takeover era fully surfaced. Chasing highly leveraged customers and pursuing expensive acquisitions, he allowed American Express's balance sheet to be saddled with debt and a variety of bad loans. Within six years of my resignation, Jim was forced from the company. His inability to control his managers and his infatuation with glamorous but risky businesses proved his undoing.

In the years after my departure, it has been more difficult to offer Peter Cohen the same generosity of spirit that I have accorded Jim. Writing this book, however, has softened some of my feelings. For nearly two decades, I resented Peter's actions and felt he went out of his way to attack and undermine my position at American Express. I felt deeply hurt that Peter traded his loyalty to me for budding relationships with Jim Robinson and Edmond Safra. I also felt wounded by how quickly he seemed to lose interest in my advice, to the point where he stated overtly that he'd never accept working for me again.

More than anything, though, I blamed Peter for nearly destroying Shearson, the sum total of twenty-five years of my life. In the late 1980s, the chickens started coming home to roost, as Peter's increasingly reckless course at Shearson hit unexpected potholes. With Jim's blessing, Shearson paid an incredibly high price to buy then troubled E. F. Hutton in 1988, which had been hurt badly in the market crash of the preceding year. Peter leveraged Shearson's balance sheet dangerously in order to buy Hutton. At about the same time, Shearson lost all semblance of discipline in lending to risky leveraged buyouts and becoming involved in shaky real estate ventures. The junk bond market's eventual crash caused massive losses and put Shearson at serious risk thanks to its weakened capital base.

It has been hard to reopen the door on Peter's actions toward me and how he nearly destroyed Shearson. Nonetheless, I am more stoical now. Ultimately, I come to two questions: Could I have treated Peter differently? And, if I had, would it have mattered?

I now realize that I communicated poorly with Peter during our negotiations with American Express regarding his role on the board. I understand now that I always worked Peter hard and perhaps didn't tell him often enough how much I valued him. I obviously took Peter's continued loyalty for granted after the merger closed and I began to spend most of my time at American Express's headquarters.

In hindsight, it might have been wise to have taken extra time to communicate with him and be sure our relationship was on a firm footing, particularly as I began to worry about Jim driving a wedge between Peter and me. Yet Peter enjoyed his freedom once he gained his autonomy. It seems unlikely that he would have suddenly given up his newfound prestige, especially as Jim lavished him with attention.

I am sure I could have worked harder at staying on top of the relationship at the beginning. However, I wonder whether it would have mattered in the final analysis. Nearing forty, Peter had a biological clock that was pushing him to prove his independence. Peter always was a smart and driven manager—and ultimately, people with that level of intensity often feel the need for independence.

As my final postscript on this period, it's notable that American Express wasn't alone in struggling with the financial conglomerate model. The Sears–Dean Witter and Prudential-Bache combinations both faced tough times. In 1984, Prudential reported a $113 million loss. Sears spent years trying to build a vehicle to get close to nonaffluent consumers but faced repeated culture clashes between conservative retailing executives and the more upstart Wall Street types. Sears ended up pouring huge sums of money in support of in-store financial centers only to see massive employee turnover and insignificant earnings. Sears finally woke up and exited the business.

Despite these travails, I never lost hope that a new model for financial services would someday take shape. As I walked away from American Express, my greatest sadness was not only for my own outcome but for the missed opportunity we could have achieved had we delivered operational and managerial excellence.

7

Out of the Limelight

ife is filled with ironies big and small. My severance agreement with
American Express provided for office space in the midtown Seagram Building, and I wasted little time heading there to set up my
new office. On my arrival, I was stunned to see another name posted
on the door: John Loeb Sr. I had promised John office space for life
when we bought Loeb Rhoades, and American Express assumed the
obligation after it bought Shearson. So here I suddenly was sharing a
graveyard office with the eighty-three-year-old famed financier who
had inspired me with respect and awe for so many years.

Something inside me sank at that moment. I may have left American Express with sufficient wealth to guarantee a comfortable retirement, but at fifty-two, I was damned if I was ready to fade into obscurity.
I had preached to my colleagues for years that our company needed to
constantly move forward or else atrophy—and the rule applied to me
as well. "I love working, and I've proven I know how to build a successful business," I told myself. "I'll figure a way to reinvent myself."

The office setup was comfortable enough. Facing Park Avenue, the
suite offered a small reception area behind which ran a hallway leading
to five offices, a conference room, and a storage facility. American
Express had agreed to cover my staff expense for a number of months,
and luckily my secretary and two professional assistants, Allison Falls

and Jamie Dimon, elected to join me. Their loyalty meant a great deal as each gave up a promising career in a large company in order to join me and head into the complete unknown.

Jamie especially sacrificed and demonstrated unbelievable commitment. Only twenty-nine years old and newly married, he willingly gambled with his future. I advised him to get on with his life and reminded him that I had plenty of money while he was only starting out professionally. "You don't want to work with someone who doesn't have a job," I insisted. "Go talk to Jim Robinson about finding a new assignment at American Express, and I'll take you back the minute I find a new opportunity."

But Jamie has always been determined, and he steadfastly refused to consider my advice. I finally relented and told him I'd pay him $100,000 per year. He hated the notion that I'd pay him out of pocket, but I reminded him that he had to eat. Besides, American Express would cover the expense temporarily.

Jamie had come to work for me full-time as my executive assistant in 1982, and I already had known him for years before offering him that job. His father and grandfather had worked as brokers at Shearson Hamill, and Joanie and I had become close to his parents shortly after we bought Shearson. Ted and Themis Dimon soon purchased a country house near our home in Greenwich, and we spent a great deal of time enjoying one another's company. Joanie and I liked that Ted didn't seem like the typical broker—he was intellectual and enjoyed a talent for playing the violin—while Themis was warm and never put on airs. Jamie was studying at Tufts University, and in 1976, I offered him a summer job at Shearson following his sophomore year. He spent many weekends with us in Greenwich socializing with Jessica and Marc.

Jamie exuded a natural intelligence and was especially cocky for his young years. I had assigned him to a financial group that summer working under one of Peter Cohen's reports, and he worked on our first major budgeting project. To this day, I remember sitting in my backyard and pointing out proudly that our analyses showed that all of our branches were profitable. "No they're not," he piped up. "The analysis is flawed. Portland doesn't make any money; neither does Seattle." I don't know whether he was right or wrong, but I sure liked the way he confidently spoke his mind even if he had the nerve to question the professionals for whom he worked.

After graduating from Tufts, Jamie took a job as a management consultant for two years before enrolling at the Harvard Business School for an MBA. During his first year in Cambridge, Jamie arranged for me to speak to his classmates. I hadn't seen him for a while, and it was clear that he had matured. He no longer came across as a wiseass kid but rather as a poised Baker Scholar who had suddenly gotten serious about his life.

He introduced me to his attractive classmate and fiancée, Judy, who as it turned out was working on a special project commissioned by Shearson where the students were asked to make strategic recommendations. Judy's team later came to New York and recommended that we should merge with American Express. This was in 1981, and we in fact just had begun discussing the idea of selling to American Express. It was uncanny that this group of young students could reach the same insights as our seasoned executive team. I liked the fact that Jamie had found someone to marry who obviously had a great head on her shoulders.

As Jamie's degree beckoned, he called to tell me about his job offers and ask for my advice. He was trying to decide between Lehman Brothers, Morgan Stanley, and Goldman Sachs. I did my best to steer him in the right direction, and a week later he came to my office to let me know he had decided to go with Goldman, where he had worked the prior summer. By then, however, I had a very different idea for Jamie. "Before you go further, let me ask you a couple of questions," I said. "How important is money to you? Would you be interested in doing something where you might accelerate and broaden your learning process?"

In an instant, I stoked Jamie's curiosity and came out with my proposition: "I can't offer you the most money in the world, but I have this new job at American Express, and I need help in learning the business. You could come in as my executive assistant, and we could learn together. It would be an invaluable experience. Would you consider it?" Jamie eagerly responded, "Well, that's a completely different story," and we quickly set to work on the details. My pay offer was a third less than what Goldman had proposed, yet, proving his decisiveness, Jamie pinned his future to mine and accepted the job without even a murmur of hesitation.

Jamie came to work for me in the fall of 1982 and once again impressed me with his maturity. He soon set off helping on a wide array of demanding projects. I was never much of a teacher, at least in a formal sense, and preferred to put my staff in a sink-or-swim atmosphere. Jamie quickly learned to work with others and solve problems, often under tight deadlines. A quick study, he soon absorbed a new financial language and spoke with other staffers with an air of authority.

He was involved in the negotiation for the new headquarters building, helped me restructure the company's investments, and sorted out complex tax issues. Later, Jamie helped me negotiate the IDS acquisition and figure out how to repair Fireman's Fund. The more we worked together, the more I appreciated Jamie's incisive mind and his capacity to absorb a wide array of financial details. He quickly learned how to push his way through a crowd and to hold his own with American Express's executives, all the while demonstrating solid political instincts.

I enjoyed working with Jamie and felt we had a fantastic relationship. Jamie worked hard to understand my values and thought processes—so much so that he'd frequently jump in to complete my sentences. By the time I resigned as American Express's president, Jamie had gotten a terrific grasp of the industry which seemed years beyond his age. As I left, I felt secretly happy that Jamie had decided to cast his lot with me. The isolation in my new office on Park Avenue seemed less intense knowing I had a protégé with whom I could share my fears as well as my grandiose ideas.

———————

As we settled into our new quarters in July 1985, I received a rush of phone calls and notes from friends and associates wishing me well. I took for granted that my reputation soon would lead to a variety of offers to manage other companies, yet it didn't take long for the self-doubting to begin. Within two weeks or so, the phone calls tailed off, and periods of disturbing quiet came with increasing frequency.

I did my best to stick to a routine. I'd arrive punctually at 8:15 each morning and spend most of the day gazing at my stock quote machine or arranging dates for lunch. Jamie suggested we work on setting up a merchant bank, and I encouraged him to assemble a pitch book for prospective investors and to seek out companies in which to invest potentially. We even selected a name for a possible investment firm: Weill Industries. Meanwhile, assembling a scrapbook for the letters from my many well-wishers soon became a focus for my administrative assistant, Allison.

As the weeks wore on, the quiet became increasingly unsettling. Jamie and I discussed the merchant bank idea, and we frequently arranged lunches with various investment bankers who were all too eager to pitch possible investments. Yet, after a while, most of these "opportunities" seemed familiarly quirky and uninteresting. I had difficulty buying into the idea of becoming a financial investor.

I had made my reputation as a builder/manager, and the notion of becoming beholden to others by managing their money seemed far from natural. Jamie pressed however, and at one point, we considered using a merchant bank as a vehicle for eventually converting passive financial stakes into control positions. My close friend Arthur Zankel—an outstanding investor in his own right—told me I'd be crazy to pursue such a harebrained scheme as it would take years at best to get back to an operating role. I respected his advice and soon dropped the idea.

By early fall, my mood soured. I finally came to see that my hoped-for rush of exciting offers amounted to little more than a fantasy. I started to wonder whether American Express had wounded my reputation and somehow induced others to fear hiring me. Increasingly bored, I began to take longer lunches, and my usual martinis soon induced sleepiness, especially given my lack of intellectual stimulation.

Often I'd return to the office and find myself taking unaccustomed naps on my sofa. Joanie probably worried more than a little about my emotional well-being and did her best to raise my spirits. I'll never forget her calling suggesting that we go see an afternoon movie. Maintaining the fiction that I was hard at work I insisted, "Joanie, I can't; I'm working." Then, in her inimitable manner, Joanie said, "But Sandy, you don't have a job!" She soon began insisting that work didn't have to define my identity and made sure to remind me that we had sufficient money that we didn't have to change our lifestyle. I'm not sure I ever agreed with her comments on identity, but I appreciated her perspective.

It may sound silly, but Joanie boosted my self-image by pushing me to keep my private driver and pay for the things to which I had become accustomed. "You don't need to work for a company to enjoy these things," she said. "If you want to fly in a private plane, then charter one!"

Despite feeling disoriented, I did my best not to wear my heart on my sleeve and to keep my eyes open for new opportunities. I also reminded myself about my good fortune not to have the financial worries that most people encounter when they lose their jobs. Joanie and I kept up our social engagements as well, and I often playfully bragged to Allison about the celebrities whose paths we'd sometimes cross. It became a game which lightened the mood in the office as I'd frequently spur a round of Twenty Questions by posing, "Guess who we met last night?" One day it might have been Barbara Walters while on another night actor Wayne Rogers (otherwise known as Trapper on the TV show M*A*S*H).

Then there was a day Allison received an incoming call from a woman who identified herself as Mrs. Jim Marlis inviting Joanie and me to dinner. Allison normally was aware of the people with whom Joanie and I socialized, but the name seemed completely unfamiliar, and she tried the better part of a day to figure out the identity of the mystery caller. Mrs. Marlis was in fact the actress Glenn Close. She had grown up living in the cottage on my property in Greenwich and now sought to rent the building for the summer so that she might reconnect with her roots to help her get through an emotionally difficult divorce.

I'd happily forget most of my feelings during this period except for the chance I had to better connect with my kids, who both offered their support and talked to me about my hopes for the future. Jessica and Marc, of course, were adults by this time, but for the first time in their lives they could see my vulnerable side and felt a measure of equality, which allowed us to relate to one another on a new level. For instance, Jessica joked, "I guess I'm going to have to buy your cigars now since I have a job and you don't!" We took a family vacation to Rome and Paris—our first in years. As rare as it was to vacation together, it felt equally odd not to suffer the usual business-related interruptions.

While the touring was fun, the flight over was itself memorable as Joanie and I ended up sitting next to Senator Ted Kennedy in the front of the plane. Somehow the senator and I managed to have a bit too much to drink. We became rambunctious enough that a priest sitting in the row in front of us finally yelled for us to "shut up," while our kids later told us we could be heard in the back of the plane. After enjoying that vacation, I'm sorry we didn't plan other family events thereafter. By insisting on going to the office every day, I gave in to my insecurities and lost the chance to engage Marc and Jessica further.

Family life picked me up, and my growing involvement with Carnegie Hall offered additional therapy. Since joining the board in 1982, I realized that the institution had enormous untapped potential to add to the vitality of New York City and the music world at large. I also marveled at Isaac Stern, Carnegie Hall's savior and the intellectual and spiritual giant behind the organization. In the late 1950s, the hall had been owned privately and was slated to be sold to real estate developers who planned to raze the edifice and replace it with an office building. Nearly single-handedly, Stern mobilized a rescue which led New York City and the state of New York to purchase the hall in 1960. Isaac Stern was much more than a wonderful musician. Apart from saving Carnegie Hall, he pushed the institution to include music education and community outreach in its core values. That emphasis created a new focus, but Carnegie Hall had still lived hand-to-mouth for the two decades since the building was saved and relied on public subsidies and the generosity of its board to cover regular operating deficits.

In my new role as a director, I asked why Carnegie Hall hadn't worked harder to connect with its broader community and to take fund-raising more seriously. My views rankled some of the other board members who might have felt that soliciting for funds was beneath their dignity, but my opinions resonated with Isaac. He soon invited Joanie and me to join him for a weekend in Palm Beach to get to know us better.

Isaac had a warm and gregarious personality, and he immediately put us at ease. Sitting on a deck overlooking the ocean, he waxed freely about his dreams for Carnegie Hall where music as a universal language could connect people and transfer culture from one generation to the next. "When you sit in Carnegie Hall, you can feel Tchaikovsky in the walls," he purred. "All the great artists of the past century have played here from Artur Rubinstein to Jascha Heifetz to Yehudi Menuhin to Vladimir Horowitz. We have an obligation to transfer the knowledge embodied by these great artists to the next generation." Isaac went on to share his grand plans for revitalizing the concert hall and building a preeminent center of music education and community outreach.

Isaac's passion was contagious. He knew I'd respond to a well-articulated action plan and that I could be counted upon to support him in building a more professional organization. Before I knew it, he proposed that I head a new steering committee to raise funds for Carnegie Hall's restoration. I was flattered by Isaac's praise and personal attention, but I never had raised serious amounts of money before and had reservations whether I'd be up to the task.

After some cajoling, I agreed to co-chair the committee with Carnegie Hall's chairman, Jim Wolfensohn. Later, Joanie and I decided to make an initial gift of $2.5 million to kick off the fund-raising project. Our gift was the single largest donation to the hall since Andrew Carnegie's original endowment in 1891. I reasoned that I'd never be able to ask others for money in good conscience if I weren't willing to commit my own funds.

All was fine until I announced my resignation from American Express. Without having a large corporation behind me, I questioned whether I had the credibility to remain co-chair of the capital campaign. I immediately telephoned Isaac and Jim Wolfensohn to resign the post as well as my board seat, but both promptly rejected my offer. Isaac especially pushed back, promising that I still enjoyed his confidence and telling me my enthusiasm and commitment were what counted. His words mirrored Joanie's observation that my self-worth didn't always have to be tied to a large company. The sincerity of his friendship meant a great deal and showed that I didn't need a fancy corporate title to stay relevant.

Over the next year, I threw myself into raising money for Carnegie Hall, and the challenge often provided much-needed relief from the boredom and frustrations of day-to-day life in our office suite in the Seagram Building. Our fund-raising efforts soon bore fruit. Money flowed in, and Carnegie Hall accelerated its long-delayed restoration project. The capstone came at the end of 1986. We had raised roughly $60 million and completely refurbished the main concert hall in addition to a smaller recital facility.

After seven months of construction, a sparkling Carnegie Hall re-opened in December with a huge gala program which began with a ribbon cutting by the mayor and two formal dinners whose guest rosters filled the society pages. The music that evening featured the New York Philharmonic and a wide array of performances by the likes of Frank Sinatra, Lena Horne, Vladimir Horowitz, and Leonard Bernstein. Only three weeks later, Joanie and I celebrated an even more intimate event, the opening of the Joan and Sanford I. Weill Recital Hall. Isaac and Jim generously decided to name the newly renovated theater after us in appreciation for our gift, which had energized the fund-raising campaign.

Rebuilding Carnegie Hall introduced us to the joys of philanthropy. Somehow it felt even better to give money away than it had to earn it in the first place. I also enjoyed working with Carnegie Hall's professionals, with whom I developed deep and long-lasting ties. Until his death in 2002, Isaac Stern and I enjoyed a wonderful friendship. Isaac inspired me to think boldly and to dream large just as Tubby Burnham had inspired me years earlier. The people I've always respected most have been those who are filled with passion, intelligence, and good humor and who are well rounded. In this regard, Isaac was truly one of a kind. He was a futuristic dreamer and so much more than the "fiddler" he called himself.

I also had a wonderful relationship with Judy Arron, whom we hired as Carnegie Hall's artistic and executive director in the mid-1980s. Judy taught me a tremendous amount about music, as we'd often share a house box, where she'd explain the nuances of a given piece of music. Judy had terrific business sense and an aptitude for budgets and operational details. In board meetings, Isaac typically would speak words filled with passion and spirit and get everyone pumped up, while Judy would then take care to infuse the ensuing discussions with a dose of practicality.

My deepening involvement with Carnegie Hall in the 1980s set the foundation for many rewarding experiences in the years that followed. When Jim Wolfensohn gave up his chairmanship in 1991, Isaac asked me to take over, and I'm proud that we've increased Carnegie Hall's endowment from $2 million to over $250 million during my tenure thus far. When I think about what has cemented my commitment to this wonderful organization, I always come back to my inspirational relationships and especially Isaac's faith in my abilities during a relatively difficult period in my life. In late 1985, I needed to be reassured that I still had true friends, and Isaac answered the call.

As much as Isaac and my family played to my ego, I still felt ill at ease during the fall of 1985. Jamie and I kept looking for investment ideas, but nothing grabbed me. I could see that it would prove far more challenging than I had expected to find an exciting new business. Then, out of the blue, I received a call from Warren Hellman, a former president of Lehman Brothers who had retired to the West Coast to establish his own investment banking boutique. Warren was plugged into the San Francisco business and social scene and was distressed how the city had seen several of its major companies swallowed up by mergers.

Now a new crisis was emerging: The city's preeminent commercial bank, BankAmerica, was in serious financial trouble, and Warren feared that disarray at such an important institution might severely wound the city and its local companies. He recognized that the bank desperately needed a change in leadership and had been searching for someone who might be capable of reviving the bank's financial strength and credibility. Marty Lipton, our mutual friend and lead attorney at Wachtell Lipton, had reminded Warren of my availability and pushed him to make the call.

Warren described the sequence of events that had undermined the venerable eighty-year-old institution. For thirty years following World War II, BankAmerica had led the industry in size and progressiveness. But in the 1970s, the bank surrendered its leadership position to Citicorp and lost its discipline. Inflation and financial innovation undermined the banking industry in the 1970s and 1980s and led BankAmerica, along with many other banks, to lend aggressively in order to maintain earnings growth. Before long, the company ran afoul of credit problems related to less-developed countries, the oil patch, commercial real estate, and agriculture. By the mid-1980s, the company's stock price was skidding; longtime investors were angry; and more than a few board members were restive. The company and its CEO, Sam Armacost, were on the ropes.

It didn't take much for Hellman to pique my interest. I liked the franchise and thought the stock looked undervalued. I related to the branch and credit card businesses, and I was confident that I had proven my capacity to run a retail financial services company. Jamie and I quickly caught a plane for San Francisco. Meeting Warren in his office overlooking the bay, my friend promptly reassured me, "It's the perfect time for a change in management, and you're the perfect person to step in. You're a builder; you're available; and there's no one else out there with your stature."

With an opening like that, it was all too easy to begin thinking large once again.

We rolled up our sleeves and soon hammered out a three-point plan under which we'd seek the support of selected directors, inject fresh capital, and overhaul the bank's operations. Warren asked how much capital I thought we'd need to raise, which of course was the most pressing question. I replied that we should be conservative—putting investors' minds at ease regarding the bank's financial stability was job number one. Jamie and I already had done a lot of number crunching, and we suggested $1 billion should be about right. It was a big number, but we all agreed that my reputation and our combined contacts made raising that sort of money feasible.

During November and December, Jamie and I spent a lot of time on the West Coast preparing to approach BankAmerica. We brought in Bob Greenhill from Morgan Stanley as an additional advisor, and Greenie and Warren arranged conversations with several directors who appeared supportive. Former Defense Secretary Robert McNamara and Chuck Schwab, CEO of Charles Schwab, especially cheered us on.

Indeed, Schwab raged against BankAmerica's management. He had sold his company to BankAmerica never anticipating the problems that soon followed, and he eagerly sought a way to buy his company back. He cited chapter and verse on all that plagued the bank: "It's a sieve losing money . . . they've destroyed their ability to do business . . . their top people are inept." He went on to provide us with valuable insight into the board's politics and the bank's financial and operational details.

I also sought out Federal Reserve chairman Paul Volcker, reasoning that I should touch base with him before making a concrete overture to BankAmerica to avoid any possible embarrassment later. I traveled to Washington on a Saturday morning, and we met for lunch in the Watergate Hotel. I had met Volcker during my tenure at American Express, so we weren't complete strangers. I told him about my plan and made certain to stress that I had the capacity to bring fresh capital and management talent. Volcker listened politely but, as one would expect, took care not to pass judgment on BankAmerica. Nonetheless, I heard nothing that made me think the Federal Reserve would blow our approach out of the water. In these types of meetings, the most important thing to listen for is what is *not* said.

My advance selling job was nearly complete. I only needed to get Joanie on board. Over my whole career, I cannot remember another time when she pushed back so hard on one of my initiatives. To my surprise, the idea of moving to California upset her deeply. She rebelled at leaving her friends and children in the East. Jessica didn't help matters any as she argued I was being headstrong and that I was interested in

BankAmerica for the wrong reasons, suggesting the idea of running a huge company put stars in my eyes. Ignoring the objections, I tried my best to win my wife over. Joanie never offered her blessing, but I effectively delayed the day of reckoning and stayed focused on my project by declaring, "Let's not worry until we actually have something worth worrying about."

We finally put our plan into motion around New Year's Day. Warren placed a call to CEO Armacost relaying my interest in BankAmerica and proposing a meeting. Without going into detail, Warren pointed out that I was prepared to raise capital in return for a management role. Caught off guard, Armacost initially accepted the invitation but almost overnight called back to cancel the get-together without explanation. He must have felt threatened by our offer and only agreed to the meeting initially in order to buy time. Days later, BankAmerica stunningly announced that it had lost nearly $340 million during 1985 and that it was suspending its dividend. The bank had been reeling for a long while, but the surprise dividend cut signaled that the troubles ran deep.

My advisors and I agreed that it was time to put our offer in writing. In a letter to the board, I specified that I'd raise $1 billion from investors and add $10 million of my personal funds in return for being named BankAmerica's CEO. Knowing that the company's directors would hold a regularly scheduled meeting during the first week of February, I moved to solidify my negotiating position. The AT&T pro-am golf tournament was held at Pebble Beach that year and was an event in which I always eagerly participated. Conveniently, Jim Robinson also participated, and I called him aside to see whether Shearson would agree to provide a commitment letter to raise the $1 billion. Wasting no time, Jim summoned Peter Cohen to fly out and join us. A day later, I had my capital commitment in hand. Shearson was then pushing to get out in front of the late 1980s merger boom, and Jim and Peter must have viewed backing me as a convenient way to advertise Shearson's capabilities. I still harbored lingering anger at Peter, but I wasn't about to let my emotions stand in the way of getting the ammunition I needed.

The board meeting came and went without any news. Our supporters inside the organization soon told us what had happened. Armacost had arranged for Salomon Brothers' John Gutfreund to argue that BankAmerica was capable of handling its issues on its own. Armacost then detailed a five-year plan supposedly blessed by the Salomon investment bankers which called for an imminent and long-lasting profit recovery. Soon thereafter, I received a letter from the board referring condescendingly to my "job application" and stating the board had no intention for me to be involved.

I always knew that BankAmerica represented a long shot, but I still felt deflated reading the rejection letter. We had come a long way, though, and I was determined to press every option. I decided to head off to Puerto Rico for my annual midwinter vacation, but instructed our team to assemble an action plan for fixing the bank. At the right time, I'd angle for an opportunity to personally make my case before the board. During our vacation, word of our interest suddenly leaked (presumably by a dissident insider). On February 20, BankAmerica's share price surged 10 percent to $15¼ on heavy volume, and by day's end the company disclosed that I had expressed interest.

I soon returned from vacation and received word that Robert McNamara had suggested that "the time is now right to send another letter to the board requesting an opportunity to present [Sandy's] case directly." BankAmerica had set its next board meeting for March 2–3, and I immediately sent off a new letter offering to personally present my overhaul plan. On February 27, only two days after we sent the letter, the local press once again broke the story. This time BankAmerica's stock price surged 13 percent to $17¼.

The board never allowed me to appear. After a five-hour session on March 3, BankAmerica announced once more that it had rejected my approach, this time with the unanimous approval of its outside board members.* In some respects, I felt as though I had been set up and couldn't understand how certain directors could tell me one thing but not have the courage to vote on my behalf.

This time the rejection completely deflated my hopes, and I withdrew my offer for good. Though disappointed, I concentrated on the

---

*Charles Schwab continued to oppose management but was considered an insider.

positive aspects of the experience. After all, I'm good at rationalizing away my defeats. The BankAmerica episode kept my profile high and showed that I still enjoyed the backing of supporters in the financial community. I figured these assets would come in handy in some future opportunity.

Losing out on BankAmerica at least pleased Joanie, who never got comfortable with the notion of moving to the Bay Area. However, a related incident soon created a new source of distress. Joanie had been seeing a therapist for nearly twenty years and very much had relied on him for talking through the stresses of a possible move to California. Shortly after the BankAmerica episode concluded, she received a surprise phone call from the doctor saying that "I can't meet with you anymore. My lawyer will call yours." My wife turned ashen as she related the conversation and questioned what was behind the call.

We soon learned that the good doctor had been accused of trading on insider information based on Joanie's confidential discussions pertaining to my moves at BankAmerica and other business matters. The news stunned and devastated Joanie, although she eventually had the opportunity to confront the doctor in a lawsuit we filed which led to a $100,000 settlement. That confrontation was emotionally charged but turned out to be the best therapy. It proved once and for all that Joanie could deal with her stresses on her own.

As a final postmortem on BankAmerica, I ultimately was vindicated. Only four months after the final board meeting, the bank announced a $600 million loss, and management's plan for an earnings recovery appeared in shambles. Armacost managed to hang on as CEO until the fall but was then let go. The turn of events demonstrated once and for all how companies can suffer when their management and directors succumb to a siege mentality and lose perspective.

Putting the BankAmerica experience behind us, Jamie and I returned to square one, and we reconsidered our options once more. I looked at a few insurance companies and had a brief conversation with Wausau

Insurance. The business, though, seemed lackluster at best, and I soon lost interest. Later, the Pritzker family in Chicago approached me about leading a hostile run for ITT, but I never liked hostile deals. Rumors also surfaced that I had an interest in going after Merrill Lynch, which was struggling in the mid-1980s. It got to the point where Merrill chairman Bill Schreyer called to say, "We're friends; don't try to come after me." I had no more interest in an unfriendly approach for Merrill than for ITT.

Just as the excitement from pursuing BankAmerica was turning into a distant memory, *Fortune* writer Carole Loomis unwittingly did me a favor by profiling me in a feature story entitled "Sanford Weill: Experienced Manager, Good References." It proved a great piece of advertising and turned out to have a huge impact. Days after the magazine article appeared, I received a call from someone who identified himself as Bob Volland, treasurer of Commercial Credit, a small finance company based in Baltimore. Volland suggested I'd be perfect to restructure the company, which had fallen on tough times under the ownership of its parent, the computer giant Control Data.

Volland pointed out that no one had authorized his approach, but he apparently figured I'd be the ideal person to lead his company out of what must have seemed a hopeless morass. Having built Shearson, served as president of American Express, and pursued BankAmerica, I didn't think getting involved with the blemished and unknown Commercial Credit exactly fit my idea of the perfect opportunity. Yet, by now, I was losing the luxury of waiting for the ideal situation, and I was hungry to find something to run again. With little to lose, I decided to invite Volland up to New York and listen to what he had to say.

8

Resurrection

Bob Volland was a rogue employee regardless of the goodness of his intentions. "Commercial Credit would be a good opportunity for you, and I'd love to tell you more about it," he declared in our first phone call. "I'm doing this on my own, and I have no hidden agenda. I only want to do what's right by my company." Somehow this secondary member of Commercial Credit's management—and from a company which I had already looked at and dismissed buying two years earlier—managed to talk his way into my office.

A year had gone by since I had left American Express, and I had suffered several wheel spins trying to find a new challenge. I considered myself a very good manager and thought others shared that view. Yet if that was the case, I wondered why a wider range of opportunities hadn't come my way. With a whiff of desperation, I recognized that I needed to lower my sights and no longer focus on large branded organizations. I decided to leave no stone unturned. Bob Volland and I agreed to meet in my office a couple of days later on May 2, a date that fed my superstitious nature and which made me feel strangely hopeful. After all, we'd be meeting on the twenty-sixth anniversary of the creation of my first partnership.

Volland and his assistant arrived promptly at 2:00 P.M. My guests were nervous about the unauthorized action they had taken. Volland genuinely felt Commercial Credit was falling apart under its current management and figured he had little to lose by trying to call the company's plight to my attention. Still, his surreptitious visit resembled corporate espionage. Volland spoke carefully: "I can only go so far. I want to do what's right, but I don't want to lose my job." He then started to describe Commercial Credit, a seventy-five-year-old Baltimore-based finance company with operations in twenty-eight states which had lost its way.

He emphasized that the core business remained attractive but that the ownership structure was undermining the firm. Management at the parent, Control Data, saw Commercial Credit only as a source of cash to support its computer business and failed to appreciate that the cash flow depended on Commercial Credit's debt ratings. These had been slipping steadily due to poor credit judgments. Volland went on to tell of misguided forays into commercial lending, leasing, and lending to developing countries which were overshadowing the consumer finance business.

Unwilling to accept his assertions at face value, I wanted to know why he believed the core of the company remained solid. "I can only speak as a financial person," Volland noted, "but the consumer finance business has been profitable during both good and bad economic periods, and our customers have remained surprisingly loyal." He elaborated on the vast scope of the consumer middle market in America and described a whole class of people who'd borrow at 25 percent interest rates in order to buy a car, a piece of furniture, or a home appliance. "Commercial Credit might have gotten sidetracked, but a decent consumer lending operation definitely remains buried within the company," he insisted.

Our interest piqued, Jamie suddenly blurted, "It's like getting to Middle America and to people that go to Wal-Mart!" I doubt Jamie had ever stepped foot in a Wal-Mart—I certainly hadn't, but it's fair to say we were intrigued by the seemingly vast market that had gone largely unnoticed by larger financial services companies. Listening further, it became apparent that the consumer finance business was fragmented, and I wondered whether a cleaned-up Commercial Credit might represent a vehicle to pursue potential industry consolidation opportunities. Now, that was something to which I could relate!

Playing devil's advocate, I informed Volland that I had been among those who had looked at Commercial Credit in 1984 and had concluded it was "a piece of crap." Not put off, he emphasized how much restructuring had been done over the prior two years. Pressured by its deteriorating financial condition, Commercial Credit had sold off branches and built reserves. Even if finances remained tenuous, he argued that enough progress had been made to lay the foundation for a turnaround under the right leadership.

Bob Volland spent two hours briefing us and responding to our questions. By the time he left, I realized that this could in fact be far more interesting than I had first thought. Over the next few weeks, I directed Jamie to study the consumer finance industry and dig deeper into Commercial Credit. We spoke further to Volland—whom Jamie and I now jokingly referred to as "Deep Throat"—and he provided us with additional financial insights while being careful to filter out anything that might be considered material nonpublic information.

Our research confirmed Bob Volland's initial observations. The unregulated consumer finance business had indeed produced remarkably consistent growth and profitability in recent years. Commercial Credit may have lagged, but the industry's better companies had posted high returns on capital—above 20 percent—year in and year out, a performance which contrasted sharply with the far more cyclical banking and securities industries. Finance companies were among the fastest growers in the financial services industry in the 1980s, and their funding needs increasingly dominated public credit markets. The industry, however, was fractured and contained thousands of small operations while the biggest firms—names like Household or Beneficial—had amassed only modest market shares.

The industry was fascinating, but I concluded that Commercial Credit represented a study in missed opportunity. Founded in 1912, the company had grown steadily over its first fifty years and even had pioneered financing automobile purchases before General Motors and other carmakers created their own captive finance companies. Commercial Credit's problems took root in 1968 when Larry Tisch's Loews Corporation offered to buy the company. In those years, Commercial

Credit maintained a WASPish culture and was reluctant to accept the Jewish financier's approach. Instead, Commercial Credit sold to Control Data, then a four-year-old high-flying computer company with a stock selling at a lofty $160 per share.

Had Control Data left well enough alone, things might have worked out better for Commercial Credit, but the new parent's executives erred in a couple of important respects. Under their protection, Commercial Credit lost its financial discipline and competitive drive. It didn't take long for the quality of Commercial Credit's assets to deteriorate, and Control Data mismanaged its subsidiary's cash flow, often siphoning it off for other investments. By the early 1980s, Commercial Credit was saddled with hundreds of millions of dollars in problem loans, especially in places far from its core business.

By 1984, Commercial Credit was locked in a downward spiral and had become more of an albatross than an asset for its parent. Control Data explored selling the unit and hired Goldman Sachs to drum up interest. That's how it had come to my attention when I was with American Express. But no one was willing to offer a price close to Control Data's minimum requirement of book value. Commercial Credit had no option but to shrink further in order to protect its solvency. Over two subsequent years, the company shaved more than a third of its assets and employees, sold its lucrative West Coast branches, and built loan loss reserves even as it reported ongoing losses. Meanwhile, Control Data's stock price hit new lows, having plummeted to $8 per share.

Despite Commercial Credit's poor recent history, I smelled opportunity. The more I looked, the more it seemed that Control Data's weak management had failed to invest properly in the still viable consumer finance business. For all its difficulties, Commercial Credit maintained a market share of 3 percent, not dominant but respectable relative to the 6 percent shares of the industry's biggest players. The core consumer finance business still appeared focused on its target Main Street America segment of households possessing between $15,000 and $45,000 of annual income, a market that encompassed 45 million potential clients. The moves to build reserves and jettison problem loans had given the company some breathing room. At last, I had found a company with a compelling risk/return profile.

Now I'd only have to convince Control Data to bet on me.

———

The logical next step would be to arrange a meeting with Control Data's CEO, Bob Price. I asked Bob Volland if he'd make an introduction, but Deep Throat quickly stammered that he'd lose his job if it became known that he had been passing me the information on the company. That idea plainly was a nonstarter. Instead, I returned to my friend Bob Greenhill, who was more than happy to contact Price. Around the end of May, we flew out to Control Data's Minneapolis headquarters on an uncomfortable People Express flight. Price listened politely while we argued that Commercial Credit might not easily regain an acceptable debt rating so long as it was owned by Control Data. The smart strategic move, we maintained, would be to hand off the unit to a new management team who might restore the finance company's credibility with investors. We proposed a plan where Control Data would name me CEO of Commercial Credit and then spin out the unit. Greenhill asserted I was unique in having the credibility to pull off such a restructuring and that the IPO route would offer Control Data its best chance to off-load Commercial Credit at a price that would avoid a large write-off.

Price thanked us for our presentation and said he'd think about what we had proposed, but he offered little more. Heading home, Bob Greenhill and I were seated in the back of another People Express flight and had to endure an awfully bumpy ride. We tried to compare notes on our meeting, but the lack of privacy and my ever-present nervousness at flying soon induced me to seek solace in a double martini. Bob, as usual, played my alter ego—he ignored the turbulence and leisurely pored over a pilot's manual, as he was then taking flying lessons.

To our disappointment, we soon learned that Bob Price had decided to table our proposal in favor of pursuing an expensive debt offering pushed by his investment bankers at First Boston. I suppose his bankers had convinced him that issuing bonds was more of a "bird in the hand" solution.

Undeterred, we waited out Control Data's bond deal and then pushed to restart our discussions. Price must have realized that the financing deal was only a stopgap measure because he willingly resumed conversations by midsummer. Now we pitched our idea even more strongly. Greenhill told Price there was a good chance Control Data could receive at least book value in any public offering, something they hadn't come close to in their earlier efforts to sell the company. Greenhill argued that I'd have the leverage with investors to sell 80 percent of Commercial Credit but also to raise additional funds that would help guarantee a longer-term recovery for the company.

This last idea proved pivotal in turning Price around. The notion that we could raise fresh capital directly for Commercial Credit's benefit held out the prospect of critically needed improvements in the company's debt ratings. Price could see a compelling exit strategy where Control Data could largely unload the problematic unit while bringing in someone with a plan that might well create value for Control Data on its residual 20 percent stake.

By early September, our talks shifted gears. We brought in our outside counsel, Ken Bialkin, who began to structure our agreement, and Price introduced me to Joe Minutilli, a career Commercial Credit executive and the company's CEO, so that I might begin to craft a turn-around plan. I wasn't quite sure what to expect with Joe given that Commercial Credit's future had been under discussion without his input up until this time. But Minutilli must have realized that the status quo was untenable and that by working with me he'd stand the best chance to salvage his legacy.

Even before we struck a deal, I had begun to sound out a variety of people with whom I had worked about coming to join me. I began to think, too, about how we'd attract investors to an IPO of Commercial Credit and quickly saw the importance of aligning my interests and that of my management team with those of our prospective new shareholders. On September 12, 1986, Control Data announced it was naming me chairman and CEO of Commercial Credit and that it would expeditiously reduce its ownership stake to 20 percent via an initial offering. I accepted a $500,000 salary ($100,000 less than I had received at American Express), and I personally committed to buy $5 million worth of stock at the company's $18 per share book value. My new management team and I would own 10 percent of the firm via stock purchases and options grants.

I knew I had my work cut out for me, but I felt exhilarated nonetheless. A year had been a long time to go without a job. Yes, I confess I was more than a little scared. After all, Commercial Credit was a small fish in a business completely different from what I had known. I expected it would be a challenge to turn this little company into a powerhouse and that my glory days with Shearson might fade to distant memory if things didn't pan out. Still, I had taken down my expectations several notches by now.

Reality hit when I learned that Commercial Credit would be covered by *The Wall Street Journal*'s Philadelphia bureau rather than from New York. That news told me where we'd stand in the pecking order. At one time, I would have felt wounded by the loss of prestige; now, I was excited to have a chance to build something out of this underrated business.

I had a number of good leads for building a new management team and firmed up a few right away. I first pulled in a couple of disaffected American Express executives I had known during my tenure as president. Greg Fitz-Gerald signed on as my senior financial person—Greg had been treasurer at Amex and CFO of Merrill Lynch before that. I also hired Jim Calvano, formerly vice chairman of Amex's Travel Related Services business, which included the important credit card operation. I wanted someone with a strong background in consumer lending.

Of even more significance, I had been approached during my pursuit of BankAmerica by Bob Lipp, who was then president of Chemical Bank. Bob confided that he'd jump at an opportunity to work with me. He plainly was tired of Chemical's bureaucracy and was frustrated at being passed over for CEO, which had recently been up for grabs. Bob enjoyed a terrific reputation and had the perfect background for Commercial Credit. I didn't want Bob to compromise himself by resigning from Chemical before our IPO was complete since there's always an element of uncertainty in large offerings, so I told him to hold off on his announcement until after the close of our deal. I looked at Bob as our morning-after surprise and secret weapon which would reassure our new investors once and for all.

Even as I continued to recruit additional executives, we filed our IPO registration statement on October 3, 1986. We proposed offering thirty-eight million shares with an initial range of $21–$24 per share, making Commercial Credit one of the largest initial offerings ever. In readying the deal documents, I insisted that we add Shearson Lehman to Morgan Stanley and First Boston as a managing underwriter. This was important since I still commanded the respect of my old sales force and knew I could count on Shearson to place a significant amount of stock with retail investors. Events would soon prove the wisdom of reaching out to my old firm.

We began our investor road show in mid-October and planned to visit investors in sixteen cities—including six outside the United States— over eleven days. Joe Minutilli, Greg Fitz-Gerald, and I formed the primary team. Jamie was upset at having to take a back seat to Fitz-Gerald, but I made sure he had the opportunity to present in a number of cities.

We made a straightforward pitch. We pointed out that Commercial Credit had been undermanaged but would be refocused and repositioned. We argued that investors misunderstood the consumer finance business and that it enjoyed better financial returns and growth relative to more mainstream commercial banks. Under our plan, fresh capital would lead to improved ratings and allow Commercial Credit to regain access to public credit markets. And finally, I recalled my proven track record and emphasized that my equity ownership in Commercial Credit would align my success with shareholder results.

The underwriters in typical fashion initially jockeyed to show how much interest they were drumming up. In fact, the head of institutional sales at First Boston pulled me aside after our second presentation to tell me "you're doing terrific." I didn't need the flattery; I simply wanted to know the answer to one question: "*Where are the orders?*" When he promised that "they'd come," I threatened to back out of the road show unless they allocated a meaningful number of shares for Shearson's retail clients. I knew that retail investors too often were poorly treated in stock offerings and was determined not to let this happen to my friends in the Shearson sales force. Only a few days earlier, I had pitched our deal to these brokers over Shearson's "squawk box" and heard firsthand how this enthusiastic sales force was still in my corner. First Boston reluctantly acceded to my ultimatum and offered a large block of shares for Shearson to place.

The marketing proceeded smoothly until October 29, the next to last day of the road show. We were in Scotland when First Boston's syndicate manager called with the surprising news that he wanted to reduce the price of the offering. We were in the market around the same time as another huge IPO for Coca-Cola Bottling, and the banker suggested we faced limitations on demand from having two such large deals in the market at once. The First Boston people wanted to cut the offer price to under $20 per share. Hearing this, Bob Price turned livid, as he had been led to think there was strong demand for the shares. Even though he really didn't have a good alternative, Price warned he'd cancel the offering if the underwriters violated the $20 minimum price.

Fearing tempers might get out of hand, I quickly proposed to personally buy an additional $1 million worth of stock if Control Data and First Boston would compromise at a $20.50 per share price. The demonstration of my own conviction helped calm the atmosphere, and we had an agreement within thirty minutes. We ended up pricing the deal that night, a day earlier than scheduled, and I immediately decided to fly back to New York so that I could be on hand at the New York Stock Exchange's opening the next morning. When our chartered jet landed in Newfoundland to refuel, we learned we'd be delayed owing to a battery-related problem. I shuddered at missing the thrill of watching our new stock open for trading. Fortunately, the plane's crew solved the malfunction after a couple of hours just in time for us to land in New York by 7:00 A.M. I ran home for a shower and made it downtown as the gavel fell to open the day's trading.

It's a great moment to launch a new company, and I felt especially proud of my highly visible comeback. We had sold over $900 million worth of stock including nearly $300 million for Commercial Credit's use beyond the Control Data payback. Ours was the third largest initial offering ever at the time, and it felt like a remarkable market affirmation of confidence in my abilities. A company with no public market all at once had come public in a huge deal. With the fresh capital, Commercial Credit's balance sheet would be noticeably less leveraged than most of its peers, a fact which helped nail down a speedy and urgently needed upgrade from the rating agencies. At least from a financial point of view, the concept behind bringing Commercial Credit public seemed to fall neatly into place. Commercial Credit's shares closed at $21 that first day and rose another $1⅜ the following day.

Despite the positive feelings, I recall an unsettling aspect of that first day's trading. Nearly a quarter of all the shares placed had turned over by the market's close. I thought sarcastically, "Thanks for your vote of confidence, all of you loyal shareholders. It's been nice having the opportunity to work for you, and I'm glad you've had such long-term vision!" It became clear that many large institutions simply had signed up in search of a quick buck whereas the retail clients of Shearson were my most committed believers. I was glad I had insisted that First Boston treat my old firm the right way, and I felt doubly proud that the Shearson brokers still held me in high esteem after all I had been through with American Express.

———————

In the weeks leading up to our offering, I learned a lot about Commercial Credit. It took a while to adjust to the idea that I'd now be giving money away instead of collecting it. Although we came from completely different worlds, Joe Minutilli behaved like a gentleman fielding our questions and introducing us to the company. I needed to tend to important organizational issues, most notably rounding out my new executive team and firming up our new board, but I understood the broader agenda of what we needed to accomplish in our first year: We had to speedily exit our exposures to overseas loans and corporate credits which were wholly unrelated to our consumer finance business. We also recognized the imperative of working further with the rating agencies to shore up their confidence. Finally, we needed to get our arms around Commercial Credit's primary consumer finance business and revive its growth.

Bob Lipp signed on as of November 1. He had tried to negotiate a seat on our board, but I turned him down arguing that I wanted to get away from my old practice of including inside directors. Bob wasn't thrilled, but it wasn't a deal breaker. He understood that the entrepreneurial challenge Commercial Credit offered far outweighed the prestige of serving on the board. I might once have had qualms about hiring a commercial banker since the stereotypical banker lacks creativity. Bob certainly didn't fit that mold, and I liked him immediately. He brought needed lending experience and struck me as a tough operator. He authoritatively described the credit business, its key metrics, and the sort of things one had to manage to avoid trouble. I especially liked his philosophy of creating profit and loss statements at the local level and decentralizing control to the field. I knew that would empower employees and matched the approach I had insisted upon for Shearson's retail brokers over many years. Bob's skill showed from the start, and he'd go on to be one of my very best managers.

Within our first few months, we broadened our management, mainly seeking renegades from either American Express or Chemical Bank. In effect, we were parachuting a new management team into Baltimore. John Fowler joined us from American Express's Warner-Amex unit to head corporate development while Lipp soon recruited his longtime lieutenant Bob Willumstad to run most of our consumer finance branches. Bob Willumstad, in turn, hired fellow Chemical Banker Marge Magner to help run the branch system. We hired others to focus on public and investor relations, our investment portfolio, bank relations, and our small insurance operation.

We pitched our new company to prospective recruits with a unique promise: "This will be different . . . we'll run the company the way it should be run: without bureaucracy." I may not have appeared discriminating as I searched for executives whom I had known from prior experience, but I reasoned I'd be better off that way than by taking a chance on complete unknowns. In fact, I usually preferred to make important hiring decisions by looking for people I'd enjoy and trust as partners. As things turned out, we hired a mix of people, some whom I knew well and others who came by way of referral. Curiously, the former Chemical employees—Bob Lipp, Bob Willumstad, and Marge Magner—far outperformed many of the people I recruited from Amex. They'd all move on to prominent positions in our company over the next two decades.

I also had the good fortune to add Chuck Prince to our team. Chuck was thirty-six and served as Commercial Credit's general counsel. We needed to resolve many legal details to untangle Commercial Credit from its parent, and Chuck methodically helped the process along. He weighed a lot in those days, and I have an early recollection of Chuck eating lots of hamburgers and French fries during our long working meetings.

If that was a first impression, I soon learned that Chuck had a great deal to offer. He was one of the fastest and most retentive readers I've ever met and was the type of lawyer who would look for solutions while balancing the risks in a given business decision. Among the original executives at Commercial Credit, he uniquely possessed incredible enthusiasm, trustworthiness, and a can-do attitude. There were few people I wanted to keep among Commercial Credit's prior executive team, but Chuck clearly stood out. Besides, I wanted to reach out and show the rank and file that we were willing to recognize and reward local talent.

Beyond putting together a new management team, I also needed to assemble a board of directors. Here again, I first approached people I knew and quickly received commitments from some old stalwarts: Ken Bialkin, Art Zankel, Frank Zarb, and former president Ford. Standards for determining board composition had begun to change well before the later Sarbanes-Oxley legislation. Many companies were beginning to emphasize independent board members to enhance their stature with institutional investors.

I set out to build a diverse board devoid of insiders. I brought in Doug Danforth, the chairman of the blue chip company Westinghouse; former Secretary of Defense Mel Laird, whom I knew from IDS's board; and Dudley Mecum, who headed Combustion Engineering. On Jamie's suggestion, I reached out to his former Harvard Business School professor Andy Pearson—before teaching, Andy had a successful career at Pepsico. I also wanted some continuity with the past and with Baltimore so I included Joe Minutilli (who by now had retired from management) and Les Disheroon, who was CEO of Monumental, a local insurer. In all, our board included a teacher, a former U.S. president, a chairman of a mutual fund board, and individuals with prominent business or political experience.

I knew the board would challenge me, educate me on other industries and developments in Washington, and help open doors for our company. In fact, Les Disheroon soon began setting up parties in Baltimore to introduce us to local movers and shakers such as the publisher of *The Baltimore Sun*, the mayor, and the governor. From the start, we tried to exercise leadership in corporate governance. We refused to consider golden parachutes and other excessive management perks which were common in the 1980s, and we soon required our full board to stand for election annually. Introducing the board to our new senior team, I asked each executive to talk for a few minutes entirely off the cuff without charts. I always prefer informal presentations, and these revealed our executives' enthusiasm.

The excitement had to be contagious for our new directors as well.

With the board and management in place, we rolled up our sleeves in earnest and began to tackle the job of remaking Commercial Credit. This may have been a sleepy little company in Baltimore, far away from the commercial intensity of New York, but that pushed us all the more to change the tone of how this company would be managed. We immediately leased rooms in nearby hotels, as we planned to commute from New York each week. Most of us lived out of the Harbor Court

Hotel. I had rented a suite with a spare bedroom and asked Jamie to take the extra room so that we might save some money.

Unfortunately for Jamie, I'm an early riser, and I'd typically light a cigar with my coffee. The smell seeped under his door and would wake him before his alarm sounded. We established our regimen quickly. We'd typically gather as a group for an early breakfast to plan our day's focus, work intensively all day, and reserve evenings for extended dinners where we could debate in further detail the important decisions that we needed to make.

We labored feverishly in those first months. Each Monday, we'd all meet at La Guardia for a 6:30 Piedmont flight, assuming that no crisis had come up, which sometimes necessitated our heading down on Sunday. For the next four days, we'd toil nonstop in Baltimore. On most Fridays, we'd shift back to New York and work out of our increasingly crammed offices in the Seagram Building where most of the team would share the conference room. I'd reserve most Saturdays for the team to convene at my home in Greenwich where we'd carry on our group discussions in a more relaxed setting. No detail was too small for us to ignore.

My lifestyle changed dramatically relative to what I had been accustomed to. Gone were the comforts and perks of working in a large company and the ease of a short commute. When I first saw Commercial Credit's ungainly glass and aluminum headquarters building on St. Paul Place, I knew I was entering alien territory. It felt like the building's contents hadn't been modernized in thirty years, and everything seemed plastic, at least the furniture and plants. Flying Piedmont Airlines or taking the occasional train during bad weather was a far cry from American Express's fleet of private jets. Still, after a year of downtime, I was glad to have a job again and didn't dwell on these things. When it came to commuting, I told myself that "more important than the mode of transportation is where the transportation is taking you."

Of course, being separated from Joanie was a hardship. Early on, we looked to buy a home in the Baltimore area. I sincerely considered this option in part to dispel the characterization, common in the local press, that I was just a corporate raider hell-bent on moving Commercial Credit out of the area. On one occasion, a reporter asked Bob Lipp what he was doing about finding a house. "I'm looking," he replied. The reporter didn't realize that what he meant was "I'm looking *for an answer to your question*." To the relief of my team, I didn't insist on a wholesale migration south. Only Jamie found it sensible to buy a home in the area since his wife was about to give birth to their second child.

Joanie felt that Commercial Credit was far better than the alternative of moving to San Francisco, the notion she detested when I was pursuing BankAmerica. She could see, too, that I was happy at being productive once again. However, the weekly separation soon became tedious. Joanie would come down for a day or two each month for what we joked were conjugal visits, but this arrangement still left a great deal to be desired.

Between working so intensively and having the physical distance between us most of the week, it was difficult to share what was going on in our lives. Joanie wanted to talk more about what was happening with our kids as well as her growing involvement with not-for-profit organizations such as Citymeals-on-Wheels and Brooklyn College, her alma mater. Joanie, too, is an outgoing person and sometimes felt stymied at not being able to socialize as a couple during the week. I understood the experience was isolating for her, but I felt there was little alternative. After all, so many things needed attention for our new venture to succeed.

The situation left something to be desired, but we both came to see that my need to be in Baltimore wouldn't last forever, and by now, at least the kids were grown. Occasionally, we'd have a lighter moment as when Bob Lipp, Jamie, and I insisted on placing a conference call to my wife to implore her to contact the chef at the Harbor Court. We were tired of the elaborate pheasant dish he kept foisting on us and wanted Joanie to pass along her recipe for roast chicken. She was a good sport and got the chef to add home-style chicken to his menu.

My wife and I also were becoming more integrated into Baltimore's social scene, which gave Joanie opportunities to come down and feel part of events and organizations in a new city.

———————

Personal adjustments were one thing, while overhauling Commercial Credit's corporate culture stood as our greatest challenge. The staff had settled into a comfortable lifestyle even as their company was falling apart around them. For instance, the last public bus to the suburbs left Baltimore at 4:30 P.M., so that effectively became quitting time for the headquarters staff. It didn't matter that the company had branches on the West Coast that needed support from the home office.

I immediately contacted the mayor and asked for better bus schedules, which he soon delivered. Then we encountered our first local snowstorm. I made it down from New York with relatively little delay only to find our building was empty. I went bananas: "How can I get here faster than everyone else when I'm traveling two hundred miles? If you want snow days, get a job with the government!" I then proceeded to call our human resources head and barked, "We can't afford to do business this way. Things have to change."

For our first order of business, we set out to methodically review the company's businesses. The work ethic of employees was a huge issue, but we soon found more evidence of an alien socialist corporate culture. A program called "Cars for Cons" represented a classic example of how the company had lost its bearings. Years earlier, Control Data's founder had wanted to do something socially responsible, so he directed Commercial Credit to lease cars to ex-cons out on parole to help give them a new start on life. The program turned out to be a bust, with three of the cars actually used to hold up Commercial Credit branches.

Of greater concern, the incentive system in the branches looked out of whack as no one in the field had any understanding of their profit contribution. Bonuses were modest and far too uniform to reward superior performance. The more we saw, the more we understood why no one had worked hard in this company for years. The ubiquitous coffee machines especially peeved Bob Lipp as the employees seemed to take constant coffee breaks. Then we uncovered the perk that gave each senior executive a company car. We immediately sent out a memo one Monday telling our people they had until Friday to either write a check for their car or surrender the keys.

Within our first month, we completed our initial review and began to communicate changes. In December, we announced we were cutting headquarters staff by 125 people or 10 percent, an action that would save nearly $5 million per year. Although the company was overstaffed, firing people wasn't easy. I worried about employee morale, but I also believed we had to be honest. Poor morale doesn't make for productive employees, and most preferred a quick and decisive cut in staffing rather than the insecurity of dribbling out the bad news.

Identifying cost cuts at headquarters and problematic loans and leases to sell or liquidate was fairly straightforward—recently built reserves and the fresh capital we raised in our stock offering facilitated our ability to exit our problematic exposures. I also insisted that we thoroughly reexamine how Commercial Credit approached its ongoing activities. Consumer finance would make or break our company, and we realized fast that reenergizing this business would represent our supreme challenge.

Bob Lipp and his team immediately zeroed in on the problem, instituting financial measurement and controls at the branch level. As the profit reporting took shape, we could see that the cost structures of most branches were out of whack, and we began to understand, too, that the lack of incentives was retarding growth and exacerbating profit pressures. We announced that we would no longer pay any bonus to the lowest performing 10 percent while we'd offer as much as 100 percent of one's salary for our top producers.

Beyond consumer finance, Commercial Credit maintained a meaningful presence in both the life and property and casualty insurance businesses. Again, these areas suffered from weak management. I quickly recruited John Sharp, a successful insurance industry entrepreneur, as a consultant and promised to give him a share of the profits if he could grow the life insurance business. John and his team produced fast results by expanding our product line, cutting costs, and getting our life product sold within our own channels. Unlike the life business, property and casualty insurance didn't exactly fit with a consumer finance company, but I knew something about the business having run Fireman's Fund and decided that Commercial Credit should try to make a go of it under its existing Gulf Insurance brand name.

By the beginning of 1987, I felt we were making progress, but I still required our managers to defend their businesses before their colleagues. On one occasion, we decided to sell a small subsidiary named American Indemnity, which was in the business of guaranteeing credit to suppliers. At first, we thought the business was profitable, but we began to worry about how its profits might react to an economic downturn. I still recall its manager making a presentation. After he left, I asked my team, "Did anyone understand a word this guy said?" When all shook their heads, I went on, "If we don't understand the business, why should we stay in it?"

We ended up approaching Dun & Bradstreet and reached a deal for it to take American Indemnity off our hands. I've always operated under the principle that it's best to exit those things that cannot be explained in plain English.

Looking back on our first eighteen months in Baltimore, I think most of my colleagues would agree that this was one of the most stimulating and enjoyable times in our professional lives. We were a bunch of vagabonds in an unfamiliar city, working exceptionally hard with a shared purpose. I looked at it almost like going to a sleepaway camp for boys—there was that same intensity of spirit and camaraderie. We were all learning a new business from scratch, and no one was afraid to speak out for fear of appearing foolish. Having mostly come from bureaucratic cultures, my colleagues relished the absence of politics and the entrepreneurial atmosphere.

The insecurity of being in a new business undoubtedly pushed me to work everyone hard, but I wanted to do everything possible to understand my new company and industry. Being a decisive decision maker was always one of my best attributes. If I was going to be successful in this new business, I'd need to develop good instincts and feel confident making fast decisions. Accordingly, I did a poor job delegating—I needed to know everything and to make the most important decisions.

My colleagues and I shared an eagerness to learn, and we naturally formed a cohesive team. Our dinners were memorable and seemed out of a B movie as we primed ourselves with rounds of cocktails and rare steaks, all the while sitting under a heavy cloud of cigar smoke. We'd array ourselves around an oval table in a private room at the Harbor Court, and I'd ask everyone to speak what was on their minds. If someone raised a problem, I expected that they'd also recommend a solution. All week, I'd roam the hallways asking questions of employees to gain perspectives of what was going on in the company. I'd then use this "field research" to push my colleagues on specific issues—it kept everyone on their toes and on top of our business.

I also learned to better control my temper. When I ran Shearson, I commonly blew off steam in public. Now I understood that more was at stake. I was in a strange city and didn't want to appear like a New York carpetbagger before the locally based managers. Still, it was tough to fully control myself. One explosion especially sticks in my mind. We had declared our first dividend. After we had issued our press release, Chuck Prince realized he had signed off on a record date that was a day short of what the rules allowed. When he came to me to inform me of his error, I cut him off midsentence with a three-minute tirade before I took note of his pale and stunned expression. Catching myself, I paused and sheepishly said, "I guess you now realize you're a full member of the team."

After working with one another for a year or so, our team lost some of its initial harmony, but I suppose that was natural. I had begun to lean on some of my colleagues more than others while our familiarity with one another enabled the weaker people to be more readily identified. It didn't take long for me to appreciate Bob Lipp and Jamie Dimon as the bright lights of the group. Bob's managerial skills were superb, and he quickly fired up the consumer finance business. Jamie, meanwhile, proved

excellent at surfacing issues and analyzing our business and capital structure. He took it upon himself to learn the risk/return tradeoffs of each
business, helped us exit unwanted exposures, and spearheaded our program to revive a commercial paper funding program. I looked at him as
a valuable junior partner, but a partner nonetheless who had the capacity
for tremendous personal growth. From the start, everyone knew he had
my ear and a lot of authority.

———————

Within a year of our IPO, our stock rose more than 50 percent and
reached the low $30s even as most other financial services stocks lan-
guished. The accomplishments made me feel tremendously proud. In
the space of a year, we had built a first-class management team, slashed
costs, boosted reserves, and communicated a clear recovery plan. The
rating agencies recognized our accomplishments and raised our debt
ratings time after time—in the first year alone, Standard & Poor's gave
us an unprecedented four-notch upgrade, taking us from "BB+" to
"A–." Armed with our new investment grade rating, we tapped the
public debt markets in January with a $100 million offering, proving
once and for all that we had regained access to institutional sources of
funding.

    We also began to build an equity culture. I wanted my managers
to think like owners and insisted they all take a meaningful portion of
their compensation in stock or options. If anyone wanted to sell their
stock, they knew they'd first need to secure my approval. With our
collective enthusiasm, this was far from an issue. More important, we
needed to completely alter Commercial Credit's culture and get our
entire workforce to feel like partners. At our very first management
meeting, we made up T-shirts that read "Work Hard" on the front and
"Buy Commercial Credit Stock" on the back. We ended up distributing
options all the way down to the branch staff.

    It took a few years for the Commercial Credit employees to un-
derstand the power of equity ownership, but they were amply rewarded
for their patience. Thanks to our exceptional performance, I'm proud

that many hardworking Commercial Credit employees, who might never have earned more than $35,000 per year in salary, eventually became millionaires owing to their stock in our company.

By the start of the fall of 1987, I felt optimistic. We were heading toward full-year earnings that would exceed $100 million, almost triple what we earned in 1986. When we arrived in Baltimore, Commercial Credit was producing only a 4 percent return on equity, which was well under the industry average; now, we were closing in on an impressive 18 percent.

Although I'd soon see the error of my timing, I pushed to buy Control Data's remaining stake in our company. We reached an agreement at the end of September to pay over $300 million in three installments at the prevailing price to take back the 20 percent stake. We issued $100 million in convertible bonds to help finance the trade. I've never liked the idea of having a large minority shareholder. Moreover, our shares still traded close to book value and seemed attractively priced.

In my excitement over our improving performance, I ignored my instincts about the market's health and a number of signals that the stock market was headed for trouble. A congressional committee was reconsidering the tax deductibility of interest on junk bonds, which threatened the pace of merger activity. The leadership of the Federal Reserve recently had changed hands as Alan Greenspan took over from Paul Volcker. Meanwhile, interest rates had bottomed two years earlier and were now heading higher.

I kicked myself when the market finally broke since I had seen many of the warning signs. On Black Monday, October 19, 1987, all hell broke loose. At once, investors responded to rising interest rates and surrendered to fear and then to panic, all in a matter of days if not hours. I was scared out of my wits. At its worst, the Dow swooned 600 points and closed the day with a gut-wrenching 30 percent drop. Unlike other market breaks, this one took on a global dimension and was fed by relatively new automated trading strategies which reinforced the market's volatility.

While I was now in a different business, my first instincts were to think like a Wall Street trader. I was terrified as I punched in ticker after ticker on the Quotron machine in my office. All our labors of the past year seemed to evaporate as I stared in amazement as Commercial Credit's stock price ticked down toward $17. I then decided to call some of our branch managers just as I would have called brokers during earlier market panics. This time, though, I heard a foreign set of voices: "Don't worry, Sandy. Our customers have nothing to do with Wall Street. It won't make a difference, and no one will jump out of any windows. Our business will be fine." I listened incredulously and felt these people either didn't give a damn or were whistling in the dark.

My distance from the securities business made me extra nervous. I wondered how my old firm would stand up to the suddenly turbulent market given that I had left my personal account there. In the years since Peter Cohen took over, I felt he was systematically destroying Shearson by taking excessive risks. My son, Marc, had remained at the firm and now worked as my broker. I insisted that he take the $5 million in municipal bonds then held in street name and get them registered and delivered to me for safekeeping as soon as possible.

The next thing I knew, there was an armed guard at my office door with five boxes of securities. Comically, I hadn't realized these were bearer bonds that couldn't be consolidated into a single bond. Instead, the big square bonds loaded with detachable coupons came in $5,000 denominations.

"What the hell am I going to do with all of these?" I screamed at Marc over the phone as my associates in the office all snickered. "I'd need a room in my house to store all of these. Get that guard to return and take these back!" When the security guard returned, he insisted we spend over an hour counting all the bonds to be sure they were all there.

More than at any other time in the prior year, I missed Wall Street. I suddenly felt far removed from the business I loved so much.

Regardless of my feelings, I quickly refocused on our business. Control Data probably wondered if we'd honor our buyback agreement. I soon allayed their concerns—my word was my bond. The plunge in our share price raised other issues. For one, I knew that some of my executives had borrowed heavily to purchase shares and I was aware of one individual who had seen half of his net worth evaporate. I took this colleague to lunch and offered to help if he was in a bind. I also wanted to send a signal to our employees and investors that we remained optimistic. Having just committed to the large share repurchase, we lacked the financial capacity for an expanded buyback program. Instead, I cajoled our top executives to agree to buy additional shares for their personal accounts. It was a modest but still tangible vote of confidence.

When I took over Commercial Credit, I assumed we'd ultimately acquire additional consumer finance companies and repeat my old consolidation formula. The crash, however, changed my calculations: Suddenly, I began to see a wider array of undervalued companies. I didn't surrender the idea of buying consumer finance franchises, but I decided to cast a wider net. Wall Street firms were particularly slow to recover given that investor confidence remained shaken, and before I knew it, I began to see chances for a return to the securities business.

E. F. Hutton especially whetted my appetite since the white-shoe firm had fallen on hard times. Late in the fall, I received a call from Bob Fomon, E. F. Hutton's retired CEO, who expressed distress at the way the firm had been managed under his successor. He offered to introduce me to some of his fellow board members. The offer was too tempting to pass up.

We ended up spending a couple of days looking over Hutton's books, but we immediately spotted financial and legal issues. I realized, too, that Fomon lacked support for his overture. In the end, E. F. Hutton's board decided to put the firm up for auction. I abhorred competitive deals and decided not to participate. Within days, Shearson announced it was paying $1 billion to buy E. F. Hutton. While it stung to lose the deal to Peter Cohen, I understood that it's always best to walk away when you can't move forward on your own terms.

Other acquisition opportunities soon came to my attention. Around the end of March 1988, I took a call from John McGillicuddy, CEO of Manufacturers Hanover, who told me he had decided to sell his consumer finance subsidiary in order to bolster his company's weakened balance sheet. Manny Hanny ran a first-rate consumer finance company which rivaled Commercial Credit in size and offered a complementary branch system. We soon performed due diligence and bid around $650 million.

Unfortunately, I learned that a third company, American General, had topped our bid by $50 million. I felt we had offered a full price and didn't want to stretch to win the deal. I had been in this spot enough times before to know that something better is always out there waiting to come along. Little did I realize that I wouldn't have to bide my time for long.

9

Back to the Future

For years, Ira Harris has been one of my favorite investment bankers. Enhanced by a long career at Lazard Frères and Salomon Brothers before that, Ira's reputation for creativity and thoughtfulness has only been matched by the size of his extensive Rolodex. By June 1988, other bankers were beating a path to my door with acquisition ideas, but I suspected I'd hear something novel when Ira invited himself to my New York office. True to form, my friend wasted little time in offering his bold suggestion: We should bid for Primerica, a company larger and far more diversified than our own. At once, I realized he was suggesting one of those enticing and most difficult of deals, the transformational merger.

Known as American Can until 1986, Primerica was the brainchild of Gerry Tsai, the onetime wunderkind money manager who skyrocketed to fame in the epic 1960s bull market. Indeed, Tsai completely upended American Can as he morphed it into Primerica, acquiring an array of financial and retail companies while shedding the mature manufacturing operations. By the late 1980s, Primerica owned Smith Barney, several insurance companies, a large mutual fund complex, a mortgage company, hotels, and retail ventures. The expansion initially had been impressive, but Tsai financed the growth with outsized leverage, and he had bought Smith Barney for an extravagant price in early 1987 just as the market peaked. In the wake of the October '87 crash, Primerica faced serious challenges, especially unexpected losses at Smith Barney—including a $100 million arbitrage loss related to United Airlines—and a hefty debt burden that threatened to undermine the company's financial stability. In the space of a year, Primerica's stock price had plunged to around $30 from a high in the mid-$50s.

It didn't take Ira Harris long to convince me. "I realize this would be a hefty deal, but these businesses would completely transform Commercial Credit and instantaneously offer you a range of businesses in which you could grow," he intoned, downplaying the fact that Primerica's value exceeded that of Commercial Credit. "I think Gerry would be open to a deal, and I could influence him on coming up with a reasonable price. Sandy, you're the perfect person to run Smith Barney and understand its potential value. You'd also get your arms around the rest of the business very quickly."

Ira knew I needed to find a way to broaden my company and that the unsettled stock market had aroused my eagerness to find attractively valued acquisitions. He must have known, too, that I had approached Gerry Tsai only a few months earlier after it had become known that Smith Barney had been hit with large arbitrage-related losses during the market's crash. At the time, I tried to convince Tsai to sell Smith Barney, but the idea never gained traction. It would have been embarrassing for him to take a large loss only a few months after buying the brokerage firm. My earlier approach might have fallen on deaf ears, but now Smith Barney's earnings pressures were intensifying as nervous investors fled the market. If that weren't bad enough, Moody's and Standard & Poor's seemed ready to cut Primerica's debt ratings.

Primerica captivated me immediately. I liked the idea that I might become the CEO of a broad-based company which would pose a complex management challenge. Returning to the securities business with Smith Barney also represented a powerful draw—after all, I had tried in vain to buy the unit in the 1970s, and the idea of ultimately prevailing appealed to my ego. Similarly, the Dow Jones Industrial Average included Primerica—as one of the thirty companies in the index, Primerica offered the brand status that I liked, not to mention the benefit of free advertising every time the newspapers listed the performance of the index's component companies.

As I dug into Primerica, I realized immediately that there were a lot of moving parts. Smith Barney offered an exciting opportunity to diversify into a business I knew very well, and I felt confident I could substantially boost performance. Smith Barney had stubbed its toe in its trading areas and ran a weak investment bank, but it possessed an excellent name and a high-quality sales force.

Primerica's insurance businesses seemed more complex as the firm owned an array of life, credit, property and casualty, and title insurance companies. I wondered whether the units in many cases were too small to be effective, but it meant a great deal that our insurance team, led by John Sharp, believed that there were decent franchises included within Primerica's portfolio of companies. John, more than most, spoke with credibility, as he had sold his company, Transport Life, to Gerry Tsai only a few years earlier and had stayed on as a consultant before coming to work for Commercial Credit.

While much of Primerica's insurance franchise may not have oozed competitive distinction, one company stood out. The A. L. Williams Corporation promoted a term life product via an army of part-time commission-based salespeople numbering nearly 150,000. Built from scratch in the 1970s by Art Williams, an evangelical supersalesman, the company had produced stellar growth as it took on traditional insurers and their high-cost whole life policies.

Rallying to the slogan of "Buy Term and Invest the Difference," A. L. Williams agents often used aggressive tactics to win business and provoked the ire of the traditional firms, which in turn frequently registered complaints with state regulators. As we studied the franchise, the complaints about its sales practices certainly caught my attention, but A. L. Williams's huge sales force, its concept of undercutting the established order, and its reach into middle America fascinated me. The notion of 150,000 agents promoting a business and potentially cross-selling other products seemed extraordinary.

Adding up Primerica's parts, I realized that a merger with Commercial Credit would give us multiple distribution systems and a range of products that would touch all the major consumer segments. Commercial Credit would focus on low-end consumers; A. L. Williams would concentrate on Middle America; and Smith Barney would serve high-net-worth clients. We'd have an enormous branch system with 1,800 offices spanning the country. Our market shares by product might be small, but we'd enjoy an unusually wide number of businesses in which to seek growth, a diversity of choice not available to other more narrowly based financial firms.

Still, there were issues, and big ones at that. My colleagues and I had no idea what Primerica's retail businesses were all about. Among other things, the company owned a mail order operation for household goods, a chain of record stores, and a couple of hotels. It was difficult to understand what risks these units posed.

We also would have to face up to a completely new management challenge. I had heard that Tsai and his executives maintained a distant relationship and even that the relationship between Tsai and the head of Smith Barney had ruptured openly in the wake of the October market crash. I wondered, too, what surprises lurked in Primerica's balance sheet. After all, Gerry Tsai's long streak of growing earnings had come to an abrupt end, which suggested that there were few reserves left to fall back upon.

Lastly, and most important, we'd need to accept a highly leveraged balance sheet if we really were to go forward and buy a company larger than our own. In virtually all my prior deals, I had hewn to the principle of seeking a conservative financial underpinning. If we were to acquire Primerica, we would be assuming an altogether different level of risk.

I quickly sought out Bob Greenhill at Morgan Stanley for his help in exploring Primerica's opening negotiating position. Not surprisingly, he came back saying Tsai wanted a lofty price in the low $40s, about a 40 percent premium over where Primerica then traded. I had no intention of paying anything close to that sort of figure, and I assumed it represented only a starting position. Tsai's reputation as an aggressive negotiator preceded him, and I calculated that Primerica's earnings challenges would only get tougher with time. Thus, I instructed Bob to counter that we wanted to meet further to better understand the company before offering a price of our own. With that, we bought time and began a protracted process of investigating the company in more detail.

Over the next couple of months, we intensively studied Primerica. Tsai's tough reputation made me wary, and I pushed my team to work the numbers hard. At the same time, I determined to treat Tsai carefully since in any deal, I understood he'd emerge as our largest shareholder. I made sure to let the investment bankers take the lead in the negotiations in order to minimize the risk of tension arising between Gerry Tsai and myself.

Fortunately, a few of our employees had relationships which helped us better understand Primerica. Our accounting head, Irwin Ettinger, knew Primerica's chief financial officer and benefited from especially good access to information. Meanwhile, John Sharp and his associates knew the right questions to ask about the insurance business given their past involvement with the company. Led by their insights and my own concerns that Tsai had run down reserves, we hammered away on Primerica's balance sheet and operating practices.

Jamie Dimon, too, rose to the occasion and proved his strong financial skills and ability to get his arms around the risk/return profile of Primerica's diverse businesses. From the start, he devoured Primerica's financial statements and spit out issues that demanded attention. I long since had stopped thinking of Jamie as a young kid out of school and increasingly looked to him first for advice on Primerica's toughest issues, feeling confident he'd speak his mind and challenge me with well-reasoned logic.

It didn't take long to realize that our fears relating to the quality of the balance sheet were well founded. The insurance business became our focal point as John Sharp and his team kept finding examples of inadequate reserves and questionable accounting practices. The insurance exposure to AIDS-related claims represented a particular concern. We also took note of our own shortcomings in understanding Primerica's retail businesses. Delving into Fingerhut, a retailer which specialized in mail order gift and household items, we soon started hearing repeated references to SKUs, which turned out to be shorthand for stock keeping units, a completely alien term which represented a key reference point for the business. We realized that we were completely out of our depth regarding the retailing businesses.

Finally, we began to understand Tsai's flawed management style, especially his failure to imbue his managers with a shared sense of purpose. The open rift between Smith Barney head George Vonder Linden and Gerry Tsai—the two had stopped speaking—indicated the lack of cohesion within Primerica. I had come to see that Tsai's forte was financial engineering, not running a company.

I was disappointed by what we learned in our due diligence, yet I believed the issues only gave us additional negotiating leverage over price. Our homework provided us with a roadmap on how to shore up the balance sheet and manage the company. I felt Primerica offered a unique opportunity for my brand of leadership. By early August, we were finally ready to discuss price in earnest.

Based on what we had learned, making an opening offer was tricky. We were coming up with values well below Tsai's asking price, but I wanted to manage the process in a way that would avoid putting him on the defensive. We would be offering stock with a dividend far below what Primerica had been paying, and I had no idea how Tsai might react to the loss of the dividends. I ended up doing most of the negotiating with Ira Harris instead of with Tsai directly. Kicking off the negotiation, I played a game of throwing out hypothetical prices in order to judge his reaction.

I started at $28 per share. "You're crazy," Ira barked. "Tsai will never talk to you there. You might as well forget it." Watching him carefully, I then replied, "Well, I might be prepared to go to $29." Harris laughed and told me there was no way we'd strike a deal if I refused to offer Tsai a premium to Primerica's market value. I didn't think Tsai had many alternative bidders and I knew things weren't going to get any easier for him, but I understood that we had to offer at least a modest premium to induce a handshake. After some additional posturing, we agreed to offer one share of our stock for each Primerica share plus $7 per share in cash ostensibly to make up for our lower dividend. Based on Commercial Credit's share price of $25, our offer came to just over $32 per share, a modest 7 percent premium to Primerica's market price and nearly 25 percent below Tsai's original asking price. The price seemed high relative to Primerica's current earnings power, but I believed the offer left open the prospect of a very healthy return assuming we could execute well and draw out the latent value embedded within the company.

With nowhere else to turn, Gerry Tsai took the bid.

Having reached a tentative agreement, we moved into the more formal and final stages of due diligence where we gained access to confidential information. We continued to find more reserve and accounting issues, but the biggest surprise related to the magnitude of management's golden parachutes. Primerica had disclosed such arrangements, but we and others on the outside had assumed a relatively manageable $30–$40 million figure.

To our surprise, we now learned the real figure was close to $100 million, with $30 million set to accrue to Tsai and the remaining amount to be split by ten executives. I never liked the idea of special arrangements for insiders and felt especially disgusted by what we had found. How could Tsai defend taking such a large payment for himself after so poorly managing his shareholders' interests? His company had lost half its value in the prior year, and he'd be taking money out of his shareholders' pockets for personal benefit.

I pushed back initially and had Greenhill convey that we had no intention of making such a large payment. Tsai stood his ground and even had the nerve to make additional demands such as a long-term management contract whereby he'd receive annual compensation, use of the corporate plane, and reimbursement for a wine cellar to "entertain clients."

The demands were outrageous and infuriated me, yet I saw that Tsai wasn't about to budge on most of the points. Greenhill finally looked me in the eye and calmly reminded me not to let my emotions get in the way. "This is paltry stuff," he noted. "Are you prepared to kill a deal valued at more than $1.5 billion over this issue?" Of course, Bob was right, and I relented. I told him sarcastically, "Go into the men's room with Ira and cut the deal. After all, that's the appropriate place to settle an issue like this!" We succeeded in eliminating the wine cellar perk, although I had to swallow hard in playing accomplice to the unseemly side deal.

Toward the end of almost every one of my negotiations, I tend to experience a wave of self-doubt, and Primerica certainly was no exception. Strategically, the deal felt right, and I knew we had a talented management team with spare capacity to handle a far more complex challenge. Most of my team agreed, although John Sharp notably withheld his approval. Throughout our due diligence, John had argued we'd be better off focusing on acquisitions to build our credit insurance business. I finally had to take him out to the woodshed and explain that his vision was far too narrow and out of sync with my thinking. Beyond Sharp, my other executives were excited by the deal, and our board similarly gave me a vote of confidence on the belief that we could do far better at Primerica than Tsai had done.

I thought once more about absorbing a company larger than our own and inheriting a highly leveraged balance sheet. Nonetheless, we all recognized that Primerica brought an array of businesses where competitors had proven the capacity to produce high profit margins. I finally decided that we had identified the bulk of Primerica's weak spots and that we'd start with sufficient reserves to show decent earnings growth initially.

At last, I turned to my wife and asked what she thought. In her inimitable way, Joanie turned the question back to me and asked if I felt good about the opportunity and what we had negotiated. With my affirmative reply, she simply said, "You've done your homework and you feel confident—so do it."

I took a deep breath, put my nervousness aside, and set myself to the task of proving to investors that we would succeed at our bold undertaking.

———————

On Monday, August 29, 1988, we announced our blockbuster deal and that we'd adopt the Primerica name. The prior Friday, rumors of a deal circulated, so the analysts were prepared for something that morning. Unfortunately, few were in a positive mood as they filed into our analyst presentation. Looking out over the sea of quizzical expressions, I laid out our case and explained we were buying a company with an intrinsically better valuation potential relative to Commercial Credit. I argued that we'd quickly move to divest nonstrategic assets, cut costs, and repay debt. Over time, we'd demonstrate our ability to cross-sell products across our newly diversified sales force. I reminded the audience that we had created excellent value since our IPO; indeed, over two years Commercial Credit's stock price had outpaced the market by advancing 25 percent. In my mind, these were powerful positives.

The analysts unfortunately chose to concentrate on more immediate issues.

The bulk of the questions zeroed in on Primerica's weak earnings and its leverage—several analysts peppered us with questions on how we planned to overcome the hit to our earnings per share and why we were accepting such stepped-up risk. Others asked why Smith Barney was still losing money a year after the crash or why we weren't more concerned about insurance exposures. Our decision to abide by the golden parachute payments, too, elicited scornful comments. I countered that we were buying a group of businesses at the bottom of their business cycles and that Primerica would add to our earnings within two years.

The analysts didn't trust Gerry Tsai or his numbers, and I suppose we added to their unease by the magnitude of the write-offs and reserve charges we planned to take. Within three days of our announcing the deal, our share price fell 8 percent, and by the December 15 closing date, our price plummeted 16 percent in an otherwise flat market. The hit to our stock price exceeded my expectations. This was a different reaction compared to when I announced my arrival at Commercial Credit. Then, investors were willing to bet on my record; now, the same analysts said "show me."

I might have been elated to have found a path back to the securities business and to running a diversified company, but the stock price reaction told me I had my work cut out for me.

———————

It took more than three months to receive the regulatory approvals needed to close the merger, but we began making changes immediately. I wanted to move quickly to get Smith Barney back on track. I came to see that Smith Barney suffered from a wholly inadequate management mind-set. From George Vonder Linden down, the company's top executives still managed the company as though it were a private partnership—they gave no second thought to paying out virtually all the profits in incentive compensation.

I was flabbergasted that these guys never felt a sense of obligation to produce a meaningful return for Gerry Tsai after he had bought the firm. In 1987, Smith Barney stubbed its toe badly on a misguided trading position relating to United Airlines and lost nearly $100 million. A year later, the firm had not yet returned to profitability, and plans called for excessive bonus payouts that bore no relation to profits. I wasted no time in formulating an action plan: We'd shore up management and change the company mind-set; we'd overhaul compensation and eliminate unprofitable segments; and we'd aggressively cut fixed costs and repair operations.

Even before we announced the merger, I had made an extra effort to reach out to Frank Zarb, my old friend who had played an important role in building our back office back in the late 1960s and who had overseen our operations in the 1970s. Frank had worked for Lazard Frères for nearly ten years by now and had made his fortune. I began asking Frank for his advice on Smith Barney in his capacity as a member of our board, hoping indirectly to pique his interest. As I had suspected, Frank soon became excited about the opportunity to repair Smith Barney, and we began to talk more openly about the possibility of his returning to work for me.

I knew I had to deal somehow with George Vonder Linden, whom I found consistently underwhelming, but the Smith Barney CEO ended up making it easy for me to decide on a course of action. At the end of September, he invited me out to California's Spanish Bay where he was hosting Smith Barney's President Council, an annual gathering of the firm's top retail brokers.

I suppose he assumed he could score points by having me out there, but once I arrived, I was shocked by what I saw. The securities business had been in a funk for a year, and Smith Barney was struggling. Instead of planning a substantive meeting, the company was entertaining its employees with puff presentations and afternoons of golf. The firm was about to come under a new owner, yet Vonder Linden strangely had made no provision for me to speak to his troops even though I had traveled cross-country for the meeting.

Seeing that the program called for a break after the morning's main session—a political commentator from CNN blathering about the pending election—I strode up to Vonder Linden, who was standing outside the entrance door to the meeting room, and asked to speak to the brokers. Remarkably, he said he'd "appreciate" my not coming into the meeting as *he* wanted to talk to the brokers and say "nice things" about me. He probably reasoned it would be business as usual and that I'd be a completely hands-off owner.

Well, did he ever miscalculate! I angrily insisted over his objections that I wanted to say a few words and had to push past him to gain entrance to the room. It was at once insulting and weird. I ended up marching up to the podium and simply told the assembled group that I was eager to get to know them and work together. "Since no time has been scheduled for me to meet with you officially, please stop by the hospitality suite this afternoon for drinks—and please bring your spouses, too," I announced.

Later that day, Joanie and I received our new colleagues in an open-house session that ran well into the evening. The brokers plainly enjoyed the chance to trade war stories and ask about my plans for the business. Our interest in spouse participation—including the example set by Joanie's presence—also struck many as a change in emphasis since Smith Barney had never allowed spouses to participate in business meetings.

Still incredulous at Vonder Linden's poor judgment, I called Frank Zarb at home that night and implored him to leave Lazard immediately and come run Smith Barney. Frank and I already had arranged with Gerry Tsai for Frank to join us before the formal close of the merger, but the day's events gave us the pretext to close our deal immediately. On the plane back to New York, I informed George Vonder Linden that I wanted him to step aside. I promised we'd allow him to leave with respect but told him that Zarb had agreed to come in as CEO effective the following day. The next morning, we held a meeting for Smith Barney's top two hundred executives in order to introduce Frank. The executives realized that their cozy world had come to an abrupt end.

The lack of management depth extended beyond Vonder Linden, and I began reaching out to others to join Smith Barney. Frank's strengths applied mainly to administrative and operations areas, but I wanted to shore up the institutional and retail areas, too. By year end, Lew Glucksman, once the co-head of Lehman Brothers, signed on to manage our trading business, and I brought back Mike Panitch, one of my colleagues from the old Shearson days, to co-head retail. Jamie itched to be more involved with the securities business, and Frank encouraged him to help straighten out Smith Barney's financial measurement and control functions.

We soon turned our sights to specific opportunities. Jamie eagerly sought to involve himself in the securities business, and Frank seemed genuinely glad to have the benefit of his strong financial skills. It didn't take long for the two to devise a host of cost cuts. We shuttered a problematic bond trading unit in London, streamlined back office operations, and eliminated overlapping branches. I also had issues with the excessive pay awarded to Smith Barney's investment bankers, although Frank Zarb twisted my arm to avoid slashing the bonus pool at the start of 1989 given his concerns over prompting a mass exodus.

Still, the message soon went out that pay had to relate to performance and that we'd become far more discriminating in distinguishing between our best and worst producers. Over our first two years owning Smith Barney, expenses dropped decisively.

While expense realignments were important, we immediately saw that the key to reviving Smith Barney's profitability lay in better managing the retail business. Above all else, productivity represents the key to a successful brokerage operation. Smith Barney sported better than average revenues per broker even before we arrived, but we saw tangible ways to improve the business. We instituted a branch-based profit and loss statement and began paying incentives based on an objective profitability scale. Our new model matched the successful approach we had used in my old days at Shearson and removed subjective factors from how we'd pay people.

Overall, Smith Barney enjoyed a high-quality core retail business as its brokers typically sold blue chip stocks and shunned risky issues. The industry's largest firms overshadowed our modestly sized 2,200-person sales force in terms of raw numbers of brokers, yet we quickly determined that we'd make up for our smaller size with quality product, more cohesive management, and industry-leading productivity.

Whereas Smith Barney represented a relatively straightforward repositioning challenge, Primerica's retailing and specialty insurance businesses were far more diffuse and demanded a lot of attention over an extended period. We went to work immediately shedding marginal businesses, but we needed a few years to fully restructure Primerica. Ultimately, we sold off almost every business other than Smith Barney and A. L. Williams and put the capital to work far more productively in our core businesses.

Primerica's retail businesses especially needed prompt attention. They were a can of worms, and I especially did not like Fingerhut or the guy who ran it. After searching in vain for a buyer, I received a call from Ted Deikel, Fingerhut's former CEO, who expressed an interest in returning to run his old business. Deikel struck me as an impressive businessman, and we soon worked out a win-win deal in which he would buy an initial stake and become CEO once more, after which we'd sell the company to investors in a public offering. In mid-1990, we sold a 29 percent stake in an IPO, though the investor appetite was underwhelming. It ultimately took us another two and a half years to completely sell off Fingerhut. It required patience, but we finally shed the business at a fair price.

We also needed to address our specialty insurance businesses, as Primerica had collected a hodgepodge of disconnected businesses many of which suffered from dubious market positions and management. Only A. L. Williams seemed like a real keeper, and I viewed the other insurance units ambivalently. I may have been irritated at John Sharp when he persistently opposed our merger with Primerica, but I respected his years of experience in the insurance business and relied on him to sort out our newly expanded insurance business.

John still felt reasonably good about Transport Life, the company he had sold to Gerry Tsai and which wrote substandard life, accident/health, and credit-related policies. It took little time for John to uncover issues in nearly every other unit. We remedied some areas but soon determined that a couple of businesses suffered from unacceptable risk/return profiles. One unit, Penn Corp, relied on a door-to-door sales force and heavily promoted death benefit policies to pay for funerals. I didn't think the future of the insurance business would belong to salespeople making house calls, and to make matters worse, the company too often sold the death benefit policies to poor people at outrageous prices, a practice which certainly felt wrong. We ended up selling Penn Corp by the middle of 1990.

Another company we inherited, named Voyager, underwrote automobile-related warranty extensions. I soon understood that this was a small Southern company run by an unsophisticated person who would never mesh with our culture. Early on, this guy came to one of our planning group meetings and declared in a thick drawl, "All I care about is cash flowing into the bank. We've got plenty of cash so don't worry." Maybe he didn't worry, but I did plenty. The business was at the mercy of second-rate used-car dealers and body shops whose honesty in providing appraisals we had to question constantly. We ended up restructuring the business and selling it, though it took a couple of years to off-load the unit. Our issues with Voyager provided me with one important business lesson: If it has wheels, look the other way!

———————————

Although we had plenty of surprises, not all of these were negative. At first blush, the A. L. Williams Corporation stood out as the quirkiest organization I ever encountered, yet it somehow had found the road to success. I may have felt underwhelmed by our other insurance businesses; however, the more I saw of A. L. Williams, the more I believed we had tapped into something unique and powerful. Art Williams had founded the company in 1977 and within ten years had amassed 150,000 part-time insurance agents who wrote over $90 billion in policies, surpassing Prudential and making A. L. Williams the largest underwriter of life insurance in the country.

Based in Duluth, Georgia, the company possessed a unique culture and business model. Art Williams advanced the theory that ordinary people were being ripped off by large life insurance companies which overcharged and provided mediocre investment returns on whole life policies. He understood that individuals would be better off buying low-cost term insurance and using the savings to either pay down debt or invest in other savings vehicles, thus his rallying cry "Buy Term and Invest the Difference."

Art also devised a multilevel approach to selling insurance whereby agents received commissions not only on the policies they wrote but also on business written by others whom they introduced to the company. Indeed, agents were eligible for overrides on business originated by several "generations" of referred agents. In other words, if agent A brought in agent B who brought in agent C, Agent A would earn a commission on agent C's policies, and so on down the line.

Pudgy and bald, Art's looks belied his exceptional talent as a salesman. A former Georgia high school football coach, he understood the art of motivating others and brought a Southern evangelical zeal to spurring on his legions of agents. A religious and moralistic culture pervaded the company, and Art and his agents commonly talked of being on a "crusade" to undermine the powerful entrenched insurance companies. A. L. Williams termed its agents "termites" since they had become so good at eating away at the business of the large traditional firms. The crusade also took aim at helping those on the lower rungs of society's economic ladder. It wasn't enough that agents would find a buyer for a term policy; they had to convince that person, too, that they could supplement their income meaningfully by signing on as an A. L. Williams agent.

Soon after we had acquired Primerica, Art invited me to speak at one of his company's sales conventions in Detroit. When I arrived, I learned I had to go to the city's basketball arena where fifteen thousand agents were gathered. Art already had whipped the crowd into a frenzy, and as I walked onstage, a surge of cheers rose up from the crowd.

I began to perspire profusely at the thought of having to speak before such a massive crowd. I've never gotten over my nervousness at speaking publicly, and this event made me nearly frantic. Still, I managed to stammer out a few words which somehow the crowd seemed to love. As if that weren't tough enough, Art next had me appear in the Georgia Dome to speak to fifty thousand producers. It was extraordinary!

From the moment I first looked at Primerica, I was captivated by the idea of tapping into this huge sales force in order to cross-sell products developed elsewhere in our company. Indeed, the idea of A. L. Williams agents selling mortgages from Commercial Credit and mutual funds from Smith Barney soon became a reality. Seeing more of A. L. Williams, I came to love the culture and the moving personal testaments.

Joanie and I began hearing hugely inspirational stories from people who had worked their way up the economic ladder. One person told us of living out of a car for six months before coming to the company and having the ability to move into a beautiful home because of the commissions he earned. Another had been a carpenter eking out a subsistence living and now directly or indirectly had introduced three thousand agents to A. L. Williams and could afford to put his kids in private school. It was fantastic, too, that the company had a spouse-inclusive culture; the partners of agents urged them on to earn higher commissions or to become eligible for reward trips.

Since she typically joined me at sales conferences, I wanted my wife to share in the experience of talking to the agents. At first, she teasingly balked, saying, "This wasn't part of the bargain when I married you." As always, Joanie readily went along and connected immediately with the hordes of agents as she told the story of how we had worked our way up from our nearly penniless days as newlyweds. At the Georgia Dome event, Joanie told a story of a repairman who used to service our apartment air-conditioning unit. One day, the laborer announced that he wanted a better life for himself and his two daughters and that he had decided to quit his job and work for A. L. Williams. Joanie related how she wished the guy well when all of a sudden a voice echoed from the arena's upper tier, "Hey, it's me. I'm that guy. I'm here! I'm here!" Joanie waved to him, and needless to say, the crowd went wild.

I loved A. L. Williams's sales force, but I saw that the company still had its weak spots. Notably, Art perhaps unconsciously had created a win-at-all-costs sales culture, and the company needed to exercise more care in controlling unprofessional practices.

A. L. Williams had taken on directly the powerful large insurance companies, which curried influence with state insurance regulators and the rating agencies. Following complaints by the major firms, various regulators constantly seemed to be investigating our sales practices. Consumers rarely complained, but that didn't stop our large competitors from alleging that we were encouraging people to uneconomically cancel existing policies.

In fairness, A. L. Williams sometimes succumbed to using almost slanderous practices. We'd receive complaints that our agents had picketed competitors' offices, while corporate advertisements showing Met Life's Snoopy as "roadkill" or anti-Prudential slogans like "Piss on the Rock" most certainly went overboard. Warding off the legal threat to our business kept Chuck Prince, our general counsel, extremely busy.

Early on, I emphasized to Art that we needed to clamp down on our sales practices. I pointed out that our ratings were suffering because of the high level of regulatory complaints we were receiving. A number of regulators, too, threatened us with more restrictive agent licensing rules, something which would delay our ability to put productive agents in the field and would cost us real money. Art professed to agree, and I thought we could manage things successfully. However, as I'd soon learn, Art was set in his ways and unable to change.

It was a classic founder's problem: He understood how to grow his company far better than how to control and manage it.

———————

The disturbing news came just before the July Fourth weekend in 1990. Trying to enjoy my annual vacation in the South of France, I learned that the U.S. attorney in Jacksonville, Florida, had opened an investigation of A. L. Williams and was looking into allegations that our unit had interfered inappropriately with a competing company. This clearly was a matter far different from our earlier regulatory issues; now it was the feds considering charging A. L. Williams with criminal actions. I could only speculate on what was afoot, but I promptly called Chuck Prince to have him get me the facts.

Within two weeks, I received Chuck's report. What I learned was troubling indeed. A former employee had gone off to create his own company modeled after A. L. Williams and began poaching our employees, encouraging them to write fictitious insurance policies before leaving. Typically, we paid a full year's commission up front on a new sale, so departing employees stood to benefit at our expense from the payment on the made-up policy.

I'm not sure how long this had been going on, but I now understood that A. L. Williams had sanctioned its own "hit squads" to infiltrate the competing company and play a tit-for-tat game. The other firm had hired a private investigator and had collected alleged evidence of wrongdoing in our company including a videotape of Art Williams exhorting employees to infiltrate our competitor. The private investigator, we surmised, had taken his information to the U.S. attorney, who then opened the formal investigation.

The entire mess doubly disturbed me as Art's involvement had begun only weeks after I had last insisted that he clean up A. L. Williams's sales practices. Indeed, I had spoken to him at the end of 1989 as we bought out his residual ownership interest, and I recall telling him specifically, "Art, you have to be sure we're doing good things here and not outside the bounds of honesty." I guess I had been naive to think that Art could change the way he approached the business. Even so, I was now incredulous that he had gotten involved in such a public pissing contest.

The back-and-forth "hit squads" didn't impact either organization's clients, and it was never clear whether the law had been broken. Nevertheless, I felt scared by what might happen next and worried that Art or his associates might attempt a cover-up of the facts. Thinking of the Watergate scandal, I understood that the cover-up could be worse than the original misdeed. In short order, I decided to take the painful step of asking Art to leave our company, knowing full well that this would immediately hurt A. L. Williams's business and lead to all sorts of complications in how we'd manage our sales organization. Our franchise and reputation, however, were at stake, and I believed that we couldn't afford to risk complicating our situation further.

Chuck and Ken Bialkin told me they thought I was overreacting in wanting Art to leave, but I saw no alternative. As much as I hate delivering bad news to others, I saw no choice on this occasion. I asked Art to meet me in our Armonk, New York, guesthouse and waited for his arrival with Chuck and Ken, who continued to suggest I didn't need to take such a draconian step. Art arrived, accompanied by his attorney, and we proceeded to the living room where the words spilled forth in staccato sentences: "This is very serious. I want to make sure we don't interfere with the judicial process. It's best for you and the company to take a leave of absence while we work together to handle this issue. My mind is made up, and I'd like you to agree with me today."

Art obviously never expected anything like this and became quite emotional. "I've done nothing wrong. If I'm dismissed, people will assume I'm guilty." Unyielding, I replied, "You will be better off taking a leave in order to fight this." Tearfully, Art reminded me over and over how the company was the most important thing in his life. I understood that he loved the company, the people, and the adulation, but what else could be done that wouldn't threaten to undermine the company further?

After an hour or so, we took a break, during which Chuck, Ken, and I walked out alone on the patio. Once more, the two pushed me to reconsider. "You're making a big mistake; it's not that bad; the business will suffer," they counseled. I recognized that I had the option to give Art another chance and to monitor his behavior closely, but that didn't solve the issue in my mind. "I'm afraid that even if he didn't do wrong, things could still get worse," I countered. "Any cover-up would be far worse. We can't take that risk for our company." Had this been a normal business issue, I would have preferred to arrive at a more consensual approach. In my heart, though, I understood that the toughest decisions in business often don't lend themselves to popular solutions. We went back inside where I promised Art that we'd hire him a first-rate criminal lawyer before sending him on his way.

I breathed deeply and felt enormous relief to have this confrontation behind me. It took a long while for the U.S. attorney to complete his investigation, and eventually the matter was dropped. Art would have liked the chance to return, but that would have been far too disruptive. To this day, Art would probably say that I treated him unfairly, yet I'd say that I saved his life by taking him out of the place where he might have been tempted to cover things up. Meanwhile, he held his shares in our company, which in later years propelled him into the *Forbes* list of the wealthiest people in the country.

Picking up the pieces at A. L. Williams was anything but easy. It took nearly five years and a succession of managers to finally stabilize the company. Without Art Williams's forceful personality, the sales force lost a great deal of its fervor, and many agents bridled at our attempts to rein in and better control sales practices. We also experienced waves of agent turnover. Within a year of Art's departure, our agent force had shrunk by a third.

Management turnover became almost comical. In five years, we went through six executives. We first installed Art's administrative person as an interim step, and soon had Bob Lipp take over. Bob incorrectly assumed that A. L. Williams would respond to traditional business controls, but his efforts to impose business goals and expense cuts only met with dismay and added turnover. Upon arriving, Bob went to an off-site meeting for regional vice presidents and decided that we should offer the group an in-house credit card with a $5,000 line of credit to enhance their loyalty. Unfortunately, by the end of the weekend meeting, a lot of the cards' lines were fully drawn, and we ended up losing money on a great many of the accounts. The cards were a bad omen as Bob continued to have difficulty figuring out what made this odd company tick.

Our agent force shrank at an alarming rate, and I finally decided we needed a better managerial solution. I thought I found the perfect answer in Pete Dawkins, the larger-than-life former Heisman Trophy winner, army general, Rhodes Scholar, and U.S. Senate candidate. I reasoned only another legend could replace Art and that Dawkins's sports background and charisma made him uniquely qualified.

From the start, Pete had his work cut out for him. During his first week, we heard that A. L. Williams planned a convention for 25,000 agents in Atlanta, and I suggested that we show up so that I might introduce him to the assembled agents. What I didn't realize was that this was not really a standard convention at all but rather the organizing meeting for a new company being set up by one of our departing top producers, a guy curiously named Hubert Humphrey.

Accompanied by Joanie, we arrived at the huge convention unannounced and strode out onto the stage. Humphrey's jaw dropped, and I'm sure everyone was confused, but the crowd still roared. After making a few comments, agents pressed toward me to shake hands or have me sign their notebooks, one of which Joanie asked if she could keep.

Leaving the convention, we returned to our car reveling in the adulation which by now I had taken for granted. Joanie quickly interrupted our conversation to ask, "Have you seen what's inside this notebook?" Shaking our heads, she informed us that this was in fact material copyrighted to a new company being set up by Humphrey. Stunned, we spent the next several days on the phone with our attorneys in a frantic effort to prevent the loss of so many producers. It was quite an introduction for Pete Dawkins.

Initially, the sales force reacted positively to Pete, but as time went by, he lacked the spontaneity to hold their attention. I also saw that he didn't have the background to understand a number of complicated financial issues. Accordingly, I decided to bring in a former colleague from American Express, Ed Cooperman, to share responsibility for managing the company. Cooperman would tend to administrative issues while Pete would focus on sales management. Once again, though, I made a poor judgment as Cooperman soon proved a disaster. Not only did he and Dawkins clash, but Cooperman wanted to go around the sales force and sell our product directly to customers via an infomercial strategy. Cooperman left in a matter of months.

At Pete Dawkins's urging, we had decided to rename A. L. Williams and adopted Primerica Financial Services (PFS) as the unit's new brand identity. However, the name change did little to address the underlying problems. Our agent force finally bottomed out, and Pete managed to stabilize volumes of newly written policies. PFS, though, remained a drag on our corporate earnings. We experimented with additional managers who soon became tagged "the flavor of the month."

Things didn't really improve until 1995. The recipe that finally worked was to bring in Joe Plumeri, who had a background managing stockbrokers and an outsized personality to motivate a sales force combined with a toughness to enforce quality standards and tightly manage costs. Within a year of taking charge, Joe turned PFS into an industry model on sales practices and also executed my long-held desire to cross-sell a broad range of products, such as home equity loans and mutual funds.

A. L. Williams (and the successor PFS) proved to be the major disappointment of the entire Primerica acquisition. We eventually sorted out the challenges, and other businesses picked up the slack, yet I never would have imagined we'd have to put so much effort into this part of the business.

———

Looking back, it's easy to gloss over the enormity of the issues we faced to reposition Primerica and build value for our shareholders. I'm normally highly averse to taking on excessive debt in acquisitions. On this occasion, I violated my rule since Primerica represented such an unusually good vehicle for Commercial Credit to break out of its narrow business model. There's no denying the deal tested our managerial abilities and our shareholders' patience. It took nearly two years for our share price to recover from its drubbing after we announced the deal.

The truth of the matter is that, for a period of time, Primerica diluted the earnings of our original owners, something I've never willingly accepted before or after. In 1989, for instance, our consumer finance business experienced strong 20 percent earnings growth, yet our consolidated earnings per share remained flat owing to the inclusion of Primerica's weaker earnings. We might have promised strong future earnings, but investors remained skeptical. By the middle of 1989, our stock price remained mired in the low $20s, barely above the price at which Commercial Credit had come public two and a half years earlier. I'm sure most of the shareholders had expected better, a realization which only made me more determined to execute the merger as flawlessly as possible.

In late 1989 and the first part of 1990, things looked up somewhat. We had returned Smith Barney to profitability, our insurance earnings stabilized, and we made some headway in disposing certain businesses and paying down debt. The rating agencies, thankfully, saw the progress and rewarded us with upgrades. Meanwhile, the stock market regained its footing in 1989 with a 27 percent advance for the broad averages. By mid-July 1990, our stock price had worked its way back to $37, and our shares were beginning to outperform the market indexes. Unfortunately, the upbeat news turned out to be short-lived as the bottom was about to fall out of the market, financial stocks, and most important, Primerica's share price.

Perhaps I should have seen my problem with Art Williams as an omen, since the economy soon began a steady slide into one of the most severe recessions in a long while. For nearly two years following the 1987 crash, the market somehow had managed to shrug off wide-ranging problems in corporate and financial sectors. Remarkably, investors had been willing to look the other way even as the chickens were coming home to roost after the debt binge of the 1980s.

A variety of circumstances in the early 1990s threatened investor confidence: the demise of the once-high-flying Drexel Burnham and the end of Michael Milken's reign over the junk bond market, news that the savings and loan industry required a massive bailout, and the failures of a host of weakly capitalized banks and overburdened corporate borrowers ranging from real estate developers to retailers to leveraged buyout firms.

The news that provided the spark to this combustible market finally came in August when Iraq invaded Kuwait and paved the way for the United States and its allies to go to war. The resulting geopolitical fears pulled the rug out from under the economy and the stock market and thereby exposed the shaky financial footings of many companies once and for all. In the space of only two months from its July high, our stock price fell below $26 per share, a 30 percent drop and twice as bad a percentage decline as the overall market performance. October proved to be the cruelest month as our share price sagged all the way to $18 per share.

I felt extraordinary stress during this time to the point of wondering whether we had accepted too much financial leverage to buy Primerica. I insisted to my colleagues that we had to stay focused on our business and work doubly hard to monitor and control our risks. Fortunately, our earnings remained reassuringly steady owing to the recession-resistant nature of our consumer finance business, the steep insurance-related reserves we had booked when we bought Primerica, and the significant cost cuts that were under way at Smith Barney. Finally, in December, the Federal Reserve came to the rescue and injected desperately needed liquidity back into the markets via a series of interest rate cuts that extended out over the next couple of years. By year end, our stock price recovered to $23 per share, and I began to breathe easier.

Aside from providing our company with an opportunity to showcase its earnings stability, this difficult period contained one other silver lining: It forced Joanie and me into a weekend getaway in the Adirondacks where we soon would find a beautiful country home. Joanie nearly had to force me to head upstate over one Halloween weekend, but she recognized that the pressure I had been under had strained our relationship and felt that we needed some time away to reconnect. I never had been to the Adirondacks and assumed she was going to take me to someplace in Appalachia.

When she told me we were staying at The Point, a luxury inn, and that I needed to bring a tuxedo, I rebelled and insisted on only taking a blazer and slacks. Fortunately, the dress code really was "black tie optional." Upon our arrival, The Point's general manager, Bill McNamee (who later would join our company), met us and showed us around. He also took us on a seven-mile hike alongside the pristine lake and through the pine-scented woods. I fell in love with the area immediately and also realized that I had stopped thinking about commercial paper and my other problems for the first time in weeks. I enjoyed the distraction and realized this was a great place to decompress and to get away from the hectic New York scene.

Before the hike ended, I asked Bill about the local real estate market. He replied there were two things worth seeing: a practical option just off The Point's property which would give us access to the hotel's services, and a second more isolated home which we assumed would be more ridiculous to pursue. We soon looked at the practical option and hated it. "Let's see 'ridiculous,'" we declared. Built by a Buffalo-based business magnate in 1920, the 140-acre property overlooked a shimmering lake and included a main home and separate guest and caretaker houses nestled in the woods. Joanie and I loved its beauty and serenity, and immediately made an offer which we closed on less than two months later. In subsequent years, I've done some of my best thinking up there and have used the area as a gathering place for our executives' annual planning sessions and for entertaining our good friends over long weekends. It's been a terrific investment, especially for its emotional rewards.

In January 1991, we reported that Primerica's earnings per share grew 14 percent during the prior year driven by a 23 percent gain from our consumer finance business. I felt reasonably good about the results, particularly as we had come through five months of market turmoil and were making steady progress repositioning our businesses. Still, we couldn't completely rid ourselves of our doubters. In April, an inexperienced reporter from *Forbes* visited us and wrote a cover story entitled

"Sandy Weill—Did He Get Taken This Time?" The piece got under my skin since it was chock-full of inaccuracies and argued that I had blundered for my shareholders in buying Primerica. Shrugging off the article, we worked with renewed fervor to prove ourselves.

Our earnings growth sharply outpaced our peers' in the early phase of the market's recovery as per share profits surged 31 percent in 1991 and 22 percent in 1992. Smith Barney's profits alone nearly tripled in 1991 as market activity recovered and we leveraged our streamlined operations and cost structure. In 1992, virtually all of our businesses delivered peak results. We had made incredible strides in reshuffling our company and rebuilding our balance sheet.

Since buying Primerica, we had shed $2.5 billion of assets, doubled our equity capital, and cut our debt by 50 percent. We also had enjoyed an unprecedented six years of consecutive ratings upgrades, an accomplishment in which I took great personal pride. Our stock price rocketed close to $40 per share by the middle of 1992 and had convincingly outperformed the broad market indexes over the prior two years. After four years of meandering in a relatively narrow range, our valuation finally had broken to the upside. In a satisfying vindication, Steve Forbes ran a new story in late 1992 admitting the magazine's error in suggesting Gerry Tsai had taken me.

I'm not sure if it was the shock of the credit crunch or the intensity of our repositioning challenges, but by September 1991, I decided we needed a more formal management structure and specifically wanted to recognize Jamie's contribution. I realized how important he had become to both our company and me personally. Jamie officially wore the title of chief financial officer, a job which demanded familiarity with our many businesses and sophistication in managing our funding and capital positions.

By now, his value had become much broader. Jamie had seized the lead in overhauling Smith Barney's financial controls even while he energetically analyzed the risk/return profile of each of our other businesses. I recognized that he also played a vital role in ensuring the openness of our culture and decision process. Jamie always offered up ideas freely and never acted defensively, and like few others, he knew how to stand up to me. I loved Jamie and felt we enjoyed a special relationship.

As much as I'd try to dismiss the comparison, I'd frequently look at Jamie and think of Peter Cohen in an earlier time. The analogy wasn't fair—after all, Jamie had proven his loyalty and was truly brilliant—yet I worried about not giving Jamie enough recognition, Peter's old complaint. The last thing I wanted was to make the same mistake twice. Against the advice of a couple of my board members who argued I was advancing Jamie too far too quickly, I announced that Jamie would become our company's new president. At thirty-five years old, he was the youngest president of any Fortune 500 company. I also promoted Bob Lipp and Frank Zarb to vice chairmanships and added all three executives to our board (reversing my insistence against inside directors). Although the press concentrated on Jamie's fancy new title, I thought it was understood inside the company that I valued each man equally.

Helped by our reviving earnings and stock price, I felt upbeat as we moved into the early 1990s. After all, we had grown from a small and narrowly based company with little cachet into an organization with diversified expansion opportunities. We had proven that we had the breadth of management to succeed under a variety of business conditions, and I once again had shown my ability to build value by acquiring a company experiencing duress and with businesses operating at the bottom of their cycles. Importantly, we were expanding at a time when many competitors were cutting back, an observation which only whetted my appetite to build Primerica further.

Just as Ira Harris had promised, the Commercial Credit–Primerica transaction completely transformed our company—we were the proverbial caterpillar which now had turned into a butterfly.

10

More Things for
More People

Things frequently go in and out of fashion in the financial services business, and by 1990, the appeal of the financial supermarket suddenly had lost its luster. For a decade, industry pundits had sung the praises of the large diversified financial services company, but in the wake of adversity, many now changed their tune. These new cynics took their lead from a variety of establishment firms—among them Sears, Prudential, General Electric, and, notably, American Express—which by then had faltered and had begun to repudiate the strategy. Meanwhile, bad loans, bloated costs, and deficient capital put many of the largest banks—such as BankAmerica, Citicorp, and Chase Manhattan—on the defensive, while depressed trading volumes and troubles in the fixed income markets similarly hurt much of the securities industry. Viewing the competitive scene, I considered how our company might benefit from our competitors' dislocations. With each step of progress sorting out Primerica, I grew more determined to leverage the industry's turmoil in order to push our company into a leadership position.

As events would soon show, I wouldn't have to wait long to turn my dream into a reality.

The conventional wisdom might have begun favoring narrower business models, yet I remained convinced that the industry naturally would consolidate, grow larger, and require more capital. After all, the trend had been unfolding for nearly thirty years. Financial innovation was proliferating at an accelerating tempo and included explosive growth in the mortgage and derivatives markets on a global basis. Suddenly, institutions and individual investors had found new tools to manage their risks more creatively. These new products only reinforced the need for larger and broader companies with the scale to invest in and integrate new services. I hated applying the term "financial services supermarket" to our company since I thought of supermarkets as very low-margin businesses. Instead, I preferred to think of our firm as a diversified financial services company. It was only a one-word substitution, but at least it didn't connote a pedestrian business model.

Having dealt with Primerica's biggest repositioning challenges, we started to articulate for investors the things that would distinguish our company. First and foremost, we announced in 1991 that we planned to become the preeminent U.S. financial institution. I understood the idea might sound grandiose to some, but I felt that we would only make strides if we set ambitious goals. We set our sights on doubling our earnings per share every five years, implying a 15 percent annual growth objective. Few companies had grown at such a rate over any length of time. I reasoned, though, that the industry's best companies ought to be able to grow at twice the pace of the economy and then grow additionally by acquisition.

The target felt right since our company already had delivered more than 20 percent annual growth since the 1986 IPO of Commercial Credit. By 1990, we had assembled three major business lines—Consumer, Investment, and Insurance Services—with annual pre-tax profits ranging from $100 million (Investment Services) to nearly $400 million (Insurance Services). Total pre-tax profits exceeded $600 million. By contrast, Commercial Credit had generated little more than $60 million in total pre-tax earnings just four years earlier.*

Beyond the performance goal, we laid out other reasons investors

---

*The issuance of new shares to purchase Primerica explains why the company's earnings per share grew by "only" a 20 percent compound rate during 1986–90.

should view us differently. We promised to build leading market shares and decisive cost advantages for each of our businesses. We'd stay financially strong and insist on "A" ratings for each of our units with publicly traded debt. And we committed to compensating our top executives with meaningful equity incentives and building inside stock ownership so that management's interest would be aligned with that of the shareholders.

Lastly, I was determined to demonstrate that we would execute flawlessly and prove that our diversified model worked even though others had tried and failed before. To drive home this point, we needed to deliver product excellence and tie our company together so as to cross-sell products across our various distribution channels. Other firms like American Express had tried a similar approach unsuccessfully, as they operated with a flawed management model which failed to reward internal cooperation.

Our efforts, in contrast, focused on stock- and options-based compensation which fostered shared values and teamwork. Our monthly planning meeting pulled together our top executives and drew them into informal discussions which aligned their agendas and highlighted ways to do more business with our existing customers. At one session, we might discuss how to offer credit cards to Smith Barney clients while at the next we'd focus on getting PFS to sell mortgages originated by our consumer finance arm.

As one example, even before closing the Primerica merger, I saw that A. L. Williams and its army of agents might provide the core of a cross-sell strategy. I wasted little time and asked Marge Magner, then a senior executive at Commercial Credit, to visit A. L. Williams's Atlanta headquarters in order to explore how we might harness the agent force in distributing Commercial Credit loans. Marge thrilled me when she came back with the idea for a great new product, the "$MART" loan (short for Save Money and Reduce Taxes), a second mortgage which would allow customers to take advantage of the tax laws and borrow against the equity in their homes while paying tax-deductible interest.

It was a terrific concept where we could educate middle America on how to benefit from the tax code while channeling the improved cash flow into saving more for their future. We also encouraged our agents to sell in-house mutual funds, another way to put teeth into the second half of our "Buy Term and Invest the Difference" slogan. It took time, but eventually we had thirty thousand PFS agents selling mutual funds—the largest fund sales force in the industry—and PFS became the largest source of consumer loans for Commercial Credit, taking responsibility for nearly $500 million in outstanding credits by 1992.

Unfortunately, educating investors about our differentiation and demonstrating our capacity to cross-sell product didn't produce over-night results. In fact, investor doubts on the wisdom of the Primerica deal nagged at us as we entered the 1990s. I may have gone against the grain in diversifying our business and accepting a leveraged balance sheet, but I felt confident we were heading in the right direction and determined to prove our doubters wrong. I understood the need to rebuild investor confidence, and I set a course to steer clear of more potentially contro-versial acquisitions. Or at least that was the intention.

Between 1989 and 1992, we made only two acquisitions. In early 1989, I assumed we had sorted out Smith Barney's back office sufficiently to consider buying another retail brokerage business. It seemed a no-brainer to put more business through our back office given that we enjoyed excess processing capacity. In April, we had an unusual oppor-tunity to seize upon the failure of Drexel Burnham, a company which had gained prominence during the 1980s only to fall victim to impro-prieties incurred in its junk bond business. Once Drexel ended up in bankruptcy, we were able to buy sixteen retail offices with about four hundred brokers and $100 million in revenues for virtually nothing. The deal enlarged our retail revenues by nearly 40 percent and should have been a slam dunk. Sadly, though, it proved a challenge to integrate since the newly acquired brokers bridled at our culture. I had over-estimated Smith Barney's capacity to absorb more change so soon after the Primerica deal. In the end, everything worked out, but it entailed a lot of effort for a modest return.

In the spring of 1990, we paid over $1 billion in cash for Barclays' U.S. consumer finance business, a decent-sized operation that broadened our distribution nationally and expanded receivables at our Commercial Credit unit to more than $5 billion, a 40 percent increase. This deal went off seamlessly. Unlike Smith Barney, Commercial Credit enjoyed deeper management and had been unaffected by the Primerica deal. Barclays ran a traditional finance company that made secured loans to lower-income households, but it also had a business where it financed recreational vehicles and where its credit quality had suffered. As a condition of our purchase, we forced the parent to set up substantial reserves on this business. Happily, we bought the company just as the losses were peaking, and the declining write-offs and ample reserves allowed for a strong profit recovery which immediately enhanced our earnings. The transaction provided our executives with a positive learning experience and a meaningful confidence boost.

While we wouldn't make another large investment until late 1992, we got close on a couple of acquisitions. The most notable would have been a deal for Shearson. Peter Cohen finally had gotten axed at the end of 1989, and within weeks, I approached Jim Robinson with the idea of buying back my old firm.

Jim and I came close to a deal by early March—we performed extensive due diligence and even consulted the rating agencies. The acquisition would have been a large bite for us, and we would have needed to rely on American Express for financing. Plainly, it had the potential to be complex enough to keep our investors on edge—something, as I've said, I would have wanted to avoid on almost any other deal at that time. Nonetheless, I reasoned that I could contain our risk since I still knew Shearson well and had many friends in senior management. This deal offered the potential to transform our brokerage business into a power-house. I figured, too, that we could structure a transaction whereby American Express would limit our risk.

Unfortunately, news of our talks somehow leaked, and *The New York Times* ran a front-page story that made it sound like I was the all-American success story returning to reconquer the company at Jim Robinson's expense. My heart sank as I read the article. Just as I had experienced with Fireman's Fund five years earlier, I knew Jim and his board would avoid entering into a transaction if they thought I'd get the better of the bargain. "There goes our deal," I told myself. "It'll never happen now since Jim's ego surely will get in the way." American Express's board still planned to meet to discuss our bid, but I anticipated the outcome. Not wanting to look like the loser, we preemptively announced that we were discontinuing our talks before the board could reject us. I'm sure Jim didn't appreciate the tactic.

Two years passed before we'd come so close on another deal. This time, Kidder Peabody was in play when its parent, General Electric, considered exiting from its disappointing foray into the securities business. By 1992, I had known GE CEO Jack Welch for a few years, having first met him at a pro-am golf tournament. GE had bought Kidder several years earlier, and as friends, Jack and I periodically traded observations on the securities business. By 1992, it had become public knowledge that GE was unhappy with Kidder, and I decided to approach Jack about taking the securities firm off his hands.

Following an initial meeting at one of GE's suburban Fairfield County, Connecticut, locations, we decided to commission teams to negotiate a deal. The talks proceeded smoothly. I wasn't interested in Kidder's fixed income business, which seemed to take big risks by betting on the direction of interest rates. Fortunately, GE agreed to carve out the unit and allow us to buy the more desirable retail, equities, and investment banking franchises where revenues of more than $1 billion were nearly three-quarters as large as those of Smith Barney. We would have paid a relatively modest premium to book value, which would have allowed GE to post a gain while we'd have the opportunity to earn an attractive return on our investment.

With the talks closing in on a final agreement over Memorial Day weekend, Jack and I flew in from our respective weekend homes to finalize the details at GE's Rockefeller Center headquarters. Jack, however, unexpectedly raised a variety of issues, and he seemed put off by what my colleagues and I had thought was a done deal. Ostensibly, the talks foundered on retiree health and pension benefits, and Jack finally decided to abort the deal. I think the real reason for the impasse was

Jack's fear that the newspapers would conclude that I got the better half of the deal. It was the same issue that drove Jim Robinson from selling us Shearson two years earlier. In the end, Jack and I shook hands and parted as friends.

———————

Our interest in Kidder Peabody was part of a broader appetite for larger deals now that Primerica's earnings and balance sheet had improved. By 1992, our profits were running 80 percent higher than when we first bought Gerry Tsai's company, and our leverage had returned to its normal conservative posture. If anything, we had at least several hundred million dollars of excess capital. Our renewed financial strength put us back in position to pounce on opportunities, and we scoured the landscape for attractive ideas.

Given that I didn't like formal presentations and never had a formal strategic planning department, some investors and even certain members of my team may have concluded that opportunism, rather than strategy, guided me. This view, though, was wrong. I *did* have a strategy: I wanted Primerica to be the best and most profitable financial firm in the United States as measured by customer attitudes, balance sheet strength, low-cost products, and diversified distribution. My brand of opportunism sprang from being on top of my company and industry and from feeling comfortable in acting fast. Each morning I'd repeat my daily regimen of studying the newspapers and asking, "What if this happens? What would I do?"

My wife claims I'm a "pragmatic dreamer." The dreamer says there's no stopping what our company might build while the pragmatist reminds me to execute carefully, taking one step at a time.

Only weeks after ending our talks for Kidder Peabody, a new and very different opportunity came our way. One midsummer morning, Bob Greenhill called to tell me that The Travelers Corporation had hired Morgan Stanley to find a large strategic investor. Based in Hartford, Travelers ranked as one of the insurance industry's giants and offered a range of services from property and casualty coverage to life insurance. "There's an opening here if you're interested in buying under a 20 percent stake," he began. "Travelers has gone through a rough patch, but most of its issues are now out in the open. I think the numbers could work and that it could be a good opportunity for you over time." Knowing Bob so well, I sensed from his voice that Travelers had already shopped widely for an investor and evidently had come up short. Yet, having known him for so long, I also felt confident he might be right in this case.

I told him we'd take a look.

Travelers indeed appeared a wounded giant. For years, it had contended with rising asbestos- and pollution-related claims, and now real estate had blindsided the company. Travelers had erred badly in the 1980s during the real estate boom. Thinking the good times would last forever, the company invested heavily in commercial mortgages, assuming the cash flow would cover a large volume of guaranteed investment contracts which it marketed to investors. Initially, Travelers earned an attractive spread. Unfortunately, the real estate market soon fell apart, and the large insurer suddenly became stuck with inadequate cash flow to service its obligations.

At the peak, Travelers had invested nearly 40 percent of its $50 billion in total assets in the real estate sector, an unbelievably large and risky position. The exposure had since fallen, yet Travelers still had $14 billion in real estate loans in 1992 of which troubled credits amounted to over $5 billion. The killer was that Travelers' stated equity capital amounted to only $4 billion. Investors now valued Travelers' stock at only 50 percent of book value. At the same time, the debt rating agencies threatened to cut Travelers' ratings, a risk which already had raised the company's cost of funding and undermined the company's life insurance segment whose business depended on top ratings.

I had qualms about investing further in the property and casualty business since the industry seemed inherently cyclical and had never delivered impressive returns or growth. Yet I took to heart Bob Greenhill's comment that Travelers nearly had reached the worst of its issues, and the possibility of investing on the cheap intrigued me as it had so often in the past. I wasn't thrilled about taking a minority interest, yet I understood that a capital infusion, if large enough to restore integrity to the balance sheet, might well spur a recovery in investor confidence and provide an attractive return on investment.

We met a number of times in Hartford that summer with Travelers' CEO, Ed Budd, and his team. Budd was a classic company man. At sixty years old, he had invested his entire career in the company, rising from an entry-level position in the mid-1950s to CEO by the early 1980s. He also ran an incredibly inward-looking company in an industry known for its paternalistic culture. Our meetings helped us understand Travelers' predicament. The company suffered from fat expenses and uninspired senior management, but the real estate issue dominated everything else and underscored the company's desperation. Fortunately, the core property and casualty underwriting function remained sound.

To move forward, we told Travelers that it would have to substantially bulk up its real estate reserves and rapidly liquidate its worst positions. We also required Travelers to step up reserves for asbestos and pollution exposures to be sure no surprises would surface in these areas. Just as important, we needed safeguards to protect our investment and wanted meaningful board representation and input on how the company would be run in the future. We demanded Travelers give us four board seats and that it set up a new management committee which would be responsible for investments, reserves, and new business oversight. We wanted to play a major, if not dominant, role on this committee in order to learn the company and stop any new foolishness from taking place.

Financially, we were prepared to inject $500 million in return for slightly more than a 20 percent ownership stake. Our offer worked out to represent $17 per share, a price modestly below the market. Ed Budd initially balked at our financial terms. He felt uncomfortable letting us buy at a discount and indicated he didn't want to give up more than an 18 percent stake. I remained steadfast, however, and insisted on the higher ownership percentage in order to gain a blocking position against a third party later coming in and undermining our economic interest. These terms were difficult for Budd to accept, yet I knew he had little room for maneuver. He might demur, but I was willing to wait him out.

Suddenly in late summer, an act of providence named Hurricane Andrew forced Ed Budd's hand. The killer storm approached the Florida Keys as a class five hurricane and maintained a strong category four rating as it slammed into the mainland south of Miami. The devastation was overwhelming, and overnight Travelers faced more than $400 million in claims.

The news couldn't have been worse for Ed and completely altered the dynamic of our negotiations. "If we invest $500 million and all that money goes out to pay the claims from Andrew, Travelers will be in virtually the same position as it is in today," I told him. "Your company won't have the money it needs to work its way out of its problems."

Ed listened quietly as I pressed my advantage: "I'm still willing to invest and stick to the price I offered you earlier, but the only way this will work will be if you allow us to take a more meaningful ownership stake." I then told him that we were willing to buy a 27 percent interest for a little over $700 million. To cap off my new proposal, I indicated that we wanted to pay $550 million in cash and offer our Gulf Insurance unit and part of Transport Life as the remaining consideration. I looked at both of these units as sub-scale and reasoned that they'd pose a conflict of interest if we ran them independently while owning a large stake in Travelers. I also figured investors gave us little credit for these businesses given their small size.

Travelers' prospects had turned dire following Andrew, and Budd had to accept our tough terms. He only insisted that Primerica accept a normal five-year standstill provision, under which we'd commit not to add to our stake without Travelers' approval. On September 21, 1992, we announced the transaction. By now, Travelers' stock price had fallen so it appeared we had offered a price in line with the market. In the first day's trading, Travelers' price surged an impressive 18 percent as investors concluded that the capital infusion might well save the company.

Primerica's price went sideways initially. Within days, however, investors jumped on board and bid our shares up as well. Following the official close of our investment that December, our stock price topped $48, more than a 17 percent advance from when we first announced the deal and equivalent to $8 billion in total market value.

Our company finally had regained its credibility with investors.

———

Before Travelers, I had never taken a minority stake in another company. The idea normally put me off since I don't like to surrender control to others. With Travelers, though, I calculated that we were really buying a low-cost option for an inside look at the company. Equally important, I reasoned that we'd have leverage over Budd's management decisions and eventually find a way to buy the company outright. Insurance historically had lagged behind the profitability and growth of other financial services businesses, but I had a strong sense that Travelers could benefit from deep cost cuts and better investment returns. I suspected, too, that the insurance business soon would begin to consolidate just as the banking and brokerage businesses had over recent years. My management team and I were proven acquirers, and I liked the idea that we might now apply our skill in a new business.

I understood that we'd have to move a step at a time, but I couldn't help but consider the possibility of an eventual full merger. Travelers offered a great brand, one of the oldest and most recognized names in the financial services business, and it opened up a variety of additional cross-selling opportunities. Affiliating with Travelers seemed a compelling way to further my vision of continuing to build a diversified financial services powerhouse.

Upon closing the transaction, we immediately convened the new special management committee that included Jamie, Bob Lipp, and Budd and his top three executives. Our agreement specified that this group would oversee the company, and the structure allowed us to learn the company better and monitor important decisions. I commissioned Bob Lipp to move to Hartford full-time so that he might fully engage Travelers' management and look for ways to improve the company. As a minority owner, we needed to walk a fine line, taking care not to push so hard as to make our new colleagues defensive. Bob Lipp's personality couldn't have been better for such an assignment. He operated with strong management instincts and always thought and argued in a reasoned way. Most important, Bob understood diplomacy and knew how to encourage people to make decisions without feeling forced.

Still, we needed to tread carefully to steer Travelers in the right direction. My colleagues and I blanched at the first presentations we observed since they all painted a far better picture than circumstances warranted. In one board meeting, I sat in amazement as the company's chief financial officer spun a positive assessment of business trends which I saw as a fantasy. Fortunately, our four board seats and our representation on the new management committee gave us the platform to challenge the Travelers executives and encourage them to reconsider their assumptions. The size of our investment also worked in our favor as it represented a wake-up call to management and the board that they needed to take us seriously. Before long, I could see a shift in tone as presentations adopted more realistic assumptions and as Travelers' executives began to see the need to act more forcefully.

The changes in attitude, however, were far from revolutionary, and Bob would continually come back from Hartford with tales of poor management and waste that often were as humorous as they were appalling. For instance, Travelers maintained a large weather forecasting department. We couldn't understand why Travelers' underwriters couldn't just watch the Weather Channel. And then there was the case of the broken water fountain in front of Travelers' headquarters. Rather than spend thousands of dollars on repairs, Bob instead convinced the facilities people to fill it with soil and use it as a tree planter. The icing on the cake came when we found that the company employed as chief medical officer someone who turned out to be a dentist.

Bob repeatedly urged me to approach Budd and push for more extensive changes. I understood Bob's frustration, but I counseled him to be careful in choosing his battles and to stay focused on the big picture. After all, our five-year standstill meant we needed to be careful with day-to-day issues and disappointments. Still, after a few months seeing Travelers from the inside, I wanted more than ever to find a way to take full control, and I understood I needed to woo Ed Budd in order to convince him to let us take over. Fortunately, Ed and I enjoyed a great deal of mutual respect and worked well together. I sensed he had tired of the challenges in running his company. I figured my best strategy simply would be to put my arm around Ed and lay on the charm. After all, what choice did I have?

———————

As busy as we were with Travelers, a stunning event at American Express hit the tape in late January 1993 and forced me to consider yet another possible deal. Incredibly, the American Express board ousted Jim Robinson as CEO and replaced him with my old friend Harvey Golub. American Express had just announced a more than $100 million loss for 1992, its second deficit in three years as bad decisions came home to roost. I normally don't take satisfaction in the travails of others, but I confess I felt vindicated.

For the next two days, I wondered how Harvey would reassess the company's strategy, and I obsessed on the idea that I might convince him to part with Shearson. In the decade since I hired Harvey to run IDS, we had remained friends, and the no-nonsense way he managed IDS indicated that he was a man of action. Finally, I telephoned him ostensibly to offer my congratulations but quickly raised the issue that was on the top of my mind. "I know you have all these issues with your balance sheet, Shearson, your New York real estate exposure, and so on," I said. "You should know that I'd be very interested if you decide to sell Shearson. I'm still very familiar with the company, and you could do a deal with me quickly."

From our prior attempt to buy the company in 1990, I also knew that American Express had an issue with the buildings on Greenwich Street in lower Manhattan that now housed Shearson's New York operations— they were carried on the balance sheet at around $1 billion or about twice the current market value. I considered this information especially valuable and used it to my advantage: "Harvey, I'd be prepared to take Shearson's buildings off your hands for whatever value American Express records them on its books." Harvey heard me out and said, "I'll have to think about it."

I wondered if I had come on too strong. I decided, however, that Harvey and I had known each other for years and that by now he had to appreciate my direct style.

My gambit worked. Harvey invited me to his apartment in the sleek Museum Tower that weekend to discuss terms. He had to realize that I offered an unusual solution since few firms would have the interest or capacity to take on Shearson. To Harvey's disappointment, I insisted that I only wanted to buy Shearson's retail operation and leave out Lehman Brothers, a business which I was convinced contained excessive trading risks. I told him we'd pay book value, which modestly exceeded $1 billion. Shearson's retail and asset management businesses normally would have deserved a healthy premium, but I argued the depreciated real estate on Shearson's two properties on Greenwich Street negated that value. Paying book value seemed fair and would allow American Express to exit the business without having to take an earnings hit.

Harvey asked if I wanted a cup of coffee, and we continued our negotiation around his kitchen table. "I'm okay with your valuation," he said, "but I'll need something more to take back to my board. I'd like for you to include an earn-out formula whereby American Express would be paid a share of Shearson's profits. That way, Shearson's future success will work to the advantage of both our companies." The proposal seemed fair, and I went along with giving American Express 10 percent of our combined brokerage earnings in excess of a base of $250 million (Smith Barney's current earnings) for the next five years. Once more, Harvey probed whether I'd include Lehman Brothers in the deal. "It's relatively small. Are you sure you don't want it?" he pushed. On this point, however, I remained adamant.

Seemingly in no time—and without even a refill on the coffee—we reached the outline of a deal.

For a definitive agreement, though, we had to settle a host of details, not the least of which involved the massive complexities of disentangling Shearson from Lehman Brothers. Panicked by the thought of a leak, I insisted we negotiate as long as possible in secrecy and only engage essential colleagues in the discussions. Over the next two weeks, Jamie and I faced off against Harvey and three or four of his lieutenants—a remarkably small team for a billion-dollar deal. At the end of February, we brought in the lawyers to draft the agreement. I figured it would be only a matter of time for word of the deal to get out, and sure enough, *The Wall Street Journal* broke the story on March 9 even as we needed a few more days to finalize our deal.

The investor reaction floored me. I knew we had negotiated a blockbuster deal—the largest ever in the securities industry—but Primerica's share price surged 12 percent the day the *Journal* story ran. For once, pre-publicity didn't kill the deal. Over the next three days, the stock rocketed 11 percent higher and closed the week at an all-time high of $49.50 (taking into account a recent three-for-two stock split, our unadjusted price would have topped $74 per share).*

Investors immediately understood the strategic and financial logic of our deal and how it enhanced the positioning of our newly named Smith Barney Shearson unit. Indeed, they trusted that I couldn't fail with my old company. In one fell swoop, we went from a niche position in the securities business with fewer than three thousand brokers to an industry leader with nearly twelve thousand spread out in five hundred offices. We also doubled our mutual fund assets and now managed over $100 billion, the fourth largest operation in the country.

With Smith Barney alone, we might have earned in the neighborhood of $250 million in a good year; now we'd have a shot at $1 billion in peak earnings from our brokerage side. It didn't take a genius to see that our company suddenly would enjoy a unique opportunity to tie together the brokerage business with PFS and Travelers and offer a potent mix of product manufacturing and distribution. Many investors believed that the price we paid implied a compelling financial return and

---

*American Express's stock also traded higher on the news, rising nearly 5 percent the day the news broke. Evidently, investors were happy that the company was finally addressing its issues and getting back to its core strengths now that Jim Robinson and Peter Cohen were both no longer with the company.

pointed out that the mutual funds business alone could have justified the price we paid.

The adulation expressed by investors felt great, though the chance to be reunited with my friends in the company I had founded touched me far more deeply. In all my years in business, the ecstasy felt like none other. I fantasized that my return was akin to MacArthur going back to the Philippines. Shortly after we closed the deal, I traveled around the country meeting the brokers—I probably visited with more than half of them in a two-week period. I always enjoyed spending time with brokers, and this was an absolute lovefest. Old friends hugged me and told me how happy they were to come home.

I listened intently as many brought me up to date on their personal lives or explained the business challenges they currently faced. Others told tales of the outrageous excesses that Peter Cohen and Jim Robinson allowed after I had left the company. I recoiled in anger at hearing of lavish off-sites at which celebrities like the Pointer Sisters or Liza Minnelli would perform or the meeting where Shearson hired the Ringling Brothers Circus and had Jim ride in on a large elephant followed by Peter on a smaller one. The image made me ill as I reflected on how the two had undermined the performance culture I had spent years building.

On balance, though, the joy of being back made it easy to cast aside the negative images.

Of course, absorbing Shearson brought its own set of issues. The two most pressing items related to financing the acquisition and operationally pulling Shearson and Lehman apart. Having recently sold our remaining interest in Fingerhut, we had sufficient cash on hand to pay for the bulk of the transaction, yet we still needed to raise $300 million. We elected to issue new shares outside the United States, which allowed us to avoid the normal delays in registering a domestic underwriting.

Dealing with Lehman, unfortunately, proved more complex. No one had ever separated a retail and institutional business like this before, and we purposely had left the mechanics of the breakup vague in our merger agreement. It didn't take long for our operations people to complain about the operational challenge. Shearson and Lehman had shared a common back office as well as payroll, general ledger, and stock loan systems. Before we could close the deal, we needed to solve Lehman's operational needs, devise an approach for distributing Lehman's underwriting deals and research, and figure out who to hire and how to divide profits.

I never imagined the difficulties, and it took months to solve the issues. Along the way, normally serene executives like my operations head, Bob Druskin, nearly lost their cool, and I didn't make things any easier with my demands for progress. I originally had hoped to conduct our first big conversion over Memorial Day weekend, but Bob told me we weren't close to being ready. I blew my stack only to hear Bob say, "You're CEO. If you want me to go forward, I will. But it will blow up the company!"

Naturally, I backed off while reminding him that each day's delay would cost us money. Finally, all the hard work and a series of ad hoc agreements—including provisions that we'd continue to clear Lehman's trades and distribute its research—put our operations in order, and we closed the purchase at the end of July. In addition to Bob, I have to give Jamie Dimon special credit for his role in the deal. Jamie helped me stay on top of important details during the negotiations, and he eagerly delved into the logistics of handling the merger.

In hindsight, I made a mistake by not buying Lehman Brothers. Harvey's asking price turned out to be remarkably low, especially given how well Lehman performed in later years. Unfortunately, I didn't understand the investment banking and trading side of the business very well in 1993 and focused too much on the potential negatives.

On a more mundane level, putting Smith Barney and Shearson together felt like a marriage of the Hatfields and McCoys—the cultures differed that much. Many Smith Barney brokers were especially upset. They reminded me that I had frequently promised to keep Smith Barney small, highly productive, and very personal. The brokers didn't understand that the business was changing rapidly and that we needed much larger scale in order to remain competitive. Visiting with countless colleagues, I apologized for blindsiding them and emphasized how we would now be far better positioned to develop new products and service our customers. I promised we'd remain personal despite our new size and reemphasized our Capital Accumulation Plan—our stock and options ownership program—and the value it offered in allowing discounted share purchases in the face of a surging stock price.

I also needed to make a tough call on who would manage our retail securities franchise. Mike Panitch had worked for me during Shearson's formative years and didn't think twice about coming back once I had bought Smith Barney. Time and again, he had proven his loyalty and his expertise in running a retail sales force. Shearson, however, came with a president, Joe Plumeri, who was an old friend as well. Joe lobbied hard to keep the top slot and promised he could hold together Shearson's nearly nine thousand brokers without having to resort to typical and costly retention bonuses. I made the choice to go with Joe and to coddle Shearson's brokers, who now comprised three-quarters of our sales force. I'm never good at communicating tough news to people, and filled with emotion, I struggled to convey my decision to Panitch. Fortunately, Frank Zarb stepped in and took the lead. Mike gallantly professed to understand; turning down another assignment, he instead chose to leave the company.

Joe Plumeri initially proved the right choice as he delivered on his promise to hold the brokers together. Less than 10 percent of our brokers turned over, a remarkably low rate and half the attrition we had assumed. I imagine we saved as much as a few hundred million dollars by avoiding the normal retention bonuses. The longtime Shearson brokers remembered how well they had done under my leadership as compared to the tough times working under Peter, and that perspective secured their loyalty.

Over the following year, I dealt with a variety of leadership issues at Smith Barney Shearson, but I categorically believe the deal to acquire Shearson proved one of my best. Right after we announced the transaction, the stock market took off, and we enjoyed significant positive earnings surprises. Within six months, our stock price surged nearly 30 percent, compounding the great performance we had enjoyed in late 1992 after investing in Travelers.

11

A Reach for Greatness

Buying Shearson helped convince me more than ever to go all the way and merge with Travelers. By mid-1993, we had seen enough from the inside to feel confident that purchasing the remaining 73 percent of the company would greatly enhance our shareholders' value. I also believed that owning Shearson and its army of brokers could energize the cross-selling of life insurance and annuity products to our high-net-worth clients. We had made steady progress in cutting Travelers' real estate exposure, and my colleagues agreed with me that a number of other big opportunities were out there only waiting to be seized. Without a change in control, however, all the cajoling in the world likely would not change Travelers' inherently plodding ways—it was a tradition-bound company inside a tradition-bound industry.

I worked hard but always respectfully to convince Ed Budd about the wisdom of a deal. I highlighted the Shearson cross-selling potential and stressed that we'd probably get bogged down over splitting incremental revenues if we remained separate companies. I also cultivated the Travelers board, which in many ways didn't need a great deal of convincing on the merits of merging.

The directors had become familiar with our decisive style, and I think many believed that Travelers lacked a viable next generation of managers. The board included a number of high-profile directors who couldn't afford to fool around. One in particular offered some encouraging advice: "You have to treat Budd with respect. You'll get to own the company if you approach Ed right and in a way that makes him feel it's good for the community."

By late summer, my constant nudging finally bore fruit. Tired by the seemingly endless struggle to fully resurrect his company, Ed asked me to prepare a board presentation that would lay out the value of combining. I didn't realize that Ed and his board at the time were soliciting other parties for similar pitches, but I can't see how any other firm could have competed with what we were ready to offer. Our pitch book highlighted Primerica's strong balance sheet and documented how our uniquely broad range of products and distribution would offer important earnings-related synergies.

We also laid out our superior record of financial performance. Earnings per share had compounded at 20 percent over the prior five years and had ended 1992 up by 22 percent. Meanwhile, our book value per share had increased at an 18 percent pace since 1987, and all the while our earnings volatility had been below average, attesting to our superior capacity to manage risks. To the extent it had any real alternatives, Travelers might have considered merging with another large insurer, but management had little credibility to pull off such a deal.

By now, Travelers was working with First Boston, and in early September I received a call from that firm's well-regarded M&A banker, Gary Parr, asking to see me. I invited Parr to Greenwich where we sat on my back patio and discussed what might induce Ed to part with Travelers. To my relief, I learned that Budd wasn't preoccupied with valuation. "Ed cares deeply about his people. The price is fine, but the real issue will be whether you can protect his employees' benefits," Parr stated. "If you can do that and treat Ed fairly, you'll probably have a deal."

My meeting with Parr proved to be the prelude to an unusually brief negotiation with Ed and his top executives. It only took a handful of sessions to cover the issues. By the third Saturday in September 1993, we came together one last time, once again at my house in Greenwich. The investment bankers did much of the talking, but it was clear that Budd had concluded that a merger served Travelers' best interest.

The conversation soon zeroed in on the employee benefit issue. Recalling employee-related issues that arose after we bought Primerica in which certain retiree health benefits were canceled, Budd and his team insisted Travelers needed guarantees for its people. Not missing a beat, we promised lifetime benefits for all eligible retirees.

With virtually all the issues settled, Ed made one last request: "I'd like you to honor the options that I have been granted in lieu of cash bonuses in recent years." The modest request and the way Ed had saved his personal issue for last underscored his noble character. Ed finally said that he wanted to take a walk with his team. The group headed off for a stroll in our apple orchard. When they returned, Ed extended his hand and announced, "You've got yourself a deal."

We offered stock worth $38 per share for the remainder of Travelers. A number of Travelers investors complained that Budd and his board hadn't done more to protect shareholder value—our deal represented only a 6 percent market premium—but I thought the shareholders really had little basis to be unhappy since their investment had more than doubled in the space of a year, thanks to our investment. As for our constituency, the reaction once again proved favorable—equity investors bid up our stock price while the rating agencies soon followed with upgrades on Travelers' debt. By the end of 1993, we had delivered on our objective of producing "A" ratings for all our units.

Once more, I felt great pride.

In the space of only six months, we had acquired leadership positions in the securities and insurance industries, a remarkable accomplishment. With Travelers, we had overcome the limitations imposed by our standstill agreement and had bought one of the great names in the financial services business for an all-in price around book value. Seeing the chance to enhance our corporate image, we changed the name of our parent company to the Travelers Group and adopted the familiar umbrella logo. Overnight, we even became the lead sponsor for the premier Masters golf tournament, one of the country's most widely watched sports events.

We closed the Travelers merger in December of 1993 and launched a blitzkrieg of changes. New senior management assignments and cost cutting took priority. We accelerated our real estate disposition efforts and stepped up our use of reinsurance to reduce our risks. We set to the task of updating our operations areas and spurring product cross-sales. And we devised incentives to promote growth, including provisions for extensive employee stock ownership. There remained so much low-hanging fruit that tangible results flowed quickly.

I also pushed hard for Travelers to deal with its health care business, an area in enormous flux during the early 1990s as Hillary Clinton was exploring a national health insurance system. Everyone knew of the impossibility of predicting cost trends and I struggled to understand how our business would work in the future.

Unlike the situation prior to our acquisition, Travelers now could afford to give up the health segment's modest level of profits, and I insisted we find an exit strategy. Unable to find a buyer, we entered into a joint venture with MetLife in June 1994 and hired a CEO from United Health, thinking we'd eventually pursue an IPO. Happily, the newfound scale from the joint venture enhanced the franchise's appeal, and the new CEO's contacts led to a sale of the company to United Health only four months later. Now that was superb execution!

Just when it felt our good fortune couldn't get any better, one more seemingly golden opportunity arose. This time, though, I wasn't looking at a company but rather at the chance to hire my longtime friend and superstar investment banker Bob Greenhill. An unfortunate victim of a power struggle at Morgan Stanley, Bob resigned in early 1993 rather than see his president's title taken away. Just as we were completing the Shearson deal, he asked if I'd invest in a boutique investment bank he planned to form—in return for my backing, he offered to give Smith Barney Shearson first rights on distributing his deals. I quickly turned around his proposition and proposed instead that he come work for us and build a first-class investment bank within Smith Barney Shearson.

Still euphoric from winning Shearson back, I only imagined the positives of having Bob join us. I especially had begun to train my sights on Merrill Lynch, still the largest securities firm, and marveled how this competitor had successfully melded its retail and investment banking businesses. With Smith Barney Shearson now operating a retail sales force nearly as large as Merrill's, I convinced myself that we had a tremendous chance to use our retail business as a springboard to build a leading investment bank and match our competitor's success.

Jamie, too, loved the idea of going after Greenhill. For more than a year, Jamie had complained about Frank Zarb's managerial weaknesses, and he now argued that we had the chance to trade up with Greenhill. Jamie insisted he had become the one responsible for Smith Barney's most important day-to-day decisions. He'd increasingly circumvent Frank in making decisions and come directly to me with complaints, especially about his need for more managerial support. With Greenhill's availability, it suddenly became easier to give Jamie the manpower he wanted.

Jamie and I soon began to negotiate a contract with Bob. The inveterate deal maker at once showed his negotiating savvy. He pushed for a ten-year contract under which we'd have to commit to share a portion of Smith Barney Shearson's profits. He also insisted that we immediately hire two lieutenants from Morgan Stanley with exceedingly lucrative compensation guarantees. Bob's brazenness stunned me. I never had cut a side deal like that for anyone. When I resisted, Bob quickly reminded us that we were the ones pulling him away from starting his own firm and that his terms represented the price we'd have to pay for him to join. By the end of our negotiation, we managed to reduce the contract period to seven years; it wasn't much of a concession on Bob's part, but by now I had gotten so excited about this opportunity that I swallowed hard and went along.

On June 25, we announced Bob's arrival at a press conference at the Drake Hotel. I thought Bob represented a real coup—throughout the 1970s and early 1980s, I had tried to build an investment bank at Shearson without success, but now I assumed I finally had found someone with the skills to deliver. Sporting a pair of bright yellow suspenders, the fifty-six-year-old Greenhill confidently strode to the podium and predicted that we'd build the "firm of tomorrow."

It was a memorable photo op. We had agreed to pay Bob 2 percent of Smith Barney Shearson's profits over a $50 million threshold plus a signing bonus of $20 million in stock. To show his commitment, Bob in turn bought $35 million more of our stock on the open market. Validating our decision, investors immediately bid up our stock nearly 8 percent—it suddenly had come to feel as though we could do no wrong.

I give Frank Zarb a lot of credit for sucking in his emotions that day. After all, he joined Bob and me at the press conference and put on a brave face. I had summoned the courage to tell him about Greenhill only two days earlier, and the news obviously floored him. Ashen, he managed to express his disappointment that I hadn't been able to come up with a better solution and warned prophetically that we should build our investment bank on distribution strength rather than star power. Frank stuck to the high road, though I knew he really had to feel angry and hurt. Frank accepted a different role and stayed with our company for another year and a half before taking the job of CEO at insurance broker Alexander and Alexander. Frank and I had been close for so long, and our friendship managed to survive.

———————

Bob Greenhill and Joanie share the same birthday—June 20—which I figured made for a positive omen. Geminis are known for having split personalities, and I reasoned that I had learned to get along so well with my wife that I'd probably enjoy a similar experience with Bob. The early returns in fact looked promising. Within three months of joining our company, Bob brought in some high-profile deals. He had a good relationship with Sumner Redstone, and we were soon advising Viacom on its $8 billion acquisition bid for Paramount Communications. Later, Viacom hired us again as it pursued Blockbuster Entertainment. Redstone and Blockbuster chief Wayne Huizenga negotiated in our offices, which made me feel as though Smith Barney Shearson finally had hit the big leagues. I also listened to Bob talk about his close relationship with Henry Kravis at KKR and began contemplating how we might win all sorts of new business from the prestigious buyout firm.

Having spent a lot of time together working on various deals over the years, Bob and Jamie liked and respected one another. The two now had adjacent offices and enthusiastically sought to collaborate. Bob understood he lacked experience in the retail area and seemed happy to let Jamie focus on that side of our business even if Bob kept formal responsibility for the unit. Bob tried his best to learn more about the retail side of our business, but it didn't come naturally to him, and he soon began spending the bulk of his time looking for new investment banking assignments. The shift in Bob's attention to the area in which he had the most experience didn't bother me since I figured Jamie would help oversee Smith Barney Shearson. I also planned to remain heavily engaged with our brokers.

Greenhill meant well, but it didn't take long for issues to surface regarding his management style. Bob avidly pursued his mandate to build a first-class investment bank and thought little about constraining costs. Almost overnight, he hired more than twenty investment bankers from Morgan Stanley with multiyear contracts involving unseemly amounts of money. He even paid his secretary a six-figure salary. Bob would argue we needed "to bring in expensive talent in order to build for the long term," but I soon began to harbor doubts about the wisdom of the approach. He'd keep stressing "talent" while I'd focus on the "expensive" part of the equation. At the same time, Bob did what came naturally, and he would hit the road for days at a time prospecting for new business. Soon, Jamie began complaining about Bob's frequent absences and difficulties in efficiently making decisions.

We also faced serious integration issues in our retail securities business. Joe Plumeri made good on his pledge to deliver the Shearson brokers with minimal attrition, which I considered a terrific accomplishment; however, other issues—largely tied to Joe's managerial style—began to take center stage. Joe managed by the force of his personality and surrounded himself mostly with yes-men.

In no time, our new retail head began allowing individual brokers in the field to circumvent the normal hierarchy and to appeal decisions directly to him. Regional and branch managers soon were up in arms at their loss of influence and control. Jamie saw that we were courting disaster. We had eleven thousand brokers and a like number of support people in the field who were receiving the message that they could go above their immediate superiors' heads and get results.

Tensions between Jamie and Joe soon mounted. Joe may have reported officially to Greenhill, but Bob's frequent absences and his lack of comfort with the retail business had created a power vacuum that Jamie eagerly filled. Jamie also questioned Shearson's broker compensation system. Unlike the objective approach we had relied upon during my old days running the company, Joe used a subjective model which paid bonuses for specific types of product sales. Jamie and I agreed that the system heavily politicized resource allocation and undermined brokers' confidence in how they'd be compensated.

Between Greenhill's frequent absences, our expense pressures, and the growing conflicts in the retail area, I decided to make Jamie chief operating officer of Smith Barney Shearson by the beginning of 1994. Bob wasn't keen on anything that would undermine his stature as CEO, but he went along with the promotion. Unfortunately, Jamie's new title did little to ameliorate frictions within the company, and business conditions soon began to deteriorate, which fanned resentments all the more. In February, the Federal Reserve shocked investors with a hike in interest rates, the first of several that followed. Soon, stocks plummeted and investment banking transactions dried up. Greenhill's expensive hiring campaign now pinched our earnings while the unhappiness among our brokers resonated all the more loudly.

In particular, Joe and Jamie began complaining even more vociferously about one another. Jamie described eroding morale among our regional managers and their complaints about Joe's idiosyncratic style. Ever the street fighter, Joe would counterpunch and loudly complain about Jamie meddling in his business. The war of words escalated steadily to the point where a fed-up Jamie insisted that I remove Joe.

I initially put off responding; however, complaints from the field were mounting steadily. I realized that Joe's micromanagement methods in fact were ineffective and incompatible with our emphasis on teamwork and objectivity.

Since I've never been good at delivering bad news, I hated having to confront a colleague like Joe whom I had known for years and who had done an excellent job delivering Shearson's sales force. I finally arranged for our old retail head, Mike Panitch, to return, and I sheepishly asked Bob Greenhill to do the dirty work of communicating the changes to Plumeri. In no time, Joe came running to my office insisting, "Are you going to let him do this to me?" But I stood by my decision. As consolation, I told Joe I wanted him to become a group vice chairman in charge of marketing, a role he took on for a year until I later moved him over to run PFS in 1995.

As if my issues with Joe weren't enough, I realized during 1994 that I had a larger headache brewing with Greenhill. The spurt of new business Bob brought in right after his arrival soon gave way to less-inspired performance, and I noticed that Bob and his newly hired team were struggling to bring over their old clients from Morgan Stanley.

In addition, Bob had convinced me that we needed to globalize, and he pushed to build a new Asian investment banking operation. We opened luxurious offices in Hong Kong and Beijing and began prowling for acquisitions in the region. As in the United States, though, our ambitions outstripped our ability to deliver revenues. With the stock market under pressure, our ballyhooed investment banking initiative began bleeding red ink. My early doubts regarding Bob's administrative skills suddenly multiplied, and I pushed Jamie to find ways to rein in our costs and limit Bob's free-spending ways.

In March, *The Wall Street Journal* ran a high-profile story which included a long but telling tagline: "Smith Barney fails to crack big leagues of investment banking—after two years of trying, it remains minor player despite pricey new hires." The depressing article enumerated a litany of woes too many of which, I'm sorry to say, were accurate. The article cited culture clashes between the Smith Barney and the ex–Morgan Stanley bankers, the story of a high-profile preferred stock offering we attempted on behalf of KKR that went awry, and our decision to reverse course and pull back from our expensive experiments in Asia.

At my urging, Jamie began to press Bob to focus more on the bottom line. Unfortunately, their relationship deteriorated as a result. Jamie started to criticize Bob openly in management meetings, a tactic that insulted his colleague. The problems between the two, in turn, injected friction into my relationship with each as they would take turns coming to me for support.

Before I knew it, I was cast into the impossible role of having to mediate between the two. I tried dealing with them on a one-off basis and alternatively by sitting them down together, but my weakness at confronting people undermined my wherewithal to broker a solution. I found myself stuck in the middle of each executive's tit-for-tat assertions.

Soon, Jamie started pushing for me to take decisive action. By the second half of 1995, he began insisting angrily that I fire Bob. I thought he was going too far. Greenhill was still one of the industry's outstanding investment bankers, and I thought we'd be negligent if we forced him out rather than find a constructive way out of our dilemma. For weeks, I tried to cajole each into a new arrangement where Bob would focus on managing clients—a "Mr. Outside"—while Jamie would manage the firm's day-to-day functions. Bob countered that he had come to our company as CEO and that he wouldn't tolerate a demotion. I argued we didn't have to change titles but could simply implement the change in practice, but Bob reminded me of our contract and resisted.

The situation spiraled downward, and I became angry and frustrated at both my colleagues. I wanted to shake Bob at times for his inflexibility, and I kicked myself for having been so compliant in offering him such a lucrative employment contract. I had other reasons to be upset when I looked at Jamie. I detected a pattern where Jamie seemed unable to get along with a variety of senior people. Bob only represented the latest conflict, as Jamie had worked hard to annihilate Zarb and Plumeri over the prior couple of years. Jamie, too, had begun to form a tight team of loyalists within Smith Barney Shearson on whom he relied for political support. Somehow, it seemed as though Jamie had a problem with anyone with whom I shared a close relationship, as though that person amounted to a personal threat. I understood the legitimacy of many of Jamie's points, but it bothered me that he couldn't operate more collegially.

Tortured by my associates' inability to get along, I devoted what felt like hundreds of hours trying to find a better outcome rather than simply severing my relationship with such a close friend. Joanie and I spent several Sunday dinners with Bob and his wife, Gayle, trying to come up with a solution, but at each get-together we'd hear chapter and verse from the two how Jamie and his team had worked to embarrass and discredit Bob. Bob and Gayle had become bitter and didn't hold back. One night at our New York home, Gayle finally broke down in a cathartic outburst. When she confessed how Bob so much wanted to prove himself after being unceremoniously shunted aside at Morgan Stanley after so many years, Joanie and I finally understood what this meant to them.

Finally, over one last dinner in December, Bob declared, "Either Jamie or I have to go. I know you won't fire Jamie, so it's clear what has to happen." As much as I hated final confrontations, it had become obvious we needed to make a change, and at that, we began negotiating our divorce.

During the final talks between the lawyers, I hoped we might salvage some value from our contract by offering to take an equity stake in a new firm that Bob subsequently planned to establish in lieu of making a severance payment. However, Bob played it tough and insisted we honor our agreement fully. In the end, the failure of our arrangement rested on my shoulders. Our friendship with Bob and Gayle survived after an initially awkward period.

I hated the controversy that took place among my colleagues in this period. Power struggles are always terrible and debilitating for a company. It's never a good thing when the "enemy" is in the office next door, and it's clear that a company will never achieve its best results when a lot of infighting takes place. I'd advise business leaders never to put up with such behavior and to consider firing any subordinate who undermines another. Allowing struggles is akin to tolerating a cancer: Even seemingly small issues can undermine an entire organization. Similarly, I'd tell young executives not to succumb to such behavior and to consider going elsewhere if one's firm doesn't place a top priority on teamwork.

After Bob left, Smith Barney Shearson's performance improved owing to better market conditions and tightened expense controls. Market shares in the equity business turned up as well. Much of the gain probably stemmed from the enhanced power of our retail distribution, but I believe our experience with Greenhill managed to send a positive message that, however long it might take, we intended to build a competitive investment banking business.

Some of my colleagues talked about our experience with Greenhill as a "reach for greatness" that came up short. Even with the disappointment, Travelers Group delivered exceptional performance in the early to middle 1990s. Ten years after I resurrected my career by taking Commercial Credit public, our company had produced an enviable record: Our earnings per share had grown at a 24 percent compound annual rate while our original shareholders earned a breathtaking 1,000 percent return on their investment.

In the course of a decade, our company's annual revenues had grown from $1 billion to $21 billion while our profits skyrocketed from $46 million to $2.3 billion. Our 1996 assets of $151 billion exceeded the 1986 level by thirty-one times while our shareholders' equity had zoomed nearly fourteenfold. In early 1997, a *Fortune* survey recognized my accomplishment in building shareholder value—I had grown the market value of our company by $33 billion in a decade.

The market capitalization of our company now surpassed that of American Express, a feat which I found deeply gratifying.

I felt especially pleased by how we had refuted the conventional wisdom which only a few years earlier called into question the outlook for large diversified financial services companies. Though other competitors had come up short, we succeeded in transforming Travelers Group into an industry leader in every one of its businesses, and I took particular pride in how we had amassed a first-class management team despite our occasional personnel issues. Our speedy overhaul of Smith Barney gave us the wherewithal to buy Shearson and trade up to an industry leadership position.

We also delivered a number of other victories. We made good on our promises to manage our balance sheet conservatively, to at least double our earnings every five years, and to avoid acquisitions that would hurt our earnings per share. Successful cross-selling set us apart as well. By 1996, real estate loans booked by PFS rose to $1.5 billion from a standing start six years earlier. Similarly, PFS sold an impressive $2.3 billion in mutual funds while it became the second largest distributor of Travelers annuities. Smith Barney, too, got into the act by selling mortgages and credit cards to its affluent investors.

In addition, we completely transformed our insurance business over a few short years by exiting a host of risky ventures and by getting back on offense. In late 1995, we announced a $4 billion deal to buy Aetna's property and casualty business for approximately book value. Buying our principal rival in the insurance business represented the capstone to our overhaul of this segment and cemented our leadership position in the industry. It confirmed one of the important assumptions we had made when we bought Travelers, namely that the insurance business would consolidate.

In later years, we analyzed how our insurance investments created potent value for our shareholders. In round numbers, we had paid $8 billion for both Travelers and Aetna while divestitures offset incremental investments. By 2002, the value had risen to over $26 billion, more than a threefold return in less than nine years. Insurance may have been a mature business, but that didn't stop us from making well-timed acquisitions and leveraging our superior management to produce stellar investment returns.

As much as I enjoy looking back on our collective accomplishments during this period, I'm proud, too, that my outside philanthropic activities grew in tandem with our company. My involvement with Carnegie Hall and Cornell University particularly flourished.

When Isaac Stern first asked me to chair Carnegie Hall's board of trustees in 1991, I felt there were other people on the board who deserved the honor more. I asked Isaac why he thought I'd be right for the job. He smiled and reminded me how closely we had worked in recent years.

"You've demonstrated an honest passion for the institution and understand what I'm trying to accomplish," he confided. "Sandy, you're the right person to execute my vision." As he had done many times before, Isaac honored me with his confidence and of course, it was impossible to turn him down. Fortunately, Carnegie Hall came with a strong staff, including its remarkable executive director, Judy Arron, whom I could rely upon to ease much of the demand on my time.

A few years later, in 1995, I also stepped up and became chairman of the Board of Overseers for Cornell's medical school. I had served on the board for almost ten years but had become active only in recent years. Initially, Joanie and I were intrigued by an initiative to integrate computers into the education program and to allow the students to work at their own pace and gain access to more information and teaching materials. We made a relatively modest-sized contribution to install computers in student dorms but soon decided to make a more substantial gift to establish a full-fledged computer lab/education center.

Later, I started to push the university to decentralize its decision making and to find ways to extend the tenure of the school's deans, who, until then, seemed to turn over every few years. I argued forcefully that it would be tough to have any continuity in leadership with such turnover.

My more visible contributions to the board's deliberations soon caught the university's attention, and that's when I was offered the chairmanship of the medical college's board. I liked the idea, but I also felt nervous about whether I knew enough to succeed in the role. Finally, I spoke to my predecessor, Arthur Mahon, who had planned to retire, and said I'd only take on the job if he'd agree to stay on as vice chairman. I reasoned that I'd gain from his perspective and that the school would benefit from a greater degree of continuity than in the past. Mahon thought it was strange to go from chairman to vice chairman, but he finally agreed, saying he assumed I'd make the job exciting.

Between my expanded philanthropic activities and Travelers' full agenda, I enjoyed plenty of stimulation and excitement. I've always enjoyed working hard and finding new challenges, and this period in my life felt especially gratifying even with the occasional setback. I had turned sixty years old in 1993, an age at which others might have considered slowing down. Maybe I had become hooked on the rush of competing and winning, but I felt as though I was only getting started. Energized, I wanted to find still more opportunities to expand our company. I also had come to appreciate the joys of donating money to worthy causes and increasingly found myself hoping for a strong stock price for an altogether new reason, namely to enable Joanie and me to donate more to our favorite causes.

After contrasting Travelers' strong performance with the setbacks of so many competitors, I decided my lifelong ambition to build a great and lasting company more than ever was within reach. With each success, however, my ambitions multiplied, and I now found myself thinking how we might export our success and win on a global stage.

12

Execution Angst

The fall of the Berlin Wall in 1989 unleashed dramatic changes for global capital markets and set the stage for a bull market of unprecedented proportions in the 1990s. Suddenly, the Cold War's end provoked investors to dream of an era of prosperity, and capital soon eagerly flowed across national boundaries. New technologies linked markets and accommodated huge increases in trading volumes while large multinational companies began scouring the globe for the cheapest sources of capital.

With the most respected financial system in the world, the United States benefited handsomely. Dick Grasso, chairman of the New York Stock Exchange, began making speeches claiming the public value of U.S.-listed equities would double to $20 trillion within a decade. The figure seemed reasonable taking into account the droves of foreign companies that already wanted to register for trading on U.S. exchanges.

Before 1994, I could only watch from the sidelines since we had our hands full integrating Primerica and then dealing with Travelers and Shearson. In investor meetings, we continued to highlight our company's domestic orientation, but I already had begun to consider how the securities markets might evolve and become more complex and global long term. It was becoming obvious that our clients had begun to think more globally and that underwriting and merger transactions were growing in size and frequency. Undoubtedly, we'd need to follow our clients abroad and invest significantly to service their needs.

I refused to let our internal disputes—especially those between Jamie Dimon and Bob Greenhill—stop me from investigating possible ways to globalize and, starting in 1994, we spoke secretly to a lot of potential partners. One of my first stops was Salomon Brothers. The firm had been thrown into turmoil in 1991 after the government accused it of rigging its bids during U.S. Treasury security auctions. Warren Buffett saved the firm with a large investment, but I reasoned he wasn't a long-term owner.

At the end of 1994, I approached CEO Deryck Maughan, whom I had earlier invited onto Carnegie Hall's board. Deryck seemed receptive initially, and we talked about a deal at some length. However, I could never get comfortable with Salomon's large proprietary trading activities. I tried to convince Deryck to keep the proprietary trading business and part instead with his investment banking and equities units, but he stood firm, saying it was all or nothing. With that, I chose nothing.

Looking past Salomon, I remained on the prowl and held discussions with a variety of companies, sometimes thinking in grand terms. For instance, I approached Jon Corzine just after he was named Goldman Sachs's CEO. Jon seemed genuinely interested; however, his partners had other ideas, and they put the kibosh on further talks. I also approached David Komansky at Merrill Lynch. I was now thinking grander than ever. The largest securities firm had proven its ability to meld its retail and investment banking business, something virtually no other firm had accomplished at the time. I salivated at combining the industry's top two securities firms and running an operation with over 23,000 brokers. Despite its size, Merrill suffered from high expenses which undermined its returns—Smith Barney Shearson, for instance, enjoyed rates of profitability 25 percent higher than Merrill's. To me, this represented pure opportunity.

Merrill seemed like a home run no matter how I came at it. Komansky ended up meeting me at my home in the city one evening. We sat in the den and talked over drinks about what a deal might mean. Inspired by the potential power of such a combination, I offered a significant inducement up front: I'd only insist on running the combined company for two years, after which he could take over. It was a powerful concession, especially as I hadn't given any thought to retiring until then. Still, I told myself that a Travelers-Merrill deal easily could represent enough of a crowning career achievement to induce me into an early retirement. Seemingly intrigued, David promised to report back after he had time to consult his colleagues.

Unfortunately, it didn't take long for David to close the door on further discussions. Without much elaboration, he relayed that his senior colleagues had vetoed the idea. Even though we had barely begun to talk, I felt unusually disappointed this time. Over my career, many deals got away from me, but the inability to snare this one stood as the only lost opportunity that I had trouble getting over. Merrill, after all, had long dominated the retail securities business and offered a hugely compelling fit.

Meanwhile, the 1990s bull market rolled on. By the end of 1996, investors had seen the broad stock market indexes increase by over 150 percent from their 1990 lows. The expansion had become the longest-running bull market in U.S. history, and no end seemed in sight. Combined with low interest rates and a cheap dollar, the ebullient market conditions put the wind in the sails of the securities business. I couldn't remember a time of such unbridled prosperity. Underwriting volumes hit records in both 1995 and 1996, and merger activity surged. Over the following couple of years, firms as diverse as Disney, Boeing, and British Telecom announced acquisitions worth tens of billions of dollars. The age of the mega-merger had arrived.

The environment might have been terrific, but I still found it frustrating. Despite all our efforts, we had not yet found a way to establish a leadership position for our investment bank (we ranked fifth in underwriting fees in 1996), and our securities franchise remained domestic in scope. The prolonged bull market, moreover, acted like a tide which raised all boats—unlike the past, we no longer saw many undervalued potential acquisition targets. I felt determined to address our competitive weakness as we entered 1997.

That January, I convened our management committee for our annual planning session. I had made it our custom to hold this session in the Adirondacks, a place where we could all relax and think out of the box. This time, I insisted we'd focus on how we might solve our missing global component, and I asked my colleague Mike Carpenter to lead a discussion where we'd identify a list of potential worthy targets. Formerly a management consultant and later the head of Kidder Peabody, Mike had joined our company two years earlier and sometimes acted as discussion leader at our planning sessions.

He kicked off this meeting by asserting what we all knew: We'd only get to the next level globally by way of an acquisition. Mike then listed all our competitors with international exposure and with at least a $5 billion market value. Weeding out firms domiciled outside the United States (due to the lack of a cultural fit), about twenty companies made the cut. We then discussed each name in turn and whittled down the list. We eliminated property and casualty insurers since we already had plenty of exposure to that slower growth sector. Next, we tossed out companies with aggressive risk cultures. The sifting continued until we arrived at a short list. The final group included American Express—I knew I wanted nothing to do with them again and discarded the name immediately. Next, there was Citicorp, but the giant bank dwarfed us in size and seemed an impractical option. Finally, my eyes settled on the one name that seemed compelling: J. P. Morgan.

I already had my eye on the white-shoe company. For one hundred years, J. P. Morgan had enjoyed an elite status like no other financial institution—it defined the term "the bankers' bank." Politicians and Federal Reserve chiefs routinely turned to the company during times of crisis and financial panic. In 1990, for instance, regulators had approached Morgan about possibly taking over the then ailing Citicorp. On that occasion, Morgan passed, but the incident—still recent—served as a high-profile reminder of Morgan's formidable reputation. Having traded up our company's name so frequently over the years, we thought Morgan seemed like the ultimate chance to go after the crème de la crème of brands.

J. P. Morgan appealed to me in other ways. It had served prestigious clients globally for decades and possessed huge private banking and asset management businesses that ran hundreds of billions of dollars in investments, franchise strengths which would complement Travelers'. Nevertheless, J. P. Morgan's financial performance in the mid-1990s had been far from pristine. The company's earnings were volatile and only in line with a 14–15 percent return on equity in 1995–96.

Investors might have winced, but I saw the potential for repairing the company's weaknesses and leveraging earnings. Besides, the lagging performance had cut into J. P. Morgan's valuation, as its market value stood at only a third of Travelers'—in a market which offered few bargains, J. P. Morgan looked undervalued and feasible to absorb financially.

Around this time, we had been discussing strategic options with Marty Lipton and his team of banking lawyers at Wachtell Lipton. The firm's lawyers captured my attention by claiming they could help us circumvent the legal issues involved with merging with a bank. Two powerful federal laws, the Bank Holding Company Act of the 1950s and the Depression-era Glass-Steagall Act, stood in our way—these laws prohibited commercial banks from diversifying and specifically ruled out affiliations with securities firms and insurance companies.

The laws struck many as anachronistic—especially as the prohibitions on banks encouraged excessive risk taking in their lending businesses and had led to repeated financial crises in recent years. Time and again, however, Congress proved it lacked the political will to overturn the outdated statutes. In the absence of reform, the Federal Reserve had stepped into the breach and had begun to allow well-capitalized banks to experiment with securities powers on a limited basis. By the late 1990s, for instance, a commercial bank could underwrite securities so long as the related business remained less than 25 percent of the bank's total revenues. It was this opening that Marty Lipton's team of lawyers claimed might give Travelers Group flexibility to find a bank partner.

For nearly a month, I mulled over J. P. Morgan and a couple of other names that had made our final cut. During the first week of February, however, I awoke one morning to startling news that served as a call to action: Morgan Stanley and Dean Witter had agreed to merge. The announcement shook me thoroughly. I had approached Dean Witter's CEO, Phil Purcell, only a couple of weeks earlier to test his interest in a deal, but he slyly convinced me he had no interest in affiliating with anyone. Even worse than our being misled, the news suggested Smith Barney was at risk of ending up the only large brokerage firm lacking a global capability.

Wasting little time, I decided to ask Dennis Weatherstone, J. P. Morgan's former CEO and a longtime friend, to introduce me to his successor, Sandy Warner. Meeting that spring, I could see at once that the Morgan Stanley–Dean Witter combination similarly had jolted J. P. Morgan's CEO. In fact, Warner caught me off guard by proposing that I should sell him Smith Barney and take an ownership stake in J. P. Morgan.

The Glass-Steagall limitations were on the top of his mind, and he reasoned that his idea could be structured in a way where both Morgan and Travelers could comply with the Federal Reserve's rules. Before he could go too far, however, I cut him off and simply declared, "Smith Barney isn't for sale, but I'd love to buy you." Warner countered that my idea wasn't feasible under current laws, but I made a point to disagree, telling him that our attorneys had assured me there was a way to accommodate a full merger. Warner remained skeptical. Still, we shared an incentive to find common ground, and we agreed to set up a task force to explore some sort of venture.

With that decision, we began weeks of extensive meetings which ran from April into July. Each company with which I've negotiated has had a style of its own—some talks go quickly while others get caught up in details. My associates and I saw quickly that Morgan's executives ran a process-intensive company; our negotiations, therefore, involved teams of executives, and the Morgan people determined to leave no stone unturned in their due diligence.

At the same time, I did my best to woo Sandy Warner on the merits of a merger, explaining how Travelers would add a diverse product array, cross-selling skills, and operations expertise, all of which Morgan lacked. "With our products and execution skills and your customer list, we can't lose," I ventured. In recent years, the concept of mergers of equals had become popular in the financial services industry, and I told Warner that I'd be willing to share the CEO title with him. We didn't negotiate price up front, but I communicated that I envisioned a low- or no-premium deal, which I thought would be best for both company's shareholders. I took for granted that as our executives learned more about one another, excitement over the deal naturally would grow and that we'd then be able to sort out the "social" issues of price and management structure.

Our talks continued at a slow but steady pace, and I remained optimistic we'd eventually strike a deal. Still, Warner kept questioning the legal issues, and I grew increasingly frustrated by the lack of detailed answers from Wachtell Lipton's lawyers. Finally, I called Ken Bialkin for his opinion. Kenny told me that Skadden, Arps had a top attorney in Washington who used to work for the Federal Reserve. Soon, he gave us the roadmap for getting the deal done. He pointed out that the Fed had the authority to review compliance with the banking laws and normally would grant a two- to five-year period before forcing divestiture of a business deemed not to be in compliance with the banking statutes.

In practice, that meant we could convert into a bank holding company and merge with a bank. We'd then have time to convince the Fed that our business complied with its regulations or, alternatively, lobby for a change in the law. When Kenny told us his legal expert would meet happily with Warner and his team, I decided to switch legal advisors and immediately brought in Skadden.

As much as we tried to educate Warner on the deal's feasibility, he professed skepticism. Finally, in June, we proposed a joint meeting with the Fed in order to get a more definitive read. Warner, however, balked for reasons which I couldn't explain at the time. I then asked for his permission to go to Washington without him and at least get my own answers. At that point, J. P. Morgan held what I think was its first board meeting on the matter—armed with his directors' evident blessing, Warner agreed so long as we promised not to mention J. P. Morgan's name. Kenny and I flew south and met Fed chairman Alan Greenspan and his general counsel, Virgil Mattingly.

To my delight, Greenspan corroborated Skadden's formula, though he warned that we should be prepared for the formidable task of convincing Congress to revise the nation's banking laws. He recalled that the Dutch financial conglomerate ING had tried to mix insurance and banking in the United States several years earlier and eventually had to divest its bank once its regulatory review period came to an end. "If you do this, you have to realize your chances of changing the law may not be that good," Greenspan warned us.

While I understood our legal formula might involve future issues, it still seemed good enough to warrant charging ahead. After we relayed the Fed's feedback, however, Warner suddenly shifted his demeanor and began to make demands which seemed wholly inconsistent with the spirit of our earlier negotiations. His first issue regarded price. Suddenly, Warner sent his general counsel over to demand a substantial market premium to Morgan's current share price. Losing my cool, I called Warner and bitterly complained about his nonsensical proposal.

Rather than negotiate over the phone, we hastily arranged to meet. When we sat down, however, I could see something was amiss. Warner's body language and his overall negotiating posture had undeniably changed. Stonily, Warner clung to his valuation demands, but he now also wanted something more. "If you buy my company, you aren't going to get very much unless you keep the Morgan culture," he began. "As I look at your executives, few, if any, are as good as my direct reports." Warner went on to argue that his executives should dominate the lineup of any future management team.

Then, in a real kick in the stomach, he proposed I start out as chairman and CEO but retire after a year. Flabbergasted, I thought this was all some sort of strange negotiating ploy. I tried to soften him, yet Warner remained distant and inflexible. The deal, once so promising, was now in trouble.

Before leaving, my negotiating partner reminded me he was heading off to his country home on Michigan's Upper Peninsula for a scheduled vacation. Angry and distressed, I stormed back to my office.

My temper cooled after a day or two, and I phoned Warner in

Michigan to suggest I fly out so that we might continue our conversation. I wasn't about to let this deal slip away without giving it my best shot. Warner greeted me at the airport, and we drove to his home where we met for two hours. I tried to convince him to drop his new conditions, but his perspective had hardened even further. Indeed, he now demanded that every one of the top nineteen jobs in the company go to a Morgan executive.

The arrogance was incredible—here was the CEO of a company which hadn't acquired anything of significance in thirty years suggesting his management team could be relied upon to complete a successful merger! He kept saying Morgan's value resided in its culture and that it was his obligation to protect his company's essence. It came out as "culture, culture, culture." Exasperated, I finally offered sarcastically, "I didn't realize you were in the yogurt business!"

Before I left, Warner at least conceded that he'd hold another board meeting to discuss the deal. The offer held out a sliver of hope that the merger still might be saved. Pulling out the stops, I invited Dennis Weatherstone to my home in the Adirondacks for one last strategy session. Dennis subsequently did what he could to broker a compromise, but it was clear Warner and I remained at loggerheads. Around the end of July, I learned that J. P. Morgan's board had voted down Travelers' merger proposal.

I felt debilitated by the rejection. Once again, our push to become global had been stymied. I never understood Warner's change of heart—either Morgan's byzantine internal politics or arrogance dampened his interest. I did my best to get over the disappointment and consoled myself that I shouldn't be too remorseful considering how Morgan's leadership had acted in our negotiation. At least we now had an understanding of how to merge with a bank, an incredibly valuable insight that we'd soon use to our advantage on a far larger scale. In the wake of our aborted talks, Morgan lost ground to stronger competitors and, three years later, merged with Chase Manhattan. Within a year of that combination, only one of Morgan's top executives remained in a senior position.

It goes to show that corporate culture is meaningless if you can't execute.

The failure to reach a deal with J. P. Morgan culminated an especially frustrating three-year period. I had tried so many tactics to propel our investment bank to leadership since 1994, yet the interlude with Greenhill and the successive merger talks had gotten us nowhere.

Unfortunately, another dynamic was at work during this period: My relationship with Jamie Dimon was becoming much more complex and difficult to manage. I might have been slow to detect the original seeds of the problem, but our relationship began to slide visibly in the wake of Greenhill's departure. By 1997, Jamie had become fixated on the notion that I hadn't recognized his contributions. He also exuded a sense of empowerment, probably wrought from his success at pushing past other executives, and increasingly challenged me to the point of rudeness in front of other executives. Worse still, Jamie began to freeze me out of Smith Barney meetings and to instruct his associates to avoid being open with me. In a surprisingly short time, I felt Jamie had changed from being a loyal lieutenant to running a company within a company, and I began to wonder if he ultimately sought to push me aside altogether.

How had our relationship devolved to this sad and unlikely state of affairs? Finding an answer to this question would probably challenge the best psychiatrist; however, it's important to understand that our relationship eroded slowly and that I didn't realize what was happening until our issues had become entrenched. While it's easy to find fault with Jamie's actions, I accept my share of the blame. In hindsight, our tensions stemmed from Jamie's desire for autonomy, our mutual insecurities, and interference from other executives.

Hiring Bob Greenhill proved more disruptive to our management process than anyone ever imagined. Bob had turned Smith Barney Shearson on its head. All of a sudden, Greenhill's imported Morgan Stanley team was pitted against our established executives. Whereas we had operated with a clear decision structure and respected the planning process, Greenhill didn't live by the same rules—instead, his unpredictable comings and goings injected friction and made it tough to manage effectively.

Jamie reacted to Bob's loose managerial style and tried to take matters into his own hands. During 1994–95, Jamie assembled a team of loyalists within Smith Barney Shearson and did what he could to run the firm's day-to-day affairs. Empowered by his success in managing the integration of Shearson, he subsequently forced out Joe Plumeri, projected himself into the retail business, and marginalized Bob Greenhill. It would be unfair not to recognize his accomplishments during this period, but his steamroller approach gave Jamie a sense of power and an overinflated ego.

Jamie's aggressive lobbying for me to fire Greenhill took me by surprise. In a year and a half, he had gone from excitedly backing Bob's hiring to wanting to assassinate him professionally. Although I understood we had a problem, Bob was too good a banker to cast off without exploring all our options. Jamie, however, simply refused to be patient and to consider compromise. The experience caused me to see Jamie in a new light. As CEO, I couldn't afford to have my senior hiring decisions constantly held hostage.

Jamie progressively became more confrontational in our monthly management meetings, and our colleagues sensed the deteriorating personal chemistry. In the past, Jamie rarely held back from expressing his thoughts or disagreeing with me. That never bothered me since I appreciated his thoughtful challenges. Yet now he had an altogether different tone; he spoke with more of an edge and framed his arguments more on emotion than on facts. Memorably, he confronted me almost to the point of rudeness as we debated the merits of buying Aetna's property and casualty business in late 1995. He believed we were at risk of growing too large in a business with uncertain economic appeal. At one meeting, he stood up in full view of my team and said accusingly, "You're making a mistake. *You, Sandy.*" All pretense of respectful disagreement had vanished.

A few weeks later, we held our annual planning meeting in the Adirondacks. My team typically put a lot of effort into their presentations at this event. This time, Jamie came ill prepared and spoke off the cuff. It looked like he considered himself above it all.

Jamie turned forty in 1996, and I suspect his biological clock had begun to influence his behavior—I could see he wanted to be his own man just as Peter Cohen had at the same age. Jamie's actions had grown more nettlesome. What bothered me most was the increasingly closed way that Jamie sought to run Smith Barney. By now, he had repeatedly asked me to stay away from his management meetings, a request I found insulting. "You intimidate my team, and they don't speak what's on their minds when you show up," he claimed. "You shouldn't go to everything; that's not reasonable. I'll brief you on whatever information you want."

Even if Jamie's argument might have had some merit, it incensed me that he had instructed his managers to deflect my requests for information. I hit the roof when Charlie Scharff, Smith Barney's chief financial officer, told me one day that he lacked authority to give me certain information. Squirming, he informed me that I'd need to talk first to Jamie. Preventing the CEO from speaking to anyone in the company was unconscionable. Smith Barney represented one of our largest businesses, and I'd be god-damned if Jamie was going to cut me out.

I saw that Jamie had assembled a coterie of about half a dozen executives who formed the core of his team, people like Charlie Scharff, vice chairman Lew Glucksman, capital markets head Steve Black, and his deputy, Jim Boshart. Jamie held sway over these loyalists, and I soon began receiving feedback that the group was stoking Jamie to be more independent. From what I heard, Jamie's "mafia" openly criticized me in front of others, implying that Jamie was better equipped to run the company. Jamie's reliance on this closed circle of insiders made me wonder if he had the capacity to reach out to and benefit from others with different skills and backgrounds, a capacity critical for management success.

The growing signs of a company within a company and my rift with Jamie had become an open wound, to the point where I'd frequently come home complaining to Joanie. At first, my wife tried to make light of things and to see it from Jamie's perspective, but she soon realized the issue was profoundly upsetting to me. Finally, in early 1996, I asked Jamie and his wife, Judy, to join Joanie and me for lunch during an off-site meeting we were holding at the Dorado Beach Hotel in Puerto Rico.

I wanted to include Judy so that my message would register clearly. We met for a room service lunch sitting on our private balcony overlooking the ocean, and we spoke for two hours about the growing strains in our relationship. I tried to communicate as directly as possible. "Jamie, I can't be effective as CEO if you're going to keep freezing me out of the flow of information. You know my management style, and we can't allow the current situation to persist where you or your colleagues won't respond to my questions." I barely got these words out, however, when Jamie's wife chimed in, "But Sandy, you're not giving Jamie enough credit. He's been working incredibly hard, and you don't appreciate him." Judy then added the punch line: "He doesn't even own as much stock as you!"

The final comment floored Joanie and me. It revealed how my lieutenant somehow had come to see himself as my equal. Of course, Jamie had played a very important role in our company, and we had enjoyed a special relationship. I undoubtedly had considered him my partner for many years but always a junior partner. At once, it had become clear that Jamie's self-image had raced ahead unchecked to the point of fantasy. I had a difficult time getting past Judy's observation, but I tried my best to hammer home that we needed to restore a more cohesive relationship. "Jamie, you obviously play a special role in our company, and my decisions to make you president of the parent company and chief operating officer of Smith Barney show that I've rewarded your contributions. You need to behave. If you do, all of this can be yours one day."

This wasn't the only occasion on which I confronted Jamie. Nonetheless, I fault myself for not recognizing the issue sooner and dealing with it more assertively. I've never had trouble facing down colleagues in the context of business decisions on which I've disagreed, but I've always struggled when confronting people on personal issues.

Moreover, I got caught up in my own insecurities. From the moment I hired Jamie, he proved a fabulous go-to guy, someone on whom I could always count. As he grew more involved in Smith Barney, however, I felt as though I couldn't always rely on him in the same way, which probably got under my skin. I especially wanted to stay on top of Smith Barney because of its importance to our company and out of my love for the securities business. Jamie might have detected a double standard if he perceived I didn't meddle with our consumer finance or insurance businesses to the same degree, but I felt these other businesses lacked the same pressing issues that confronted Smith Barney.

Unfortunately, Jamie's growing defensiveness unleashed my own set of insecurities as I began to think back on how Peter Cohen froze me out of Shearson in the 1980s—I never suspected Jamie of disloyalty, but I was determined not to lose my grip on the securities business after that unfortunate experience.

When I look back on my deteriorating relationship with Jamie, it saddens me that my kids—particularly Jessica—got caught in the crossfire. Having grown up in the brokerage business, I had seen countless brokers form family teams. I loved that practice, and from the day we set up our partnership in 1960, I never wanted to have anything in our governance that would rule out hiring family members.

Why would we arbitrarily prohibit hiring someone who had seen the business through the eyes of a parent and who would be dedicated, versus just hiring someone off the street? As our company grew, we employed lots of relatives in both the brokerage and operations areas. We thought of our company as a family business—it seemed a model that naturally would foster teamwork and shared values. As youngsters, Marc and Jessica took summer jobs with us, and I always hoped they'd come work for me one day.

After receiving their college degrees, my kids took their first jobs in our company. To my disappointment, each left after a short time to work elsewhere. Upon earning his MBA from Columbia in 1980, Marc spent a year with Shearson before leaving to work for Sandy Lewis, my old friend who had brokered my deal with Amex. He figured Sandy would teach him about trading and arbitrage. Marc stayed there for about three years but eventually decided to return to Shearson, where he managed money for the next six years.

Meanwhile, Jessica graduated from Cornell and initially took a job in American Express's credit card unit shortly after I joined the company. She hated that job and found her way to Shearson's mutual fund business where she stayed until her unit was sold. After that, she decided to strike out on her own and ended up working for several years marketing mutual funds for Prudential-Bache.

Marc and Jessica were wise to gain some experience in companies apart from mine; by the early 1990s, both decided to work for me again. I was thrilled with each arrival, though Joanie expressed some misgivings: She felt I could be overbearing and she wanted our kids to know that they could succeed on their own. Yet, after Marc and Jessica settled in, Joanie stopped pushing back. Marc arrived first, joining Smith Barney in 1990. Originally, I had hoped Lew Glucksman would mentor him, but Lew failed to live up to his promise and let my son flounder. Thankfully, Marc long has had an aptitude for investing, and within a couple of years, he found a more suitable job running our investment unit. Thanks to our acquisition of Travelers and its gigantic investment portfolio, Marc's job soon became important, and he was successful and well respected.

Jessica arrived around the beginning of 1994. She had excelled at Pru-Bache, but when her boss (my old colleague Wick Simmons) passed her over for a promotion "in favor of someone with a pedigree," she opted to leave. I encouraged Jessica to join Smith Barney, and Jamie seemed especially excited. For once, he worked closely with Joe Plumeri to design a meaningful job for her centered on mutual fund marketing.

I was elated to have both my children in the company, yet I didn't have any grandiose visions for how they should develop. In a publicly owned company, it was important that their immediate superiors should determine their progress; I tried to remain as hands-off as possible. When I'd occasionally ponder their future, I typically pictured Jessica running the private client group while I felt Marc's position in the investment area would satisfy him for the long term.

I realize now that bringing in my kids caused others to speculate that I was grooming them for important future assignments, including a path potentially to succeed me, but in truth, I was only thinking a step at a time. I never considered seriously about succession since I couldn't imagine retiring in those days. Whatever gossip-mongers might have said, I assumed at the time that Jamie stood first in line to succeed me eventually.

Marc and Jessica initially enjoyed their jobs. The investment area operated largely autonomously from the rest of the company and allowed Marc to focus on the investment process rather than having to fight political battles, something he never relished. Far more gregarious, Jessica took to her primary role marketing Smith Barney's mutual funds and seemed to get off to a fast start. Until then, our fund offerings hadn't been integrated effectively, an issue accentuated by the Shearson merger, and Jamie decided to promote Jessica to take control of the entire proprietary mutual fund function. The promotion came shortly after we removed Joe Plumeri from running retail—Jessica now reported to asset management head Jeff Lane.

Jamie and Jeff didn't have the best relationship, and Jamie apparently had to push for Jessica's promotion over another candidate favored by Lane. Jamie may have stood up for Jessica, but my daughter immediately was cast into a situation in which she had to justify her new boss's support. At nearly the same time, Jamie began assembling his management team, intent on bringing in a small group of people whose loyalty he could command. Perhaps because Jessica now worked for one of his rivals, Jamie never reached out to make Jessica an integral part of his team.

During 1995, Jessica worked hard at her new job. Smith Barney grappled with integrating its mutual fund offerings, and it faced a revolutionary new product offering from rival Charles Schwab. The discount broker had unveiled a new service which brought together hundreds of mutual funds, offering them to clients on a no-load basis, meaning it would levy no sales charge. Schwab assumed it would undercut the traditional brokers who generally relied on a sales load in return for advising clients on which funds to buy. Under its revolutionary conception, Schwab would make more money raking in large volumes of assets rather than settling for smaller asset flows with a traditional fee structure. The sudden appeal of no-load funds immediately placed traditional brokerage firms like Smith Barney on the defensive and pro-voked an extensive debate within our company.

By the time these internal conversations began, Jessica had started to feel alienated from Jamie's newly formed team. With Jamie, there was no gray area: Either you were on his team and roundly supported or you weren't. Jamie had begun distancing himself from my over-sight, and I assume he now looked at Jessica as someone who might interfere with his autonomy.

Smith Barney needed to decide how it would respond to Schwab, and unfortunately Jamie and Jessica staked out different positions. Jamie pushed for aggressively rolling out a no-load product of our own whereas Jessica emphasized the need to first sort out internal incentives and ac-counting before radically recasting our product. I remained above the fray during the early discussions and initially had no idea where Jessica and Jamie stood on the issue.

At some point, I decided to sit in on some of the discussions. Coin-cidentally, I adopted a point of view that turned out to resemble Jessica's position. Unwittingly, I created the erroneous perception that Jessica had lined up my support. Nothing was farther from the truth, but sadly, the incident probably hurt my daughter politically as she faced off against Jamie and his cohorts. I relied on Jamie's maturity to make the final decision, and we finally rolled out the no-load initiative (which turned out to be the right decision).

This story illustrates that I normally didn't ask Jessica about the specifics of her job—I didn't want to interfere. Accordingly, I was slow to appreciate my daughter's growing frustrations. I realize in hindsight that she felt increasingly isolated during 1995. Jamie apparently decided Jessica only possessed an aptitude for marketing, and he all too openly criticized her financial analyses. The repeated criticisms soon became humiliating, and before long, Jamie's cohorts eagerly piled on, thus abetting what I perceived as character assassination. Jessica increasingly felt trapped in a situation in which she couldn't possibly succeed.

Meanwhile, our asset management business remained fragmented under Jeff Lane's stewardship, and Jamie relentlessly pushed for a change in leadership. I finally agreed to reassign Jeff and allow Jamie to lead the search for a replacement. Jessica never asked for the job, but I knew she felt qualified so I suggested that Jamie consider promoting her. Jamie shot down the idea at once, calling into question Jessica's qualifications and insisting that we needed a "meritocracy."

Instead, Jamie gave me reasons why he wanted someone else to have the job. Under my brand of family involvement, where I'd count on others to manage my children, I felt it would be inappropriate to push further on Jessica's behalf. For the first time, I realized that having a family member in the firm had tied my hands in a way that led to a weak decision for our company and a hurtful treatment of my daughter.

Jessica rarely revealed her frustrations to me. There were a sufficient number of events, however, where Jessica didn't have to say anything for me to guess at her unhappiness. She spoke more openly to her mother, but Joanie always took care not to interfere with how I ran the business. Rather, Joanie used her influence to ease the pressure she sensed I placed on Jessica. "Don't make Jessica a captive of the company," she'd say. "You can't hold it against Jessica if she decides to leave the company." Facing that sort of jawboning from my wife, I did my best to stay out of Jessica's way and left her to fend on her own.

Increasingly frustrated by early 1996, Jessica approached our retail head, Mike Panitch, about switching into a management role in the field. Jessica reasoned correctly that she possessed good interpersonal skills and had a knack for relating to brokers. She calculated, too, that a retail job would distance her from Jamie. Jessica probably made it sound like she'd only consider a very senior job because Panitch apparently lectured her that she'd only have a shot at moving into the retail business if she'd start with a lesser branch or district manager job. I doubt that that was the message Jessica wanted to hear, and she evidently tabled the idea of moving into retail for several months. In October, she approached Panitch once more upon learning of the pending retirement of our West Coast division head. Mike resisted Jessica's pleas for a senior job while the two continued their dialogue.

Finally, Jamie made a pivotal decision which forced Jessica into her endgame. In February 1997, he announced three new additions to Smith Barney's management committee and noticeably omitted Jessica. Under some circumstances, it might not have been a cause célèbre, but this time Jamie included one of Smith Barney's women lawyers, Joan Guggenheimer. Many felt at the time that Jamie was explicitly trying to demonstrate diversity by including a woman. Jessica felt slighted since she had been out front in promoting women's issues within Smith Barney. To my daughter, it seemed a deliberate snub.

Following this incident, Jessica stepped up her discussions with others about changing jobs, including intensified conversations with Mike Panitch. I didn't realize it at the time, but she also began taking calls from executive search firms and soon lined up an offer to become president of a modest-sized money manager, John A. Levin & Company. I believe Jessica preferred to find an internal option, and Mike Panitch finally began talking to her about a more senior retail job on the West Coast.

Jessica wanted to get a feel for Jamie's attitude and initially seemed heartened by his self-professed enthusiasm for her taking the offer. However, when she went to close the deal with Panitch, she learned that the plan called for splitting the West Coast division into two and that she was being offered something less than a full division directorship. In the end, Jessica decided she had endured enough and all but decided to accept the outside job with John A. Levin.

I was attending the Masters golf tournament in April when Jessica called to say she was on the verge of leaving to take the job at John A. Levin. She correctly anticipated that I'd question her interest in joining such a small firm. She mentioned that Levin wanted to meet me for lunch, as though he were a suitor asking my blessing for my daughter's hand. I can't say that I was shocked by Jessica's decision to leave, yet it seemed we were losing an incredibly talented person for the worst of reasons. I pleaded for Jessica to hold off making her final decision a while longer.

Within days, I spoke to Jamie during our annual management meeting at the Greenbrier resort. I said, "If you think Jessica is a dummy, okay—if you think she's good, you should come up with something for her, or else she'll leave." Jamie seemed responsive, saying, "I *do* think she's good, and we *should* keep her." Assuming Jamie would speak to Jessica and straighten things out, Joanie and I headed off for our annual two-week vacation in France. To my dismay, however, I returned to learn that Jamie never approached Jessica and that my daughter had now firmly made up her mind to resign. Jamie's lack of follow-up infuriated me—Jessica might have ended up staying if only Jamie had demonstrated his support for her.

Jessica insisted on coming up to our house in the Adirondacks the following weekend to explain her decision. She knew how intensely I cared about the company and worried I'd never forgive her for leaving. Unfortunately, the intensity with which I've committed myself to work sometimes caused my kids to question where they stood in my priorities. I've always loved and respected my daughter and now especially appreciated her gesture. Still, I couldn't bring myself to bless her new venture. I couldn't understand why she was going to such a small firm when she had the ability to take on something much more substantial.

It didn't take long for Jessica to realize moving to Levin was a mistake. She soon left in favor of a job running a small start-up company called National Financial Partners. At the time, I scoffed again. I feel completely different today, however. In a remarkably short time, Jessica took her company public and within two years boosted the company's market capitalization to $1.5 billion, a value which implied that the original investors' stakes had soared roughly tenfold. She proved her ability to get along with all sorts of people and buy companies nationwide. Most important, she showed her breadth as a manager. Whatever Jamie may have thought, Jessica has demonstrated once and for all that her talents extend far beyond marketing—she's proven herself an exceptional CEO.

Jessica's experience opened my eyes to the problems of hiring family members in a large public company. After she left, Marc observed that others probably would come after him as well if he were to have a string of poor investment performance. I may have learned the obvious: Employing family too often ties a CEO's hands and compromises decisions. Jessica received no benefit for being my daughter. Rather, we sacrificed her talents precisely because of our relationship. That's what troubles me the most in retrospect. If I had it to do over again, I never would put my kids in that unfortunate position.

Needless to say, the press had a field day with Jessica's departure, playing up the idea that this was some sort of "family feud" and that Jessica had driven a wedge between Jamie and me. Of course, nothing could have been farther from the truth. Rather, Jessica's experience was a sideshow in my overall deteriorating relationship with Jamie. The news accounts only deepened my anger at Jamie, since someone on his team was feeding the reporters selective information that unfairly cast Jessica in a bad light. Wasn't it enough that they had driven her from the company? At the same time, reporters dwelled on comparing my relationship with Jamie to a "father and son" team. Joanie never liked that comparison since it demeaned the relationship I had with my children. In the wake of Jessica's departure, the analogy felt especially jarring and angered Joanie.

———

I'm typically an upbeat person. However, in early August 1997 I felt downcast. Our talks with J. P. Morgan had come to an abrupt end; our competitors were sprinting ahead of us in the race to globalize; the tensions between Jamie and me continued to intensify. In a fortuitous stroke of timing, I took a phone call from Salomon Brothers' CEO Deryck Maughan during the second week of the month and was pleasantly surprised by the message. "Sandy, I'm probably going to sell Salomon Brothers. I haven't talked to anybody about this yet, but I'm planning to go on vacation and consider my options. Think about it. If you're serious, I'd like to talk to you when I return." Caught off guard, I mumbled that of course I'd be interested and suggested getting together as soon as possible. Deryck, however, insisted we should wait until after his vacation.

As I hung up the phone, I marveled at the turn of events. Coincidentally, I had considered approaching Deryck during the prior year to see whether I might lure him into joining Smith Barney. My growing difficulties with Jamie had given rise to the idea. Tall and distinguished-looking, the urbane Englishman impressed me with his intelligence and ability to see the big picture. Moreover, Deryck had done an excellent job turning Salomon Brothers around after its debilitating problems with the regulators a few years earlier.

Of course, acquiring Salomon Brothers represented an altogether different proposition than simply recruiting its CEO, and I quickly recalled the blemishes we identified when we had discussed a merger two years earlier. Still, I suspected a lot had changed in the intervening period, and I was eager to learn more. Accordingly, I called Deryck back the next day and proposed having dinner. Deryck demurred, reminding me he preferred to await his return from his pending Hawaiian holiday. I pressed to get together sooner.

Deryck and I met at the Four Seasons restaurant on August 14. It only had been three weeks since the collapse of our discussions with J. P. Morgan. Before getting down to brass tacks, we exchanged a few observations relating to our shared involvement with Carnegie Hall. Deryck rarely missed an opportunity to thank me for reaching out to him and sponsoring his board membership in the early 1990s. Setting the pleasantries aside, Deryck jumped in and explained how Salomon Brothers had changed over the last couple of years and his reasoning for approaching me.

Aware that his company's risk profile had killed our last merger discussions, Deryck repeatedly emphasized how Salomon's earnings balance and risk management disciplines had improved. Continuing to hit my hot spots, he described how a Travelers-Salomon combination would balance and internationalize our securities business and give Merrill Lynch a run for its money. Finally, he confessed that he was nervous about sustaining recently strong trading profits. Without that boost, Salomon's ongoing heavy investment requirements would make it difficult to keep delivering a sufficient return on investment for his investors. When he mentioned "investors," I only thought of his primary owner, Warren Buffett, who controlled nearly 20 percent of Salomon's shares.

I reflected how much had changed over the prior couple of years. Salomon Brothers' earnings mix had improved as the company had reinvested its strong proprietary trading profits into its customer-driven businesses—the international, equities, and investment banking businesses had all grown substantially. Travelers Group had expanded, too, both by internal means and by acquiring Aetna's casualty insurance business. Salomon's risky trading activities remained significant but no longer represented the outsized percentage of profits they had when we last looked at the company.

Apart from the financial profile, I especially wanted to resolve our international weakness once and for all. Salomon's global franchise represented a shadow of what we had seen at J. P. Morgan, but I decided we couldn't afford to wait for the ideal partner. Nor could I ignore the chance to diversify my executive team in light of how badly my relationship with Jamie had decayed.

At the end of our dinner, Deryck mentioned he looked forward to speaking more following his holiday. I smiled agreeably, and I was already thinking about Salomon's franchise and the things I wanted to learn more about. How had Salomon directed its proprietary trading activities? How did it run its other businesses? What had the company accomplished internationally? Why did management commit capital so freely to build its equities business? Deryck might have thought he was heading off to relax, yet I had no intention of leaving him alone if it would stand in the way of my getting more information. I pestered Deryck throughout his Hawaiian vacation, forcing him to respond to each of my issues.

Deryck returned after Labor Day, and I looked forward to beginning formal due diligence. He insisted that I first commit to a price. "If I get jilted, I'll be in hot water. I need to know that you're in the ball-park," he declared. Given that Salomon represented a far from pristine property, I didn't want to tie my hands too tightly, but I told Deryck we'd pay around $80 per share subject to due diligence.

The price implied only a modest market premium and amounted to less than two times book value, about half our own valuation and those of other major securities firms. With that sort of spread, I naively assumed a deal could only add to our earnings per share. Having put a price on the table, we began the due diligence process.

For the next two weeks, we intensively studied Salomon's franchise and sized up its managers. We directed most of our energies toward understanding the company's balance sheet and its proprietary trading strategies. Over many years, Salomon had earned a reputation for committing huge amounts of capital on aggressive trades and more recently for pioneering creative uses for newly invented derivatives products, one of the hottest growth areas in the financial services industry.

Salomon Brothers' former star trader, John Meriwether, had set up the firm's arbitrage business before leaving to establish Long-Term Capital Management, the leading hedge fund of the day. He had taken along many colleagues, but Salomon had managed to hold its own with cutting-edge strategies. Smith Barney, by contrast, had avoided extensive proprietary risk taking, and our team struggled to understand Salomon's infinitely more complex business.

The complexity troubled my colleagues, and our nerves soon were unsettled further when we learned that Salomon had just lost $100 million on a problematic risk arbitrage trade. To assuage our concerns, Salomon flew in its head trader from London, Shigeru "Sugar" Myojin. Sugar walked with a typical trader's swagger, though he calmly took our team through a presentation that documented how Salomon's trading performance had become less volatile in recent years. His analysis revealed that the proprietary trading desk had produced a consistent 20–25% return on equity over the past seven years.

Despite Sugar's flamboyance, his numbers impressed us all. Jamie had taken responsibility for studying the trading area, and he finally weighed in saying that Salomon's positions "don't seem crazy."

Salomon's customer franchises ranged in quality, and the company still needed to invest substantially to complete the build-out of its international, investment banking, and equities businesses. Each of these businesses, however, had improved in recent years. Moreover, digging into Salomon's large fixed income operation, we saw at once that the franchise represented the company's crown jewel. For nearly two decades, fixed income markets had sustained remarkable growth, and Salomon Brothers consistently led the field. Smith Barney never had ranked more than a bit player in the bond business. It was clear that merging with Salomon Brothers would propel us to instant leadership.

As we wrapped up our due diligence, I sensed a considerable degree of ambivalence among my colleagues. While we had tried our best to understand Salomon's most complex activities, we were all aware of the difficulty in nailing down every element of risk. We had come to appreciate Salomon's improved earnings mix, yet a number of my executives still worried that we might compromise the quality of Travelers' earnings by merging with a company which still had the potential for considerable earnings volatility.

Countering the skeptics, I argued that we should be able to comfortably absorb Salomon's risky businesses because of our firms' relative size differential, and I stressed again that we could ill afford to put off solving our weakness outside the United States. I also observed we were offering to buy Salomon Brothers at a relatively low price in exchange for our stock, which seemed richly valued at the time. I never took a final show of hands, but it's important to note that, on this occasion, Jamie concurred with my reasoning.

At the beginning of our talks I had mentioned casually to Jamie that I'd want him to partner with Deryck in running our expanded securities business. We didn't dwell on the matter at that early stage. With the deal in sight, I raised the issue again and became more emphatic in telling him I planned a co-CEO structure for the new Salomon Smith Barney.

Jamie professed support for the merger; however, he objected to my power-sharing concept. "It's a terrible idea," he declared. "I've run Smith Barney successfully through all kinds of challenges; why muddy the waters now?" Jamie always thought he could come to a complete understanding of any business overnight, so I wasn't surprised by his objection. I saw things differently. Salomon represented a very different sort of deal for us given the complexity of its business and balance sheet and its continuing high proportion of volatile earnings. Keeping Deryck on board seemed the prudent course. The last thing I wanted was to buy Salomon and only have Jamie there to run activities about which we lacked full understanding.

Jamie pressed harder. He recalled our earlier merger talks with Salomon and how I had promised then that he would lead the combined securities firm. While that was true, I felt circumstances now had changed. He insisted that he and his Smith Barney team could handle the challenge. Nonetheless, I remained firm. Too much would ride on getting Salomon's large fixed income and proprietary trading units right, and there was no way I'd have entrusted these units solely to Jamie or people on his team.

I reminded him that only weeks earlier I had offered to share the CEO position with Morgan's Sandy Warner. If that arrangement had been acceptable for me, Jamie needed to see it the same way now. "It's the right thing to do for Deryck and for our company," I insisted, "and I want you to agree that you'll work as a team." Jamie didn't disguise his unhappiness, although he saw that he had little choice.

He finally declared, "That's fine. You're probably right." I took him at his word that he'd cooperate with Deryck.

With the management issue settled, Deryck and I quickly finalized our deal. On September 24, 1997, we announced the $9 billion deal, my largest ever. Rumors had been circulating for a few days that we were close to some sort of deal—J. P. Morgan, Bankers Trust, and Salomon Brothers all had been bandied about in the press—yet the actual announcement still managed to shake up investors. *The Wall Street Journal* declared "the Street was stunned" by the deal. On the day of the announcement, Salomon's stock price surged several points into the mid-$70s while our shares dropped nearly 4 percent. In our presentations, I did my best to focus investors on the franchise benefits of the merger. We promised the deal would boost our earnings per share by 10 percent within two years based on cost savings and revenue enhancements, and I stressed repeatedly the deal's modest premium.

Despite my efforts, I only did a so-so job selling the deal. Several months earlier, I had been quoted as saying I had no interest in Salomon and that I thought its trading activities resembled a casino. Unfortunately, it mattered little that I had now come to view Salomon differently—many investors simply obsessed that I had violated some sort of promise. When the dust settled, a number of the analysts who followed our stock came to our defense, and our stock settled at a price only modestly below its pre-announcement level. In all, I wasn't surprised by the Street's verdict.

———————

I'm not sure we ever really enjoyed a honeymoon with Salomon Brothers. Even before the deal, problems were brewing in Asian financial markets as a long spell of speculative capital flows was coming to an end. Various currencies from the Philippines to Korea began to weaken, and market pundits soon spoke of an Asian crisis. Sadly, these events scarcely registered during our due diligence on Salomon; barely a week after we announced our deal, investor fear spread ominously. In early October, Indonesia's currency cratered and set off a panic that immediately pressured emerging markets' currencies around the world. By month end, investors the world over started to raise cash, draining liquidity from many capital markets and sending financial asset values sharply lower. In a single week, the Hong Kong stock market lost 23 percent of its value, and the nervousness soon hit U.S. markets when the Dow plunged 7 percent on October 27.

The period between announcing our deal with Salomon and closing the transaction was two months. To my dismay, the intervening period yielded one nasty earnings surprise after another. Curiously, Salomon's proprietary trading group—the focus of much of our due diligence—didn't produce the disappointments. Instead, we took losses in our supposedly customer-driven equities businesses where we had positioned ourselves incorrectly, assuming modest market volatility. The introduction of highly integrated global markets suddenly undermined the established order. Faced with growing unexpected losses, our risk managers now struggled to come to terms with events.

I was shocked by the speed at which these losses arose. Our failure to understand our exposures ahead of time and the appearance that we had tolerated excessive risk to build our equities business troubled me more. A number of our traders asked for time to recoup their losses, but I insisted that we speedily cut our positions. By the beginning of 1998, market conditions eased noticeably but not soon enough to prevent

Travelers from reporting a 35 percent drop in fourth quarter profits now adjusted to include Salomon Brothers. Ironically, I had pushed hard to buy Salomon to make our company more global, and yet international events immediately conspired against us.

While Jamie wasn't happy about having to share Salomon Smith Barney's CEO role with Deryck, I assumed the two would find a way to work together. The initial cooperation, however, proved short-lived as my colleagues' sharply contrasting personalities and management styles, not to mention the challenges of managing our trading risks, soon pulled them apart.

Jamie by now had gotten used to managing largely autonomously with his small group of yes-men in tow, and he resisted changing his style or opening his team to accommodate Deryck. The early trading losses caused a lot of finger-pointing, which made it easy to put Deryck on the defensive. Jamie would turn toward Deryck in management meetings and demand in an accusing voice, "How could this have happened? What are *you* doing about it?" Before long, Jamie's cohorts would offer their "insights," which all too often amounted to thinly veiled slights designed to undermine Deryck.

Determined to preserve a statesmanlike facade, Deryck typically stayed composed and coolly did his best to look the other way during these public encounters. He opted for a passive-aggressive style—out of public view, he'd complain bitterly about Jamie's take-no-prisoners style. The contentiousness exasperated me no end. I exhorted the pair to "set your personal issues aside and act like grown-ups and work out your differences."

Against this backdrop, my relationship with Jamie sank to a new low. For two years, he had tried to discourage me from attending his weekly management meetings. Now he went to even greater lengths to exclude me. He'd frequently cancel the sessions only to reschedule them on days when he knew I'd be out of town. Discovering the deception, I realized that Jamie was manipulating me with the same tactics he had once used on Bob Greenhill. Yet, as in an estranged family relationship, I couldn't summon the will to cut the cords that still bound us together. Rather, I pleaded with Jamie to honor his agreement to work with Deryck, and trying to placate him, I promised that he'd take my place one day if only he respected my wishes.

In certain ways, we stumbled into 1998. The early disappointments with Salomon's risk positions and the increasingly dysfunctional relationships centering on Jamie contrasted with the generally strong performance of our other businesses. Despite the heartaches, I somehow convinced myself that we'd find a way to resolve our issues. I guess I'm simply an inveterate optimist. A market recovery early in the year fed my hopes. The panic which had gripped investors during the fall abruptly ended and allowed Salomon Smith Barney's earnings to snap back and underpin a solid recovery for Travelers' first quarter earnings.

During this market reprieve, our proprietary trading head, Sugar Myojin, retired. Following Sugar's departure, I proposed that my son take over his role, reasoning that Marc's investment skills might be transferable and that we might benefit by taking a longer-term view on our proprietary positions. Jamie, however, resisted, claiming the move would prove disruptive and potentially put Marc in over his head. I didn't agree; nevertheless, I wasn't eager to create another source of friction, so I backed off. The episode reminded me that employing a family member once again had tied my hands.

With the approach of spring, volatility in global markets began to increase anew, putting me on edge once more. We had cut back sharply on our exposures in our equities and fixed income businesses, but I noticed that our positions in our proprietary trading business, solid for so long, were starting to perform unevenly. On balance, I felt we were in better control of our business, but our experience over the past several months had proven sobering.

I kept asking myself whether global markets were becoming naturally more volatile. If so, I wondered if Travelers Group had yet attained the proper scale to master its destiny. Though the Salomon merger had proven far more complex that I had hoped, I felt the deal had expanded our strategic options. After all, it had given us an exceptionally strong position in the fixed income business, a basic international platform, and an overall market capitalization which would allow us to go toe-to-toe with the financial services industry's largest players.

Always being prepared for the next deal had explained much of my success over the years. With the approach of April, I was prepared to test that proposition as never before.

13

An Audacious Leap

The years of acquiring one company after another never interfered with the way I managed our company. The trick was to focus a smart group of executives on a common agenda, encourage them to think like owners, and regularly share ideas and challenge one another. The monthly meetings of Travelers' Planning Group, held in our Armonk conference center or periodically in a relaxed resort setting, gave me a regular overview of the company's issues and allowed me to drill down on matters of interest.

Between meetings, I spent countless hours trying to keep my finger on the company's pulse, always probing by roaming the halls, telephoning employees at different levels, or meeting with individuals or small groups in my office. Each day, the business heads provided a one-page summary of the key trends in each of their areas, a managerial device I had picked up years before from our operations people who used to keep a weekly tally of important back-office-related metrics. These succinct reports forced executives to seek timely information and zero in on the things that really mattered to their business. They also sensitized me to the most important drivers of our profitability and helped me anticipate emerging trends.

For example, our consumer finance unit tracked new lending commitments, lending margins, and delinquent credits, while our retail securities business followed customer asset flows, commissions, and margin activity. Forcing my team to summarize their business trends on a single page focused everyone and instilled discipline.

At the end of 1997, the Planning Group comprised Travelers' top twenty executives. The Salomon acquisition, and the friction it introduced between Jamie and Deryck, strained the mood at meetings, but the sessions remained integral to how I ran the company. As we approached our December meeting, I was keenly aware that disappointments following the Salomon deal might darken our discussions. We had bought the industry's premier fixed income operation, but the stunning collapse of several important Asian economies presented us with a challenging trading environment and adverse earnings volatility. We also better appreciated that Salomon required substantial incremental investment for it to give us the global positioning we had long desired.

I felt disappointed but far from dismayed, and I never reconsidered my eagerness to diversify globally. In fact, Salomon's shortcomings encouraged me to think about how we might use additional acquisitions to build our balance sheet and further diversify our earnings. We had issued $9 billion in stock to buy Salomon, and our company's market capitalization had risen to $40 billion, a substantial 40 percent increase over the prior year. I instinctively sensed our new heft would give us a wider range of acquisition options.

Convening in Armonk in mid-December, we took our seats in large comfortable armchairs set up in the wide semicircle we favored for these meetings. I had asked our corporate planning head, Mike Carpenter, to lead the discussion, and Mike announced the first order of business: "What do we do next?"

To an outsider, posing such a question so soon after our last deal might have sounded odd. But the idea of acquisitions always preyed on our minds and appeared regularly on our agenda. This time, Mike explained the ground rules: "Don't worry about legal or regulatory constraints. Simply throw out good merger ideas. The only criteria should be companies with diverse earnings, strong balance sheets, and significant international franchises."

The group began to shout out ideas. Mike moved to a flip chart and jotted down the names in three neat columns with brief notes summarizing the rationale behind each idea. Most of the names weren't surprising—after all, we had been down this road before. Merrill Lynch. Goldman Sachs. American Express. J. P. Morgan. Some executives suggested foreign companies, like HSBC or ING, though we discounted these since our discussions with foreign firms earlier in the decade had made us wary about cultural differences.

Finally, someone proposed Citicorp, the largest bank in the United States and the undisputed leader in financial services globally. Immediately, I heard a chorus of guffaws: "You have to be kidding—Citi is out of our league . . . It wouldn't be legal—that would be a small problem . . . Let's stay realistic . . ." Mike jumped in and quickly reminded the group that thinking outside the box represented the whole point of the exercise. With that, we listed some of the things that would make Citicorp interesting.

As we talked, I saw that the idea really wowed the group—forget whether it was feasible, Citicorp stuck out like a strategic home run. The company operated in over one hundred countries where customers and governments alike harbored huge respect for its brand. Whereas Travelers Group enjoyed strong positions in financial products apart from banking services, Citicorp had amassed enviable positions in nearly every banking product. A combination of our two companies would create a powerhouse with unparalleled scope, scale, and diversification. It would provide a fortresslike balance sheet and neutralize the risks from periodic bouts of market instability. We'd be thrust into position to seize on competitors' weaknesses.

No one could remember when Citicorp last made a meaningful acquisition, which prompted someone to suggest we were wasting our time. Yet only a few weeks earlier, the press had reported that Citicorp and American Express had held unsuccessful merger talks, and the news made me wonder whether the company was reconsidering its options.

We finally checked Citicorp's market capitalization and, lo and behold, it was amazingly close to Travelers'. I reflected that Salomon—despite its earnings issues—had given us the financial heft to pull alongside the world's leading bank. I considered, too, what we had learned from our aborted attempt to buy J. P. Morgan: We had found a way legally to merge with a bank.

To most of its attendees, the Armonk meeting probably seemed to end inconclusively. Privately I felt energized. My colleagues rarely reached a consensus on an idea, but once we got past the potential obstacles to a deal with Citicorp, they all seemed enthralled by the company's scope and reputation. During the meeting Jamie had suggested that "Citi would be the mother of all deals." Always ready for a new challenge, I heard that comment, said to myself "aha," and started musing how I might set the idea in motion.

———————

I had known Citicorp's CEO, John Reed, for more than twenty-five years. In the 1970s, we had served together on the board of a troubled real estate company named Arlen Realty. When that company hit the skids, most of the other directors ran for cover, but John and I worked closely together to salvage our respective interests. The shared experience under trying circumstances forged a great deal of mutual respect. In the years after Arlen, we'd run into each other periodically; John and his first wife even invited Joanie and me to their home for dinner on one occasion.

Curiously, in November 1997, only a month before Travelers' Planning Group met, I joined John at a benefit for the Jewish Theological Seminary held at the Pierre Hotel. My friend and public relations expert Gershon Kekst served as chairman of the board and had lassoed me into serving as the event chair each year. On this occasion, John had agreed to be the year's honoree.

While I may have thought it odd that the Jewish Theological Seminary would honor a good Presbyterian like John Reed, the evening turned out wonderfully. Ehud Barak, then head of Israel's Labour Party and soon to be prime minister, had been invited to make the keynote speech and was a lively contributor to the conversation around our dinner table. An exceptionally down-to-earth person, he soon put all of us, including John and his wife, Cindy, in a congenial mood. Joanie recently had undergone surgery on her finger and wore a cast—I loved it when Barak grabbed her knife and cut her steak for her.

How often does one see a future prime minister tending to one's wife like that?

The warmth of that evening didn't end with the banter over dinner. In my introduction for John, I noted the terrific way he had shepherded Citicorp through its dark hours in the early 1990s when foreign loans and bad real estate ventures nearly torpedoed his company. In response, John reciprocated with praise about my own accomplishments. I was surprised how much I enjoyed the entire event, and the evening gave me an unambiguous feeling that the respect John and I had for one another in the days of Arlen Realty had managed to survive.

The warm feeling from that evening and the insight from our subsequent Planning Group session inspired me to approach John Reed. First, I double-checked with Kenny Bialkin to be sure Skadden's conclusion on the legality of merging with J. P. Morgan would apply to Citicorp. Kenny reassured me that the same principles held, and I promptly phoned Reed. With as much nonchalance as I could muster, I said, "John, I have something interesting to talk to you about. It should be done in person. Can we look at our calendars and come up with a date to meet?"

A couple of years before, we briefly had discussed the idea of Citicorp distributing some of Travelers' products, so I figured my call didn't seem too out of the blue. We had difficulty finding a mutually convenient opening in our schedules, but John proposed getting together at the upcoming Business Council meeting of leading CEOs to be held in Washington in February. We agreed to meet in my hotel room after dinner on the first night of the conference. Fixing the date, I had two long months to figure out how to turn what seemed like an audacious long shot into a reality.

Over most of the intervening weeks, superstition got the better of me, and I kept my date with John a secret. The logic and power of putting our companies together seemed so compelling that I didn't want to do anything that might spill the beans prematurely. My executives reconvened in late January—this time in the Adirondacks—for our annual off-site to consider our priorities for the year. Once more, we revisited potential acquisition targets, and we discussed Citicorp again, among other names.

I was careful to say little and simply soak up the discussion. The complementary fit between Citicorp's global distribution and Travelers' products seemed more compelling than ever. The consumer equation seemed especially enticing, but I understood that amassing a stronger balance sheet would have to be a boon for the corporate side of our business as well.

As this second meeting ended, I realized that Travelers Group in its current form never really would break out from the pack. We were weighted heavily toward insurance, securities brokerage, and consumer finance, areas which offered few consolidation opportunities on an international scale. If we were going to become the financial services industry leader, we needed a commercial bank partner, and Citicorp fit our needs like none other.

———

Over the next two months, I obsessed on my upcoming meeting with Reed. Our company was all of twelve years old and little more than an industry upstart, and here I was gearing up to pitch a merger with Citicorp with its nearly two hundred years of history. I was nervous as hell. This could be the greatest deal in the history of the financial services industry and would surely transform the business, but I had only one chance to propose my idea. The pitch needed to be perfect.

I didn't have any inside scoop on what had gone wrong in Citicorp's merger talks with American Express. The press speculated that my friend Harvey Golub had pressed Reed hard for American Express's executives to dominate management. It sounded an awful lot like my fruitless discussions with J. P. Morgan's Sandy Warner only a few months before. Still, that John Reed had negotiated seriously with Amex said something.

Citicorp had turned over a variety of top executives in recent years, and I reasoned John had to be open to a deal that might dramatically improve his earnings prospects while bolstering his management.

Returning to the similarities in our companies' market valuations, I realized that only one structure made sense, a merger of equals where our companies would split evenly the ownership and boards of a merged entity and where John and I would join as partner CEOs with a management team balanced across the two companies. Yes, I had proposed co-CEOs to J. P. Morgan, but the idea seemed far more promising with Citicorp. John Reed already had discussed something similar with American Express, and more important, Citicorp's franchise seemed light-years better than Morgan's.

I continued to keep my own counsel for the most part, though Kenny Bialkin knew how my thoughts were evolving in his capacity as our outside counsel. I also reached out to Art Zankel. For years, I'd rely on Kenny and Art not just as board members but as friends who had phenomenal business judgment and who could be relied upon for consistently honest feedback. In this instance, both advised me to be careful with the idea of sharing executive responsibility, but their caution ended there—they both understood the enormous competitive potential of a combined Travelers/Citicorp.

I also told Joanie, and she echoed Kenny's and Art's comments on partnering with Reed. "Sandy, you're not the best at sharing," she said. "What makes you think you could work alongside John?" All three of my closest confidants had raised the same issue, and they were quite rational. Still, I knew my proposal would be the only way I'd get my idea off the ground, and I had myself conned by now that John and I were mature enough to work out an arrangement.

Finally, Wednesday, February 25 arrived, and it was time to head to Washington. For most of the plane ride, I went over and over how I'd welcome John that evening and phrase my proposal. As the plane descended, my thoughts seemed to clear with the clouds. I looked out on the District's street grid and the layout of the various monuments and marveled at how the city's designers had come up with such an elegant plan. Why couldn't my idea of an entirely new sort of financial services company embodying unprecedented diversification and scale convey the same sense of logic? This bold merger idea made such preeminent sense.

I went to the Business Council's dinner that evening, but don't recall a thing. I'm sure my mind was centered on the meeting at my hotel that would follow. Around 9:00 P.M., John finally knocked on my door. I opened it and invited him in. "Hi, John. Would you like a cocktail?" "No." "What about a glass of wine?" "No." "Coffee?" "No thanks."

John was in a serious mood and, after a long day, obviously wanted to hear the reason I had asked to meet. "Okaaay," I replied, stalling slightly while I arranged my words one last time. "Why don't I start at the end and tell you the conclusion of what I'd like to talk about, and if you think it's interesting, I'll go back and tell you why I think it makes sense." I paused for effect before laying my concept on the table.

In a rush of words, my idea tumbled forth. "I think we should merge and be partners. We'd create a company that instantly would be the industry leader. We'd have scale and diversification on our side and a powerful balance sheet. Our companies' market values are nearly the same, and we could do a deal where we each own 50 percent, have an even board split, and share the chairman and CEO roles. It probably would take three years to pull together after which we could both leave together."

John hadn't expected anything like this, and he sat silently with a dazed half smile on his face. Finally, he exclaimed a long "Hmm." I knew John to be a thinker, and for an intellectual, this was off the charts. Finally, he collected himself and laughed. "And I thought you had asked me here to buy a table at some charity dinner. I convinced myself before coming here that I'd take a $25,000 table." Thinking of the $150 billion deal I had just proposed, I ribbed, "No, John, this is much larger than that!"

John wanted to hear more so I launched into a monologue on why Citicorp and Travelers franchises would complement one another and played up how a merger would be an ideal marriage of product and distribution while offering market positions and financial strength that would be the envy of our competitors. John listened intently before interrupting: "What about the legal issues? Since when can a bank merge with a brokerage firm, let alone an insurer?"

"Not to worry," I replied. "We've already been down this path with the Fed. We've found a provision in the law that would allow us to do this deal and have up to five years to seek legislative relief or else another solution." I then confided how we had spoken to J. P. Morgan the prior summer and determined that the law allowed for a merger so long as Travelers would be the acquirer for legal purposes (and then subsequently apply to become a bank holding company).

John then hit me with the co-CEO issue but surprised me with how he framed his point: "Co-equals usually don't work. You know you don't have to do it this way. I respect you and would have no problem working for you. After all, I probably won't be around for that long since I've been thinking of retiring."

This represented an alluring offer, yet intuitively John's proposal didn't sit right. Without hesitation, I countered, "No, John. The only way it will work will be as a full partnership. If you're not my partner, I can't be sure I'll get your management team to sign on. Besides, neither of us is a spring chicken. We've had long and successful careers, and I'm sure we have the seasoning to make this work."

John pressed a little more and saw I meant what I said. When I make my mind up on something, I follow through, and I had convinced myself that John and I could be excellent partners. In hindsight, I suspect John's offer to work for me might have been little more than a test. He probably threw out the idea to see how serious I was about sharing. After all, rumor had it that John's deal with Amex fell apart because Harvey Golub was not interested in sharing power. Had I taken the bait, we might never have had a second meeting.

After nearly forty-five minutes, John stood and declared, "This could be interesting. I'd like to speak to my wife tonight. I'll get to you tomorrow morning at breakfast." As he moved toward the door, John made one last loaded comment. "I want you to know that our deal with

Amex fell apart for business reasons and not because Harvey and I are so different." The comment puzzled me. I interpreted it as reassurance that if we were to enter talks, Citicorp's board would not penalize me for being a Jew or for being from the other side of the tracks from John and his WASPish predecessors.

When John left, I could barely contain my excitement. The meeting had gone far better than I had hoped. John seemed to have a positive feel about what I had proposed, and his offer to respond the next day was incredible. I called Joanie and exuberantly recounted the meeting nearly word for word. The next morning, John and I met at breakfast and scurried off to a private side room. John's response was everything I wanted to hear.

"Sandy, what you proposed last night really intrigues me," he said. "Clearly, you've thought this through a lot more than I have. I'm leaving this afternoon on a two-week trip to Europe and Asia. I propose having my colleague Paul Collins meet with you while I'm away to explore the logic in more detail. Once we do our homework, I can better decide on whether and how to take this forward."

John's response was music to my ears. What had been a long shot had now turned into exploratory talks. I never had expected to leave Washington with a concrete next step in hand. I was flying high and in shock that my idea actually had taken hold. I just prayed John would follow through.

———

Happily, I received a call from Paul Collins that afternoon. Paul had the title of vice chairman of Citicorp but effectively served as John's consigliere. We agreed to meet the coming Monday, March 2. I assured him we'd provide whatever information he needed to help John understand what I had proposed.

The professorial-looking and soft-spoken Paul Collins perfectly complemented the intellectual Reed. He arrived at my downtown office at 11:30 A.M., and we headed to a private dining room where we spent the next three hours talking about my concept for the merger and how to move forward. Despite his reserve, Paul seemed fascinated by the notion of combining our companies. In fact, he spoke openly about Citicorp's challenges and especially pointed out its need to beef up management and improve product diversity. Echoing the comments I had made to Reed a few days before, I stressed how a merger would create unmatched product and geographic diversification. I also asserted that a merger would create years of strong earnings growth from leveraging both firms' client relationships not just in the United States but around the world.

We moved on to specifics and went over the information Paul would need and how to facilitate his mission. Given the magnitude of the proposed deal, its unconventional regulatory issues, and my hard-learned lesson over the years that leaks usually kill deals, we agreed not to tell others about our talks except on an absolutely must-know basis. At this early stage, this meant I'd include Jamie and Mike Carpenter while Paul would bring in a lieutenant, Bob Khanna. Paul suggested he needed a couple of days to organize himself, and we agreed to meet in my apartment three days later.

That Thursday, the small working group arrived at my home at 7:30, and we spent the morning responding to Collins's questions and going over spreadsheets that would help him build basic pro forma financial statements. He seemed especially interested in the hypothetical capital and funding structure, the relative efficiency of different businesses, the impact on overall earnings diversification, and Travelers' track record on growing organically versus by acquisition.

We had a few more meetings over the next few days in which Jamie typically responded to Paul's financial questions while Carpenter smoothly played up the logic of the business fit. Finally, Paul informed us he had what he needed to brief John. He didn't lay his cards on the table, but I sensed Paul had become a believer.

A couple of days later—now in mid-March—I received a far-ranging, cerebral, handwritten fax from John, who was then in Singapore. The stream-of-consciousness document ran several pages and amounted to a discourse on John's vision and the issues he saw in the proposed merger as well as in a freestanding Citicorp. John stressed how he wanted to build the world's preeminent consumer financial services firm but felt frustrated by Citicorp's slow pace of sourcing new customers and by the lack of success at building domestic distribution. Perhaps enviously, he complimented Travelers for its success in distributing product via multiple channels and for proving products could be cross-sold in different parts of the company. He then segued into a discussion of how the U.S. market was slowing and how merger activity surely would accelerate. On this point, he acknowledged Travelers' skill as an acquirer while bemoaning Citicorp's lack of consolidation experience in recent years.

A third of the way through the document, I took a deep breath and thought "so far so good." John then lapsed into a discourse on the corporate and investment banking business. For years, he had openly stated his disdain for this side of the business, so I felt far from surprised by the continued pessimism expressed in his written thoughts. John's conclusion: If we were to merge, we should consider selling the property casualty insurance business and divest the corporate business. I thought these were nutty ideas—after all, even John agreed a merger would strengthen our combined corporate/investment banks. It seemed a bad time to sell our insurance business, and why would we merge only to want to turn around and sell our corporate business, still a work in progress and a key part of our franchise?

Fortunately, John's memo didn't end there and returned to more constructive themes. He noted that Citicorp had been stymied by excessive bureaucracy which slowed decision making and fostered inefficiencies. Here, he made a pivotal point: Citicorp needed new DNA for its management, something more akin to what drove Travelers' managerial success. He understood that a great deal of our success at Travelers had come from moving fast on opportunities and delivering a remarkably efficient operation.

John saved his strongest point for the end. He announced that he wanted to meet upon his return from Asia and discuss the merger idea in more detail. Over his career, John had proven his capacity for bold innovation, and he didn't let me down. Elated, I couldn't believe how quickly things were moving. I never would have dreamed two weeks earlier that John would be so receptive. After years of searching for a way to globalize, the granddaddy of all conceivable options seemed to be taking shape.

I went running to Jamie's and Mike Carpenter's offices and triumphantly showed them John's memo. Both pointed out John's different vision for our corporate business, but I already had chosen to ignore that part of his discourse. I figured the rest of the memo was so upbeat that I'd have no problem talking him out of his more esoteric ideas. Why upset the progress I was making with John by focusing on a few differences of opinion? Besides, by now I had come to worry that Travelers' earnings momentum might slow without a large merger, and I didn't want to upset a deal that could reenergize our earnings.

I wanted to will this deal to happen.

John returned from his trip, and we arranged for our now somewhat expanded deal teams to meet in Armonk on March 20–21. Secrecy remained important, and we agreed to limit the insider group to about a dozen people. Before the full group would convene, I wanted time alone with John, and I proposed that he come up to our conference center the night before for dinner. We devoted most of the private session on that Thursday night to figuring out how we'd organize the next couple of days of talks, but I also raised one issue which had been preying on my mind: Jamie.

I knew John had been thinking of retiring for some time. Though we had agreed we'd stick around for a few years to see a Travelers/Citicorp merger properly integrated, I worried John might view Jamie as a possible successor. By this point, the close relationship that Jamie and I once had shared had long since evaporated. I didn't want to dwell on the problems, so I simply related to John the issues I had been facing with Jamie and stated clearly, "Don't do this deal in order to get Jamie as a successor. You'll have to see for yourself, but there are issues here you aren't aware of." John heard me out but didn't pursue the matter.

The next morning, our teams arrived at 7:30 for breakfast. John brought only four others: Collins and his associate Bob Khanna,

Citicorp's CFO Victor Menezes, and Charlie Long, Citicorp's corporate secretary and John's point person with his board. From Travelers, we had our general counsel, Chuck Prince, Jamie Dimon, Mike Carpenter, Deryck Maughan, Heidi Miller, and Irwin Ettinger (the last two respectively our CFO and chief accountant). After brief introductions, we moved into another room configured with the comfortable chairs that always promoted relaxed discussions, and we dove into two days of intensive work.

There was plenty to discuss, and we agreed on far more things than not. We first tackled the business fit and went segment by segment to assess what each company brought to the deal. Citicorp, of course, enjoyed unique global positioning, but it also offered a number of other salient strengths. These included its credit card, foreign exchange, private banking, and derivative businesses, not to mention its relationships with large multinational corporations.

On the other hand, Travelers Group offered an array of distribution platforms and brought industry-leading franchises of its own in consumer finance, insurance, asset management, and institutional and retail securities. Next, we focused on financial matters and seamlessly settled on a common dividend policy and an exchange ratio for our shares that would deliver the 50/50 ownership that John and I had discussed in our first meeting. We discussed a structure for the board of directors and agreed on a plan to exclude inside directors and pare the combined board to a total of eighteen individuals. We then moved to the flip charts and drafted ideas for how we might organize our businesses. We settled on three broad groups: the Consumer Business; a Corporate Investment Bank; and Asset Management and Private Banking. It was premature to assign jobs, but we agreed each company's top management would be well represented in the new company.

John never brought up the idea of divesting the corporate business as he had in his fax, although he did express discomfort with the risks and suggested we should constrain its overall relative use of capital. I reminded him that I never had been a big risk taker and was already deeply engaged in cutting Salomon Smith Barney's trading risks. John then briefly raised the notion of selling our commercial insurance business. I countered that this would be a poor time to make such a move, and fortunately, John dropped the suggestion.

For a deal of such epic proportions—the largest in corporate history—things fell into place remarkably easily, and I felt good about the direct and cooperative atmosphere our teams had established. Moving on, we discussed how we'd name our new creation. John felt strongly about the Citi brand, which seemed fine with me—after all, I always had shown flexibility on names so long as the prestige of the new name outstripped the old.

Striving for balance, I told John that I thought we should use the "Group" from Travelers Group and definitely employ the Travelers umbrella as our logo. That red umbrella represented all that I had aspired to for more than twenty years: building a diversified powerhouse with an "umbrella" of services that would cover all of our customers' needs. "Citigroup" with the umbrella logo seemed an elegant compromise.

By the second day, we had worked through most of the important structural issues, and we turned our attention to procedural matters such as setting a timeline, determining how to perform due diligence, and engaging third-party advisors. Throughout the talks, succession never came up as an issue since John and I had settled that up front. Still, many on the team felt the idea of co-CEOs was sufficiently unconventional that we should at least explore how John and I might react to hypothetical issues.

Accordingly, we went through an exercise where our colleagues raised issues seeking our response. We explored differences in how we might address matters such as budgeting, acquisitions, compensation, risk tolerance, and more. I undoubtedly was in sell mode and took care to defuse potential disagreements and avoid skirmishes. I bent over backward to demonstrate I'd be a good partner since I just wanted to get on with the deal. If John or others raised a thorny issue, I took delight in offering constructive solutions. In the end, John and I felt we could compromise and work effectively together—we agreed we'd each have a veto over all major decisions.

The meeting broke up on Saturday afternoon, and John suggested that we sleep on things before making the final decision on whether to move ahead. Given how far we had come in such a short time, I figured I could wait John out one more day. Of course, I didn't need any more time to see the compelling logic of our now newly named Citigroup. The next morning, John called early. It was a terrific phone call: "I really look forward to this, pardner." There was no qualifying "but . . ." and that word "pardner" stuck in my mind—it was as if John had reached out through the telephone and put his arm around me.

I didn't need to hear another word.

The timeline we had settled on in Armonk called for wrapping up due diligence and announcing the deal within two weeks, an aggressive schedule that was underpinned by my fear about the transaction leaking. In this final phase, we'd have to introduce additional insiders, and the risk of word getting out multiplied enormously. We had little time to lose and immediately scheduled a board meeting and a critical trip to Washington in order to meet with the Fed later that week.

On Wednesday, March 25, the Travelers Group board convened for the first of three sessions to discuss the merger. Salomon Smith Barney's investment bankers prepared a book for the board that reviewed the concept behind the merger and artfully crafted code names of "Jupiter" for Travelers and "Saturn" for Citicorp—undoubtedly, putting together such giants would propel us into a universe of our own. I had told Kenny Bialkin and Art Zankel ahead of time, so the surprise wasn't complete, yet the board still seemed awed and excited. Many had been with me since I took over Commercial Credit and felt a shared sense of accomplishment. Even the need to trim the number of directors who'd get to serve on the new company's board didn't provoke debate.

Not unexpectedly, the only significant issue related to how John and I would work together as co-CEOs. Several board members shared experiences of their own as to how difficult it was to jointly manage. A couple of directors cited the ongoing difficulties between Jamie and

Deryck as an example. I countered that I understood the issue, but that my formula was the only way this incredible deal would happen. "John and I have known each other for years," I argued. "We've both been around the block and are mature enough that we can make this work." I cited Goldman Sachs where Bob Rubin and Steve Friedman and, before them, John Weinberg and John Whitehead had run the firm jointly (never mind that these men had grown up together at Goldman).

In the final analysis, the directors felt the deal was so compelling that it was worth the risk. The board authorized me to move forward.

———————

I had known Chairman Greenspan for years. After President Ford lost his reelection campaign, Greenspan left his presidential advisory post to return to his consulting practice in New York. I hired him on behalf of Shearson in the late 1970s, and Alan would come and speak to our research department every Monday morning. I usually attended these sessions and enjoyed debating policies to improve business conditions with the future Fed chairman. At the time, how to conquer inflation and reinvigorate business investment spending were frequent hot topics. My son, Marc, also worked for him one summer.

When I called Greenspan to set up the meeting to discuss the merger with Citicorp, I asked, "Do you know who I'm coming down with this time?" Greenspan stayed silent. "It's not J. P. Morgan again," I continued. "It's John Reed." Greenspan immediately commented, "I need to talk to my general counsel on this. I'll call you back." For a moment, I panicked. However, Greenspan phoned a few minutes later telling me he would meet with me later that week.

On the morning after our first board meeting, John and I met at the Fed accompanied by our lawyers. In the room outside Greenspan's office hung paintings of famous Americans. Waiting for the Fed chairman to emerge, I tried to break the tension by asking John whether the historic proportions of our deal would earn us a portrait one day. Even though I had been here before talking about J. P. Morgan and had been reassured about our legal rights, I feared that Greenspan might throw us an unexpected curveball.

Finally, we were ushered into Greenspan's office where he and his general counsel, Virgil Mattingly, greeted us. As nervous as I had been about the magnitude of our proposed deal, Greenspan put me at ease. "I have nothing against size," he declared. "It doesn't bother me at all." We discussed a variety of legal and regulatory issues, and the dreaded surprise from Greenspan never materialized.

Fed chairmen typically make equivocation an art—it was what Greenspan did *not* say that struck me as so positive. His only caution came toward the end. "I have to warn you that you'll have two years to comply with the Bank Holding Company Act [which disallowed affiliations between banks and insurers] or else you'll have to make changes. It's very possible that you could get three one-year extensions, but remember, this has happened once before. [Dutch insurer] ING bought a U.S. bank and was confident that the laws would change, but that never happened, and they eventually had to choose between the banking and insurance businesses. Based on history, I'm not sure you should feel that you'll be any more successful."

Greenspan's comments were as good as I had a right to expect. Even if we'd find ourselves one day in the position that ING faced, I reasoned we could live with divesting our property casualty business if it came to that. Before we left, however, Reed unexpectedly changed course and put the upbeat tone of the meeting at risk. John must have felt uncomfortable with the elliptical nature of Greenspan's comments and, all at once, declared abrasively, "We don't want any legal runaround. If you don't want us to do the deal, tell us and we'll go away." The comment was extraordinarily direct and bordered on being disrespectful. Fortunately, Greenspan simply pointed to Mattingly, saying, "If that guy over there says you can do it, it'll be okay as far as I'm concerned."

When we left Greenspan's office, I felt we were in good shape. To reassure John Reed, Kenny Bialkin wrote a letter to Mattingly laying out our understanding of what we had discussed in the meeting and how we planned to proceed. When the Fed's chief lawyer responded verbally that he agreed with our understanding, we were home free. Another important piece of the puzzle had fallen into place.

With a week to go before our planned Monday announcement, everything looked on track. The lawyers were finalizing the contractual details; required due diligence was proceeding smoothly; and most important, there were no leaks! During that final week, John suggested I come down to his apartment in Greenwich Village for an afternoon working session. As we wound up, John invited me to stay for a steak dinner which he'd personally barbecue.

Offering me a drink, John stunned me with his next words. "I've been thinking about this a lot. I may not want to work as long as you do, and I don't want you to feel forced to retire. That would give me a guilty conscience. As far as I'm concerned, you don't have to leave with me as we initially discussed." The comment came as a bolt from the blue and clarified the one aspect of my initial offer that I had never quite resolved in my own mind. When I first proposed our partnership, I felt we needed to be completely even in how we'd work together, but at heart, I really never could imagine walking away from working, let alone from a company as great as the one we were putting together.

I'm not sure what provoked John to make this late offer. At the time, I took it as an affirmation of the close relationship we were forging. In hindsight, though, I suspect John may also have realized that his board wouldn't accept legislating our joint departure into the merger contract, as directors may have assumed succession was the board's prerogative. Whatever the motive, I declared, "God bless you, John. You're a terrific person."* I then embraced him and reciprocated with a kiss on the cheek. While I communicated John's con-

---

*Oddly, as lawyers drafted the merger proxy statement two months later, Citicorp's general counsel tried to write into the document that John and I planned to jointly retire after three years. Chuck Prince and Ken Bialkin replied that that was not our agreement, and the matter died. I assumed at the time that the issue represented a miscommunication between John and his legal counsel. Later, John began telling people soon after the deal—to my consternation—that we had agreed to leave at the same time.

cession to members of my board, I'd later learn that John kept our conversation to himself.

By the end of that week, our merger teams were abuzz with activity. On Thursday, we updated our board a second time and brought our investor and public relations departments into the fold. On Friday and Saturday, we had two teams at work with our communications people holed up at Kekst & Company, our public relations firm, while most of our other top executives joined John and me in Armonk to resolve the final financial details. The cooperative spirit never flagged. At one point, John's Consumer Business head, Bill Campbell, insisted we needed to design our logo ahead of the analyst and press conferences which would be held on Monday. Many companies would have spent countless dollars hiring an outside firm to perform the design work. John and I simply sat down with Campbell and in ten minutes designed how the Citigroup name and umbrella would look.

That Saturday afternoon, our work was nearly complete. Citicorp's board met and approved the deal. Travelers' board convened telephonically on Sunday and granted speedy approval. With everything set, I decided that it might be wise to stay out of the city that night, and Joanie and I remained in Greenwich. On one of my earlier deals, I recalled having drinks with my merger partner on the Sunday night before our announcement and running into someone we knew who easily could have tipped off the press prematurely. Ever superstitious, I didn't want to do anything that might jeopardize the enormous surprise we were about to unleash.

In the days leading up to that final weekend, it occurred to me that there might be one person who we shouldn't catch off guard: the president of the United States. One of my directors, Ann Jordan (and her husband, Vernon), was friendly with President and Mrs. Clinton, and I asked Ann to see if she could arrange an advance phone conversation. On the night before announcing the merger, John and I placed our call to the president. Completely exhilarated, I said, "Mr. President, we want to make you an insider on an amazing transaction we will be making in the morning."

I didn't know of anyone else who ever had given the president of the United States a heads-up on a merger. Clinton took the news politely and offered, "That sounds exciting." He then went on to describe his recent trip to Africa. I interjected that Citigroup, with its scale, would be in a better position to lend to and invest in developing areas of the world. Clinton seemed excited that we could relate our deal to his agenda. Our conversation lasted all of ten minutes. Just when I thought I couldn't get any more excited, the president had pumped me up all the more.

That evening Joanie and I relaxed together quietly at home. I couldn't get over the fact that the deal had never leaked. It seemed a good omen and a sign of approval since it would have been easy for one of the insiders to reveal our secret had anyone been unhappy about the transaction. I also marveled at how much we had accomplished in barely more than a month—it would have taken many companies a year to do what we had done. Joanie shared my excitement, having long since moved past her caution on what it would be like working alongside John Reed. She asked me that evening how I thought the merger would impact our lifestyle and the time we'd have to spend together. I told her what she already had to know: "I'll have to work very hard for a few years, but this is the culmination of what I've worked forty-five years for. If we can put this together right, it will be very fulfilling."

I then gulped and smiled coyly. "Joanie, I'm only asking you for a few more years." Ever supportive, my wife smiled and whispered, "Sandy, have I ever stopped you from getting what you've wanted?"

My driver pulled up in front of Citicorp Center at seven that Monday morning, April 6. Joanie and I bounded out of the car and headed for

John's office. The early news reports on the merger sounded promising: "We have a blockbuster deal to report . . . a groundbreaking transaction . . . financial history in the making . . ." My adrenaline was surging, for this day represented the crowning of my career. Making our way to the twenty-third floor, I found John sitting alone in his office and immediately gushed, "This will be the biggest event in financial services history. I could hardly sleep last night." We turned to watch the morning television reports, flipping channel to channel to get the broadest possible sense of the reaction, all the while basking in the rush of excitement. It all sounded too good to be true.

John told me he had set aside a conference room down the hall for my use and that my assistant, Connie Garone, was already there. "I think perhaps you'd be more comfortable using my office," he intoned graciously. "Why don't you move in here, and I'll use the conference room today?" I appreciated the gesture but refused to upend my new partner. Instead, I insisted on walking the floor and poking my head in and saying hello to Citicorp's top executives, who mostly were sitting in their offices watching the morning financial news programs. Everyone beamed and greeted me eagerly.

Returning to John's office, I presented my new partner with a couple of gifts: a red Travelers tie embellished with blue umbrellas and an umbrella lapel pin. Reed immediately yanked off his tie and proudly donned the new one as the assembled executives smiled. John and I soon would need to walk out in front of the press and the analysts and demonstrate our new partnership—everything had to be just right.

Showtime began at ten o'clock with a presentation to the analysts. On the walk to the auditorium, I recalled how Reed's own staff had warned me about their boss's tendency to say whatever came to mind rather than follow a script. Their comments that John was "hard to control" worried me, but I already had resolved to step in and cover any missteps if necessary. Three decades of increasingly institutionalized markets rendered these ritualized analyst presentations critically important for influencing the overall market reaction. I figured we'd have our share of skeptics but felt hopeful that I had proven myself enough over the years that most investors would be excited about our transaction.

Walking out onto the stage, I knew once and for all this day was special: The analysts were actually applauding! In all my years, I never could remember the cynical analysts acclaiming a deal so publicly and with such apparent unanimity. My nerves instantly calmed. John and I took our seats at a table festooned with the broad blue banner we had hastily designed with a red Citigroup umbrella. John spoke first in his typical nasal-staccato manner. "This is an opportunity to put the best management teams in the business together . . . we're committed to performance . . . we come together to create a whole which is where many feel the industry wants to go . . . I've known Sandy for years ever since we were on the board of a troubled company—that's when directors get to know each other . . ."

John spoke briefly and in sufficiently broad terms to allow me to address the deal's specific rationale. Understanding that the crowd would scrutinize our capacity to partner effectively, I began by addressing how long John and I had known one another and spoke of my respect for what he had accomplished. I then rattled off my version of what would make Citigroup so formidable: "We'll have 100 million retail customers and 30 million corporate clients . . . revenues will be about $50 billion while earnings will exceed $8 billion. . . . Our objective over the next two years is to add $1 billion in incremental profits from cross marketing and boosting our investment bank abroad. . . . We'll have predictable earnings . . . and conservative leverage. . . . We'll have multiple distribution channels and the ability to build globally and be a leader in all our businesses." I finished by telling how we had phoned the president the night before. To peals of laughter, I whispered, "We made him an insider and, even though this was Washington, the news didn't leak!"

Our presentations completed, we turned to the part of these meetings I always enjoyed most, fielding questions and interacting with the analysts. I scanned the audience and realized I was now dealing with a substantially new crowd compared to those analysts who had followed Travelers. Until now, insurance and specialty finance analysts largely had covered our stock, but we'd now have the opportunity and challenge of dealing with a slew of bank analysts, many of whom possessed considerable stature and influence over investor opinion. I had a good idea how our old constituency might react to the deal, but I now wondered how this sea of new faces—perhaps unfamiliar with my track record—would respond.

The questions bubbled forth: "No one thinks of either one of you as a 'co-anything' [laughs]—how will it work?" "How will you deal with the regulatory issues—will you have to divest part of your business?" "How will you merge and integrate a company this large?" "Where will the $1 billion in earnings improvements come from?" They were all fair questions; in retrospect, I felt many of the people questioning the regulatory issues somehow thought that we were trying to do something illegal.

In response, John and I conveyed our confidence that nothing would stand in the way of the merger. We spoke of our mutual respect and determination to work well together and to set an example for our colleagues. We described the merger as a "revenue-driven deal" where new business opportunities would hopefully make our goal of $1 billion in earnings enhancements a conservative estimate. The questions may have been pointed, but we had good answers worked out, and—despite the warnings that John Reed could be a loose cannon—I thought he handled himself very well.

As the meeting wound up, I felt it had gone quite well indeed. John and I stood; I patted him on the back; and we publicly shook hands. Glancing at a note someone had passed me, I saw that our stocks had jumped upward at the start of trading on enormous volume. People were voting that the merger was a very good thing. Exuberant, I slipped the note into my pocket and enthusiastically greeted the many analysts who by now were surging toward the stage to shake hands. We were on our way.

———

The excitement built all morning.

Immediately after the analyst meeting, we headed to the press conference at the Waldorf-Astoria. A group of television cameras and photographers awaited us out front, but that was nothing compared to what we'd see in a moment. Walking up the stairs into the hotel and turning left toward the meeting room, we were barraged by an army of cameras and flashes. My adrenaline was pumping, and I gushed with excitement. As John and I stepped up onto the stage, another sea of flashes exploded simultaneously. It was like the Fourth of July and being elected president of the United States rolled together. The rush of pride and excitement at that moment was like no other experience in my life.

The analyst meeting had prepared us well for the press conference—it was shorter and our answers were crisp. The reporters posed questions similar to those of the analysts, but knowing now that investors were rushing to buy our shares, we responded in a more easygoing manner, enjoying the moment for all it was worth.

"Will there be layoffs?" someone asked. "This deal isn't about cost cutting," we responded. "We started with two CEOs—doesn't that speak for itself?" "What's next for acquisitions, Sandy?" I smiled and dodged the question, but to laughter put in a plug for Salomon Smith Barney: "Our investment bank handled this deal for us—I hope others will call our bankers since they obviously know how to do big deals." "Sandy, you've reportedly talked to all sorts of companies about merging; were you surprised when John was willing?" To this question, I simply smiled broadly, paused for effect, and declared emphatically, *"Yes!"*

At the conclusion, John and I stood and put our arms around one another, and a new surge of flashbulbs captured the image for posterity. We then made our way out of the hotel and began walking the five blocks up Park Avenue back to Citicorp's offices. The army of reporters and cameramen followed us every step of the way. More precisely, they engulfed us. Joanie had been with me all morning and now grabbed my arm and pressed close—the gesture confirmed she was sharing every ounce of the excitement. With photographers darting in to snap our pictures and the host of reporters yelling out questions as we walked, one more analogy came to mind.

I felt like a rock star swamped with adoring fans.

For the rest of the day, John and I made calls to important investors, clients, and politicians. I never took my eye off the stock quote machine and our surging stock price. By the close of trading, Travelers' price had galloped 18 percent higher, and our combined market capitalization had expanded by a whopping $30 billion. Not bad for a day's work! I marveled how far we had come since the days of Commercial Credit in making this long shot a reality. For nearly fifty years, I had wanted to build the largest and best financial company in the world, and now I had arrived. I was giddy contemplating our new global platform.

The next morning's papers framed our deal in historic terms—in a stroke, we had challenged the status quo which had created artificial silos in the financial services industry. Now we had jumped on the fact that technology and competition had rendered that fractured approach out of step with reality.

Favorable reaction came from almost every quarter. Even John Dingell, the powerful chairman of the House Commerce Committee and someone who had tussled with John Reed over the years, called and offered his support. Not only did our deal provoke an initial surge in share prices across the financial services sector, we put a number of our key competitors on the defensive.

Suddenly, companies like Merrill Lynch had to respond. I loved that feeling of doing something unexpected and forcing others to react. The press and the analysts had taken in our deal at face value—they recognized the value I had created for my shareholders over the years while they accepted John Reed's mystique as a CEO who had been a boy wonder and industry innovator. I didn't appreciate it at the time, but in those days when investors were caught up in a bull market that had run for years, CEOs were really treated like celebrities. In every respect, it was a unique moment.

The excitement continued for several days. On Tuesday evening, Joanie and I treated John and Cindy to dinner at Le Cirque. John didn't enjoy food as I did, but I relished introducing him to one of my favorite restaurants. Savoring the delicious food and Bordeaux, we finally had our first chance to kick back and celebrate. We talked about our kids, our travels, and our charitable involvements and felt energized about our new partnership.

The next day, Joanie and I headed to Augusta for the Masters golf tournament, which Travelers sponsored. Over three nights, we hosted nearly four hundred clients at dinners where I waxed on about how the merger had come together and how Citigroup would offer its customers exceptional service. Strutting around the grounds in my green jacket, I enjoyed seeing my friends. Even a number of the professional golfers whom I had known for years—like Ray Floyd and Hal Sutton—came running up to offer their congratulations. I don't know what a parade down Broadway feels like, but this amounted to the next best thing: a celebration in the temple of golf.

Later in April, several of our competitors announced mega-deals of their own. NationsBank merged with BankAmerica; First Chicago and Banc One joined forces; and Bank of New York made an unsolicited bid for Mellon Financial. Undeniably, the forces of consolidation had taken over the industry; notably, none of these deals rivaled the power, foresight, and overall audaciousness of what we had assembled in creating Citigroup.

14

Fear and Loathing

U nfortunately, the elation that accompanied the merger didn't last
long. I was stunned by how quickly squabbles among my executives and unsteady financial markets intruded. We had an enormous amount of work in front of us and didn't need these sorts of
distractions. The week that had begun with our blockbuster announcement and ended with my parade around Augusta turned out to be the
happiest period I'd see for a long time.

Our emphasis on speed and secrecy during our merger talks implied we had to defer management assignments until after the deal's
announcement. That meant, of course, that we had to determine who'd
lead our businesses as quickly as possible once the deal was out in the
open. But the complexity of this merger outstripped any we had done
before. Unlike Travelers' typical modus operandi where we determined
management assignments ahead of time and where we placed a premium on accountability and fast decision making, our approach this
time by necessity had to differ.

I had committed to a merger of equals that called for balanced
managerial assignments between Citicorp and Travelers executives. I
was largely unfamiliar with Citicorp's international and commercial
banking franchises so it made sense that we should first study our new
businesses before making dramatic changes. We'd soon learn that these

self-imposed constraints would slow progress and generate a lot of uncertainty for our managers.

Nevertheless, we had to start slotting people into jobs. John and I decided to hastily convene a handful of our top executives somewhere away from the office. I already had committed to be in Bermuda for a Directors Council meeting of our top brokers, and we decided it made sense to tack on a couple of extra days there for our deliberations.

On the last Sunday in April, John and six others joined me at the Princess Hotel for a two-day session where we'd decide who would run our principal line and staff units. We purposely kept the group small. It was natural for me to bring Jamie Dimon and Bob Lipp, who had been by my side all the way in building Travelers and who respectively could offer insight into financial matters and the Consumer Business. I also insisted that Mike Carpenter come to represent our corporate and institutional businesses. John, meanwhile, brought his longtime aide Paul Collins, Citicorp's Consumer Bank head Bill Campbell, and a third executive named Larry Philips, whom he had recently hired to head human resources. Ensconced in one of the hotel's suites, we set to work with a congenial "let's get this done" attitude, and the progress came surprisingly fast.

By Monday afternoon, we had come up with a rational structure that fairly represented the two companies. Jamie would lead our Corporate Investment Bank with three direct reports: Deryck would take Investment Banking, while Citicorp's Victor Menezes and Dennis Martin respectively would run Corporate Banking and Emerging Markets. On the Consumer Business side, Bob Lipp and Bill Campbell would work as co-heads. Similarly, in Asset Management we opted for joint leaders from Travelers and Citicorp. On the staff side, operations and human resources went to Citicorp executives, whereas we gave the chief financial officer's job to Travelers' Heidi Miller. Everyone seemed pleased by the outcome.

I felt encouraged by the plan, especially the way it dealt with Jamie and Deryck, whose relationship since the Salomon Brothers deal had been consistently nettlesome. I didn't relish making Jamie sole head of the Corporate Investment Bank after he had treated Deryck so shabbily, but I reasoned that Deryck would be happier not having to contend with sharing responsibility with Jamie any longer. Importantly, the plan also put a new layer of management between Jamie and his groupies. I figured Victor and Deryck would limit Jamie from having free rein and finally give me two trustworthy executives to whom I could go for information.

Sadly, the progress proved fleeting. Upon our return to New York, I presented the plan to Deryck, who immediately objected. He flatly refused to report to Jamie, arguing it wasn't appropriate. "When you bought Salomon, you promised I'd be equal to Jamie. Since then, he's done everything imaginable to undermine me. There's no way I'll work for him."

Deryck was clearly insulted by not being included in Bermuda. "I was supposed to be an equal with Jamie . . . you go to Bermuda and I'm suddenly no longer his equal." I was flabbergasted by his vehemence, but the bad blood with Jamie obviously ran deep. I stressed he'd now have Jamie's old reports working under his command, but Deryck countered that the arrangement would be a recipe for disaster: "Jamie will never allow his people to support me. They'll do everything in their power to make me fail."

It sickened me to hear how Jamie had poisoned the relationship and thoroughly reneged on his promise to act as a partner. I understood it wouldn't be right for Deryck to become a victim and promised to speak to John about a change in plan.

I surprised John with my change of heart. I could see that John didn't like reopening an issue once a decision had been made. By contrast, I valued talking through issues with people and incorporating their feelings before finalizing things. At first, John reacted, "We made a decision. If Deryck doesn't like it, screw him." I resisted and impressed upon John that Deryck was too valuable to lose. Had John remained inflexible, I might have backed down, but my partner deferred to my judgment, and with that, we began a week-long scramble to find a new arrangement which would make everyone happy.

Burdened by two years of increasing frustration and creeping hostility, my relationship with Jamie suffered even more during the next several days. Jamie became apoplectic when I told him that we needed to change the plan. I obviously had raised his expectations, but Jamie had worked with me long enough to know that I reserved the right to change my mind.

Hearing that I now wanted him to share responsibility with Deryck for the Corporate Investment Bank, he let loose. "You have to be kidding!" he yelled. "Deryck doesn't have a clue how to run this business. The smartest thing he ever did was to get you to pay Buffett and Salomon's other shareholders a big premium for a mediocre franchise. You can thank me for cleaning up things downtown, and it's time you give me some fucking credit."

Assaulted, I angrily shouted back, reminding Jamie that he had never lived up to his commitment to partner with Deryck and that time and again he had proven himself incapable of working with others outside his narrow circle. We yelled ourselves to a stalemate, but that turned out to be just one of many arguments that week.

The next day, I came back with a different idea and suggested we name Jamie president and have various staff functions report to him. Under this plan, we would have taken him out of the Corporate Investment Bank altogether. John and I hadn't planned to name a president, but I reasoned this approach would placate my obstreperous colleague. Once again, however, Jamie hated the idea, saying he only wanted to run a line unit. It was "a matter of self-respect to run a business," he insisted. Unwilling to draw the parallel to my own experience at American Express more than a decade earlier, I tried to reason with him. "If you're president and have the major staff functions, you'll be in an important position. You'll have the capacity to get involved with all sorts of things and learn different businesses, something you've always enjoyed. It's the best way to go if you want to run the company one day." It was a waste of time. Jamie didn't want to be president if he couldn't run a line unit.

I withdrew the notion of making Jamie president and over the next few days tried a variety of other ideas to promote some sort of sharing for the Corporate Investment Bank. However, Jamie wasn't happy with anything I proposed. I kept John Reed posted and felt increasingly embarrassed by the unfolding soap opera. Finally, John and I agreed that we'd simply set up a three-way leadership arrangement for the corporate business where Jamie would share power with Deryck and Victor. Emerging Markets would report directly to John and me. I knew the arrangement was inherently unstable but figured it would buy us enough time to rationalize the business's management structure later. The last thing I wanted was an ugly stalemate that risked undermining our progress even before the merger closed.

Jamie railed against the triumvirate structure but soon realized he faced a fait accompli. In a final bid to mollify my unhappy executive, I offered Jamie the president's title once again but with scaled-back staff responsibilities given that he'd now remain heavily involved in managing the Corporate Investment Bank. He accepted the title but remained unsatisfied. I'm sure his coterie of lieutenants was stoking his insecurities, and he had it in his mind that his self-respect was constantly on the line. In a last gasp, Jamie insisted I include him on the board, to which I laughingly replied, "You have to be joking. You've known from the start that our merger agreement has called for no inside directors apart from John and me." Jamie didn't want to hear it. "It's absurd," he claimed. "I've helped build this company, and I deserve to be treated better than the others like Deryck."

Jamie may have wanted to be seen as first in line for succession behind John and me, but I couldn't imagine broadcasting him as a first among equals at that point. On May 6, we announced Citigroup's initial management structure. Jamie received the president title, but we purposely said nothing about succession and let outsiders draw their own conclusions regarding his standing.

The week-long struggle left me depressed. Jamie was self-destructing at a time when he had a golden opportunity to repair his relationship with me and prove to John his capacity to lead. In hindsight, it might have been far simpler had I been more dictatorial with Jamie from the start. I missed many chances when I simply could have said "accept it or leave." By not taking that approach, I may have led him on. Unfortunately, Jamie and I shared a complex relationship filled with lots of emotional baggage. I had known him since he was

a kid and watched him grow and stand by me even when I had little
to offer after I left American Express. I felt obliged to acknowledge
his loyalty and couldn't overlook the brilliance he frequently displayed. Settling Jamie's position in the wake of the merger was far
from my finest hour, but I'm not sure I had the capacity to play it any
other way.

Although the negotiations with Jamie grabbed the spotlight during
this time, other members of my team, particularly Bob Lipp, were also
restive. John wrote a follow-up memo describing our understandings
in Bermuda which set Bob off. We had agreed that Bob and Bill Campbell jointly would manage the Consumer Business. Bob accepted the
arrangement, though he had low regard for Campbell, who had little
experience in financial services. (Bill Campbell had joined Citicorp
only a year before following a career spent mostly as a marketing executive at Philip Morris.) One morning amid my wrangling with Jamie,
Bob came storming into my office waving a copy of John's memo.

"This isn't what we agreed on," Bob angrily declared. "I'm not
going along with this. This is crazy." He laid the memo on my desk,
and I saw that he had underlined the disputed sentences in red ink. Sure
enough, the document appeared to give Campbell preferential treatment including responsibility for the international area. Bob looked
forward to taking on the international franchise and obviously didn't
want to miss out on this exciting aspect of the merger.

Bob suggested John was trying to pull a fast one and was looking
to protect his authority over the Consumer Business. I didn't see it that
way and assumed that the wording more likely reflected an honest difference in recollections. "Relax, Bob," I offered. "I'll speak to John, and
we'll work it out." It didn't take long for John to back off as we agreed
that we needed to demonstrate flexibility between ourselves to set an
example for our teams.

The frustrations which Jamie and Bob expressed were mirrored by
many of my other associates who now recognized that we were approaching this merger unlike any we had done before. Almost all were
disoriented by the "two-by-two" management structure—soon euphe-
mistically labeled "Noah's Ark"—where we had co-heads for each major

business (or tri-heads for the Corporate Investment Bank) reporting to co-CEOs.

No one from Travelers had ever considered approaching a deal without our side being the conquering hero ready to move promptly on decisions. With Citigroup, we suddenly had to learn a new business and first decide who had the capacity to make the intelligent decisions. The potential value of our new company was so vast that it warranted holding back in order to fill our knowledge gaps before charging ahead. I assumed my colleagues' qualms would be answered in time.

Unfortunately, another huge challenge soon began to come into focus. In the spring of 1998, global financial markets had been choppy for months reflecting heightened investor awareness of the risks in Asian markets like Indonesia and Korea. After buying Salomon Brothers, I thought we had addressed our vulnerabilities. In fact, markets settled down noticeably during the first quarter. The calm, however, proved short-lived. I began to notice a disconcerting string of daily trading losses in our proprietary trading group, notably in the fixed income arbitrage area.

Salomon's fixed income arbitrage group had pioneered the use of complex statistical models designed to ferret out market inefficiencies and profit when these pricing anomalies eventually corrected. For the past several years, the effort had produced exceptional returns with little volatility; however, that low-risk profile suddenly appeared to have ended. I discussed my concerns with Jamie, who insisted that he was on top of the situation and that the losses would soon reverse. Initially, I took him at his word not realizing that matters in fact were far more serious.

Jamie might have harbored reservations over Salomon's risk profile when we first acquired the company, but he had changed his tune considerably by early 1998. Having repositioned our exposures, he now claimed that he understood the risks and appreciated the profits which the proprietary trading group had generated over the prior several years. When I suggested transferring responsibility for arbitrage to my son, Marc, earlier in the year, Jamie flatly rejected the idea and claimed he felt comfortable running the unit.

Although Jamie may have boasted that he understood the business, the results didn't seem to show it. Common sense told me something had changed when suddenly we were experiencing an increasingly long string of losses. It appeared as if our models were out of sync with reality. This business had produced high risk-adjusted returns in the past, yet I now wondered whether others had figured out Salomon's secrets.

Indeed, many experienced Salomon traders had gone to competitors over the years and presumably had taken their trading insights and models with them. One only had to look as far as the giant hedge fund, Long-Term Capital Management. The firm's founder, John Meriwether, had founded Salomon's arbitrage business in the 1980s but left in the early 1990s to ply his brilliance for himself. While its success was destined not to last, Long-Term Capital racked up more than a 40 percent annualized return on investment between 1994 and 1997. Losing Meriwether undoubtedly had been a big blow to Salomon Brothers.

Our rising losses jeopardized our credibility with investors and prompted me to press Jamie repeatedly for explanations, though I never felt satisfied by his answers. It all sounded like gobbledygook filled with formulas. Frustrated, I turned to Deryck. While pushed aside by Jamie, Deryck knew plenty of people in the trenches and was soon providing me answers in plain English.

Jamie hated my going around his back, yet I long since understood that he would do anything to preserve his autonomy and limit his people from sharing their perspectives with me. Undoubtedly, Deryck enjoyed the opportunity to play off my tensions with Jamie. Still, I refused to hold that against him since I desperately wanted an independent evaluation.

Some of Deryck's comments amazed me. I had been bothered all along by the way our arbitrage business was disconnected from serving our customers and instead took proprietary positions using our firm's capital. Now I discovered things that made me wonder if this business might in fact be in conflict with our clients. Separately, I learned that we had taken a big bet that interest costs on floating rate obligations would remain stable or decrease relative to those in the fixed rate market. I realized that a substantial rise in short-term rates would have hurt us badly. We were exposed to the tune of $1 billion on the position if interest rates went only moderately against us. It was a terrible risk/return tradeoff, and I couldn't understand how we had accepted that sort of risk for our company.

In late June, Joanie and I headed to France for our annual vacation. The problems in our arbitrage business weighed on me during the entire trip. If we screwed up, I'd be held responsible, and I reminded myself how perilous it is to stay in a business one doesn't understand. Arbitrage may have been important for Salomon before we bought it. Now, however, it was much smaller as a share of our earnings and therefore expendable.

It was time to get out. I returned and mandated that we promptly shut down the domestic portion of the business.* Jamie thought I was overreacting and even went so far as to suggest I should stay out of his way while he managed the exposure. In this case, I no longer gave him any room to push back. We substantially exited our exposure by August, trimming our assets by tens of billions of dollars. The retrenchment initially looked costly as we booked further losses in the face of limited market liquidity. Yet the wisdom of this decision soon became clear.

Market conditions appeared increasingly tenuous as the summer of 1998 progressed. Once the darlings of investors, Asian markets sagged as suppliers of capital questioned the financial underpinnings of one country after the next. The capital flight fed on itself as local interest rates

---

*I decided against closing our nondomestic arbitrage activities at that time since it would have been too much to execute in a short time and since our business outside the United States seemed more resilient to competitive pressures.

soared and currencies plummeted. By early August, the problems in Asia suddenly became transformed into the "Asian Contagion," and broad selling gripped equity and debt markets in nearly every emerging market around the world. Each day brought new mini-panics: first Indonesia, next Turkey, and then on to Brazil. Soon, investors debated whether events were overtaking the International Monetary Fund, which had been designed to facilitate the global financial order.

Suddenly, Russian bonds began to sink fast as rumors spread of enormous selling by banks and hedge funds. Many market participants looked to Russia's political sensitivity and assumed that the IMF would step in and ease the pressure. However, matters instead turned ugly. On August 13, the Russian government imposed currency controls, and four days later, it followed up with a moratorium on repaying its external debts. In effect, Russia had devalued. With no IMF bailout, risk premiums surged anew on emerging market securities, and this time investors ran from risk in seemingly every market.

The liquidity squeeze that had begun in Asia had become a global phenomenon. Interest rates on almost every debt security save for ultra-safe U.S. Treasuries surged, and panicked investors now began betting on a global recession. On August 21, the gathering storm hit the U.S. equity markets as the Dow plunged 6 percent, bringing it nearly 20 percent below its level only a month earlier.

The next ten days were horrendous as the panic deepened. With market liquidity evaporating, securities experienced exceptional price volatility, and all sorts of trading strategies engaged in by the financial community seemed to go off track at once. Hedges no longer worked, and risk calculations seemed null and void. Nearly record trading volumes swamped the U.S. stock market while the broad averages continued to slide.

Major financial firms, including our own company, began to see mounting losses, wild rumors, and sliding share prices. By the end of the month, banks and brokerages began disclosing their losses. We pegged Salomon Smith Barney's trading losses at $360 million, though profits in other areas provided a partial offset. Still, nothing we could disclose could lift the gloom. Our stock had plunged by a third during August alone and now stood at $30 per share, 40 percent below its price on that seemingly distant day when we unveiled our merger with Citicorp.

———————

It had been nearly five months since we had announced the creation of Citigroup, yet we still hadn't received the regulatory go-ahead we needed to close the merger. With each new loss and downtick in our share price, I dreaded to think that the unfolding market debacle might undo the deal of a lifetime. Since deciding to scale back our arbitrage business earlier in the summer, I had kept John Reed posted on our market exposures and assured him that we'd keep reining in our risks, but I still feared that John might panic and back out of the deal. To his credit, John reassured me that we were partners and that we would jointly weather the storm.

Still, I remained paranoid that the merger might come unglued and was worried over our mounting losses from hedge fund clients with Russian exposure and whether Jamie really understood our trading risks. Accordingly, I decided to lead a comprehensive review of our hedge fund exposure in late August. Jamie resisted my intrusion with his now standard comment, "Let me run the business. I have it under control." However, I needed to hear the answers for myself.

Convening a team of our market experts including the head of our fixed income business, Tom Maheras, I realized that we possessed only a cursory understanding of our hedge fund business. We had evaluated collateral specific to the trading positions we were financing instead of examining our clients' broader borrowing, both with us and with other broker dealers. I was stunned by the razor-thin interest we charged these clients which seemed to ignore the underlying financial risks. Our competitors, moreover, were moving faster than us to line up extra collateral from our clients. Too often, we were finding ourselves left with claims against busted hedge funds where the only remaining "collateral" was worthless pieces of paper typically issued by now defunct Russian companies.

Around the same time that we were analyzing our overall hedge fund exposure, we received our first hints that serious problems might be brewing at the giant of all hedge funds, Long-Term Capital Management. By the beginning of 1998, LTCM had gathered $5 billion from investors and, through the magic of leverage, controlled assets exceeding $100 billion.

The sign that something might be amiss came during that horrific final week in August. Tom Maheras informed me that he had received a call from two of his contacts at LTCM saying the firm was interested in a capital infusion and inviting us to take an equity stake. The invitation was completely out of character as LTCM had always arrogantly resisted giving any outsider a clear picture of its financial position. I had no intention of stepping up our exposure but reasoned that this might be an opportunity to learn more about the firm we had already financed so extensively. To our dismay, we soon found out that LTCM was racking up losses and that it couldn't sell assets fast enough to keep up with its now declining capital. The firm's leverage was rising dangerously.

Within a few days, LTCM's troubles became public knowledge. Incredibly, the fund's value had dropped 44 percent during the month, and its capital had sunk to $2.3 billion—a stunning 52 percent decline from the start of the year. Closed to new investors since 1995, LTCM suddenly announced it would open the fund. This public invitation along with the firm's earlier private efforts to bring in new investors represented a surefire acknowledgment that the firm faced severe liquidity problems.

By the second week of September, the hedge fund's trading results took on a life of their own, performing miserably day after day. Many assumed that other firms, benefiting from the information they had gleaned in looking over LTCM's books, had become predatory and were directly trading against LTCM's positions. By mid-month, LTCM's capital had dwindled to $1.5 billion, and Bear Stearns—LTCM's clearing broker—announced it would stop processing trades if capital fell below $500 million.

Events finally came to a head. On the evening of September 22, the New York Fed invited me along with CEOs from nine other major banks and brokers to attend a crisis meeting to discuss the situation.

The Fed provided the invitation and the venue, though it allowed the CEOs to take the lead in the talks. The question that quickly came into focus related to whether we should form an industry consortium to take over LTCM in order to manage an orderly liquidation.

I had dismissed the idea a couple of weeks earlier when Tom Maheras raised the notion, but I changed my mind, especially as we were now talking about spreading the risks over a large group and barring Meriwether from continuing to call the shots. Each firm would have to kick in $250 million assuming everyone participated in the rescue. I promptly announced that Salomon Smith Barney would go along. The crisis reminded me of the early 1970s when the entire brokerage industry nearly melted down because of out-of-control back offices and interlocking settlements. Now, as then, I didn't want to take the chance on seeing what the failure of a major firm would mean.

The next morning, we reconvened at 9:30 with an expanded group of sixteen major creditor firms ostensibly to finalize the consortium. However, the meeting failed to begin on time. We learned that Goldman Sachs, along with AIG and Warren Buffett, had submitted a bailout proposal of their own, causing the unexpected delay. Most of the CEOs were furious that Goldman would engage in such double-dealing.

I had a prior commitment that afternoon and fumed that Goldman would make us all cool our heels while they tried to gain an advantage. Nevertheless, the delay provided the rest of us the chance to caucus, and I soon realized that getting unanimous agreement on the bailout might be problematic. Bear Stearns' Ace Greenberg announced his firm wouldn't contribute since it already had a large clearing exposure. Lehman's Dick Fuld contended his firm should be cut a break given its smaller size. And Morgan Stanley CEO Phil Purcell questioned whether the consortium was the right approach and whether the consequences of failure were really that dire. I took issue with Purcell and lobbied him in the hallway to go along with the deal. "Phil," I said, "this isn't about making money. None of us want to see this company liquidate in an inappropriate way. We're all better off working together to bail it out." In the end, he went along.

The Goldman deal fell apart early that afternoon, and the meeting of the full group finally got under way. Late for my other commitment, I handed off our representation to Jamie. I didn't receive a report until after 6:00 P.M. when Jamie finally called to relate that we had a deal. Bear Stearns stood firm and refused to ante up while Lehman and three French banks held out against participating fully. The other firms made up the difference and each committed $300 million.

I had mixed emotions. However, I was relieved we had avoided a big unknown and thought it was terrific that Wall Street could work together without substantive government intervention. Ultimately, the deal worked out well as the consortium provided sufficient capital to stop the fire sale of assets and allow for a longer-term recovery of value. The rescue group ended up being repaid in full two years later along with a small profit.

Our review of Salomon Smith Barney's hedge fund exposure began before we understood what we were up against with LTCM, but the crisis with this huge fund brought home that we had charged too quickly into the hedge fund business. LTCM wasn't the only hedge fund that had balked at giving us a detailed picture of its financial position. I asked my associates, "How can we finance these firms if we don't know what we're backing?"

Throughout this period, a broader concern weighed on me: namely, whether our missteps might undermine John Reed's confidence in our deal. I wanted to do everything possible to reassure my new partner. Accordingly, I announced at the end of our hedge fund review that we would exit the business. "Take down our exposures as far and fast as you can," I directed. Jamie reminded me that we served more than a thousand hedge funds and that many were good clients. We skirmished once again, but I wasn't about to back down.

With the resolution of LTCM and my decision to cut our hedge fund exposure, the most contentious phase of the market crisis seemed to pass. Still, it took until early October for the global liquidity crisis to ease and only then after markets seized up further and forced the Fed to cut interest rates aggressively. The crisis had cost Salomon Smith Barney $1 billion in losses, though profits rebounded quickly once interest rates began to fall. On September 24—the day after the LTCM bailout—we received word that the Fed had approved our merger with Citigroup, and we set a closing date for October 8. It tortured me that our stock price, now at $27, had fallen nearly 50 percent from the day of our merger announcement. To his credit, John never once wavered on the deal even though Citicorp's losses from Russia and hedge funds were a fraction of ours. Our honeymoon had been interrupted by the summer's market crisis, yet our partnership remained firmly intact.

The market meltdown and my bruising battle with Jamie over his post-merger role took our relationship to a new low. Jamie hated the tri-headed structure for managing the Corporate Investment Bank and evidently simmered over what he saw as a loss of stature in the combined organization. His demeanor in management meetings deteriorated drastically. He'd denigrate the abilities of Citicorp's senior executives, openly put down Deryck, whom he despised more than ever, and complain caustically about "stupid decisions" we were making. It was a sorry spectacle which I'm sure depressed the rest of the team, especially those who had been with us long enough to remember the days when Jamie and I enjoyed a close and vibrant relationship.

Jamie also stayed downtown at Salomon Smith Barney's offices as much as possible. I thrive on positive interaction with people, and Jamie's alternating combativeness and aloofness infuriated me. The situation was bad enough before. In the wake of the merger with Citicorp, it became a much larger issue.

In fact, a slew of integration issues confronted our new company with some of the most urgent arising in the Corporate Investment Bank. No one had ever merged a commercial and investment bank before, and we had to confront a myriad of questions about how to integrate areas such as foreign exchange, fixed income, and derivatives products. How to organize our corporate calling officers proved especially complicated.

Salomon's aggressive and well-paid investment bankers projected an air of superiority with many bragging about their multitude of CEO relationships. The Citibank people, by contrast, came from a far different culture built on decorum and middling pay scales.

Given the complexity of these challenges and the obvious sensitivities on the Citicorp side, I disagreed with Jamie's frequent insistence that Salomon Smith Barney should play the dominant role and worried about his inability to get along with his new partners in running the Corporate Investment Bank. His "our way or the highway" attitude may have worked in earlier mergers, but the newness and complexity of Citigroup demanded a more nuanced and patient approach.

Jamie's aggressive behavior almost certainly shocked John Reed. During our negotiations, I had warned John that he shouldn't look to Jamie as a successor. However, I doubt he grasped my message. In fact, for a short time following our announcement, John looked like he had found a soul mate in Jamie. Both were intelligent, brash, and analytical. However, as much as John might have liked to establish a relationship with Jamie, it never took hold. Jamie's approach clearly clashed with the buttoned-down culture John had maintained at Citicorp, and his constant carping soon tarnished him in John's eyes.

Amid continuing chaotic market conditions, we closed the merger in early October. Thankfully, the Fed soon cut interest rates and—as if on command—global markets sharply recovered. We had a lot of work ahead of us, but relief and excitement over successfully completing the merger put a spring in my step. Earlier, John and I had decided to use an already scheduled Travelers event at the Greenbrier Resort in West Virginia to bring together our top executives. The five-day meeting would begin two weeks following the merger. It seemed the perfect venue to begin to forge a common culture and focus on the integration.

Before we headed off, we held one more management meeting in Armonk to discuss integration, and as usual, the conversation soon settled on difficulties in the Corporate Investment Bank. For once Jamie, Deryck, and Victor agreed on a common message. "This doesn't work—you need to come up with a different management structure," they collectively intoned. It wasn't what I wanted to hear, and I dismissively instructed them to go into a conference room and stay there until they could report back with an integration plan. When they returned sometime later, it was clear the three had solved nothing. Oddly, Deryck now took the lead: "You need to come up with a different answer. Tri-heads simply doesn't work. If you pick one, we'll accept it. If you want two, just clarify the roles, and that would be okay. Three, though, is a recipe for gridlock."

His message, however, hit a stone wall. "Why do you guys have to be so difficult?" I asked. "Sharing works for John and me. Why is it so tough for you?" At that, the meeting broke up but only after Jamie got in the last word by stating, "It shouldn't be just about what works for you and John."

We headed to the Greenbrier with the issue unresolved, but I hoped that the large meeting would spur a more cooperative spirit. One hundred fifty of our top executives convened in West Virginia along with their spouses. The Citicorp contingent included numerous managers from outside the country whom I hadn't yet met, and I looked forward to learning more about our international businesses. I also wanted to use the meeting to showcase how Travelers included spouses and used sessions in relaxed settings to promote a healthy sharing of ideas and consensus.

The meeting began well enough, and I started to reach out to my new colleagues from Citicorp. Joanie and I had arranged for small groups to join us for lunch in our cabin each day, and we enjoyed going around the table asking each to tell us about their background. Those who worked outside the United States shared especially interesting stories including tales of forced evacuations in remote corners of the world and how local cultures affected business. Our new global franchise fascinated me.

We divided the conference into a combination of large presentations and smaller breakout sessions, the latter split evenly between Citicorp and Travelers people. Bob Lipp and Bill Campbell opened with a well-presented report on the Consumer Business. Bob never liked having to share with Campbell, though he did a good job hiding his personal feelings that morning. Next, we turned our focus to the Corporate Investment Bank, and Deryck took to the podium. He gave a well-received speech that focused on our vision and the need to break down factions within the company. Jamie then followed, and my heart sank as he rambled on incoherently. The talk had no bearing on what we had just heard and lacked focus. At one point, he even lapsed into a strange analogy with the Peloponnesian War. His aloof manner and insulting lack of preparation left the crowd bewildered and seemed anything but presidential.

That Saturday, we wrapped up the business sessions. For the final gathering, John and I sat on stools and responded to questions and comments. The feedback came loudly: We needed to do a better job of sorting out managerial assignments and speed up decisions. The comments came universally but particularly from those working in the Corporate Investment Bank. "We hear you," we promised, and committed to improving things.

Sadly, the events that evening forced our hand and placed an unforgettable damper on the entire meeting. Around ten o'clock, Joanie and I were sitting in the bar with Bob Lipp, Jay Fishman (then head of our property and casualty business), and their spouses, having left that evening's final event—a black-tie dinner-dance.

Suddenly, someone came running by and said there had been a fight on the dance floor, and that Jamie had ripped Deryck's coat. A few minutes later, Deryck and his wife, Va, came running into the bar, and my colleague proceeded to give me his side of the story. His account substantially jibed with what I heard from others later. During the dance, Steve Black, our head of Capital Markets and one of Jamie's confidants, asked to cut in and dance with Va as a peace overture of sorts but quickly became incensed when Deryck refused to return the gesture with Steve's wife. Black then publicly dressed down Deryck for his rude attitude before the Maughans haughtily walked away.

Moments later, Jamie got involved, accosting Deryck in the foyer outside the ballroom. Evidently, Black had run to Jamie and, true to form, got him riled up over the alleged snub. Jamie pressed unsuccess-fully for an apology before grabbing his "partner" by the lapel and calling him an "asshole." Deryck pulled away, ripping a button off his coat in the process.

The episode came after a lot of drinking which almost certainly contributed to the unseemly behavior. I suspect the stresses of the prior few days had set Jamie and his team on edge. I never figured out if Deryck really intended to insult Black's wife—he claimed it was all a misunderstanding—but it didn't matter. There was no excuse for a verbal or physical assault.

When Deryck finished giving me his story, his wife insisted on add-ing her opinion. Never a wallflower, Va pushed, "This is no way for people to behave. *How are you going to react to this?* If this company doesn't think this sort of stuff is important, it may not be the kind of place at which we want to work." Later that night, I asked Lipp, Fishman, and Mike Carpenter back to my cabin to get their input. Not having spo-ken to Reed yet, I didn't verbalize where I was heading but knew Jamie had reached the end of the line. Jay and Mike said little, but Bob probably read my thoughts and tried to make excuses for his friend. This time, though, Jamie had gone too far. The time for excuses had ended.

After everyone left, Joanie and I stayed up talking until three in the morning, and I finally uttered the words that had escaped me for so long: "I think it's time for Jamie to go." Appalled by Jamie's long steady slide in behavior, Joanie simply nodded her head and refused to argue. The next morning, I put on my game face, tried to ignore what had happened, and saw off many of my new associates from Citicorp. Inwardly, though, I felt mortified by the taint on our meeting and how Jamie and his team had embarrassed us in front of our new partners.

That afternoon, I made two telephone calls that set my endgame with Jamie into motion. First, I called John and gave him an emotional dump on what had happened the night before. John had left the Greenbrier early and wasn't there for the final dramatics—he couldn't believe what

I told him and quickly reminded me, "You can't allow this to persist." His comment seemed pregnant with implication, yet I resisted the urge to tell him I wanted Jamie out. The time wasn't quite right. Instead, I secured his agreement to have Chuck Prince, Citigroup's general counsel, investigate and report the facts.

On Monday and Tuesday, Jamie remained in his downtown office. We only had one brief phone conversation during which it was clear that he was unprepared to apologize for his actions. On Wednesday, Chuck presented his report, and John and I sat down to chart our response. John may have respected Jamie when we first announced the deal, but the months of arguing and rude behavior on Jamie's part had squandered his standing with Reed.

To John, ever the Presbyterian moralist, the notion of a fistfight was inconceivable. He had grown up in the staid commercial bank world where people normally referred to "The Bank" with reverence. People simply didn't brawl in his company. I took the lead. "John, we need to do something about this. Our companies never will come together if we let this sort of behavior go on. Jamie has become an impediment to making the merger work. We've got to ask him to leave."

To my immense relief, John stood and unflinchingly delivered the coup de grâce: "You can't live with this. You're absolutely right. Jamie has got to go." I felt an immediate sense of relief and gratitude since John had helped me get to a place I'd never have had the guts to reach on my own. "Thank you . . . Thank you . . ." I offered. "I'm thrilled finally to have a real partner." John then offered to communicate the decision to Jamie, but I insisted I needed to deliver the message myself. At that moment, my relationship with John probably reached its zenith. Compared to all the trouble I always had firing people, John's cold rationality made it look so easy.

John and I decided we needed a few days to communicate our decision. We first had to settle details such as who'd replace Jamie and how we'd present the change. I suggested that it would look bad if we left Deryck in his job since it wouldn't have been right for him to appear victorious at Jamie's expense. I recognized, too, that Deryck hadn't always acted as a saint over the prior year. We ended up moving him to a strategy job, typically a backwater in our company. Settling that issue, John and I quickly agreed that Mike Carpenter and Victor Menezes would make a good team and preserve the balance between Citicorp and Travelers executives.

Carpenter represented the logical choice, but I knew he'd be controversial and wasn't sure if he'd even take the job. Three years earlier, Kidder Peabody had blown up on his watch owing to poorly controlled trading activities. While Mike took the fall, I always thought he got a bum rap. Mike had a lot of experience, and I felt he could thrive if John and I gave him the proper support. John readily agreed, though we still had an issue: Mike insisted when he joined Travelers that, thanks to his Kidder experience, he never wanted to work in the securities business again. We now had to convince him to change his mind.

John and I sat down with Mike on Thursday and made our proposal. "We'd like you to do this. We *need* you to do it. We know you may have reservations, but you're more qualified than anyone else in the company." Mike initially remained noncommittal. The next day, though, he accepted the charge provided that we'd promise to replenish the annual bonus pool that had been decimated by our hedge fund and trading losses. The last thing Mike wanted was to take the job and immediately confront a rebellion over compensation.

Over the next couple of days, we prepared for the announcement and opted to issue the press release on Sunday evening when we'd stand the best chance of controlling the media's spin. I knew we were making the right decision, but I tortured myself that weekend. Jamie had annoyed me no end over the last three years, and our relationship had gotten so dysfunctional that it plainly was hurting others in our company. Still, I felt sick given all that we had accomplished together. Jamie had wanted me to treat him as an equal partner, a desire for recognition which I understood but was unwilling to satisfy. I was nearly twenty-five years his senior and spent my entire life building relationships and driving value for our shareholders. His demands for equal treatment were disproportionate with what he deserved. Jamie may have felt I was stingy in sharing credit, yet he still received enormous recognition in the years he worked for me.

Nonetheless, I understood that I had made mistakes along the way. I brought Jamie along quickly and in doing so probably gave him a sense of entitlement which discouraged him from building a consensual management style. I also forced him into challenging power-sharing arrangements with Frank Zarb, Bob Greenhill, Deryck Maughan, and finally the Citigroup's Corporate Investment Bank triumvirate. My real mistake, though, was that I repeatedly missed the chance in our early years together to curtail his aggressive behavior and mentor him into becoming a team player. Once Greenhill left, it was too late. After that, I should have wielded more of a stick. Rather than imploring him with words like "behave and all this can be yours one day," I should have threatened "shape up or else find another job."

While Joanie and I both were wrecks that final weekend, my wife did her best to buck up my confidence. We talked endlessly about how Jamie had made things difficult for far too long and how I obsessed on his actions each night when I came home from work. Just as he squandered John Reed's confidence, Jamie forfeited Joanie's backing, especially after he treated our daughter so shabbily. She may have feared the consequence of actually casting him off, but once I made up my mind, Joanie did what she always did best: She offered me her unconditional support.

On Sunday, October 31, I phoned Jamie at home and told him that it was urgent that he come to Armonk. He claimed the timing was poor as he was hosting a brunch for a group of new recruits, but I insisted he drop everything since we needed to decide on a plan following Greenbrier. John and I met him upon his arrival and showed him into a small conference room. Jamie sat at the table, while we moved to the other side. Containing my emotions, I said flatly, "We've done a lot of thinking about the organization just as you wanted, and John and I have decided on the following: Carpenter will run Salomon Smith Barney; Victor will take the Global Bank; Deryck will move to a strategy job; *and we want you to resign.*"

A pregnant pause ensued. Clearly, the decision stunned Jamie, who finally only uttered "Okay" in a subdued voice.

"Do you want to know why?" I asked. "Nope," he replied, "I'm sure you've thought it through." Disregarding the comment, I went on, "The merger isn't coming together as it should. You've been a terrific asset to our company, but your attitude is not making things work. The status quo isn't good for the company, and it's not good for you either." The words that I had worried might elude me continued to flow. "You need to announce your departure today. We can write the press release together, or we can do it on our own—that's up to you, but we want to issue it tonight." John then chimed in, reinforcing in a strong and unemotional manner how the discord was putting our merger at risk.

Still in shock, Jamie could see John and I were in lockstep and that there was no basis for an appeal. He then spoke softly and without the rancor that had tainted his voice for so long. "I guess this is it. I'm not going to fight it. I'd like this to be done in a professional way, and I'll act accordingly." The entire meeting lasted fifteen minutes. We then asked Jamie to sit with Chuck Prince to go over the press release and to stay on and meet with the Corporate Investment Bank's planning group later that afternoon.

Jamie remained in Armonk for the next couple of hours and worked through the release with Chuck. Bob Lipp arrived, too, and offered his regrets. At 4:00 P.M., the senior members of the Corporate Investment Bank management team gathered, completely ignorant as to why they had been summoned. The group sat in the large meeting room in a semicircular array of armchairs as Jamie, John, and I entered.

"Thank you for coming," John said. "Jamie has something he'd like to say." With that, Jamie stood and calmly announced to the group that we had asked for his resignation. Rising to the occasion, Jamie took the high road. "Citigroup has great potential and people, and you should all be proud. I wish you the best. I'm sorry it wasn't the best for me. If I can help, let me know."

He then walked from the room and went home.

After issuing the press release, we met with the press via telephone. We wanted to emphasize the fact that the decision had been agreed upon mutually, and thankfully, Jamie corroborated the narrative. I thought the call went well under the circumstances. Nevertheless, our stock price sagged on the news when trading opened, falling 6 percent over the next couple of days. Our investors liked Jamie and concluded that his departure meant our merger integration was in trouble.

After his departure, our lawyers worked out the severance terms, and Jamie and I didn't speak again for more than a year. The voluminous demands of integrating the merger made it easy to put Jamie out of my mind, but I still periodically wished that we could have ended things better. In December 1999, Jamie took the first step in seeking a rapprochement when he called and suggested, "Isn't it time we break bread?"

We met for lunch at the Four Seasons, and Jamie quickly did his best to get off on the right foot. He told me that he wanted to talk about the past for only two minutes. He stated that he would never have done what I did and that I had done the wrong thing by letting him go. Yet he also told me that he understood some of my reasoning and acknowledged that he often ignored me and didn't always place the company's interests ahead of his own. Finally, he mentioned that he had learned from the experience and suggested that we should look ahead and not apportion blame. Grasping the olive branch in my own way, I simply responded, "You're right. It does take two to mess up what we had." With that, I changed the subject, and we spoke about his job search and world affairs.

A few months later, Jamie signed on to become CEO of Bank One after that company had stumbled. Over the next four years, he improved the Midwestern bank's performance visibly to the point where he was able to negotiate a large merger of his own with J. P. Morgan. We have spoken only infrequently since we parted, but apparently my congratulatory call following the J. P. Morgan announcement was Jamie's first. It's now up to Jamie to demonstrate whether he can reach out to others and build a broad team. If he's learned that lesson, he'll enjoy great success.

15

The Winner's Curse

I'm an optimist by nature, and I looked forward to the future as 1998 came to a close. Many had warned of the perils of entering the co-CEO arrangement, but I scoffed at their skepticism. Instead, I continued to rationalize that John and I had the maturity to work together and that Citigroup's vast potential would silence those nervous voices. The merger energized me, and I felt I had the stamina and force of will to deliver its promise.

Little did I realize how the next fourteen months would challenge that perspective and risk the things I valued most: my faith in people; my self-confidence; and most of all, my reputation.

John Reed's personality and management style differed sharply from mine, yet I felt good about our partnership at the end of 1998. John insisted upon developing an Internet strategy and systematizing the quality of our people and operations, and I challenged myself to learn more about initiatives he had begun in these areas. John had helped me deal with Jamie and accomplish something I doubt I could have done on my own. While we recognized that we were very different people, we committed ourselves to set a collaborative tone for our new company.

After all, we'd never get our business co-heads to work together if we didn't lead by example.

Cooperation, however, didn't mean that I blinded myself to John's quirkiness. I recognized his eccentricities even before we entered into the merger. As I got to know my new partner better, they became more apparent. Just seeing where John worked came as an eye-opener. He had built a nondescript executive suite on a low floor in Citicorp Center. The building was named for the company, although it was largely leased out to other firms and sat across the street from Citicorp's primary offices on Park Avenue. I hated that the entrance to the elevator stood at the back of a shopping arcade—it didn't look the sort of place to run the most important financial services company in the world. Even my grandchildren made the point in a backhanded way: "Poppi, you're so lucky. You work in a mall!"

John's rationale for relocating there seemed stranger than the location itself: He purposely wanted to remove himself from the distraction of dealing with employees and customers so that he could concentrate on the company's organization and strategy. In his mind, being CEO meant focusing on the broader form of things rather than dealing with the intricacies of day-to-day operations. John prided himself on being analytical and forward-thinking; he didn't care about connecting with people. In fact, when he traveled, you couldn't reach him, and he'd almost never call the office. The world might be falling apart, but he ordered his secretary not to disturb him. Many times, she'd take a vacation while John traveled so his office effectively shut down. That astonished me.

John didn't relate well to investors or the financial markets either. Members of his staff warned that John wouldn't—or couldn't—control what he'd say in public. Shortly after we announced the merger, he testified before Congress and said something to the effect that "Citicorp's checking business is criminally profitable." Later, he was quoted elsewhere as having said, "Adding up our corporate banking profits over many years, we've essentially been break-even."

Why would he say such things? I didn't dwell on the remarks, yet it was odd that John couldn't recognize how such statements hurt the company. It was curious, too, that John had no interest in going to the floor of the New York Stock Exchange when Citigroup's stock opened for trading upon completion of the merger. He even bragged that he had only been to the exchange once during his entire career.* In contrast, I thought ringing in trading for our new company represented a big deal—we employed people on the trading floor, and markets were integral to our business.

Despite John's oddities, I decided these issues were not critical. I figured I could work around John's behavior and that his peculiar value system wouldn't get in the way. We felt bound to our partnership and insisted on demonstrating our ability to compromise. John had dropped the idea of selling our insurance business or spinning out our corporate activities while I bent over backward to incorporate Citicorp executives into our top management.

I genuinely liked John as a person. Joanie and I entertained John and his wife, Cindy, at our home in the Adirondacks for two days at the end of August and we hit it off well. As a house gift, the Reeds brought a silver-embossed cover of the *Business Week* issue that reported on the merger and which gave me credit for coming up with the idea—it was a thoughtful gift and underscored the good faith John was trying to bring to our partnership.

We had made considerable progress during 1998 despite the global financial crisis and the issues with Jamie, and the momentum overshadowed my hesitation with John's style. We set a new corporate planning and governance structure and selected our new board of directors. We began to evaluate our operating systems and identify weaknesses and efficiency improvement opportunities. We integrated staff functions and in December announced our first restructuring including a 6 percent cut in our workforce, an important milestone toward our promised $1 billion in merger synergies. The team of Carpenter and Menezes worked to

---

*John's dismissive attitude became particularly ironic when he was asked, a few years later, to lead reforms at the exchange.

recast the Corporate Investment Bank and began the arduous task of sorting out the business's complex organizational challenges. After a year of infighting in that business, the two set priorities and pulled together a more cohesive team.

Surprisingly, we began to see considerable new business as traditional commercial banking clients now turned to Salomon Smith Barney for investment banking services. Our strong capital position, too, allowed us to step up our lending. In short, results began to bear out the logic behind creating Citigroup.

Along with our team, John and I spent the eight-month period from the merger's announcement to the end of the year learning about our expanded array of businesses and setting integration priorities. Pressures began to build in early 1999 once we gained enough perspective to start making hard-nosed decisions. It was at this point that differences in value judgments and the contrasting quality of our executives began to undermine my harmony with John.

I always had put a premium on developing an intuitive feel for my company and acting decisively. John, on the other hand, needed to study everything to death and insisted that managers prepare large briefing "decks" that would examine issues from every angle. When we'd sit with colleagues, I'd ask a few key questions and get what I needed to make a decision while John insisted on examining issues in excruciating detail. Often, he wouldn't be able to make up his mind on a course of action. To John, process meant everything, whereas for me it was all about progress. My Travelers colleagues still hadn't gotten used to the idea that they weren't the conquering heroes in this merger, and the inability to make decisions—as well as the conflicting feedback they often received from John and me—soon became a source of frustration.

The Travelers team had sharp elbows and started complaining about the weaknesses of many of their counterparts on the Citicorp side. I dismissed the comments at first; however, as we delved deeper into issues, I recognized their criticisms often were justified. In the year before the merger, John had reached outside the industry to companies like Philip Morris, Federal Express, and Viacom for several top executives. Unfortunately, he brought people to the company who lacked even a basic understanding of financial services. In human resources, technology, electronic distribution, and even consumer banking, the shortcomings soon became noticeable.

The weaknesses in our team compounded the problems in our decision making, and I also began to question some of John's priorities, particularly an area called "e-Citi." John had established e-Citi as a stand-alone company to build an Internet business. Initially, I didn't understand the group's plan and wanted to avoid undermining something on which John placed such obvious emphasis. It soon became apparent that e-Citi was costing us huge amounts of money and lacked a coherent business strategy that would dovetail with the rest of the company. John didn't appreciate my questioning and thought I stressed short-term earnings over important investment spending. In contrast, I wondered why John hadn't done more to take advantage of Citicorp's traditional franchise before running off and spending gobs of money on an area with uncertain prospects.

Soon, the complaints from my team and John's defense of certain pet initiatives—like e-Citi—fed on one another and created a negative dynamic that weighed on our relationship. We hadn't divided responsibilities, and the absence of a rational division of labor caused us to step on each other's toes frequently. We should have done something at that point to carve out responsibilities and minimize the friction, but the only thing we agreed upon was for me to take the lead in communicating with outside analysts and the press.

I began to dwell on John's hands-off management style and disregard for delivering results. John's disinterest in speaking to customers irked me, too—it was an unrealistic way to run a company. John, on the other hand, probably bridled at my obsession with short-term results and my insistence on getting involved in the inner workings of the company.

Several issues grated on us during the first few months of 1999, and each new challenge accentuated our differences in style and personality. In particular, operations came to the fore quickly. My personal dealings with Wall Street's back office crisis in the early 1970s had etched into my brain the importance of developing a competency in processing activities. When we entered into the merger, I assumed Citicorp possessed operational skills given its scale and global scope, not to mention John's reputation as a technology whiz.

I soon realized I was wrong. Many of the systems were antiquated and didn't link with one another. Citicorp lagged badly in repairing its computer code needed for the turn of the calendar to the year 2000 (Y2K). The company processed its large credit card business inefficiently and hadn't even begun to consolidate an acquisition of AT&T's credit card business which it had purchased at the start of 1998. Costs spiraled out of control, to the point where line units received huge allocations for centralized processing over which they had no control.

John and I had assigned the operations group to Mary Alice Taylor, a woman John had recruited from Federal Express a year earlier as part of his bid to bring industry outsiders to Citicorp. She had a huge job overseeing nearly eighty thousand employees. A number of my colleagues, especially Bob Lipp, immediately complained about her, saying she may have done well with packages but didn't know the first thing about banking. At first, I dismissed the feedback. However, as word kept coming back about out-of-control allocated costs and regulatory warnings over our Y2K readiness, I took the complaints seriously and began to ask questions.

Unfortunately, I received few satisfying answers. Before our merger, Citicorp had agreed to install thousands of ATM machines in Blockbuster video stores nationally, an initiative that would cost over $50 million per year. I tried to understand how we'd benefit; the payback seemed far from clear, and I surmised we'd end up with a collection of expensive and rarely used machines. While we killed that project, costs and other problems kept coming.

I'd ask, "Why are we spending so much and what's the benefit? What are we doing to ensure we'll be ready for Y2K?" but I couldn't even get basic answers most of the time.

In January, we held our first joint Planning Group meeting upstate in the Adirondacks, and I insisted we address the issue. Over the years, Travelers had pushed operations functions down to the business units to promote accountability and control costs, and we agreed to adjust our model and move toward a more decentralized format. Mary Alice Taylor seemingly got on board; however, within weeks she reneged and fought to protect her turf. I approached John and insisted, "She's not capable of running this business. It's scary. This is no way to run a business. We have to make a change." John defended her halfheartedly, although it was clear she lacked internal support. John never had deep ties to his employees and, after all, had looked to Travelers for its "management DNA"—thus, he conceded that Mary Alice should go, and we replaced her with my longtime associate Bobby Druskin, who quickly pulled the operations area together.

Unfortunately, my issues with technology didn't stop with the operations area. At about the same time, I began to grow concerned about e-Citi, the unit John had created before our merger as a response to the Internet challenge. With dot-coms the rage, John believed traditional companies needed to create an answer for the Internet outside their traditional businesses. John also looked outside the industry for an executive to run the business, this time hiring Ed Horowitz from Viacom. Once again, we had a large unit under an executive with no real experience in financial services and were spending an enormous amount of money—$500 million per year—without an apparent payback.

At first, I treaded carefully and tried not to stick my finger in John's eye. After all, John put e-Citi at the top of his priority list, and I assumed he understood technology better than I did. Still, I couldn't hold back as I learned more. Bob Lipp repeatedly complained that the complete detachment of e-Citi from the physical portion of our franchise meant we were competing with ourselves. Confusion and service complaints multiplied. We were hurting our traditional businesses far more than creating value with new online relationships.

We had set up e-Citi in an expensive midtown Manhattan location and offered lucrative compensation arrangements to its employees. Paying $90 per square foot for space and ridiculous bonuses seemed an odd way to compete with Internet "geeks" who often operated out of their garages. The e-Citi unit included a business which processed Social Security and veterans' benefits. I figured it logically belonged in a technology unit and would cover some of our burgeoning costs. Sadly, we soon got a letter from the government telling us that our processing was so bad it might be grounds for a lawsuit. The episode was tremendously embarrassing and all the more called into question our technical competence. When you spend half a billion dollars, there should be results.

I questioned e-Citi more intensively than ever following the government processing debacle. However, John didn't appreciate my interference, claiming, "You don't understand investment spending. This is the future." By this time, John had begun to suggest that my team and I were too stingy on spending for the future, "and it's not just on e-Citi," he'd claim. Shaking off the criticism, I'd reply, "It's not a question of investing. Things like e-Citi aren't being managed. That's the problem. Microsoft and Cisco, and countless other tech companies, all make good profits; all we do is lose money!"

John and I sparred with increasing frequency over how to set a proper horizon to make investments and judge performance—he'd demand patience and vision while I operated on the principle that if you consistently deliver short-term results, the long term will take care of itself. When John and I started working together, I thought he had a lot of interesting ideas; however, the more I saw, the more I dwelled on the gaps in his execution.

My colleagues and I blanched at some of John's other ideas. He used a management tool called the "six quarter roll," a rolling budget which would be updated monthly. John insisted the approach would force executives to think about long-term trends by constantly revising targets. I had a hard time figuring out the metric since its numbers were always in flux and soon concluded it took the heat off our managers to commit to and deliver results. Similarly, John championed his "Six Sigma" project, an initiative in vogue at many large companies and intended to improve product and service quality and efficiency. Once again, many of us from Travelers bridled at the bureaucracy that accompanied the initiative. Bob Lipp loudly proclaimed we'd get the same results from simply measuring and staying on top of our business. He decided early on that the consumer business wouldn't waste time with the project, a stand which effectively killed Six Sigma for Citigroup.

My colleagues and I may have begun pushing back on some of John's favorite projects, but my co-CEO didn't hesitate to make his own feelings known on other matters. In March, Carpenter and Menezes held an off-site meeting in Puerto Rico for the top two hundred executives of the newly renamed Global Corporate Investment Bank. Never a fan of the corporate business, John flew in for his speech and proceeded to muse openly about his dislike for this side of the company and how he thought the company's future lay with the consumer. When I arrived later in the day, everyone was up in arms. Later, I confronted John as positively as I could: "You can't say things like that even if you believe them. It gets people upset." John agreed, but the damage had been done.

More troubling, John began to take aim at Bob Lipp, whom I had long regarded as our company's strongest manager. John and Bob hadn't gotten along from the start—I assumed each may have had preconceived ideas about the other dating back to the early 1980s when Bob, as president of Chemical Bank, was a competitor to Citicorp. Whatever the cause, the two sniped at one another with increasing vehemence. Bob frequently questioned the abilities of those executives handpicked by John. In return, John would complain that Bob lacked creativity, foresight, and global perspective. He'd often assert that Bob was a "small thinker" who knew more about cost cutting than how to build a business.

By the spring of 1999, Bob had tired of working with Bill Campbell and pushed to run the consumer business on his own. Bob viewed Campbell as a neophyte, a longtime cigarette industry executive who operated out of his depth in financial services. Bob rightfully claimed to know consumer financial services better than anyone in the company, and it irked him that John and I had forced him to share the consumer business with someone not in his league. With a marketing background,

Campbell had been given a mandate by John to build "Citi" into a leading consumer brand, as widely admired as Coke or Colgate. The mission represented one more of John's big ideas and an area for lavish spending. Bob Lipp thought it was all a waste: "This is crazy. Can you believe how much fucking money these guys are spending?"

When Bob first began to lobby for an end to the co-head arrangement, I implored patience: "Rome wasn't built in a day. You can't come on like a stormtrooper." Bob tried yet couldn't hold back. Branch profitability lagged badly; credit card efficiency looked subpar; and systems were awful everywhere. He understood the things that could make the consumer business far more profitable and effective; however, he saw Campbell—and Reed for that matter—as albatrosses around his neck. He first made Campbell's life miserable largely by cutting him out of decisions. When that didn't force his business co-head to the side, Bob threatened to resign if he didn't get his way.

I couldn't stand the thought of losing our best executive, and I went to Reed insisting that we promote Bob. John resisted, complaining that this represented yet another assault on his executives. By now, though, I had come to question the abilities of most of the senior executives that had come from Citicorp, and I remained adamant. John probably realized that most of the consumer business's second-tier executives owed their loyalty to Bob and that they might rebel were Bob to leave. He reluctantly went along with the change. John and I agreed to reassign Bill to a staff job. In the end, Campbell decided instead to accept a generous exit package and resigned in April.

The people John had hired from outside the industry—Taylor, Horowitz, and Campbell—never commanded much respect among Citicorp's other executives let alone among my Travelers colleagues. Thus they received little support when we questioned their business judgment. Their isolation, though, paled in comparison to that of one other original Citicorp executive, human resources head Larry Philips. Once more a recruit, this time from a unit of General Electric, Philips came across as a particularly odd sort. He was a nocturnal person and rarely worked during normal business hours. When he wasn't working out of his home in Pennsylvania, he usually was holed up in an office in Princeton, far away from our businesses. Philips seemed a kindred spirit to John—he insisted on viewing people in a largely abstract analytical manner.

In recruiting the former GE executive, John asked him to devise a completely new human resources program that would include a systematic way to evaluate executives and monitor career paths. Philips created a vast bureaucracy and came up with the "Talent Inventory Review," an annual three-week process which slotted executives into a multidimensional evaluation matrix. Before I came to understand the process, I thought the idea of systematically reviewing our people sounded interesting. However, as with most of John's pet projects, the execution proved abysmal.

During the spring of 1999, John and Larry forced our top executives to abandon their offices and troop down to Princeton for the tedious reviews. I couldn't understand why we had to disrupt our people and conduct the sessions so far out of the way (except of course that it was convenient for John and Larry, who lived nearby) rather than having Philips come to New York. Worse still, everyone hated the staff-led process, which offered little useful feedback and seemed disconnected to the real world.

Each of our executives was given an evaluation code which corresponded to a spot in Philips's complex matrix. A code of "A-3-9" might have implied a high score on teamwork, low results on recruiting effectiveness, and a strong reading on creativity. Overwhelmed and exasperated by the arcane model, I began joking that we should introduce ourselves to clients by referring to our codes: "Hi, I'm B-6-4!"

I soon realized that the human resources department at Citicorp wielded excessive power. Unlike Travelers, Citicorp did not drive equity ownership deep into the organization, and after the merger, their HR people initially resisted our attempts to instill more of an equity-driven culture. We ended up securing a reasonable compromise, yet it felt like the personnel people often ruled the place. Line people weren't allowed to make an independent hiring or firing decision—instead a designated staff person had to get involved. The rule effectively took the job of managing people away from the line managers. If that weren't bad enough, the Talent Inventory Review elicited a slew of complaints from our top executives. I found the review process and the sprawling bureaucracy distasteful and decided once again to force a change.

John had a close relationship with Philips, and I knew he wouldn't take well to my trying to sideline another one of his chosen executives. By now, I could see we were paying a huge price for keeping such mediocre executives in place and decided I could no longer live with trying to meet John halfway. Intending to play to John's sense of self-interest, I complained, "Philips isn't doing you any good. He lacks the respect of people in the company; his work habits are strange; *and he's making you look bad.*"

This time, though, John stood firm. "Why do you have to get your way on everything?" he asked. "I think this guy is very good."

When we merged, John and I had agreed to grant each other a veto over decisions, so I had to abide by his defense of Philips. Yet I couldn't stand the guy and did my best to marginalize him and force him to cooperate more with the wishes of our business managers. Eventually, he realized he lacked my backing and decided to leave the company.

Philips's departure got under John's skin and prompted him to send me a memo detailing his frustrations. After reaffirming his commitment to the merger, John shifted to the stylistic differences which separated us. "I see the merger as an evolution, while you're only focused on the moment," he noted. Referring to Larry Philips, he continued, "If you're not comfortable with people, you shut them out." He went on to express his unhappiness over my lack of support for the six quarter roll budget planning tool and his Six Sigma project. "Anything with a longer-term dimension doesn't interest you," he concluded.

John shared his frustrations with a couple of directors who had served on Citicorp's board, and the memo soon became a call to action. Ed Woolard, the tough-minded former chief of Dupont, seized on our difficulties and took the lead in helping us devise a solution. He recommended that John and I meet with Ram Charan, a management consultant known for resolving organizational conflict.

Woolard and Reed had known Ram Charan for years, and I feared that the involvement of an outsider with strong ties to John and one of his closest directors might result in an unfavorable outcome. Under a worst-case scenario, John could have painted me as a disagreeable person intent on reversing Citicorp's past priorities. Nevertheless, I also understood that our executives were struggling with the dual-CEO structure. We had to do something, and I still wanted to work with John, so I cautiously went along with hiring Charan.

A globe-trotting corporate shrink of sorts, Ram Charan emphasized from the start that John and I had an opportunity to forge a new model for managing a large corporation. "There's no reason why the two of you shouldn't be able to work together and leverage each other's strengths," he said repeatedly. After interviewing many of our executives, Ram met with me in late June while I vacationed in France. Sitting in a rented cabana overlooking the Mediterranean, Charan and I discussed my relationship with John and how we might improve the situation.

I spoke cautiously at first. However, encouraged by the relaxed surroundings, I soon unloaded as though I had known him for years. I then presented a plan which called for a formalized division of labor: I should take responsibility for running the businesses and the financial function while John should take on e-Citi and the other staff areas. I argued that this approach would allow us to focus on our strengths.

While I understood that he needed to confer with John before he could endorse the idea, Ram Charan seemed responsive. Two weeks later, we met again, this time over a weekend at my home in the Adirondacks where I presented a detailed organization chart to back up my division-of-labor idea. To my delight, Ram now embraced my suggestion, saying that he thought it made sense and could be sold to John. We spent the bulk of that second meeting discussing how the division of labor would work and agreed that John and I should reaffirm our original agreement to share information and give one another a veto over important decisions.

Though pleased and relieved by Ram Charan's acceptance of my plan, I felt even more surprised by John's subsequent agreement to go along. I had taken a risk by allowing Ram Charan's involvement, and the gamble paid off. With his buy-in secured, John and I jointly drafted a memo to our directors and presented our idea at the July board meeting. Most of the directors probably were caught off guard by our proposal and by John's willingness to disengage from the line units, and I wouldn't be surprised if some of the old Citicorp directors privately questioned whether John was ceding too much. Nevertheless, John and I presented a common front and successfully sold the new power-sharing concept. We immediately went public with the news.

The division of labor helped tremendously, and John and I delved into the areas that we enjoyed most. The arrangement gave us our own space, and I used mine to concentrate on getting our businesses in better order. Without bumping into John so often—as had been the case before—I made good progress pulling the line units together. I worked like hell into the fall. Still, I felt happy that John and I had found a means to neutralize some of our tensions.

Apart from improved decisions at the business unit level, the fall brought a series of other accomplishments. Around the beginning of October, Joanie and I received an invitation to a party celebrating Bob Rubin's return to New York following his retirement as secretary of the Treasury. The day before the event, an article ran in *The New York Times* suggesting that Rubin might have an interest in returning to the financial services business. I seized on the story, thinking about what a coup it would represent if we could lure Rubin to Citigroup, and I made it a point to raise the idea with Bob at the party. Joanie and I joined the festivities the next evening, an affair orchestrated by Bob's wife, Judy, and held near the Egyptian Temple of Dendur inside the Metropolitan Museum.

Once there, I quickly sought out my target.

I barely knew Rubin. We had met once in the early 1980s when

Bob solicited me for a presidential campaign contribution for Walter Mondale. Otherwise, we rarely crossed paths until Rubin became Treasury secretary. At that point, I met with him several times as part of a larger business delegation seeking his support for reforming the country's outdated banking laws. The absence of a personal tie, however, didn't stop me from drawing him into conversation.

Seeking a quiet corner, I suggested that we "need to talk" and that Citigroup could offer a great fit. "It's probably too late," he responded. "I have my eye on something involving private equity, and I'm 99 percent sure I know what I want to do." Never one to take no for an answer, I promptly observed, "Well that's not 100 percent. We still should talk since your experience puts you in a unique position to relate to what we're doing at Citigroup, and you'd find it very interesting. We could come up with something that would be far more compelling than what you might see in the private equity world."

Too polite to spurn my offer, Bob agreed to come by my office the next day. We ended up talking for well over an hour that Friday. I played up the scope of Citigroup's global franchise and how we could present him with a wide array of challenges. He asked a lot of good questions, and it felt like we connected. I suggested that he return for a three-way meeting with John and myself and felt pleased when he accepted.

It would take time to reel Bob in, but I had him hooked. Over the next three weeks, I tenaciously barraged him with phone calls nearly every other day doing my best to woo him. At one point, I ran into his wife at a wedding. Judy Rubin had come alone since Bob had a pre-scheduled trip to China. I told Judy how terrific it would be if Bob were to join us and couldn't resist asking, "How do you think we're doing?" Judy's positive response came as music to my ears and gave me the incentive to keep pushing. A week later, we had a deal: Bob would join us as chairman of the executive committee and a member of the Office of the Chairmen.

Snaring Bob was big news. The press had been relentlessly calling into question our merger progress for months, and hiring someone as widely respected as Bob translated into a highly visible public endorsement of our company. Rubin, too, came with a phenomenal Rolodex and would help Citigroup win a great deal of new business. Even though Bob didn't want any formal managerial responsibilities (and specifically insisted that he had no designs on becoming CEO), I knew he'd bolster our investment banking team and that his expertise in trading and arbitrage honed over his many years at Goldman Sachs would help us manage risk.

Bob's tremendous personal assets outweighed one potential risk: our lack of a long personal relationship. In contrast, Bob and John Reed had enjoyed a far closer relationship over the years. I understood that introducing Bob into my complex relationship with John might complicate matters and could even give John an important new ally. However, my relationship with John seemed on a more even keel at that point, and I still trusted that our partnership would endure. Even if we had given our board a possible successor by introducing Rubin, I took our new colleague at his word when he insisted he had no interest in becoming CEO.

Bob proved a valuable addition from the start and unexpectedly played a useful role in bringing John and me together. The power sharing had smoothed some of our decision making, although issues remained. Realizing that John and I often lacked a common agenda, Bob suggested a weekly meeting of the Office of the Chairmen. John and I readily agreed, and we set aside a couple of hours each Monday to discuss priorities for the week and ways to make the business run better long term.

The meetings offered a bit of role reversal. John usually thought in a linear and organized fashion, yet he'd show up most of the time seemingly unprepared and lacking an agenda. He seemed oddly detached. On the other hand, I viewed the meetings as an opening to think in a more structured way, and I suddenly cast aside my normal instinctive approach and would present a series of actionable items. "Here's my list," I'd declare, and use the meetings as an instrument to move the company forward.

Bob proved a smart, experienced, and honest broker—lacking an agenda of his own—who helped set priorities and speed decisions. We soon developed a close bond which I'm sure reminded him of his old partnership with Steve Friedman in the days when the two ran Goldman Sachs. Bob could see firsthand my energy and eagerness to understand and improve our business. At the same time, I'm sure he couldn't help but notice John's lack of engagement. Although we may not have enjoyed a long-standing personal relationship when he arrived, we quickly built an excellent rapport.

———————

Bob Rubin's arrival in the fall of 1999 came at another important juncture for our company. We had been lobbying Congress intensively for months to overturn the Depression-era Glass-Steagall Act, which had prevented commercial and investment banks from merging. During the 1990s, a reform-minded Fed had eased some of the law's more onerous restrictions, but the statute still made it cumbersome for a financial company to offer a full range of banking services.

We also had been pushing for reform of the Bank Holding Company Act, the 1950s relic that restricted banks from selling insurance. When we created Citigroup, many industry observers claimed that the loophole we had found conflicted with the intent of these laws and that somehow we were doing something illegal. Even though I disputed that argument, it got under my skin enough to motivate me to do all I could to lobby for a new regulatory structure. With changes in technology and global competition, many others in the industry shared my conviction that the time had come for reform, and it was easy to find allies for the lobbying battle.

I readily formed an alliance with Phil Purcell from Morgan Stanley and Merrill Lynch's David Komansky to work for change. Early on, we needed to overcome the financial services industry's traditional fractiousness. In particular, insurance agents and small independent banks had long resisted industry consolidation and had sought to protect their turfs from larger competitors. I took responsibility for lobbying the CEOs of MetLife and Prudential to support our cause and felt great satisfaction when these two important industry players fell into line.

Along with other industry leaders, I soon focused on Washington.

In a number of meetings with Congress and the administration, we argued that the United States risked falling behind globally if it failed to modernize the financial system—after all, many foreign banks already had integrated financial products for years. On these visits, I developed a particularly good relationship with Gene Sperling, President Clinton's point man on financial services reform, and worked closely with him in devising our lobbying efforts. At the same time, Merrill's Komansky focused on setting up meetings with Bob Rubin, who in 1998 and early 1999 still ran the Treasury Department. Unfortunately, we soon realized that wrangling among the different banking regulators would represent a serious issue. Rubin insisted upon a leading role for the comptroller of the Currency (housed within the Treasury Department) in regulating the banks, a stance that directly conflicted with Alan Greenspan's preference to make the Federal Reserve the primary regulator.

Meanwhile, we lost an important political ally in November 1998 when Al D'Amato, until then the chairman of the Senate Banking Committee, lost his senate reelection bid. His successor as chairman, Phil Gramm, appeared uninterested in serious reform and never missed a chance to remind me that there were no important banks, brokers, or insurance companies domiciled in his state of Texas. In other words, financial services companies were far from his natural constituency.

By early 1999, prospects for meaningful reform seemed to have dimmed considerably. The Fed and Treasury were locked in an endless debate over regulatory jurisdiction; the Senate leadership seemed uninterested in reform; and perhaps more important, I could see that the impetus for change would soon diminish given that 2000 was an election year, a time when no politician would care about helping our industry.

Just as I began to give up the fight, Bob Rubin announced his plans to leave the administration in July. I was thrilled when his replacement as Treasury secretary, Larry Summers, indicated a far more flexible stance versus the Fed. Solving that issue proved the spark that reignited the political momentum for change. Senator Gramm's complacency aside, others on the Hill lined up to support new legislation. Jim Leach, the chairman of the House Banking Committee, worked especially hard to drive progress, while Representative Thomas Bliley, head of the House

Commerce Committee, also influenced the proposed legislation. Finally, the Senate and House committees passed separate bills and referred the legislation to a conference committee to align the seemingly minor differences.

Of course, nothing is ever simple in Washington, and last-minute snags developed. For one, the Congressional Black Caucus expressed reservations about whether large financial institutions would serve the interests of the poor. When I learned about this concern, I decided to call Jesse Jackson and ask for his support. I had met Jesse several years before when he protested our deal with Shearson out of a mistaken fear that we'd cut services to low-income clients. At the time, I worked hard to allay his concerns and subsequently agreed to support his initiatives to promote minority employment on Wall Street and advance financial literacy training in poor neighborhoods. Jesse and I had since become good friends to the point where I felt comfortable asking for a return favor. Jesse Jackson came out publicly in support of the financial modernization bill, and his support proved timely and effective.

Just as we were about to cross the goal line, one last obstacle arose. Senator Gramm, ever the savvy horse trader, took exception to a provision in the bill which forced banks to invest in poor areas, a long-running political football in Washington. One afternoon he called and threatened, "Call your friend Clinton and get him to change the provision or else I'll fire my rockets and blow your bill apart." Fearful, I immediately relayed the message to Gene Sperling, who laughed and said that the president wouldn't respond. I thought the worst and assumed Gramm would follow up on his threat, but an hour passed and nothing happened. Gramm called again the next day to repeat his demand, and this time the president and Texas senator found some way to compromise.

On November 12, President Clinton signed into law the Gramm-Leach-Bliley Act, and in a stroke, modernized the structure of the financial services industry. The new law removed the uncertainty over our future organizational structure and business mix. It gave me enormous satisfaction that Citigroup had led the way toward an industry structure that would prove more globally competitive and relevant to customer needs. Five years after the bill's passage, I ran into Phil Gramm at a dinner where the then ex-senator told me facetiously, "Congress made a mistake. It should have called the new law the '*Weill*-Gramm-Leach-Bliley Act'!" Ironically, Congress enacted the Glass-Steagall law in the year I was born and overturned the archaic legislation with the birth of Citigroup.

Our political triumph nearly coincided with Bob Rubin's arrival at Citigroup, and the two accomplishments, along with the still recent power-sharing arrangement with John, gave me the sense that Citigroup finally had found its stride. Meanwhile, I jumped into learning more about our global franchise and sought information on what made our overseas businesses tick. I might have been approaching my seventieth birthday, but that didn't slow my capacity to process new information, and I loved the challenge.

I approached my early trips abroad tentatively fearing that I'd be disadvantaged by my lack of international experience. However, my nervousness quickly dissipated. In 1999, I traveled to areas that I thought held unusual growth potential. I visited Poland and Hungary to understand how Eastern European countries were emerging from communism. While there, I decided to make a side trip to Turkey. The country had devalued its currency, and I wanted to see how Citigroup's loan quality would fare during that sort of crisis. Later, I made two trips to Latin America, one to explore an acquisition in Argentina and another to broadly examine the regional opportunity and the aftereffects of the region's 1980s debt crisis.

At the end of October 1999, Joanie and I set off on our most extensive tour, a two-week jaunt around the world where we visited eleven cities in eight countries and met five heads of state. The trip proved memorable for opening my eyes to the extent of Citigroup's potential and also for some very distinctive personal experiences. We began by flying to Tel Aviv to celebrate the opening of a branch in Israel, the first to be opened by a major foreign bank. Citicorp's vice chairman, Bill Rhodes, had championed the idea for a long time, and I pushed the investment to fruition owing to my friendship with Prime Minister Barak and my belief at the time (sadly premature) that an era of peace would open up a wide array of regional business opportunities. I also hated threats and saw the chance to do our part to turn back the Arab economic boycott against Israel.

After Israel, I wanted to visit Citigroup's largest shareholder, Saudi prince Alwaleed; however, Saudi Arabia would not allow us to enter from Israel, so we arranged for a side trip to Cairo in order to look at a small investment opportunity. I felt nervous about traveling to Egypt given recent attacks on Westerners and became even more concerned when, a day or two before our trip, an EgyptAir commercial jet crashed mysteriously after taking off from New York.

To ease my worries, my friend Ehud Barak telephoned President Hosni Mubarak of Egypt and arranged for a presidential security detail to meet Joanie and me on our arrival. We ended up having security the likes of which I had never seen, complete with a huge motorcade of security personnel—at one point, the police barred access to the route as though I were the president of a country, and we sped down a closed eight-lane highway against the normal flow of traffic. We were flushed with excitement, and Joanie joked that she'd never be able to go home and get on the Fifth Avenue bus again after this experience.

A day later, we traveled to a Saudi city on the Red Sea where we met with directors and friends of Samba, a local bank in which Citigroup owned a minority stake. We were entertained in the largest private homes I've ever seen. One had a shark-stocked swimming pool while another had a boathouse larger than most normal homes. Of course, the men were entertained apart from the women, and Joanie joined a group of Saudi ladies who eagerly removed their abiyas once out of sight of the men. The next day, we went on to Riyadh where I met Prince Alwaleed for a business session. I had met the Western-educated prince once before, and my visit presented an excellent chance to get to know him better. At the time, he owned about $15 billion worth of our stock, just one of his many investments.

That evening, the prince invited us to a camp he kept in the desert and personally drove us in his SUV. On the drive out, he conducted business juggling two cell phones at once which provoked Joanie to exclaim, "Watch the road!" Arriving at the desert camp, we were ushered to a large open-air space where the desert ground was covered with beautiful Arabian carpets topped with a fifty-foot-long spread of delicacies. Enjoying the sumptuous food while sitting on soft pillows, I could only imagine the waste, but I later learned that the excess food would be given to nearby Bedouins.

After dinner, we walked to another area, passing huge bonfires along the way used to warm the cold desert night. We came to another part of the camp which—still out in the open—included several falcons sitting on perches and a number of large-screen color televisions broadcasting business and news channels from around the world as well as a Saudi religious station. The prince related how he constantly traded his stock holdings and that he wished to sell $1 billion worth of our shares. Although I wasn't thrilled by the news, I immediately said that Salomon Smith Barney should manage the sale and asked to call our trading desk in New York to discuss the matter. The prince wanted to pay a very low commission, and I spent the next thirty minutes negotiating a fair price for the trade. It was thrilling: Here I was on my first trip to Saudi Arabia sitting in the desert after a sumptuous dinner talking to New York about executing a billion-dollar trade for our largest shareholder.

Before the evening came to an end, I had the unique pleasure of watching my wife ride and milk a camel, two activities which I was more than happy to observe from the sidelines. Alwaleed and I then shot guns at bottle targets before we went off to a tented area so that I could observe him meet one at a time with a group of Bedouins who sang songs, recited poetry, or begged for favors. All the while, he'd enter the requests and responses in a computer by his side and keep one eye on the business news on the surrounding television screens.

On the ride back to Riyadh late that evening, I received a call from Senator Gramm letting me know that Clinton had signed the Gramm-Leach-Bliley bill. I marveled at how I had just spent a magical evening in the Saudi desert reliving a thousand years of Arab history and how I had made my own history by helping break down a generation's worth of banking laws.

Wall Street Journal advertisement at Grand Central Station; 1997
(Weill personal photo)

Announcing the blockbuster merger on April 6, 1998: Launching Citigroup, I felt
sure John Reed and I had the maturity and experience to make our partnership work
(Courtesy of Citigroup company archives)

Walking up Park Avenue after our press conference announcing the Citigroup merger: with Joan and John Reed
(Photo by Julia Gaines. Copyright, 1998, Newsday. *Reprinted with permission.)*

Jamie Dimon and Deryck Maughan were oil and vinegar from day one; 1998
(Courtesy of Mark Peterson/Redux Pictures and Fortune *magazine)*

Next generation of management, maybe? Both from Travelers.

A day out on the links with President Clinton; 1999
(Official White House Photograph)

Touring the globe: a magical evening in the Saudi Arabian desert with Prince Alwaleed; 1999
(Courtesy of Prince Alwaleed)

At Citigroup with Bob Rubin and Mikhail Gorbachev; 2001
(Courtesy of Citigroup Photography Office)

Celebration of Bob Willumstad's promotion to president in 2002
(Courtesy of Citigroup Photography Office; from Bob Willumstad)

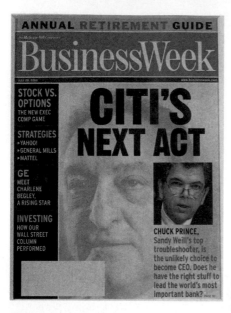

Citigroup's "next act," Chuck Prince, is a class act as far as I am concerned
(Reprinted from the July 28, 2003, issue of BusinessWeek by permission. Copyright 2003 by the McGraw-Hill Companies.)

At the New York Stock Exchange with Jessica, celebrating her company's IPO, on September 18, 2003; Jessica has proven to be a very successful CEO in her own right
(Courtesy of AP Images)

Joan and I with Nelson Mandela; 2004
(Courtesy of Julian Cole Photography)

Leading a business delegation to St. Petersburg, Russia, to meet with
President Vladimir Putin; 2005
(Courtesy of AP Images)

Receiving an award from the EastWest Institute along with Prime Minister Tony
Blair; with Joan, John Mroz, president and CEO of the EastWest Institute, and the
prime minister
(Courtesy of EastWest Institute 2005)

A great mentor: Isaac Stern
(Weill personal photo)

Naming the Weill Cornell Medical College
(Courtesy of Richard Lobell Photography)

At the inaugural ceremony for Weill Cornell Medical College in Qatar with
Her Highness Sheikha Mozah bint Nasser al-Missned and His Highness
Sheikh Hamad bin Khalifa al-Thani; 2002
(Courtesy of Qatar Foundation for Education, Science and Community Development)

"Up north" in the Adirondacks with Joan and Judith Jamison, artistic director of
Alvin Ailey American Dance Theater
(Weill personal photo)

Announcing an exciting new partnership between the National Academy Foundation (NAF), Gates Foundation, and Weill Family Foundation in 2006; with Joan, John Ferrandino (third from left), Tom Vander Ark of the Gates Foundation (third from right), and NAF students *(Courtesy of the National Academy Foundation)*

At Carnegie Hall for my last annual meeting as chairman of Citigroup on April 18, 2006 *(Courtesy of Citigroup company archives)*

For more than fifty years, Joanie and I have known what a great partnership is all about *(Courtesy of Gillian Laub)*

Our next stop was India. I didn't think we'd match the pageantry of that evening in the desert, but Joanie and I were in for a surprise. After a day of meetings designed to get to know our people in Bombay, our staff there told me about a local Hindu custom where couples reaffirm their marriage vows when they pass their sixtieth birthdays. Wishing to honor Joanie and me, our people proposed hosting a marriage ceremony, an offer we eagerly accepted. The next day we flew to New Delhi for meetings and then on to Agra, home of the Taj Mahal, for the wedding. Joanie and I had no idea what to expect, and we were bowled over by the magnificent Hindu ceremony.

The pageant called for traditional dress; for me, that meant a Nehru jacket, pantaloons, slippers turned up at the toes, and a large turban. I rode in on a white horse while men sang and danced alongside. By custom, the bride arrived late, but Joanie finally appeared dressed in a beautiful sequin-lined wedding dress complete with veil. Happily, she didn't turn and run when she saw me in my getup, and we approached the officiating pandit who took us through our vows.

Everything went smoothly except for one small screwup. The religious man told us to place our hands over each other's hearts and then turned to Joanie and asked "How many hearts?" Unsure how to respond, she said "two," which prompted the wise man to raise his voice, "No! *One heart. That's what this is all about!*" After the ceremony, we had dinner and watched fireworks with the invited guests. The experience left one more indelible memory and gave us a unique chance to bond not just with one another as "newlyweds" but also with our local Indian team.

The following day, Joanie and I joked that it was time for our honeymoon, and we headed off to Sydney on the next leg of our voyage before going on to Manila, Taipei, and Seoul. Each stop gave us the chance to learn about our local businesses. In Australia, I heard about past booms and busts and Citicorp's mixed earnings record. The Philippines offered a chance to speak with several hundred branch employees and talk about my ambitions for Citigroup and how I wanted to instill an equity ownership culture for employees, a pitch that generated obvious excitement. The stops in Taiwan and Korea provided an opportunity to assess the impact of the recent economic turmoil that had buffeted the region and also allowed me to size up a planned insurance joint venture with the Taiwan-based Fubon Group. I also had the chance to visit with the political leaders of each country and developed an especially good rapport with Australian prime minister John Howard and Korea's President Kim Dae Jung.

I thought things were beginning to look up during the final months of 1999, but sadly, my optimism proved premature. In December, I learned from one of our directors that John Reed had begun to lobby the board for a change in direction. Apparently, John claimed that he and I had agreed to retire together and that the time had come to search for a successor CEO. I was floored. John never consulted me before starting this campaign, and he misrepresented the idea that we had agreed to retire simultaneously. How could he forget the evening in his apartment before we announced the merger when he explicitly released me from having to retire with him?

Several times over the prior year, John had made comments in front of others to the effect that we'd leave together. Each time, the comments got under my skin, and I made it clear that I wasn't obliged to walk out the door with him. It was as though he harbored second thoughts on our deal and figured he could create a fact by simply repeating the falsehood often enough. John's assertion this time represented an altogether different matter as he had taken his fiction to the board.

I also discovered that one of John's close directors had put feelers out to one of my longtime board members, Andy Pearson, asking whether he'd support a shift in leadership. At that point, I confronted John, who surprisingly denied that he had made any overtures. That made me upset for it indicated that John had ceased dealing with me honestly and had begun to scheme for something which he knew I deeply opposed. His actions further torpedoed our partnership.

What explains John's turn? I only can imagine his reasons. I don't think he ever wanted to remain with Citigroup far into the future. Even before we negotiated the merger, he had hinted publicly about his wish to retire at a young age. John, too, probably failed to appreciate how his desire to tap Travelers' managerial "DNA" would clash with his grandiose visions. The more we injected our management culture, the more difficult it became for him to realize his impractical dreams. I'm sure that recognition disturbed him and encouraged him to view our relationship in terms of winners and losers. The power-sharing arrangement may have provoked that sentiment further. Even though he willingly endorsed the split, he may have felt marginalized and frustrated after the fact by not getting the rest of the organization to buy into his vision for e-Citi.

Indeed, e-Citi's problems only intensified during the latter part of the year. The latest issue related to a joint venture with AOL to establish an online financial supermarket. I originally had suggested the idea thinking that AOL, as the dominant Internet provider, might teach us something, but our execution proved hopeless, and the venture flopped. We had attracted woefully few clients, and the project was running losses at an annual run-rate of nearly $300 million.

John had taken full responsibility for e-Citi, so he couldn't run from the disaster. The contrast with the success I was enjoying in driving our core businesses had to frustrate him. Over the course of his career, John had produced a number of remarkable and innovative breakthroughs; nonetheless, with e-Citi, he seemed to have reached his Waterloo.

16

One Company, One Leader

My relationship with John Reed had noticeably cooled by December 1999. We had retreated into our separate spheres. Some of our colleagues later commented about our body language in meetings—they'd claim that I'd often roll my eyes when John spoke and that John had a way of muffling his face with the sleeve of his sweater to hide his scowls during my comments. I'm vaguely amused by these stories now, although it's important to stress that John and I never acted in an uncivil manner toward one another. The real problem stemmed from our disengagement and inability to sell one another on our convictions. We gradually had given up on each other.

While I was angry at John for discussing the succession issue with the board, I didn't know how to respond. A conversation with Bob Lipp, however, soon spurred me to action. Joanie and I customarily celebrate New Year's in the Adirondacks with a circle of friends and decided to have a special celebration for the new millennium. It snowed heavily that weekend, and everyone had a festive time. On the last day, Bob asked to speak with me privately, and when I heard what he had to say, my celebratory mood ended abruptly. "Sandy, this is no fun anymore," he said. "I can't stand Reed, and I can't get things done the way I'd like because of him. I think it's time for me to leave."

Although Bob had threatened to leave before, I took his comment particularly seriously now. His words posed a direct and very personal question: If I couldn't keep my best executive in the fold, what did that say about my ability as a leader? "I don't want you to talk that way," I replied. Trying to mollify him, I quickly added, "I'd like you to give me six months to see if we can work things out for the better. If I can't get things to work like you think they should, you can leave, *and I'll go with you.*"

That comment appeased Bob, who promised not to leave me in the lurch. When I later told Chuck Prince about the conversation, he warned that I shouldn't tie my fate so closely to Bob's since we might have different agendas. I dismissed the feedback, preferring to focus instead on how John was undermining the cohesiveness of our management team.

Our Planning Group was scheduled to gather in Arizona in early February for our annual strategic review, and I quietly positioned the agenda to encourage our executives to speak frankly about the dysfunction at the top of our management ranks. I plotted three outcomes for the meeting. First, I wanted Lipp to articulate a long-term vision and lay out how our company might change over the coming decade—if successful, the presentation would confront Reed's usual claim that Bob lacked the capacity to look beyond the short term. Second, I wanted to be sure our executives would openly share their frustrations. To this end, I added an agenda item entitled "How Can We Run the Company Better?" and visited with most of our top executives ahead of time in order to encourage them to speak up. "Whatever you feel, say it," I implored. "If you have issues, now is the time to speak up so we can address them."

Finally, I sought a way to line up Bob Rubin's support. In our weekly Office of the Chairmen meetings, Bob could see the obvious contrasts between John and me. Now I wanted him to hear firsthand how the co-CEO problems were hurting our team. While I didn't know where the meeting would lead, I'd occasionally encouraged my team to confront one another in order to solve particularly intractable problems. Getting people to open up can be difficult and the results unpredictable, but I also believe it can illuminate hidden issues and ultimately prove cathartic.

On February 9, the Planning Group convened at the Boulders Hotel in Scottsdale for the first of two substantive business sessions. In keeping with my plan, Bob Lipp gave an excellent presentation on Citigroup's long-term challenges and opportunities. He described how earnings in the consumer business likely would rise from $4 billion to $15 billion over the coming five years and how the company's staff might double over that period. He noted Citigroup would have several hundred thousand employees within ten years and thought out loud about the managerial challenges we'd face running a company that large. The presentation made Bob look like a visionary and a leader, exactly as I had intended. Moreover, it provided a natural segue into the whole question of how we'd need to restructure our management.

The following morning, we turned to the pivotal issue of our managerial challenges and went around the room so that all of our colleagues could express themselves. Victor Menezes surprisingly set the tone. A longtime Citicorp executive who normally parsed his words carefully for political correctness, Victor this time spoke with unusual candor. "The co-CEO arrangement is hard to deal with," he noted. "Tell us what hill to march up, and we'll do it, but we can only succeed if we have one North Star by which to set our compasses." Victor knew that selecting a single CEO meant that John Reed might lose, given that the management team by now had become skewed toward the Travelers side. Coming out for a single leader implied that John had lost the support of one of his important protégés.

Several other executives followed with comments of their own, and just as I had hoped, the room soon rose up in a sea of complaints. Everyone piled on and spoke about how John and I were dysfunctional CEOs and how we were impeding their ability to function. Even consumer finance head Bob Willumstad, one normally not given to ruffling feathers, chimed in. "Decision making is too slow, and I often feel pulled in different directions. This isn't viable," he said. The others' complaints weren't that surprising, but most knew Bob as an unflappable executive who usually got along well with everyone (including John). The fact that he'd complain at all spoke volumes.

John sat through the meeting mostly in stunned silence while I eagerly urged the group to keep sharing their thoughts. John probably felt ambushed by the unruly meeting. Given his disposition, I'm sure he couldn't have felt comfortable about people disregarding normal corporate etiquette and talking so openly in front of others. Yet I thought both he and Rubin had to hear the collective message. I was sick of people bitching and moaning only to me and figured the raucous meeting would force us to change course. By the end, our executives' message had registered loud and clear, and John and I committed to come up with a response.

Returning to New York that Sunday, I had no idea how John and I would solve our dysfunctional relationship, though I vaguely thought that Bob Rubin—his eyes opened—might help by proposing some fresh ideas. A few days later, though, another development pushed me to action. On Thursday night, I was honored by the Greenwich Library at an event attended by a number of our executives including our CFO, Heidi Miller. Afterward, I flew to the Adirondacks for a long weekend but was jolted the next morning by a call from Heidi telling me she was resigning to join Priceline, then a speculative e-commerce company.

As CFO, Heidi had been pulled in opposing directions by John and me, and I understood her intense frustration. Still, I felt angry at the impersonal way in which she had chosen to communicate her departure after all that I had done to advance her career. More unsettling, her news didn't speak well about Citigroup and proved that the co-CEO structure had to be resolved once and for all before it risked an exodus of our top executives. Heidi's departure was the last straw.

On Monday, I approached John and insisted that "we either work out our problems, or we go to the board." John appeared in no mood to compromise and stiffly replied, "We aren't going to work it out." With that, I pushed for a special board meeting, and we settled on the coming Sunday, February 27. Once we called the meeting, the outcome was out of our hands. The more I considered what I had begun, the more scared I became.

Only two months earlier, one of our legacy Travelers directors, Judy Arron, had died of cancer, and her board seat remained unfilled. That meant that John's old directors outnumbered mine by eight to seven. This calculus didn't include Bob Rubin, whose support I hoped for—even with his backing, the votes still wouldn't easily line up in my favor. John also seemed remarkably calm and self-confident as the week wore on, and I began to worry that he had made more of an effort than I was aware of to lobby the board. After all, he had engineered the ouster of many executives who threatened him over the years. On the other hand, John may have felt the board would say "a pox on both your houses," which probably would have suited him fine given his eagerness to retire.

Suddenly, I saw myself playing poker with someone who didn't care about the outcome so long as I'd lose.

I asked the legacy Travelers directors for their advice, and the consensus came back that I shouldn't try to approach John's old directors. Most argued that any overture could easily backfire. I decided I'd only meet with our seniormost director, Frank Thomas, and then simply to discuss the format for the meeting. I also encouraged Heidi Miller to speak with one or two directors to explain the reasons behind her resignation. Otherwise, I avoided any attempt to take my case to the board.

Still, I couldn't help but go over each director in my mind. I assumed loyalty to John ran deep, though I imagined a few of the directors would resist a partisan split. I respected Frank Thomas a great deal and believed he'd strive for an intelligent outcome. I also had a long relationship with Ed Woolard, the former DuPont CEO, who had been an advisory director for Travelers' private equity affiliate and who had gone out of his way to nominate me for a position on Dupont's board. Dick Parsons, the president of Time Warner, and Alcoa's Alain Belda also struck me as thoughtful people who would do the right thing.

Yet if I had gauged the directors' sentiment incorrectly, what then? It seemed illogical that the board would support an outcome based on a purely partisan split. Still, anything short of a total victory would have been impossible to bear. I imagined the board might refuse to make a decision and throw the matter back to John and me to work out ourselves. The status quo undoubtedly would have been a disaster and led to the steady attrition of our best executives. I preferred to be tossed out rather than live with a scenario like that.

My anxiety built steadily as the weekend approached. Andy Pearson was traveling in Asia on a business trip, and I had been unsuccessful in convincing him to return for the board meeting. When I realized he was stuck over there, I scrambled to secure a videoconferencing facility in a local Salomon Smith Barney branch and took pains to be sure that he'd stay on the line for the entire meeting even if it meant he'd have to be up all night. Every vote mattered. As the hours counted down, I was a wreck. I felt petrified that my dream of building the best financial services company in the world might slip from my grasp.

Finally, Sunday arrived, and Joanie drove me to the office. Consumed by fear as much as I was, she kissed me goodbye and told me she planned to see a movie to distract herself from the impending drama. When I walked into the office, I saw that John was sitting in Chuck Prince's office. I'm not a good poker player and like to get to answers fast. Dreading a long and uncertain board meeting, I made one last attempt to seize control of the situation. Gamely, I offered, "John, don't you think there's a very good chance the board could say that your proposal for us both to leave makes no sense and that just you could be forced out of here? Shouldn't we try to come up with our own compromise?"

John dismissed the overture out of hand and simply answered, "No way."

———————

We had called the board meeting for noon, and I watched the directors arrive piecemeal. Oddly, the old Travelers directors were the first to appear. Then, all at once, the legacy Citicorp directors entered en masse. "Oh shit," I muttered, realizing they must have had a meeting among themselves ahead of time to coordinate their position, anything but an auspicious omen. Moving into the boardroom, I saw Andy Pearson's image beamed in from Asia on the videoconferencing screen and felt relieved at least that he had made it.

The directors generally seemed angry at John and me for not having been able to resolve our problems on our own—after all, we had promised we'd make our relationship work, and now we were admitting our failure. At once, the board agreed that Frank Thomas, as the senior director, should chair the session. Frank, in turn, announced that John and I initially would make statements and then we'd be asked to leave the room so that the board could deliberate in executive session.

John spoke first. He argued that we had done a terrible job as co-CEOs and set a very poor example for our employees. "The board should find a successor for both of us and begin the search immediately. We should stay on as co-CEOs only as long as it takes to find our replacement," he declared. Alternatively, John suggested he'd reluctantly become sole CEO if the board preferred but that he really didn't want the job and would actively recruit a replacement. I thought John's idea sounded absolutely nuts. We had created a complex company and had a tremendous amount of unfinished business—how could the board agree to a process with such an uncertain outcome?

Given the chance to speak, I pulled a list of speaking points from my coat pocket—something I almost never do except in critically important instances—and began to counter John's logic. "I want the job, and I'm the right person to lead the company," I said. "I've worked for years with all the important people on the team; I know how to deliver results; and we could accomplish a great deal together. I can build upon what we've started and create a great legacy for our company. I'd like to have the chance to see the company through."

I didn't speak for long and, in reviewing my credentials as someone with a proven execution record, told the directors what I thought should be obvious. After finishing, I immediately second-guessed myself and wondered if I had sounded convincing. Should I have extolled my virtues and ticked off my accomplishments more forcefully? The presentation may not have been my finest; still, I hoped that I got my points across, and it now was up to the board to decide.

Our presentations over, John and I were asked to wait outside. The directors next heard from Bob Rubin, who somewhat huffily joined us about twenty minutes later—Bob was upset that the board viewed him as an insider and didn't allow him to participate in the deliberations. In the anteroom, the three of us at first sat together and snacked on sandwiches and glanced at the Sunday papers. After a while, Bob drifted off to another room to watch a basketball game while John and I tuned in a golf tournament. All the while, we compared notes on our favorite professional golfers and the golf courses we particularly liked.

Oddly, we communicated better in those moments than we had in months.

I figured the board would take an hour or two to resolve the issue; however, the afternoon dragged on hour after hour. I had thought the decision would be obvious. Now I no longer felt so sure. Periodically, directors would emerge to go to the bathroom and we'd try to make eye contact to no avail. AT&T's Mike Armstrong, a director from the Travelers side, kept coming out to reschedule a flight he had that afternoon—I kept reminding him that he couldn't leave until the meeting ended. I saw him getting nervous about the delay, which only added to my apprehension. Meanwhile, her movie having ended, Joanie called for an update. "Anything that goes on this long can't be good," I whispered. I still couldn't imagine that the board would side with John. Joanie began to cry softly into the phone, though she quickly caught herself. The uncertainty gnawed at us both.

Finally, around 7:00 P.M., Frank Thomas emerged and calmly asked John if he'd be willing to give up being CEO in return for being named nonexecutive chairman of the board. In a split second, John rejected the idea while I suppressed an ecstatic sigh of relief. We both knew that the proposal was meant as a face-saving gesture for Reed and that there would be no turning back for the board. It was all over! John's rejection of the chairman's role also meant that I wouldn't have to accept an unpleasant continuing relationship or have to pretend to be magnanimous.

I had won—inwardly, I leapt with joy.

Frank Thomas returned to the boardroom and remained inside for another hour during which time I assumed the directors were discussing how they'd present their final decision to John and the outside world. Finally, Frank emerged once more with the verdict: "The board has decided that you, Sandy, should be chairman and CEO and that John should retire at the upcoming annual meeting [in April]." I immediately followed Frank back into the boardroom where most of the directors were now standing and preparing to leave. The scene looked battle-scarred: Papers and plates were strewn everywhere, and a number of the directors cast angry glances my way. It had obviously been a bruising battle and one no one could have enjoyed.

Frank Thomas strode over to a small group of directors who were discussing the outcome and how to phrase the public announcement. They were passing around a piece of paper and evidently drafting a press release as they stood. I joined the group and immediately learned that three of the directors—Ed Woolard, Colgate's Reuben Mark, and Monsanto's Bob Shapiro—all were insisting that the announcement make clear that the board would begin a succession search and announce a successor within two years. I glanced at the handwritten document and immediately took strong exception. "This is unacceptable. I can't be bound by this," I declared. "If you say publicly that we'll have a successor in two years, you'll make me a lame duck and weaken my authority to pull the company together."

Trying to find a reasonable compromise, Kenny Bialkin then asked, "In that case, Sandy, how do you think it should be worded?" Suddenly, Reuben Mark exploded and practically shouted that the board had already acted and that I had no right to interfere with the decision. This wasn't the first time Reuben Mark had adopted a confrontational tone; indeed, he had developed a reputation on the board for his maverick stances and for often effectively insisting the board do things "his way or the wrong way." This time, though, he spun out of control. I tried to reason with him that I understood his point but that he and the board had to understand how the wording easily could undermine my effectiveness. Unfortunately, he remained too emotional to see any validity in my view.

Finally, as if out of a movie, John Reed poked his head into the boardroom. All this time, he had been left alone in the anteroom. "I think I'm going to leave now," he announced to the suddenly silenced crowd. The bickering stopped, and Frank Thomas and most of the remaining directors rushed off to talk with Reed. Reuben Mark stayed on to argue a bit more, but subsequently Frank Thomas took the lead and ensured that the final press release contained the right degree of ambiguity on the succession matter.

Reuben stormed off that evening. His objections had never gained traction with the rest of the board. With the eight-hour marathon finally over, I went home feeling completely wiped out. Joanie and I quietly celebrated with a couple of drinks before dropping off into an exhausted sleep.

I later learned that the board deliberations had been the most difficult our directors had ever seen. Frank Thomas tried to build a consensus ahead of the meeting to avoid a damaging split vote; still, his efforts came to naught. When the board initially went into executive session, virtually all of John's longtime directors supported bringing in a third party to succeed John and me as CEO. Relying on secondhand information, I understand that Frank Thomas continued to press for a consensus decision. Anything less would have tainted Citigroup for years to come.

I also understand that Bob Rubin and Andy Pearson proved pivotal in breaking the deadlock. Bob's credentials and perceived neutrality gave him enormous credibility with the directors, and he came out strongly against the idea that John and I both should be sent packing. Apparently, he told the board that he had come to Citigroup with an open mind regarding John and me but that he had come to appreciate my leadership skills and the respect I commanded with Citigroup's top executives. When asked if he'd have an interest taking over, Bob resoundingly said no. Andy also spoke eloquently on my behalf. He literally stayed up through the night in front of the video link from Asia and shook the board into understanding the perils of an outcome with anything less than overwhelming board support.

I wonder, too, whether John's pitch undermined his own position. His presentation made him sound like someone who only wanted out— his lack of enthusiasm was obvious and probably resulted from his long-standing desire to retire. The directors had to appreciate that Citigroup's open issues demanded a chief executive who could concentrate on details and commit an enormous amount of time and energy. In the end, the board largely set its differences aside and coalesced around offering me the job with the stipulation that the company would begin a succession process.

Once the board announced its verdict, John Reed acted graciously in defeat. He told me the next morning that he wouldn't get in my way and, indeed, wasn't a problem from that day forward. We met jointly with our top executives—John spoke for a couple of minutes and was gone by the afternoon. Similarly, at his final board meeting in April, he offered his farewell in a fifteen-minute speech that extolled the virtues of the company.

Before the annual meeting, he called to wish me luck, a very generous gesture. A day later, he sold every share of his stock, which seemed far from a vote of confidence; nonetheless, I think it's clear he simply needed closure. Many may perceive that I had it in for John from day one of the merger, but that notion is absolutely false. It was only after seeing John's shockingly detached management style that I lost confidence in our partnership. Even then, I didn't give up on John until the very end. If this were not the case, why would I have recruited Bob Rubin (a potential ally for John)?

John's departure meant that I needed to work hard to rally the board after its obviously bruising deliberations. Almost immediately, I received resignation offers from three of John's closest directors. Bob Shapiro, the CEO of Monsanto, made the first move by calling Chuck Prince, our general counsel, and announcing that he didn't support the board's decision and wanted out immediately. Chuck asked him to stay until our annual meeting, but Shapiro refused. Alcoa's Alain Belda also wasted no time in calling and offered to leave since he didn't think I'd want disloyal people on the board.

In contrast to Shapiro, I didn't view Alain as set in his beliefs and thought he brought a lot of energy and good ideas to our board. "I know this has been stressful and difficult for you and the other directors," I countered, "but you play a valuable role, and I respect you. I'd like you to stay." Belda remained, and we've since developed a close relationship.

Matters weren't so straightforward with Ed Woolard, whom I resented for not being more up front in telling me where he stood. Unlike the case with John's other directors, Ed and I had had a relationship for many years, and he led me to believe he respected my abilities. I was shocked to learn that he didn't stand up on my behalf at the crucial hour. I traveled to Delaware to discuss his intentions and frankly was relieved to hear his resignation offer. For the sake of appearances, he agreed to hold off his departure for a few months.

I remained nervous about a few of our other directors but worked diligently to earn their respect. Fortunately, Reuben Mark calmed down, though many of the others had to wonder if I was up to the task of mastering the complexities of modern technology and Citigroup's sprawling global franchise. I had to deliver results—after all, my execution strengths represented the primary reason the board had stood behind me. Fortunately, the company came together over the following few months. I quickly shut down the ridiculously expensive e-Citi unit and decentralized responsibility for the Internet to our core businesses. I also largely eliminated the co-head structure for our major businesses, assigning individual responsibility for the Corporate Investment Bank, the Consumer Business, and Asset Management. Meanwhile, our international earnings began to take off. John's departure lifted my spirits and, more important, those of the team. We quickly reestablished much of the old Travelers culture. By mid-April, investors bought in and our stock regained all the ground it had lost since the announcement of the merger. The good news did wonders for rebuilding cohesion within our management ranks and among our directors.

When we created Citigroup, I understood the merger would differ from any I had done before. Still, I had no idea how stressful things would get for both me and my colleagues. The experience provided a few important lessons, including the obvious point that mergers of equals are extraordinarily difficult.

In hindsight, John and I were undoubtedly naive. We erred in thinking we could jointly make decisions and share responsibilities from the start. We also took for granted that we knew each other well enough to get along and underestimated the difficulties we'd face in aligning our very different styles. The financial services industry includes other examples of co-CEOs who have worked well together, such as Bob Rubin and Steve Friedman in their days together at Goldman Sachs, yet these success stories usually are the result of years of working side by side. I wish that John and I had not waited to divide areas of primary responsibility. Had we moved more quickly, I suspect it would have lessened a great deal of the friction—often initiated by our confused direct reports—that drove us apart.

The premium we placed on speed and avoiding leaks while we negotiated the transaction tied our hands in sorting out a detailed plan for managerial assignments up front and made it more difficult for John and me to understand our philosophical and personal differences. Having to live with the dual-headed structure we created ended up being frustrating, particularly as I came to understand the weaknesses of many of John's people. Ultimately, I faced a tough choice: Either I had to accept their mediocrity or push hard on John to make the appropriate changes. Of course, John's detachment from everyday details made it extraordinarily difficult for him to understand my motives and logic.

Though it's perhaps easy to appreciate these issues in hindsight, I'm not sure the merger would have happened had John and I approached it in a radically different way. Practically speaking, we had to move through our negotiations quickly and with a modest-sized team since a leak probably would have blown the deal apart. Speed and secrecy circumscribed our flexibility. Still, I now wish John and I had explored a more rational functional split for ourselves at the beginning of our association.

Never a second-guesser, I find it hard to dwell on the past especially as our company coalesced quickly after John's departure. Although I'm sorry that many of our colleagues faced uncertainty and stress while John and I sorted out our relationship, the discomfort of those couple of years was a relatively small price to pay for the powerful company that emerged. Now in control, I set my sights on realizing our company's full potential. Citigroup subsequently created enormous earnings power and went on to help millions of people and countless companies around the world achieve their aspirations, effectively trivializing the drama that surrounded the company's launch.

17

Only a Temporary Calm

The year and a half following John Reed's departure represented a period of healing and direction setting for Citigroup. Although Reed's unexpected departure might have raised uncertainties for our employees who had come from the old Citicorp, I quickly moved Victor Menezes—the executive Reed once had thought of as his possible successor—to run our visible Emerging Markets business and to demonstrate our sensitivity to our partners from Citicorp. Victor was the most senior surviving member of the team which had come from Citicorp, and he had a résumé filled with years of experience in a variety of line and staff jobs. Moving Victor from being co-head of the Global Corporate Investment Bank meant that we now had a single "North Star" running each of our businesses. I also found the right people to manage technology and operations and finally attacked the waste and inefficiency that John Reed had tolerated.

We were now positioned to make faster and smarter decisions and to benefit from clearer accountability. Our earnings surged 25 percent during 2000 while Citigroup's stock topped $50 per share, rising more than 28 percent in a year when the broad market averages fell moderately. Along with our earnings, employee morale improved sharply. Undoubtedly, we'd face new challenges, yet in early 2001, things looked very good indeed. I felt energized by our progress.

Playing to our strengths, we cut costs and cross-sold different products to our customers. We had taken some of our best operations people from our brokerage business and given them a mandate to whip antiquated Citicorp systems into shape. The old Citicorp management lacked competence when it came to systems. Our people had executed one merger after another and were battle-tested when it came to wringing out efficiencies. Gaining control over our important credit card business represented our top priority. Citicorp ran thirty operations centers around the world for the card business alone. In roughly a year, we streamlined this sprawl into three efficient sites.

Citicorp's legacy banking systems were held together with baling wire—they were old and poorly maintained. We had been lucky to get through the Y2K issue unscathed; the time had come to invest in the long overdue modernization of our systems. Thirty years earlier, I had learned the importance of running a strong back office. Now, as then, I reminded my executives of Clausewitz's famous advice to "defend the heartland," which in our case meant getting control of our processing. An advantageous cost structure undoubtedly would confer a powerful competitive advantage. We ended up extracting about $3 billion in savings. Many companies would have considered efficiencies of this magnitude a herculean task; for us, it was business as usual.

I pushed equally hard for selling more products to our customers, and our new organizational structure gave us the freedom to concentrate on improving our cross-selling effectiveness. Results in the Global Corporate Investment Bank continued to provide the major positive surprises as our market share with our corporate and institutional clients advanced and related revenues surged. Our customers appreciated our capacity to provide credit, investment banking, payment, and advisory services all under one roof. By 2001, we had blown past the old leaders in the industry's league tables (Wall Street's term for market share rankings) and now we placed first in most important product areas. For decades, I had struggled with the challenge of building a successful investment bank. Citigroup finally brought all the ingredients together.

In contrast, cross-selling progress in the Consumer Business proved more difficult. While we performed poorly in selling auto insurance policies to bank customers, larger issues were afoot. Throughout the 1990s, consumers had become better educated in financial matters. Our retail customers now wanted more choice and best-in-class products. We traditionally had operated on the premise that we should take the products we manufactured and sell them through as many of our distribution channels as possible. However, I realized that this proprietary-product-centric model might not always best serve our clients. In fact, we, along with others in the financial services industry, were coming to see that our real strength lay in distributing product rather than on the manufacturing side of the ledger.

I understood our clients' preference for product choice and consequently embraced an open-architecture model where we stepped up making third party products available to our customers. Our clients benefited most from our decision to open our distribution system to outside investment advisors. Soon we were selling an array of mutual funds and getting paid for giving these funds access to our clients.

Despite the push toward open architecture, we didn't abandon our efforts to sell our own products, and we eventually produced some impressive results. Citibank customers avidly used brokerage services provided by Salomon Smith Barney and purchased annuities manufactured by our insurance company. Brokerage clients bought our bank's credit cards. Meanwhile, the partnership between Primerica Financial Services and our consumer finance business continued to excel. PFS clients remained the single most important user of our finance company's home mortgages. Product cross-selling results in the Consumer Business weren't as sexy as those in the Corporate Investment Bank, but we still found plenty of ways to extract more revenues on the margin.

John Reed's departure also benefited the international side of our business. Oddly, Reed had insisted on limiting Citicorp's market shares outside the United States to relatively meager positions, typically less than 3 percent. I suppose his caution came from the lesser-developed-country debt crisis of the 1980s when many emerging market countries defaulted on their foreign debt and created painful losses for the banks. With our greatly expanded size, I concluded that we could safely step up our risk and that we would leave sizable profits on the table if we were to continue to accept such modest market shares.

By now, I had visited our international franchise extensively and had done my best to familiarize myself with the issues so that I could make intelligent decisions. On one occasion, I even traveled to Beijing at the request of our investment bankers to pitch a strategy for privatizing businesses to Chinese leader Jiang Zemin. Memorably, I shared my advice with him on how to promote good corporate governance. More than a decade had passed since the fall of the Berlin Wall, and the appeal of capitalism had proven its staying power the world over.

In early 2000, we tiptoed back into making a couple of acquisitions, paying a combined $3 billion for Schroders, the well-regarded U.K. merchant bank, and Bank Handlowy, the largest bank in Poland. Schroders helped us create a first-class pan-European investment bank while the deal in Poland marked our first effort to step up our presence in a populous country, giving us a better position to go after the emerging Eastern European market. While they represented only opening salvos in our broader international strategy, these transactions reminded investors that global growth would drive future profits.

Investors reacted well to our surging profits, although some naysayers had begun to question if our large size would make it difficult to sustain our growth. I disagreed vehemently given that we just were beginning to scratch the surface on distribution synergies and cost savings, and I saw the international initiative as a powerful means of deflecting the bearish sentiment. Our franchises outside the United States represented nearly half of our profits. Our unique global reach, strong products, and modest market shares in many important countries offered a compelling opportunity for delivering sustained double-digit earnings growth and high returns on capital.

As the year wore on, I began to grow more receptive to larger deals. That summer, I received a call from the CEO of American General indicating his interest in selling. The Houston-based company was a large national player in the consumer finance business and also operated a substantial insurance franchise. We successfully had acquired numerous finance companies over the years and saw American General as just one more opportunity to profitably integrate a smaller competitor. The deal, however, wasn't meant to be. Our due diligence revealed issues that called into question the quality of the franchise.

I had spent several months working to build a harmonious board following my bruising battle with John Reed, and the last thing I wanted was to force an expensive deal on my directors. Accordingly, I consulted the board at a relatively early stage of the talks. We undressed the deal completely, and the board quickly came to the conclusion that it was too expensive. I welcomed the guidance and was comfortable with the decision. At that point, board harmony and support meant more than winning this transaction. American General later accepted a rich $23 billion offer from insurer AIG.

The disappointment of seeing this deal slip away didn't last long as a far more interesting seller, Associates First Capital, soon approached us. Our consumer executives viewed Associates as the gold standard in the consumer finance business. Once owned by Ford Motor Company, Associates had overextended itself and had fallen prey to consumer activist groups who questioned whether the company had taken advantage of uneducated customers. As a result, Associates' stock price had fallen nearly 50 percent from its high. I sensed the value, and my colleagues Bob Lipp and Bob Willumstad stoked my interest all the more by arguing that a merger with Associates would catapult us into the leading position in the consumer finance business in the United States. With operations in fifteen countries, including a large franchise in Japan, Associates would also transform our consumer finance business into a global player overnight.

The negotiations advanced quickly, and we announced the $30 billion deal in early September 2000. Investors responded favorably. What would have been a mega-deal for almost any other company looked like a bite-sized deal for Citigroup. The acquisition effectively broadcast that we had returned to the acquisition arena with a new seriousness. It also reinforced the theme that we were just scratching the surface on growing globally. Away from the applause, consumer activists who had battled Associates with the charge of predatory lending took exception to our announcement and rallied themselves for an even bigger fight. In the glow of our successful transaction, I completely failed to understand their rising power, which eventually would come back to haunt us. That issue would wait, however, and now I only wanted to celebrate our feeling that we had regained our stride.

By early 2001, a year had passed since John Reed's departure, and the difficulty of working with him had faded to a distant memory. I had worked hard to pull the company together, and Citigroup was now on a roll. I loved our company's vast global franchise and the respect we commanded around the world. Continuing to build our position in key emerging markets remained a top priority. One morning, Bob Rubin received a call from an old colleague at Goldman Sachs announcing that the principal owners of Mexico's largest bank, Banamex, might be interested in speaking with us, presumably about a merger. Commonly referred to as "the J. P. Morgan of Mexico," Banamex enjoyed a terrific reputation, and I asked Bob to set up a meeting as quickly as possible.

Several years earlier, Roberto Hernández and Alfredo Harp, two savvy businessmen who had built a local Mexican securities firm from scratch, took advantage of a depressed market to buy Banamex. Their timing proved extraordinarily good as the Mexican financial system enjoyed a healthy rebound in the 1990s, while the two later benefited from an IPO which raised fresh capital from investors. The Goldman Sachs banker arranged for us to meet initially with Hernández and forewarned us to be delicate in our approach as Hernández had sent only indirect signals regarding his interest in selling. In fact, Hernández wanted to protect the secrecy of our meeting and insisted on convening at a remote hacienda in the middle of a jungle in the Yucatán.

Bob Rubin and I flew to somewhere in the Yucatán where we were to meet a helicopter provided by Hernández for an early evening flight to our rendezvous. I'm not a big fan of helicopters, let alone the Mexican variety, and hoped we'd make the connection in time before the sun set. At customs, we were instructed to press a button which would indicate whether we could pass freely or instead undergo a search of our luggage. Bob and my security man, Gus, each pressed the button and received an all-clear green "*passe*" light; to my dismay, however, I got the "*no passe*" red light, which forced a time-consuming inspection process.

I obsessed on how we'd now have to land in some distant jungle clearing in the dark, an unnerving prospect. Finally, we boarded the helicopter, which flew in low over the dense forest.

At one point, Gus gazed earnestly at the wild area below and half jokingly intoned in his inimitable Bronx accent, "Be careful when we arrive; I bet there are tigers down there!" Dusk had settled by the time we descended, and I nervously grabbed Bob's arm at one point as we banked toward our landing. I hoped the pilot could distinguish the landing field. When we finally touched down, I discovered that Hernández's daughter (who ran the hacienda) had guided us in by the light of a lantern.

Joined by the bank's COO, Manuel Medina Mora, Roberto Hernández gave us a brief tour of the compound before dinner. That evening, he spoke endlessly about his passion for Mayan culture. He rambled on while Bob and I drank glass upon glass of wine and tried with increasing difficulty to remain engaged. I spied Bob's eyes rolling back and began to fear he'd drop off in slumber. It was all a careful mating game as Roberto plainly didn't know how best to bring up the subject of pursuing a deal while we still were walking on eggshells so as not to jeopardize things with an impolite advance. At last, I simply asked if we could discuss some business, which broke the ice and allowed for at least a general conversation about pursuing a deal. Before leaving the following morning, we agreed to meet again in Armonk to discuss the specifics of a transaction.

Roberto came to that second session with his partner, Alfredo Harp, and we hammered out the terms of a merger reasonably quickly. I relished the idea of making a substantial investment in Mexico as the local financial services market seemed ready to take off. I was amazed by the low percentage of financial product sales relative to the size of the economy and reasoned that growth would surge as the country proved its new stable political and economic underpinnings. My colleagues and I also focused on the rapidly growing U.S. Hispanic population and believed Banamex could help us penetrate that potentially lucrative market. The Mexican company had earned more than $900 million the year before, and I believed that continued growth and opportunities for cost savings almost certainly would enhance Citigroup's earnings per share.

Hernández and Harp proved to be tough negotiators and insisted on a $12.5 billion price and two board seats. We pushed back on a couple of Banamex's more questionable investments, a telecom joint venture and a stake in a small Argentine bank; however, we got nowhere in lowering the price or having the Mexicans take back those assets. Finally, we decided to go forward with the deal and announced the merger in May 2001.

Some of our board members weren't happy about our having to give away two director slots for a deal of this size, and a few complained that I had charged ahead without sufficient advance consultation. Perhaps I had let my excitement about the deal get the better of me, although the restiveness among my directors soon quieted. The telecom joint venture and the Argentine bank investment later became problems as we had feared. Nonetheless, the Banamex acquisition proved to be attractive. Less than four years following the transaction, Citigroup's earnings from Mexico had nearly doubled to $1.7 billion, and our company was earning an attractive return on invested capital in a market growing at an above-average clip.

While our successes in 2000 and early 2001 gave me a heady feeling, the challenge of running a large organization invariably meant we'd also face periodic disappointments. Frustrated by what he saw as excessive bureaucracy, Bob Lipp soon became a particular issue. In the wake of the merger with Citicorp, Bob had battled constantly both with his co–Consumer Business head, Bill Campbell, as well as with John Reed. We finally sorted out the conflict in his favor, yet the experience must have gotten to Bob because he never regained his composure following Reed's departure. Instead, he pushed back on a number of my decisions and began complaining that Citigroup's organization and infighting reminded him of the bureaucracy he had fled in the 1980s when he first joined Commercial Credit from Chemical Bank.

Bob, too, was unhappy about losing his board seat after the merger and pressed me to name him president. I resisted changing his title since I felt this would be a big step for the company, and I didn't think Bob was sufficiently integrating the corporate cultures that now comprised our company. I had come to see that some very good middle-level managers had come from Citicorp (in contrast to John Reed's senior people); however, Bob seemed intent on quickly imposing the Travelers people throughout the organization. Being nearly my age, Bob wasn't going to be my successor, and I didn't see the need to change his role.

My decision to shift responsibility for Emerging Markets to Victor Menezes also troubled Bob. The transfer seemed completely logical since Victor, a highly successful Indian-American, acted as a role model for many young non-U.S. nationals in our company and represented a clear signal to our employees from Citicorp that we didn't mean to steamroll over them. Sadly, the organizational realignment struck a nerve with Bob, who, as head of our Global Consumer business, felt he shouldn't have to share responsibility for even a small portion of the retail business. Bitterly, he complained that the international business was the most interesting aspect of the Citicorp merger and he didn't want to give any of it up.

I had announced Victor Menezes's shift to head Emerging Markets at one of our management off-site meetings in Armonk during July 2000, and by the end of the day, Bob and several of his colleagues, including Bob Willumstad and Marge Magner, were up-in-arms about my decision. Emotions ran high. "We're just beginning to make progress outside the U.S.—how can you take this away from us now? It's the wrong thing to do," they pleaded.

The argument came to a boil after a few rounds of drinks that evening, and I soon lost my temper. I thought they were overreacting—after all, Bob would continue to have responsibility for our massive consumer activities in the United States, Europe, and Japan—and I didn't appreciate their ganging up on me. At last, I insisted that the decision was final and assumed the team would get over the surprise.

I did what I could to placate Bob. After consulting with our directors, I gave him the vice chairman's title and agreed to award him a seat on our board. I even forced through an exception to our stock-holding policy and allowed Bob to sell half of his stock so that he could satisfy his personal financial objectives. My efforts, though, came to naught as Bob met with me that autumn and insisted that it was time to retire. "I've made more money than I ever dreamed," he said, "and it's now time to focus on my family."

I realized I couldn't change Bob's mind, and I appreciated his sincerity. I understood by now that Bob's complaints over his role in the Consumer Business represented only a small part of his motivation. He plainly felt some inner need to make a change. It was time to let go. We ended up agreeing that he would remain on our board and stay on as chairman of Travelers Insurance.

Bob's retirement provoked me to reassess my own workload. At age sixty-seven, I was beginning to look for a way out of the day-to-day obligation to review numbers and spending weekends consumed by work. Meanwhile, Bob Rubin pushed the idea that I consider naming a COO to better organize the company. I liked the concept, reasoning that it would afford me the energy to work longer. Rather than appoint a single person, however, I settled on a co-COO structure given the company's complexity.

Before he stepped down, Bob advocated his second-in-command at Travelers, Jay Fishman, praising his financial skills and nearly decade-long involvement in our insurance businesses. I opted to give Jay responsibility for finance and risk management and installed Chuck Prince as his partner COO to manage the legal, compliance, and human resources functions. At the operating level, I promoted Bob Willumstad to run the entire Consumer Business. While I was interested in seeing how each of these executives would perform with a larger assignment, succession planning did not figure prominently into the decision. The press chose to see it otherwise, but in late 2000, I was far from ready to step down.

Management changes in a large organization often lead to a lot of soul-searching among top managers. Our CFO, Todd Thomson, didn't have the best relationship with Jay Fishman and bridled at his promotion. I didn't want to lose Todd, who showed great potential, so

I gave him responsibility for our corporate investments and arranged a dual reporting structure whereby Todd would report to both me and Jay. This situation, along with Bob Lipp's unhappiness, illustrates how important it is for a CEO to minimize surprises and communicate effectively. Still, effective leadership demands doing what's right and not simply placating executives.

———————

Unfortunately, our management turnover didn't end with Bob. Soon, my son, Marc, also left the company. For a decade, Marc had proved time and again his skill as an investor, but he was unhappy with the new demands on his time which accompanied our merger with Citicorp. Before the creation of Citigroup, his job managing Travelers' investments was relatively independent of the rest of the company; however, the merger introduced a lot of politics and bureaucracy, things which Marc hated since they took away from his interest in investing. Marc grew increasingly unhappy. Finally, his frustration reached the point where he decided to leave the company.

In retrospect, Marc's departure may have been an omen of sorts. Over the next couple of years a variety of events conspired to dampen my normal optimism. The pivotal turning point came for us, as for most Americans, with the events of September 11, 2001. Like Pearl Harbor and the assassination of President Kennedy, the events of that Tuesday have been seared into my memory. I was at my desk that morning working with my muted television tuned to CNBC. When the special report showed the first pictures of the smoldering World Trade Center's North Tower, I turned up the volume and watched for much of the morning transfixed by the unfolding events.

Sickened by those images and the steady stream of on-the-ground reports, a wave of things crossed my mind. I immediately thought about our people. We no longer had offices in the Twin Towers, yet we still had sixteen thousand employees working in different locations downtown including our Asset Management business in 7 World Trade Center, which stood adjacent to the North Tower. I watched in shock as people began jumping from the top of the towers to escape the smoke and flames and kept thinking about how fate had kept my kids and me from becoming victims. After all, it hadn't been that long since we had moved our offices out of the top of the South Tower. I also imagined how one of those planes must have flown in low over Salomon Smith Barney's headquarters on Greenwich Street. I assumed many colleagues had witnessed the explosion. I couldn't imagine what it must have been like to be an eyewitness. Only God knew what would happen next. Not since Pearl Harbor had we seen anything like this on U.S. soil.

I managed to track down Joanie, who was on her way to a medical appointment, and told her to hurry home. She reminded me that our daughter, Jessica, had flown to Chicago that morning, the thought of which evoked immediate worry given that the identity of the planes involved in the terror hadn't yet been determined. Mercifully, Joan called Jessica's office at once and got patched through to her—she had already landed.

There was no time to linger on the phone since calls were now cascading into my office from nervous executives who wanted permission to close our offices and send employees home. The requests amplified the immediacy of the crisis all the more. At first, I hesitated, worried that a sudden evacuation might instill panic; however, it didn't take long to realize that we had to get our people home to their families.

By late morning, I convened most of my business heads in a conference room next to my office. Tom Jones, our Asset Management head, who kept his office in 7 World Trade, had been unreachable all morning, and we were of course concerned for his safety. At last, we were able to get through to him on his cell phone—he reported that he had been preoccupied getting our employees out of harm's way and that he was walking uptown accompanied by his staff.

He later arrived dazed and covered in soot and took his place at the table. We went around the table asking for ideas on how to react. Long-scheduled meetings no longer mattered. Telephone lines ceased to be reliable. Information came only in fragments.

When the first tower collapsed with its thunderous roar, we collectively groaned in horror, but the fast-moving events didn't allow time for reflection. Having evacuated our operations center, we needed to bring up our backup sites. We were learning, too, what all of this meant for settling the huge volume of financial transactions which flowed through trading and processing facilities in lower Manhattan.

Our senior banker Bill Rhodes had been in contact with the New York Federal Reserve and passed on the first reports that the clearing system was breaking down. Meanwhile, our credit people began to consider, in ways they never anticipated, how such a crisis might affect loan quality. Our insurance people were concerned about our exposures and were beginning to mobilize claims response teams while our consumer banking people figured out how to replenish cash supplies to keep our ATM network functioning. Despite the chaos and improvisation, my colleagues displayed unbelievable professionalism and composure under the worst of circumstances.

Once the shock of that first day of crisis wore off, the demands on our business only intensified. While we successfully moved to operational backup sites and were ready to trade government bonds and commercial paper the following day, some of our competitors weren't nearly as fortunate. Bank of New York encountered serious issues which soon became hard to conceal. A huge processor of financial transactions, Bank of New York housed its main operations center only a couple of blocks from Ground Zero and faced serious delays in restoring its systems.

It immediately became impossible for other financial firms to settle transactions with such a large intermediary out of commission. Serving on the board of the New York Fed, I witnessed firsthand how the situation compromised the integrity of the financial markets. Fortunately, the Fed's highly capable staff moved quickly to supply liquidity, leaving the discount window open late each evening for several days to give financial firms the chance to sort out their positions and borrow as needed to take care of settlement gaps. While a number of other firms needed to rely on this source of liquidity, Citigroup managed to fund itself through the entire crisis, an accomplishment of which I'm enormously proud.

The terrorist act sapped confidence and sent the economy and a number of key industries into a tailspin. When stocks began trading again on the Monday following the attack, markets reflected the fears, and stock prices opened sharply lower. Unfortunately, we soon learned that we had provided backup lines of credit to some of the more exposed companies such as the airlines without incorporating typical protections against "material adverse change."

In the weeks following the attack, we focused on a number of highly significant credit agreements and worked hard to enhance our collateral position where possible. In contrast to this somewhat nasty surprise, our insurance business perversely benefited from the attack as the enormous volume of industry claims soon translated into a boost for insurance rates on new policies. Travelers had a few hundred million dollars of exposure to the events in lower Manhattan, yet this was relatively modest compared to other insurers.

Though the attack on the World Trade Center and its resulting vast human tragedy were horrible, the crisis taught inspiring lessons in leadership. I marveled at President George W. Bush's response and the care he showed by repeatedly coming to New York to honor the victims and to stand with the rescuers and survivors. Similarly, Mayor Rudolph Giuliani's actions distinguished him.

As CEO of Citigroup, I wanted to do my share to help our company's employees and our city. I relied on my team for managing specific issues; however, that didn't stop me from being personally visible and reassuring to our employees. I sat in on many of the meetings with the Federal Reserve and our operations teams and listened carefully during the discussions about our liquidity. I cajoled city officials to restore access to our downtown offices on Greenwich Street once its function as a temporary morgue ceased. I also leveraged my involvement with the Weill Cornell Medical School to arrange for trauma specialists to spend time with our staff to help deal with the emotional scars.

Within two days of the attack, we established the Citigroup Relief Fund with an initial $15 million grant from our company's foundation to provide college scholarships for the children of the victims. My role was obvious: display confidence, care for our employees, and focus the company on recovering from this tragedy.

Of course, it took a long time for life to return to normal following the shock of September 11. New York City remained particularly traumatized. As chairman of Carnegie Hall and Weill Cornell, I soon began thinking of how these institutions might help the city recover. Carnegie Hall's season-opening gala had been scheduled for the beginning of October and many on the board believed we should cancel the accompanying celebration. In contrast, I argued that life had to go on and that the city had to move forward. The New York Philharmonic had gone the route of canceling their gala and instead put on a requiem, which seemed to do little to instill a sense of healing. I thought people would want to come together and prevailed upon our board. We arranged for Mayor Giuliani to welcome the guests and for a member of the city's police force to sing "God Bless America."

It proved an emotional and cathartic evening with proper respect shown for the recent events.

I also believed that Weill Cornell had an important role to play and set to work on a new fund-raising campaign to support clinical research and patient care. In January 2002, I announced a lead gift of $100 million and convinced AIG CEO Hank Greenberg to pledge $50 million toward our new $750 million campaign. This was my second $100 million gift to Weill Cornell and demonstrated my confidence in investing in the city even as some were questioning New York's resiliency. I felt I played my part in helping the city get back on its feet.

Call it coincidence, but September 11 ushered in other unexpected events. Problems were starting to emerge in our finance company reflecting surprises at our recent acquisition, Associates First Capital. The branch conversion had gone as planned, yet our Japanese and middle market lending and leasing businesses turned down abruptly. Unfortunately, we overestimated the quality of Associates' management in Tokyo, which had expanded too aggressively just as the Japanese consumer economy had begun deteriorating. Loan losses in our Japanese finance company surged with little warning, rising more than $500 million between 2000 and 2002, and profits soon fell by more than half. The errors in judgment forced us to change our team, and it took a couple of iterations before we found the right successor.

Similarly, we suffered from poor management in the middle market area. We weren't especially familiar with the business, and I mistakenly left the unit autonomous rather than assign one of our executives to take responsibility.

While these missteps were bad enough, the worst problems came from not sufficiently considering the changing regulatory landscape and the tenacity of activist groups focused on reforming the consumer finance business. Requiring low-income borrowers to buy life insurance had been a common industry practice for years. Suddenly, the focus turned to the high all-in cost of obtaining credit from firms such as Associates. The predatory-lending charge stuck, and regulators soon were all over us investigating our practices. We only extracted ourselves after two costly settlements including one for $215 million. In retrospect, we hadn't taken our detractors seriously and assumed regulators would tolerate the status quo.

Ultimately, we paid a very big price both financially and in loss of reputation. The regulatory settlements and the losses in Japan and the commercial middle market unfortunately overshadowed our successful integration of Associates' U.S. branches. While Associates gave us a leadership position in the U.S. consumer finance business (and provided the foundation for a decisive edge in private-labeled credit cards), the financial returns from the transaction proved subpar. I consider it one of the worst acquisitions of my career since actual earnings results missed our forecasts by so much and diluted our return on equity.

In addition to the problems in the finance company, I had to deal with more turnover on my management team during late 2001. Jay Fishman caught me off guard when he came to tell me he was resigning to become CEO of Saint Paul Companies, the Midwestern insurer. I thought he had appreciated his recent co-COO promotion and was initially taken aback. I felt hurt and angry by his lack of allegiance, yet I rationalized that the offer to lead his own company must have been a powerful lure.

Jay's sudden departure came at an awkward time since I only recently had begun to think seriously about succession planning. Mike Carpenter and Bob Willumstad, the heads of Citigroup's largest businesses, seemed the natural front-runners, although it was way too early to make such an important decision. I wasn't ready to pass the baton, and no one on my team enjoyed enough breadth of experience to make the cut then anyway. Over the prior year, I had wanted to reduce my workload more than ever and take some of the burdens of running such a large company off my shoulders.

I wrestled with these thoughts and realized that I needed to do more to develop our company's top executives. Accordingly, I decided to name Bob Willumstad president, figuring it was an auspicious time to broaden his experience beyond the Consumer Business and to see how he'd perform. Bob had demonstrated leadership in the Consumer franchise where he had managed costs successfully, delivered organic growth, and integrated many acquisitions. He also had taken the lead on exporting our consumer finance business to new overseas markets. In communicating my decision, I underscored that the appointment did not equate to a succession announcement. Bob seemed shocked and expressed nervousness about his ability to perform, but I reassured him that he'd do fine and that I was there to help.

Jay Fishman's departure similarly provoked another important decision, this time involving Travelers' property and casualty business. Jay, and Bob Lipp before him, had managed our insurance franchise, and with the loss of both of these individuals, I realized that we lacked capable executives to run the business. I assigned Travelers to Bob Willumstad as part of his broader responsibilities, although we agreed that he lacked insurance experience.

I now regretted not having spent more time overseeing a more robust succession arrangement for the unit. For some time, we had considered divesting the business given its cyclical returns and deficient growth prospects relative to most of our other businesses. We also had struggled to integrate the property and casualty business with our other franchises (cross-selling proved harder than we had imagined) and weren't thrilled by increasing our exposure to the industry via more acquisitions. Despite our qualms, we never got to the point of taking action. Following September 11, however, insurance premiums soared across the industry, a phenomenon that boosted the market values of most publicly traded insurers, and the notion of off-loading the business during a period of investor bullishness began to pique my interest.

Losing Travelers' top two executives posed a serious obstacle for selling or spinning out the unit. However, a call from Bob Lipp in early December 2001 solved our dilemma. He confided that he was considering a job offer from Jay Fishman to take over Saint Paul's reinsurance company in advance of a spin-out. He informed me that he would surrender his seat on Citigroup's board were he to accept the job. Getting over the surprise that Bob had suddenly tired of retirement, I devised a more compelling idea and offered him the chance to run a spun-off Travelers property and casualty business instead. In a stroke, I was offering him a chance to return to a name company he knew well and one ten times the size of the unit which Jay had offered.

Thankfully, Bob jumped at the opportunity, and we quickly announced a plan for an initial public offering for 20 percent of the company in early 2002 to be followed by a spin-out of the remaining ownership to Citigroup's shareholders later in the year. While some investors questioned our sudden willingness to part with the unit and wondered if we had given up on our diversified financial services model, I never thought in such terms. I simply recognized the attractive financial tradeoff of shedding the relatively low-returning business and reinvesting the capital in our more profitable units. I also understood that it was often necessary to change with the times and business realities.

We completed the spin-out as planned though the negotiations to separate the unit became far more complex than I had imagined. Suddenly, Bob and I had to adjust to dealing with one another on an arm's-length basis. Our talks became contentious as we hammered out the details of the separation, and our relationship turned frosty for a while. Happily, the strain proved temporary.

If management turnover, the disposition of Travelers, and the events surrounding September 11 weren't enough to fill our agenda, we also had to confront an international crisis during late 2001 and early 2002 as Argentina sank into political and economic turmoil. The South American country had been facing issues for some time—large budget deficits and diminishing foreign currency reserves increasingly sapped investor confidence. By late 2001, the local economy lapsed into recession while Argentine officials began sparring with the International Monetary Fund over its prescriptions for reform. In December, attempts to cut the budget sparked rioting in major cities, and the president resigned late in the month. Over the following three weeks, Argentina went through five presidents in quick succession before installing a populist leader.

Just before year end, one of the interim presidents stated his intention to suspend payments on much of the country's public debt, an announcement of a debt default in layman's terms. For several years, the centerpiece of the country's economic model had been the free convertibility of the peso into the U.S. dollar at a fixed one-for-one exchange rate. Two weeks later, amid the political confusion, the country suddenly cast out the policy, which had worked for so long. The new populist president announced the end of the currency peg and a plan to devalue the peso by nearly 30 percent (it ultimately plunged by multiples of this percentage).

The default and devaluation meant significant disruption, though it took a while for foreign banks like ours to figure out the full ramifications. In what became known as an "asymmetric pesofication," the Argentines required the banks in February 2002 to adjust their deposit obligations for the devaluation, yet they made no corresponding adjustment for the repayment of loans. Effectively, loans were repaid with devalued pesos while the banks had to honor deposit obligations as if no devaluation had occurred, the combination of which meant significant losses for our local bank. No one in banking circles ever had seen such a requirement, and it effectively meant the government was invading the deep pockets of foreign financial institutions. Overnight, the economy weakened sharply. By the time the worst of the crisis ended, Citigroup had lost over $2 billion.

The events revealed important flaws in Citigroup's management model. I gradually realized to my disappointment that Victor Menezes stood at the center of our issues. During the early stages of the crisis, Victor had downplayed our risks, and I trusted his judgment. After all, Citicorp had operated in Argentina for nearly a century with a strong market share, experienced local management, and close ties to government officials. I had no reason to doubt our market intelligence. Nevertheless, as the news worsened steadily, Victor stuck with an overly optimistic assessment, which forced me to wonder if he really understood the situation. In our management meetings, my colleagues and I pressed Victor for estimates on our loss risk. Initially, he was reluctant to offer a figure, and we pushed harder. Finally, he told us that under a worst-case scenario, we might lose as much as $350 million.

Given that we had billions of dollars in assets in the country, I believed the estimate might be too low. I asked Victor to allow other executives from outside his Emerging Markets organization to make an independent assessment, but he vociferously resisted any meddling in his domain. My doubts about Victor's management style began to grow. I suspected that he was managing from thirty thousand feet. At that point, I decided to have Chuck Prince give up his responsibilities as our general counsel and made him COO of the Emerging Markets business—Chuck and Victor got along well, and I wanted Chuck to force better communication.

In January, we announced a $470 million charge, which represented a considered estimate of where we were—we stressed to investors that there could be no assurance that this would be the last of our losses. With the implementation of the asymmetric pesofication, we realized that Victor's "worst-case" assessment bore no relation to reality, although pinning down a specific exposure remained difficult given the fluidity of events.

In fact, it took several more weeks to understand the scope of what we were up against. The second charge in April surpassed $800 million and caused our first quarterly earnings disappointment relative to investor expectations in a long while. We also booked asset write-downs of roughly $1 billion, which didn't flow through our income statement. Incredibly, Victor claimed we were overreacting even as we lost six years' worth of normal Argentine earnings in two quarters. The entire Argentine episode left me extremely frustrated. I hated the steady stream of negative surprises.

Coming up for air, I determined that we needed to change our approach and learn from our mistakes. I came to see that we had allowed the Emerging Markets franchise to operate too much as it always had under Citicorp rather than to impose the types of controls that applied to the rest of our company. I recognized, too, that our structure created significant inefficiencies since the Emerging Markets business made little effort to leverage investments and product successes developed in other parts of the company.

In June 2002, we rolled out a new matrix organization. I removed Victor from a line role (giving him instead client oversight and internal training responsibilities) and set up a new International division which would work closely to coordinate product development and distribution with our other principal business units. I tapped Deryck Maughan to take charge of our new organizational entity reasoning that he had done his penance in the strategy area long enough following his run-in nearly four years earlier with Jamie Dimon.

With Victor's reassignment, we had taken the last large operating unit away from a onetime Citicorp executive. Since John Reed's departure, I had bent over backward to keep some semblance of continuity to the past for the sake of our employees who had come from Citicorp, but Victor had given me little alternative. Still eager to preserve some institutional link to the past and to reassure our international staff, I looked to Bill Rhodes, Citicorp's longtime senior global banker. For decades, Bill had amassed incredible relationships with government officials the world over and consistently proved himself an able executive.

It's impossible to see the forest when you're among the trees. All the events from John Reed's departure to the crisis in Argentina were taking place amid the early stage of one of the great bear markets in U.S. financial history. Of course in this case, most people, myself included, only realized the significance of the market moves after much of the damage had been done. But the story of the epic 1990s bull market and its dramatic undoing ultimately produced an outsized impact on Citigroup and on me personally which made all our other challenges pale in comparison.

The bull market which began in 1982 had been the longest sustained period of stock market prosperity in modern U.S. history. It was the late-stage market moves that took place in 1998–2000, though, which proved particularly remarkable. In 1998, the Dow Jones Average rose 16 percent and closed at 9,200, marking the first year the index had produced four successive years of double-digit gains. The exuberant markets spurred massive M&A activity as the value of completed deals surged over 50 percent during the year. The real action, however, brewed in the Nasdaq market, whose broad index surged 39 percent in 1998 to close at 2,200.

The momentum had only begun to build. In 1999, the markets went crazy as the technology-laden Nasdaq index zoomed 86 percent. In fact, prices seemed to go hyperbolic in the last two months of the year. In early November, the Nasdaq index stood at 3,000 and had gained 1,000 points in less than a year. On December 29, it blew past 4,000, an incredible surge in only seven weeks. More than half of the gain in the index for all of 1999 came during November and December alone. The unprecedented ride only got wilder: In March 2000, Nasdaq hit its all-time high just shy of 5,500.

Meanwhile, investment banking activity underwent a once-in-a-lifetime surge of its own. Monumental M&A deals suddenly became commonplace: Exxon combined with Mobil in an $81 billion deal; Deutsche Telekom bought the largest phone company in Italy for $82 billion; and the biggest headline of all came with MCI WorldCom's $115 billion announced acquisition of Sprint. More notably, the IPO calendar rocketed, driven by the surging values placed on upstart technology and Internet companies. IPO volumes nearly doubled in 1999 as over one hundred deals hit the Street in the fourth quarter alone.

The price performance of these deals stunned everyone. Internet names such as Red Hat, eBay, and Internet Capital Group regularly surged thirteen times or more from their offer prices in their first few weeks of trading. A company named VA Linux soon became the standout, rising sevenfold on its first day of trading even as the company was reporting operating losses. Valuations on technology companies seemed extraordinary: The share price of Yahoo! went from $30 in the fall of 1998 to $250 by early 2000, and its $133 billion peak market value surpassed that of General Motors and Ford combined. While investor euphoria centered on the technology sector, other institutions jumped on board. Goldman Sachs ended its 130-year history as a partnership with a $3.7 billion public offering. Even the staid New York Stock Exchange considered going public.

Watching investors' unbridled optimism, I felt at a loss. I always considered myself a value buyer, preferring stocks with low absolute price/earnings ratios. Technology valuations were in the stratosphere by almost any measure. In the world that I understood—financial sector valuations—I could see that the market was inflated as our shares and those of our competitors routinely surpassed three times book value. By contrast, I could recall several times over my career when valuations had dipped under book. Offering our shares in our mergers with Citicorp and Associates reflected my attempt to benefit from our healthy valuation.

While I saw the froth in the markets, I didn't see Citigroup reaping outsized benefits. We never had a large technology franchise and ceded much of the related investment-banking-deal flow to competitors like Morgan Stanley, Goldman Sachs, CSFB, and even Merrill Lynch. Much of our banking franchise had been geared toward larger traditional companies, which meant we weren't fully engaged in the IPO business, and we still operated a large fixed income business whose relatively slower growth muted the stronger gains in our equities and investment banking areas. While I didn't like falling behind our competitors, I resisted delving into things that we didn't know especially well.

At one point, Merrill Lynch, realizing that Charles Schwab's market value surpassed its own, announced that it would introduce an online discounted brokerage service in order to compete for business. Voices inside our company pushed for a similar response, although I didn't think we should go in that direction. Unlike Merrill's management, I felt confident that our retail offerings gave our clients outstanding value. For a modest annual fee of 1 percent of assets, clients received advice, research, record keeping, and dividend collection. Rather than follow Merrill, I reassured our brokers that we'd stand behind them and continue to manage our retail business for the long term where managing for asset accumulation would be more important than chasing volatile transactions. The decision ultimately proved sound.

Whether by choice or accident, we resisted many of the fads. Nonetheless, we took advantage of one area of explosive growth which we felt sure would continue: telecom. Here we enjoyed a strong franchise and benefited from highly regarded talent including Jack Grubman, the Street's most respected analyst. Our telecom team captured a healthy share of deals from companies that advertised things like wi-fi Internet access, third-generation mobile connectivity, and fiber optics. I began to joke that we were putting so much fiber under the ocean the fish wouldn't have anywhere to swim and we'd harm the world's food supply! In hindsight, we may have pushed too hard for new business in this area. Still, I trusted our telecom people when they presented their positive views.

I also see more clearly in hindsight that the long bull market over time had stretched thin the delineation between research and investment banking. The phenomenon, however, had been in the making for years and impacted how the entire Street did business. Every firm emulated the others in order to remain competitive. Undoubtedly, by the peak of the bull market, the standards governing research analyst interaction with investment bankers had loosened. Nevertheless, at the time, I couldn't imagine that the integrity of research had diminished seriously.

Of course, booms never last forever and usually sow the seeds of their own destruction. True to form, the markets peaked in March 2000 and headed into a descent the steepness of which only matched the prior climb. By the end of the year, Nasdaq had fallen 50 percent from its March high. The decline continued for two additional years. When it finally touched bottom in October 2002 at just over 1,100, Nasdaq had given up a staggering 78 percent of its value, a mammoth decline in shareholder value. The success stories that only recently had mesmerized investors plunged back to earth. Yahoo!, for instance, gave up all of its gains and returned to its pre-bubble $30 price. Meanwhile, cut off from funding, many Internet companies simply folded. Curiously, much of the market outside technology and telecom emerged nearly unscathed. The Dow Jones Average—more of an "old economy" index—surrendered only 6 percent of its value in 2000, while the staid utility sector became a safe haven for investors and actually rose in value.

While saddened for those who lost money, I viewed the emerging bear market with considerable equanimity. In many respects, sanity seemed to be coming back into the market. Having seen the Japanese Nikkei market go from 40,000 to 8,000 since the late 1980s while the Dow Jones Index rocketed from 2,000 to 12,000 had taught me to appreciate how quickly markets could change. By the time of its trough, the Dow surrendered about 35 percent of its peak value, but the decline didn't seem out of bounds with prior market corrections, and most thoughtful people appreciated that real earnings underpinned most of the component companies. In contrast, I never understood how Nasdaq could have quintupled over such a short span, particularly on the back of companies that hadn't withstood the test of time. When Nasdaq retreated to its pre-bubble level, it somehow seemed logical and fair.

———————————

By mid-2001, complaints against the brokerage industry began mounting, and a host of lawyers started encouraging retail investors who had lost money to file restitution claims. Initially, I didn't think much of the complaints since similar attempts to assign blame for losses had typically accompanied earlier bear markets. However, in June, New York's attorney general, Eliot Spitzer, announced that his office would initiate an investigation of Merrill Lynch's research practices.

Before long, the attorney general claimed to have unearthed internal e-mails compromising Merrill's star Internet analyst, Henry Blodgett. According to press accounts, Blodgett's research did not match his privately held opinions on stocks he was recommending. One of the more notorious e-mail comments mentioned the need to "put lipstick on this pig," presumably to make the case why investors should buy shares in some upstart Internet company.

Spitzer's investigation proceeded over a number of months. Unlike traditional regulatory investigations of Wall Street practices, however, this one was being led by an elected state attorney general and not the federally enfranchised SEC or the National Association of Securities Dealers (NASD). Moreover, the probe ran its course in an unusually public fashion with almost day-by-day press accounts concerning Spitzer's assertions and rebuttals by Merrill Lynch.

That autumn, a completely separate corporate drama unfolded when questions began to swirl over a high-flying Houston-based energy company named Enron. Thanks to revelations provided by an employee whistle-blower, Enron's auditors from Arthur Andersen soon revised their treatment of certain financial structures. The embarrassment forced the resignation of Enron's CEO, Jeffrey Skilling, and a several-hundred-million-dollar write-off quickly followed. Soon, suddenly vigilant accountants began uncovering a variety of financial machinations which obscured conflicts of interest.

Investors quickly began questioning the profitability of Enron's core energy trading business and whether the company's widely acclaimed success had been a mirage. In October, the company's CFO resigned, and the SEC began to investigate. More dirt surfaced, and cash drained from the company as nervous trading counterparties moved to require Enron to post added collateral to support its trades. Citigroup, J. P. Morgan, and a variety of other banks had worked with Enron for years and had extended credit facilities, many of which could be called in the event of a credit rating downgrade.

By November, Enron's financial condition was steadily worsening. Mike Carpenter served as our senior relationship manager for Enron, but with our client's urgent request for fresh bank credit, I now had my first serious briefings. We needed to determine if Enron could be saved and how best to structure an emergency financing. During the meetings and conference calls that accompanied this process, I relied heavily on Mike and his team as well as outside attorneys for advice. All of our attention at that point centered on the financing decision and whether we could prudently take added risk.

I had read enough about Enron and its practices to want additional clarifications if possible. Among these, I suggested we speak with the chairman of Enron's audit committee (who turned out to be a former dean of Stanford's business school) to get a better sense of Enron's accounting practices. After learning that the director was hunting in

Montana, we managed to track him down for a conference call. He only gave us general answers to our questions, and I wondered seriously if we were going to throw good money after bad. Still, I finally told my team that I was willing to abide by their judgment so long as we secured proper collateral. The decision to support Enron soon became moot as the company filed bankruptcy in early December, the largest bankruptcy in U.S. history at the time.

When Enron folded, my colleagues and I viewed the company's demise narrowly as an unfortunate credit event. However, we gradually began to see some of the same shareholder lawsuits that Spitzer's probe of Merrill's research department was unleashing. In its heyday, Enron enjoyed a large investor following; those who had lost money now started looking for deep pockets. The banks and brokers who had financed Enron became easy targets, though the worst of the legal onslaught didn't occur until several months after Enron's bankruptcy when Congress launched hearings that overplayed the role of some of the nation's largest banks.

Meanwhile, Spitzer's attack on Merrill Lynch shifted into high gear by the spring of 2002, and it was becoming increasingly obvious that the attorney general was going to force Merrill Lynch into a settlement on his terms. Spitzer employed a New York statute known as the Martin Act to allege fraud even though the law had not been used in memory to enforce the country's securities laws. The notion of fraud represented serious stuff, and Merrill's then CEO, David Komansky, had little room to maneuver since a criminal indictment would have spelled disaster for his company. Initially, I dismissed Merrill's case as a one-off event. With Merrill being pushed toward a highly public settlement, however, I understood that Spitzer might well come after the rest of the major Wall Street firms once he prevailed over Merrill Lynch.

Bracing for the likely additional fallout, I realized that my emotional temperament had gone full circle over the prior two years. I had felt awfully good as I moved past my power-sharing arrangement with John Reed and put my own imprint on Citigroup. For a year and a half, investors acknowledged our progress and allowed our shares to appreciate nicely. The smooth sailing wasn't destined to last. In early 2002, I perceived that the tumult of September 11 had been the bell ringer which evoked our new problems. Before the end of the year, however, I'd see quite clearly that our new troubles flowed far more from the historic bear market than anything else. What's more, I'd soon go on the emotional roller coaster of my life.

18

The Wrath of
the Regulators

The financial world quaked during 2002. Two years of an intense
bear market meant that investors wanted blood, and recrimina-
tions surely followed. The regulators, the press, and politicians of
all stripes followed the story and sought to get out in front in the game
of pointing fingers. A spotlight had been cast on Wall Street and sad to
say, a number of past practices no longer looked intelligent in the light
of the new day. I learned a great deal during that year regarding the
manner in which the Street's standards had relaxed over the course of
the prior bull market and also how my reputation—a lifetime in the
making—could be dragged through the mud by aggressive public officials and an unscrupulous press.

I usually liked to control events, but surprise followed surprise
during 2002 to the point where my world felt as though it were being
torn apart. Trying to grab hold of the situation, I told myself repeatedly that I should look for opportunity amid all the flux—the adage had
served me well over the years. Although no one could tell exactly what
new standards would be imposed upon the industry, reform was inevitably in the air. I had spent my entire professional life embracing
change as a matter of business necessity. Now, the new climate meant
that I had to confront those who eagerly sought to sully my name; at
the same time, I had to focus on leading Citigroup—and the industry

for that matter—to a better place. While my personal reputation was at stake, I was determined to come out of this a winner.

More than Enron's debacle, Merrill Lynch's tangle with Eliot Spitzer over its research practices brought home the message of how the securities industry had to reform itself. Clearly, other Wall Street firms could be asked questions regarding whether analysts had become too involved in banking transactions and whether investment banking had influence over research ratings and compensation.

It was painful to watch Merrill Lynch's top leadership spend months ineffectively fighting a case where the strong-willed attorney general appeared to hold all the cards. I thought about earlier cases where financial firms had engaged in self-defeating battles with their regulators—Drexel Burnham, for example—and wondered why any management would think it could prevail in a public run-in with the government. Meanwhile, Chuck Prince enjoyed a good working relationship with our regulators and was sensitive to the shifting regulatory dynamic—to his credit, he kept me posted on events and prepared me for the inevitability of new industry rules.

In late April, Merrill's CEO finally capitulated and issued a public apology for the way his firm had conducted business. Accepting that its research department's standards had been compromised meant that it was only a matter of time before Merrill would settle with the attorney general. Our competitor's statement of contrition unleashed fresh waves of public condemnation over Wall Street's practices, a fervor that undoubtedly would encourage the attorney general's office to investigate other firms once it finished with Merrill.

Already, Spitzer was dropping the names of Morgan Stanley's Internet analyst, Mary Meeker, and our own telecommunications star, Jack Grubman, suggesting that the work and oversight of these prominent analysts should be questioned. I didn't think Salomon Smith Barney had a lot to be concerned about since it was never much of a factor in the technology and Internet areas, yet I understood that Grubman's prominence made him an inviting target. Sensing that the regulatory needle soon would point our way, I directed Salomon Smith Barney to take the lead and draft reforms that would address the questions being raised over the integrity of the Street's research product.

When Merrill announced its unprecedented $100 million regulatory settlement in late May, we were ready and announced at once that we'd adopt what had become known as the "Spitzer Principles." Our new policy would not tolerate any links between research compensation and investment banking, and we established a review committee to approve analyst recommendations and guard against conflicts.

We also began disclosing whether we were receiving investment banking fees on any of the companies on which we produced investment research. At a press conference to discuss the Merrill settlement, one reporter asked Spitzer what he thought about Salomon Smith Barney's quick response, and the New York official complimented our move—that felt good and reminded me that racing "first to be second" had been a smart strategy, since the entire industry soon would be forced to comply with the new rules.

In my eagerness to get out in front of the shifting regulatory climate, I didn't confine my efforts to changing research. Enron illustrated that we needed to understand better the full scope of our business with large clients and to establish a clearer point of accountability. Complaints by activist groups were also mounting over the alleged predatory lending in our finance company, charges which complicated our relationship with our bank regulators. After consulting extensively with our board, I decided in April to commission a serious governance and business practices review.

I charged one of our directors, Mike Masin, to lead the study. The vice chairman and president of Verizon and onetime managing partner of a large law firm, Mike helped me focus on important issues. Quiet and thoughtful, he was a good listener and approached business with refreshing common sense. Mike recognized that Citigroup was an amalgamation of many companies and labored for about three months to devise ideas that would lead to a more coherent corporate governance model.

He presented his recommendations at our July board meeting. Using a huge grid to lay out our issues and choices, he stimulated a healthy board discussion, and we soon agreed on a variety of governance changes. Among others, these included the creation of a formal governance committee, naming a lead director, deciding that outside directors should account for at least three-quarters of our board, and instituting a ban against interlocking directorships (which required that I surrender my seat on the boards of AT&T and United Technologies).

Our study of governance practices came amid an increasingly visceral public outcry against Wall Street as well as an attack on corporate practices at large. Led by Eliot Spitzer, the regulators turned their investigative sights on Salomon Smith Barney and other major broker dealers within weeks of the Merrill settlement. Regulatory investigations once were managed by appointed officials from the SEC, the NASD, and the New York Stock Exchange, yet times had changed. The politically ambitious New York attorney general pursued his investigation in the public spotlight and with a zeal befitting his training as a prosecutor.

By early summer, Citigroup was deeply enmeshed in its own lawsuits and regulatory investigations and had engaged lawyers from Wilmer Cutler and Paul Weiss to focus on research- and Enron-related issues. I didn't know these lawyers well and wanted to install a lawyer in whom I had confidence to oversee our legal issues. For years, I had relied on Kenny Bialkin; however, his recent retirement from our board complicated matters, and I didn't feel right tapping him for the job. Instead, I decided to turn to Marty Lipton, who had helped me at other important junctures of my career, such as when I resigned from American Express in the mid-1980s.

The best lawyer of his time in my opinion, Marty enjoyed a reputation for sobriety, sophistication, and great intelligence—most important, I thoroughly trusted his judgment. Bob Rubin reminded me how Marty's firm, Wachtell Lipton, had undertaken a conflict review for Goldman Sachs some years earlier which improved its processes and helped avoid regulatory conflict. I asked Marty to oversee our litigation, take a broad look at possible conflicts, and recommend improvements in process. In short, Marty Lipton would be our überlawyer who'd make sure we'd learn from mistakes and remain in the forefront of industry reforms.

If Eliot Spitzer's run-in with Merrill Lynch had been my wake-up call on the new regulatory era for the industry, emerging problems at WorldCom proved the spark that turned attention specifically toward Salomon Smith Barney. One of the bull market's highfliers, the Mississippi-based WorldCom had emerged from obscurity to become the telecommunications industry's leading light. Led by a zealous former high school basketball coach named Bernie Ebbers, WorldCom acquired one competitor after another and claimed to possess a low cost structure and adaptability to new technology that shamed the industry's traditional companies. Having served on AT&T's board, I could attest firsthand how WorldCom's major competitor struggled to figure out its rival's mysteriously low costs.

WorldCom, however, met its match during the bear market. In 2000, regulators blocked the company's planned acquisition of Sprint, an action which provided the first chink in investors' confidence. WorldCom's stock struggled along with other technology and telecom names until March 2002 when the company received a request for information from the SEC pertaining to accounting procedures and loans to officers.

Coming amid the intense bear market, the ominous news panicked investors. Soon, the regulatory probe and a deflated stock price forced a chastened Bernie Ebbers to quit. A month later, the rating agencies cut WorldCom's debt to junk status, and in early June, the company's CFO, Scott Sullivan, resigned in the face of evidence suggesting he had improperly accounted for nearly $4 billion in expenses mislabeled as capital expenditures. It took months to learn the full extent of the company's $11 billion fraud, and Ebbers was eventually sentenced to a twenty-five-year prison term.

Unfortunately, investors identified our famed telecom analyst, Jack Grubman, with WorldCom. Grubman had forged a relationship with Ebbers and his team and repeatedly told investors to buy their shares during the good times. On the ascent, the recommendation appeared brilliant, but now investors derided Jack as a gullible fool or, worse, a shill for management. He pulled his buy rating only a day in advance of WorldCom's first disclosure of its accounting problems and barely a month before the company filed for bankruptcy.

The WorldCom fiasco put Grubman and Salomon Smith Barney squarely in the spotlight. Spitzer soon broadened his investigation and examined whether our analyst had fraudulently promoted stocks under his coverage. Our company had jumped to the top of Spitzer's target list, and the press—seemingly in tandem—riveted its attention on us. I hated to see how we were becoming the focal point for each day's business news and shuddered at the notion that Spitzer would consider leveling criminal charges our way.

I also began to receive revelations pertaining to business decisions that plainly didn't look so smart and which put our reputation at risk. For example, preferential IPO allocations had been granted to top executives of firms with which we did business. Known as "spinning," the practice had become common on the Street, yet that didn't excuse the potential for conflict. Reporters soon got wind of the tactic and put Salomon Smith Barney front and center in their stories even though we were far from the most frequent practitioner.

The unrelenting regulatory and press attention seemed bad enough; however, 2002 was also an election year, which galvanized many politicians to distance themselves from big business and lead the charge against alleged corporate greed. By midyear, Enron and WorldCom had mushroomed into full-fledged scandals; seeking retribution, the public seemed ready to indict Wall Street regardless of the facts. Eager to show itself responsive to its constituents, Congress began holding hearings targeted at the Enron and WorldCom improprieties.

Things got rough after the July Fourth holiday, when a House committee focused on WorldCom. The hearing quickly turned into a spectacle, damaging our company's image and complicating our legal position. That morning, I watched on my office television as Jack Grubman, Bernie Ebbers, and CFO Scott Sullivan stood shoulder to shoulder and collectively raised their right hands and pledged to tell the truth. What a horrible sight!

Regardless of their real relationship, Jack Grubman now seemed inextricably linked to the two dubious WorldCom executives. Grubman never was photogenic, and television now captured his dark features and deep-set eyes in a way that made him look sinister. Worse still, he projected an air of arrogance. The testimony seemed to drag on and focused on how Jack interacted with WorldCom's top executives. Much of the time, some of the politicians seemed more interested in scoring points with the voters than in getting at the facts.

At one point, the questions took a surprising turn and zeroed in on Salomon Smith Barney's IPO allocation process. Grubman seemed caught off guard—apparently, no one had prepared him for this line of questioning. Sadly, our analyst stammered and refused to directly answer many of the questions. Nevertheless, he suggested inadvertently—and incorrectly, I was told later—that he played an important role in the distribution of new issues. By the time he completed his testimony, I already could anticipate the next day's horrific press.

Grubman's testimony couldn't have come at a worse time, as I had been scheduled to receive an award as CEO of the Year that same evening. I had looked forward to receiving this award for a long time, since I had been among the finalists in the prior three years and as the recognition came from peer CEOs. Upset and tired by the day's events, my blood pressure must have been soaring when I arrived at the New York Stock Exchange for the award celebration. I had planned to read a well-crafted speech about our corporate governance initiatives, though it was obvious that the speech would lose its impact in light of the day's news.

How could we have Grubman on television by day fumbling questions and declining to comment and then turn around and trumpet our reforms that evening?

The event's planners arranged a seemingly endless cocktail reception on the floor of the exchange before the award dinner. I noticed to my dismay that CNBC was broadcasting excerpts from Grubman's testimony over the television screens that were suspended above the trading floor. There was no audio so I could only speculate that the commentators were doing a hatchet job on us. My angst ratcheted higher. Finally, we entered a sweltering room for dinner which, like the cocktail reception, seemed to drag on interminably. The award presentation at last commenced after 10:00 P.M. I stood to deliver my speech, the content of which sought to demonstrate my personal commitment to leading industry governance reforms.

Under the best of circumstances, I'm not good at reading speeches, but this time proved especially difficult with the heat and the stress of the day. I was tired and emotionally drained and delivered the speech drenched in perspiration. If current events hadn't been so serious, the scene almost would have been comical. By the time the evening ended, I felt disappointed, washed out, and completely let down. Little did I realize that the evening would set the tone for the next few months—repeatedly, unpleasant surprises would set back our efforts to get out in front of events.

Congress held one more hearing two weeks later. Though this Senate-led session centered on Enron, the mood going in had been charged by the prior day's news that WorldCom had filed for bankruptcy. On the morning when our bankers were to testify, *The New York Times* ran an outrageous story accusing Citigroup of being a party to wrongdoing at Enron. During the day's hearings, Michigan senator Carl Levin angrily went after our company suggesting we and other banks had knowingly abetted Enron's deception by setting up structures which kept Enron's debts from being disclosed.

The WorldCom bankruptcy and the new invective from the Washington hearings savaged our stock price along with those of other major financial companies. In the course of two days, Citigroup's share price plunged to $27, a staggering 25 percent decline which erased $46 billion from the company's market value. At once, industry observers began talking of massive litigation risk and speculated that commercial and investment banks would now mimic the tobacco industry where stock prices remained depressed for years owing to legal liabilities. I never agreed with this dour view and considered the plunge in our stock price an overreaction. However, I had no idea how long it would take for our stock to recover. Rather than engage in nonproductive hand-wringing, I redoubled my efforts to ensure Citigroup's policies and procedures would be responsive to the issues being raised and to try to steer the company out of harm's way.

The news media unfortunately made reaching the high ground difficult. By now, countless reporters had whipped investors and the public at large into a frenzy—they cast nearly every story in the worst possible terms. Not long after Grubman's testimony, I glimpsed a news clip that stayed with me for a long time. A CNBC camera crew caught our analyst leaving his Manhattan apartment and tried to conduct an impromptu interview. Grubman first glared directly into the camera and complained about being harassed before he turned away abruptly and clumsily tried to lose the tagalong reporter.

Call it the power of the television camera, but that shot made Jack look awful. Sometime later, I unexpectedly ran into a camera crew of my own one morning as I entered our building. Recalling Grubman's dismal encounter, I made sure to keep quiet, look directly into the camera, and smile broadly in order to make that footage completely worthless.

———

The wide-ranging investigations and supercharged press created a climate in which events seemed to move at warp speed. Already battered by allegations that Citgroup had succumbed to all sorts of conflicts, I saw matters turn even uglier in late July and August when the first news stories ran suggesting I personally had done something wrong. *The Wall Street Journal* began citing "people close to the investigation" or "those familiar with the matter" as the basis for stories calling my behavior into question. With the first articles, I recalled how the New York attorney general's office had gone after Merrill Lynch and its CEO by using the press to its advantage. I couldn't help but worry that the attorney general now might use the same tactic on me. Enron. WorldCom. Research independence. And now *me*!

Suddenly, Citigroup and I faced the "perfect storm."

The first of these damaging articles ran in mid-July, about a week after Grubman's congressional testimony. The initial article related to Jack Grubman's late 1999 rating upgrade of AT&T. The new buy rating had caused a stir since Jack had been known as a longtime bear on Ma Bell, though his written commentary on the stock had for some time turned more positive. His buy recommendation made headlines since some observers thought he might have changed the rating to help Salomon Smith Barney win an underwriting mandate for a tracking stock on AT&T's wireless business then under consideration.

That he turned around and pulled his buy rating after several months and after the wireless deal had come to market only intensified the speculation. Now, twenty months later and based on internal documents we had turned over to the regulators, the *Journal* reported that I had "nudged Grubman to give AT&T a fresh hearing as the firm sought [its] underwriting business." The story implied that I had pushed for the opinion change and in so doing personally undermined our research ratings system.

The story was completely devoid of context and facts and was offensive in that it called my behavior into question while relying on unnamed sources. Later, my lawyers would produce a white paper for the attorney general's office and for the public which would fully lay out my position with regard to the AT&T matter, yet prior to that document, we had no way to properly respond given that we were in the midst of a regulatory investigation. In a scene that would repeat itself countless times over the next few months, our attorneys convinced me to sublimate my desire to lay out the facts and to ignore the story. The *Journal*, however, never investigated the actual events which are important to understand (and which the white paper documented fully).

In 1998, having joined the AT&T board, I was impressed by the company's new leadership and progress and thought that AT&T's CEO, Mike Armstrong, was doing a terrific job. Never a big investor in stocks apart from Citigroup, I even began buying AT&T shares for my own account that summer (making multiple purchases eventually totaling $3.3 million). At the time, many prominent analysts—at other Wall Street firms and professional money management firms—had recognized the improvement and were recommending the stock. With big institutional investors like Fidelity buying, the stock was appreciating nicely. However, our own Jack Grubman seemed out of touch with the company's changes as he clung to a generally nonpositive view.

Having had the chance to witness AT&T's good news as a member of its board and continuing to buy the stock myself, I believed Jack was missing out on the stock's surging performance and wanted to be sure that our analyst had an opportunity to see all the facts. Accordingly, I suggested that he take a fresh look.

Jack thanked me for my advice and promised to keep an open mind. This conversation took place around the beginning of 1999. In April, Jack sent me a memo noting that AT&T officials had been unresponsive to a list of questions he had submitted. Trying to be helpful, I arranged for Jack to meet with Mike Armstrong at AT&T's New Jersey headquarters.

I quietly sat in on the beginning of that meeting (which didn't take place until August) while Jack established a rapport with Armstrong. Weeks went by after that session during which time Grubman presumably conducted a thorough reassessment of his position and gained comfort on his execution question. Jack only completed his work in November—he issued his report toward the end of that month.

Considering these facts, it's easy to understand why I felt so angry when I read the reports of my "nudging" Grubman and the suggestion that I had pressured him to make the rating change. Anyone familiar with my history and my personality—or Grubman's for that matter—would understand immediately the ridiculousness of the charge. I always wanted brokerage clients to receive good and accurate advice, and I was a buyer of the stock myself both before and after the upgrade. Also, I'm certainly no shrinking violet—had I intended to pressure Grubman to change his stance, I surely would have been all over him at once rather than waiting months for Jack to come to his own conclusion. In reality, Jack took many weeks to respond to my initial suggestion and then spent months studying AT&T in great detail. In all, roughly eleven months elapsed between my suggesting he give the company a fresh hearing and his upgrade.

Jack was no wallflower either—he had negotiated the richest employment contract ever for a research analyst, which had made him independently wealthy and certainly very *independent-minded* as well. He was eagerly wooed by competitors to jump ship, and he had a hugely visible ego and stubborn nature. Indeed, failing to get Jack's endorsement often led our bankers to lose business. Far from reflecting pressure, Grubman's report on AT&T came after an enormous amount of work and reflected a highly detailed written analysis supporting his revised view.

The idea that Grubman's buy rating on AT&T had been designed to win the underwriting competition for the company's wireless business tracking stock similarly lacked factual support. I had spoken out in AT&T's boardroom against the wisdom of the deal, and Jack expressly disagreed with the idea of carving out a new share class in his upgrade. He called market reaction to the tracking stock idea "hype" and stated that buying AT&T's stock to get in on the wireless tracker would be "absurd." The point of view hardly sounded like he had crafted his report to win the tracking stock business. When Grubman subsequently downgraded his opinion in 2000, he cited specific concerns over the quality of AT&T's execution which harked back to the reason he had been slow originally to recommend the shares.

Unfortunately, it would take time for the regulators to understand fully the facts of what had transpired in 1999; meanwhile, the selective leaks to a hungry press provided an ongoing distraction. In mid-August, another *Wall Street Journal* story claimed that Spitzer had broadened his investigation to include a number of Citigroup and Salomon Smith Barney executives, *myself included*. Objectively, no one should have been that surprised given the nature of the investigation, yet the press continued to make things seem worse than they were.

It was difficult to get used to the relentless press, but I tried not to dwell on my personal legal exposure. I felt I had done nothing wrong and confidently assumed the part of the investigation that pertained to my actions would die a natural death. Accordingly, I focused on normal business issues and on making sure Citigroup pursued every possible avenue to lay its regulatory challenges to rest. Reflecting this commitment, we rolled out a series of new governance changes in early August. We created a new equity research policy committee, mandated expensing of options, went public with our new board governance committee, and became one of the first corporations to certify our financial results under the newly passed Sarbanes-Oxley law (which mandated new corporate governance standards). In the wake of Enron, we also began conditioning complex transactions on clients' willingness to disclose the impact on their companies' financial condition.

In August 2002, Mike Carpenter, our Global Corporate Investment Bank head, decided to sever our relationship with Jack Grubman. The idea first had come up at the start of the summer. Our analyst's stock picks had turned cold, and countless brokers who sang his praises not long before during the bull market now turned and demanded his ouster. A typical e-mail sent from the field to management read, "Fire the bastard." During the early part of the summer, I held out hope that Jack would find a way to rebuild his credibility. Once the regulatory investigations got under way, however, Mike pressed the issue.

At first, he worried about complicating Citigroup's legal position by letting Grubman go amid all the public allegations of wrongdoing. If nothing else, it might appear as a tacit admission of guilt at a time when distinctions between individual and institutional responsibility seemed particularly vague. Finally, circumstances snowballed to the point where Mike determined he should go. Jack's testimony before Congress had destroyed his remaining credibility, and the barrage of negative press had rendered him useless to the firm. Even though I left the decision to Carpenter, I came to the same conclusion on the day I watched our once lauded analyst nervously dodging that CNBC reporter on national television.

Mike approached me for my final approval on the severance arrangement. He and the lawyers had determined that we should pay out Jack under the terms of his contract, which meant canceling the remaining portion of a forgivable loan and fully vesting his stock and options. The proposal also called for $1 million in severance, a relative token compared to the multimillion-dollar size of his multiyear contract. Still, the exit terms felt like salt on a wound given how much adverse publicity Grubman had caused by this time. When the news broke, the press, of course, distorted the cost of the separation suggesting we had paid Grubman millions of dollars to go away.

In late August, shortly after Grubman's departure, I came to the realization that we needed to make a far more important executive change. I neared the end of a week-long business trip to Europe when I received an urgent call from Marty Lipton indicating his review of our practices had reached a critical stage and that it was imperative we meet promptly upon my return. Arriving home, I went to Marty's apartment where he and our outside public relations expert, Gershon Kekst, waited for me.

I noticed that my two friends looked unusually serious, and we got right down to business. Marty came straight out with his message: If we were serious about leading industry change and getting out from under this regulatory storm, I needed to understand that we'd never get there with Mike Carpenter continuing to run things downtown. Marty pointed out that Carpenter, though intelligent and well intentioned, had effectively resisted change and insisted far too often on defending past practices.

Marty's point of view, along with Gershon's support, caught me off guard. I hadn't been blind to the intensifying public criticism of our practices and to Mike's tendency to defend his business. Through Chuck Prince and others, I had been pushing Mike for weeks to be more responsive in making changes. Still, I hadn't expected Marty to come at me with such a tough recommendation. He reminded me how Mike resisted a number of our recent initiatives such as our new policy for structured finance deals and my plan to formalize the split between research and investment banking. For the most part, though, we concentrated on Mike's repeated claims that our practices downtown were no worse than those of our competitors. The point seemed correct enough, but Marty impressed upon me how that sort of thinking would never get us where we needed to be.

I agonized after that meeting for the next several days. I had been a big promoter of Mike for a long time. He was a close friend whose intelligence I admired and who had done a very good job in many respects. After Jamie left, Mike earned the respect of the team downtown and drove impressive gains in market share. Still, I also couldn't help but wonder if Mike had done a better job of growing the business than controlling it. As always, I dreaded the thought of having to confront one of my close executives. Whatever I'd decide, I resolved to try to keep Mike by offering him a different position. He was too talented to lose.

By early September, I had sounded out directors and others for their reaction to my formative plan to install Chuck Prince as Mike's successor running the Global Corporate Investment Bank. My advisors and close circle of staff broadly supported shifting Mike, although the idea of replacing him with Chuck elicited a fair amount of discussion given that Chuck was an unproven commodity, having never run a line unit on his own. "How will it appear? Can he do the job? Will people willingly work for him?" my associates asked.

While the doubts were legitimate, I wanted to take the chance. I respected Chuck's intelligence and his ability to work with people. If anyone could reason with the regulators, it was Chuck, thanks to his long-standing ties with most of the principal players and his ability to articulate our reforms. I also reasoned that Chuck would have strong partners working under him downtown with whom he already had forged solid relationships. After working at the corporate level for twenty years, Chuck deserved the chance to run a business of his own.

Some board members expressed similar reservations regarding Chuck's lack of experience, but most seemed willing to go along with the plan. A few, however, had trouble with the larger issue of reassigning Carpenter. These individuals—Bob Rubin included—questioned how it would appear and whether the step was justified. The concerns seemed natural enough, though I figured the board would back me once everyone thought over the matter carefully. Planning for the announcement went into high gear the week following Labor Day, and we called a board meeting for the coming Sunday.

The decision to change management at one of our two largest businesses entailed an array of details and careful orchestration. Our team readied the announcement and considered how to position the shift while I concentrated on the upcoming board meeting and communicating my decision to Mike Carpenter. Relaying the news to Mike was far from easy. There was no way to sugarcoat the situation, and I anticipated that he'd take the news badly. After all, the pressure of the past several weeks had hit him no less hard than it had me. I wished I didn't always have such a hard time dealing with colleagues in this sort of situation, but as usual, dwelling on my weakness wouldn't accomplish anything. Resolving to take the necessary action, I called Mike and asked him to come to my home in Connecticut that Saturday on the pretext that we might discuss the upcoming board meeting.

Mike had no idea regarding the real reason for his summons. When he arrived, I nervously invited him into my den and wasted little time in delivering my message. I'd been advised to avoid discussing the specific reasons for the decision, which made the job of conveying the news that much harder. I simply declared, "Mike, I have to take you out of running the GCIB. I'm sorry, but this is the way it has to be." I added that I wanted him to stay and take on another role in the company and suggested that he might go back to his old strategic planning post or, alternatively, manage our corporate investments.

Stunned, Mike responded angrily and demanded to know my reasoning. His honor wounded, he obviously wanted to defend his accomplishments. My hands, though, were tied, and I couldn't explain further. Mike bridled at my reserve. I stressed that I appreciated his many contributions and that I intended to keep him on the business heads committee. I implored him to sleep on the news and think about what other role he'd like to play in the company.

I felt relieved when Mike left. Relaying this news to Mike had been one of my toughest meetings in years. Mike and his wife, Mary, were friends, and they probably would hold it against me for putting his reputation at risk especially after what he had gone through years earlier when he was pushed out of Kidder Peabody. Emotionally, Mike might not have wanted to stay with Citigroup, yet I thought he'd take my offer of a new assignment once he mulled over his situation.

The board met the next day to discuss our regulatory situation and to ratify our proposed change in management. After lengthy deliberations, the board put its stamp of approval on our new management plan for the Global Corporate Investment Bank. Seeking to control the press's spin on this important announcement, we put out a press release and held a conference call with reporters that evening.

I emphasized that Mike had led our business through an important time and how, in the face of changing regulatory standards, the business needed new leadership for a new era. Mike tentatively had agreed to take over the management of our corporate investments, and participated in the call. His cooperation helped convey an image that we were all on the same page. Behind the scenes, though, Mike remained livid. He never grasped that our past practices largely were beside the point and that this was really about the need to embrace change.

Both employees and the public greeted our announcement with a fair measure of skepticism. Mike had been popular among his colleagues downtown, and undoubtedly, his transfer demoralized many of his closest associates. Installing Chuck generally did not immediately go over well given his lack of hands-on experience in the business. Investors, too, had their doubts since many viewed Chuck more as a policeman than a businessman. Meanwhile, the press accused me of having made Mike the fall guy for our problems. For years, I had enjoyed good press—and it always meant a lot to me. Now, however, I had gotten used to gritting my teeth and numbing myself to what I read in the papers.

Though I hoped that changing the leadership of the Global Corporate Investment Bank might jump-start settlement talks, our regulators needed to complete their investigations before serious negotiations could ensue. The subpoenas, which had gone out to the major Wall Street firms at the start of the summer, turned up a massive number of e-mails and other documents relating to analyst research and the process by which the Street rated stocks.

The resulting flood of paper necessitated a painstaking review which made it impossible to settle the issues quickly. The material turned over by Salomon Smith Barney included e-mails and memos that referred to the meeting I hosted for Grubman at AT&T's headquarters and others which showed Jack keeping me updated on his research progress on the company. Separately, our research director's speaking notes also surfaced—this document suggested that our management committee had discussed whether our investment bankers inappropriately influenced our research ratings. At the start of the investigation, the regulators concentrated on these documents and explored whether they could build a case that I had undermined our research practices.

Initially, I was alarmed by the idea, having never once imagined that I had done anything wrong. Seeing how some of the documents' contents had made their way into the press also troubled me deeply. I specifically never remembered being part of a briefing session at which our people discussed the interplay between the bankers and analysts. After a lot of work, we in fact demonstrated that I never had heard the presentation since the discussion hadn't taken place at our corporate management committee but rather in a separate group within Carpenter's business. As for my encouragement to Grubman to keep an open mind on AT&T, I never denied that I had made the suggestion or that I had visited the company with Jack. These events just seemed like something any CEO might do in the course of the job. Importantly, our advisors concurred.

By the fall, we began to feel that the tide had started to turn and that we might adopt a more proactive communications strategy. In mid-September, I agreed to speak at an institutional investor conference hosted by Merrill Lynch and clearly laid out the reforms we had undertaken. Under normal circumstances, investors would have listened to me talking about revenue growth, expense control, and capital efficiency; now, they saw me focused on taking personal ownership for setting industry best practices. The message, plain and simple, was: "I get it." Acknowledging that Spitzer had made life difficult, I smiled broadly and joked that I was determined to make the best of a tough situation. "Just watch my waistline," I implored. "I've hired a personal trainer and have gone on something I've named the 'Spitzer Diet'—I'll have no more of my favorite martinis until we fully resolve matters with the regulators."

A few days later, *Business Week* reported on my speech and offered the first positive press in weeks. Apart from advertising my shrinking waistline, the story broadcast the seriousness with which we were now overhauling our business model. Meanwhile, Chuck Prince and our outside attorneys began holding meetings with the various regulators to discuss settlement requirements. At long last, we thought we glimpsed some light at the end of the tunnel.

Sadly, we wouldn't be given the chance to settle yet, as the most bruising chapter of this unfortunate story began to unfold. Around the start of October, I received disconcerting news: Somehow the firm we had hired to cull the e-mails we had sent to the regulators discovered a software glitch and now, suddenly, another batch of documents relevant to the investigation had surfaced. What I learned next shocked, infuriated, and depressed me all at once. The e-mails included correspondence between Jack Grubman and a female client, named Carol Cutler, with whom he was having a sexually charged relationship.

In a brief exchange buried within the fantasy-filled notes, our analyst offered an explanation for why he had upgraded AT&T's stock. Incredibly, he boasted that he had recommended the stock to help me gain the support of Mike Armstrong (then a member of Citigroup's board) so that I might "nuke" John Reed in the climactic board showdown prior to Reed's departure. Grubman also bragged that I had used my influence to get his twin children into a nursery school at the 92nd Street Y and that I offered my help in return for his rating upgrade.

The claims were outrageous; one could see by reading the e-mails that Grubman had invented the stories to impress his girlfriend. Much of the correspondence seemed truly extraordinary as it alternated between musings over Grubman leaving his wife for Cutler to vivid descriptions of imagined sexual encounters. The two shared a penchant for referring to anatomical parts and voyeurism. Throughout, Cutler described Grubman as "the king" and "the great one."

Reading through the material, I concluded that Jack suffered from a serious ego problem and psychological deficiency that this relationship somehow addressed. A particularly remarkable letter from Cutler rambled on for nearly twenty pages and contained bizarre imagery to the point where one had to question the mental capacity of the two.

I felt sick reading through this stuff. Angered at the screw-up that prevented these documents from being identified earlier, I understood that the investigators would attach more importance to these relatively freestanding e-mails than they deserved. That they materialized late also looked bad despite the honest error. Worst of all, the e-mails undoubtedly would press the regulators to redouble their investigations and push everything into the realm of the absurd.

The notions that I used our analyst to prevail over Reed and that I had helped Grubman's kids get accepted into nursery school as a quid pro quo for his change of heart on AT&T were bizarre and ridiculous. Yet, out of context, the missives could be manipulated to make it look as though I had directed Grubman's controversial research call. Once more, I despaired at our inability to control events and put the issues to rest.

Almost at once, all hell broke loose. Spitzer's office began investigating Grubman's claims and started to interview scads of people, including our directors, employees, and friends. The questioning obviously had become highly personal and impugned my reputation. Nearly simultaneously, Chuck Prince informed me that he had received a call from Spitzer indicating that Citigroup's board should consider whether my interests and those of the company could diverge. Chuck stressed that Spitzer had been careful in his word choice, indicating that his point was forward-looking rather than saying flatly that my role as CEO had been compromised. Chuck told me he had replied to Spitzer that Grubman's e-mails were disingenuous and obviously false, but Spitzer refused to accept Chuck's viewpoint. From what Chuck relayed, Spitzer simply replied that "this information has to come out."

I felt incensed and dismayed by the news and scared at how the newly discovered e-mails could be brazenly distorted and manipulated. The idea of "diverging interests" boggled my mind. Since when could an employee's unsubstantiated claim in a dubious correspondence with a third party be used to undermine the CEO of an important company?

In fact, the notion that I used Grubman's upgrade to garner Mike Armstrong's support versus Reed didn't hold any water. The facts obviously didn't jibe. I had asked our analyst to take a fresh look at AT&T more than a year before the climactic board meeting, while his upgrade preceded by many weeks the events that led the board to choose between me and John Reed. My long and close professional relationship with Mike Armstrong was also such that it would have been unimaginable that he would not have been supportive of me in any endgame with Reed. Finally, had I been worried about a board showdown, why would I have taken the lead in recruiting Bob Rubin—who enjoyed a far closer relationship with Reed than with me—only a few months before Reed's exit?

The idea that I used my influence to get Grubman's kids into nursery school as an inducement for the AT&T rating change was also rubbish. To be sure, Jack complained to me about a month before his rating change that his frequent business travels had made it difficult to concentrate on getting his kids into private school. He asked if I knew anyone at the 92nd Street Y and showed me the roster of its trustees. I noticed my wife's friend Joan Tisch was on the list and offered to see what I could do. As a matter of course, I assisted countless employees over the years in all sorts of personal matters including medical referrals (via my contacts at Weill Cornell) and writing college letters of recommendation for employees' kids.

It's my nature to want to be helpful, and I considered assisting valuable employees a legitimate part of my job and a way to lock in their loyalty to our company. While Grubman initially approached me in late October, I only made the call to Joan Tisch in mid-December, three weeks *after* he issued his report on AT&T. Citigroup's foundation eventually pledged a $1 million gift to the Y payable over five years, but this donation was agreed to months later, long after Grubman's children had been accepted.

It's also important to understand that the contribution was consistent with Citigroup's overall corporate philanthropy. The Y represented a cultural icon in New York City sponsoring lectures and artistic performances. I thought it would make good business sense to have Citigroup's name associated with the highly regarded institution.

Unfortunately, in early November, Grubman reminded me of his request for help at the end of a memo informing me of his progress on AT&T, a document which later became a focal point in the regulatory investigation. Even though it cited the Y issue as "another matter," the memo sadly blurred the distinctiveness of the 92nd Street Y request from Grubman's work on AT&T. In reality, I never made any promises, a fact which seemed borne out by Jack's suppliant and apologetic words in asking for my help. Grubman also approached Kenny Bialkin and Bob Rubin for help with the Y, actions which further undermined the notion that he was counting on my intervention. Finally, Jack's request for help with the nursery school came after he had completed most of his analysis on AT&T, and I had no reason to think that his work bore any relationship to the 92nd Street Y matter.

Spitzer's comments to Chuck about "diverging interests" further upset me because the suggestion meant the attorney general was throwing down the gauntlet and might be seeking to drive a wedge between the board and me even before he had vetted the scurrilous allegations. What's more, Grubman had repeatedly repudiated his comments to Carol Cutler even under the investigators' threat of jail time—his recanting undermined the basis of the new "evidence."

If Spitzer's conversation with Chuck wasn't bad enough, the inexcusable quickly followed. Benefiting from selective leaks, a *Wall Street Journal* reporter named Charles Gasparino broadcast in a front-page story how Spitzer had gathered new evidence and had communicated that "the interests of the firm and Mr. Weill may have diverged in the investigation."

The story caused a visible market impact, sending Citigroup's stock to a new low of $27 (a 43 percent plunge year-to-date), and rocked my team. How could we be reading in real time about the course of an ongoing investigation? This did not happen in times past when securities regulators pursued their investigations outside the public spotlight. Nor would the leaks stop here. A Chinese water torture had begun under which we'd face one selective public disclosure after another.

I was entering the darkest time of my career.

A few weeks earlier, we had agreed that I would testify before the regulators and had scheduled two sessions for late October. I felt sure that whoever leaked the "diverging interests" story intended it as a device to unnerve me just prior to my testimony. If that was the motive, it worked. Whereas I had felt confident in the course of the investigation prior to the surfacing of the newly discovered e-mails, stress and uncertainty now weighed heavily on me. I could only imagine what news would hit us next. Although Citigroup's directors shared my confidence that no divergence in my interest and that of the company had occurred, Marty Lipton moved two of his top attorneys, Larry Pedowitz and John Savarese, to work exclusively on my personal situation until we satisfied the regulators that I bore no culpability. During much of October, the two seasoned lawyers prepared me for my testimony by going over past events and simulating likely questions.

I hated the idea that my ethics and character could be doubted and bridled at having to devote precious time to defending myself rather than focusing on running Citigroup. I probably drove Pedowitz and Savarese nuts. In an effort to salvage some feeling of control, I initially pushed back on the two lawyers and complained about their depressing and overly serious questions. Renaming Pedowitz "Dr. Doom," I finally threw myself into the preparatory sessions.

My first appearance before the regulators took place in Washington in a session with the National Association of Securities Dealers. While it was understood that a stenographer would be present to record the session, we never did obtain the official record of the proceedings. Back in New York, I was examined a second time a few days later in what the lawyers termed an "interview" led by Spitzer's office. Spitzer did something courteous for me on this occasion: He allowed the meeting to be held at Wachtell Lipton's offices rather than forcing me to go downtown where I might have had to dodge waiting photographers and be part of a media circus.

I viewed Marty's offices as friendly ground, which mildly eased my nervousness. Spitzer did not attend this meeting, though I thought every other lawyer involved in the matter must have been present. Flanked by Pedowitz and Savarese, I took a seat on one side of a huge conference table and faced off against Spitzer's team. We began at 9:30 A.M. Michelle Hirschman, a former U.S. attorney and the leader of Spitzer's investigation, directed the questioning. A couple of Hirschman's colleagues insisted on asking questions in a judgmental style, yet, on balance, I considered the probing reasonably fair.

Settling in for the long meeting, I tried to be gracious to my questioners, and hoped they'd respond in kind. During the breaks, I tried to lighten the mood with jokes. Spitzer's team acted professionally, and I appreciated that they were just doing their jobs even if I fumed inwardly that things never should have gotten to this point. Around 6:00 P.M., the marathon session finally came to an end. There had been no fireworks, and the session legally seemed pretty dull. I felt I had mastered the situation, and Pedowitz thankfully confirmed my impression. I left hopeful but still nervous as hell. Arriving home, I was in no mood to relive the tough day; however, that didn't stop Joanie from asking for details. To her frustration, I refused to open up. I was thoroughly wiped out.

Despite my strong showing, the barrage of unanticipated events wouldn't end. Two weeks after my testimony, the *Journal* remounted its assault thanks to freshly leaked misinformation. Over three days, Charles Gasparino dribbled out those parts of the e-mail correspondence between Grubman and his girlfriend that sounded the most compromising. The first story ran on Wednesday, November 13, and mentioned Grubman's claim that he upgraded AT&T in order to help me "nuke" John Reed.

Thoroughly out of context, the story obviously unnerved investors and Citigroup's share price dove 4 percent that day. On Thursday, Gasparino reported that Grubman had disavowed the e-mails' contents, but the reporter, intent on providing only the information that fit his preferred story line, now charged that our analyst had changed his rating in response to my willingness to use my influence to get his kids into the 92nd Street Y nursery school. Finally, on Friday, the *Journal* cited Grubman's memo in which he updated me on his progress with AT&T and asked for my help in getting his kids into school.

That story mentioned the $1 million five-year pledge that Citigroup's foundation had made but omitted that the contribution had been discussed well after Grubman's upgrade and was given months after his kids had been admitted into the school. It also failed to indicate that the pledge amounted to a pittance relative to our foundation's $100 million annual gifting budget and that the 92nd Street Y was an important cultural institution in New York which was deserving of corporate philanthropic support.

The specificity of these stories made it appear that the *Journal*'s Gasparino enjoyed a pipeline into the investigation. Our firm's public relations staff relayed that in their conversations with Gasparino, the reporter had said such things as "I'm waiting for this treasure trove of documents from the attorney general's office" and later that "I have this trove of information." Well before the latest stories, our lawyers had approached the attorney general's office more than once about the leaks. Senior representatives denied that they had leaked the information and commented that this sort of material shouldn't be made public. When confronted, Gasparino similarly denied he had a source in the attorney general's office even though his earlier comments to our public relations staff suggested otherwise. Despite our complaints, the damaging leaks continued.

We never learned which individual was leaking the information, and I didn't think it was a good idea to pursue the matter with the attorney general. Instead, I directed my anger and frustration at Gasparino, who seemed intent on promoting himself regardless of whom he hurt in the process. Manipulating incomplete information and half-truths, Gasparino appeared to take pleasure discussing my situation in his frequent appearances on CNBC which he used to promote his stories.

More than anger, intense frustration dominated my emotions during this remarkably difficult period. My reputation always had been my most prized asset, and I took great pride in having achieved my success without cutting corners. Now, my name was being dragged through the mud continually, and everything for which I had worked over nearly fifty years felt as though it were going down the drain. I couldn't fathom why I was reading each step of the investigation daily in the paper.

Deep down, I understood the reasons for the investigation, and even saw why the prosecutors in Spitzer's office might have gotten excited by the face value of the e-mails; still, a proper investigation should have been done in private before allowing unexpurgated garbage to be put out for public consumption and especially in a manner completely devoid of context. My advisors warned me that the de facto public trial risked creating such a furor that the attorney general's office might feel pressured to keep coming after me even if its investigation ultimately indicated my innocence. Why didn't people feel outraged that something like this could be happening? Couldn't they see that this was just a new McCarthyism? Every leak seemed unjust.

The public spectacle presented us with a serious dilemma over how best to respond. From the start, the lawyers had insisted that we should keep a low public profile and simply tough it out. The advice didn't thrill me, but I understood its logic and went along. Now, though, our silence in the face of these odious leaks began to tear at Joanie and me.

My wife in particular couldn't understand how we could keep on taking these body blows without giving our side of the story. I had the relative luxury of being able to distract myself at work each day, but Joanie had to deal with people in her life who didn't understand what was going on. She grappled to explain events to her perplexed mother and our vulnerable grandkids.

Receiving nasty calls and letters from people accusing me of being a "disgrace" hurt more than I'd care to admit, and my confidence in our strategy wavered. We seriously debated taking the gloves off and releasing Grubman's complete e-mails in order to provide the missing context for the snippets of information that had been made public. Advocates of this strategy insisted that the revelation of Grubman's illicit affair and bizarre correspondence would explain how he had come to invent such boastful comments and would discredit the basis for the recent press reports. Nevertheless, upon reflection, I decided against the tactic. My whole life experience told me not to fight these sorts of battles in the press. My lawyers gave the same advice, and I knew it was right to avoid a race to the bottom.

By late autumn, the whole place was getting shot at. The months of relentless public accusations wore on everyone. Our stock price floundered as investors obsessed that we'd go the route of the tobacco industry with endless litigation risk. Our employees were depressed and probably felt they were suffering on account of me. That realization weighed heavily on my conscience. My legal and public relations team especially labored to restore our reputation, and I worked these colleagues very hard.

Our team pioneered some innovative methods to deal with our crisis. With increasing frequency, we issued memos to employees that gave our perspective on unfolding events—the memos provided a convenient means of telling our side of the story. We discovered, too, that the major newspapers typically posted their day's stories on their Web sites in the wee hours of the morning and that we could use the advance notice of potentially damaging articles to our advantage.

I worked hard to sublimate my own stress during this time and did my best to keep a stiff upper lip in public. I couldn't afford to give in to self-pity—that would have been a sure road to ruin. Those closest to me, however, probably guessed that my thirty-five pounds of weight loss from the "Spitzer Diet" reflected stress more than simply improved eating habits. At least the diet offered me a sense of control that suddenly seemed so lacking in the rest of my life. Throwing myself into work proved the best means of countering the unbelievably intense pressure, and the workload certainly was heavier than ever.

Even as the regulatory investigation ratcheted into high gear, I concentrated on keeping Citigroup's interests foremost in sight. Along with Chuck Prince and our attorneys, I made sure that our company's board of directors remained informed and able to discharge its fiduciary responsibilities. Indeed, when the new e-mails surfaced, we called the board together and forced our directors to read the material page by page so that they would understand what we were up against. Needless to say, most were aghast at the context and the subsequent lack of attention given to Grubman's extramarital liaison by the regulators and the press. Even with these efforts, the thought of losing the board's confidence crossed my mind. I wasn't concerned that I'd get caught in having done something wrong, but the idea that I was dealing with an inherently unfair process unnerved me. To their credit, our company's directors never wavered in their support.

I also continued to spearhead changes in our management structure and business model during the worst of the assault. I convinced Mike Masin, for instance, to trade in his seat on the board and join management as our chief operating officer responsible for overseeing legal and other administrative functions. Having moved Chuck Prince downtown, I needed Masin's strong organizational skills in order to stay on top of our reforms and to oversee our massive array of lawyers, now commonly referred to as our "American Bar Association."

Meanwhile, I moved to sever completely the organizational link between research and investment banking. During mid-October, even as some of the worst allegations flew, I recruited Sallie Krawcheck to join Citigroup and to head our newly configured Private Client business, whose scope had been expanded to now include research. Once a top-rated Wall Street analyst, whom *Fortune* had dubbed "the last honest analyst on Wall Street," Sallie had since become president of the well-respected independent research firm Sanford Bernstein.

I had gotten the idea to hire her after I attended an off-site for our retail brokers. At that meeting, a broker suggested I should buy Bernstein in order to rebuild our research credibility. While that idea didn't seem feasible, I hit upon the far less costly plan to go after Sallie. Within a week of my first reaching out, the youthful and very bright former analyst accepted my offer to build a new organization which we'd now rename simply Smith Barney.

Our early and sustained commitment to adjust to the new regulatory era and our leadership in instituting reforms at last worked in our favor. By December, the attorney general completed his investigation and concluded he lacked the evidence to pursue me any longer, and Citigroup entered into serious settlement talks with all its principal regulators. Of the countless documents the regulators had reviewed, some of the only ones that defied a neat explanation were those relating to the 92nd Street Y, since the notion that I had helped Grubman with his kids' school application in return for his AT&T upgrade could be conclusively disproved only if I somehow could show what was inside my head at the time.

By its nature, it was the sort of allegation against which no one could fully defend. However, numerous aspects of the case spoke to my innocence: In asking Grubman to take a fresh look at AT&T, I only thought the advice would lead him to see the same value which had led me to make purchases of over $3 million of the stock for my own account; it was clear that I never pressured our analyst's change of rating; and finally, Grubman repeatedly disavowed under oath the controversial contents of his e-mails relating to the Y and my board fight with Reed.

As Spitzer's office began to back off, I looked forward to completing the settlement talks and to putting these tortuous issues in the past. I approached the end of the year with a sense of vindication, but I found it hard to accept the personal humiliation I had endured and worried over what it would take to rebuild my reputation.

19

Retaking Control of My Life

Eliot Spitzer began to wind down his investigation of the securities industry during the final weeks of 2002. He had put the industry where he wanted it: on the defensive and ready to accept his settlement terms. Meanwhile, the regulators focused the spotlight on industry practices in need of reform but came up short on executives to charge criminally.

I had believed almost from the start that this entire onslaught had little bearing on criminal wrongdoing and almost everything to do with figuring out a way for the Street to surrender gracefully. Thanks to Chuck Prince's good relationships with the regulators, Citigroup finally entered into serious settlement negotiations aimed at putting this entire affair to rest. The regulators and most of the large securities firms agreed on the desirability of a global settlement in which the industry would accept new rules and standards as a common basis for bringing these difficult months to a close.

While settling would cost Citigroup plenty, I saw that the open regulatory issues were causing incalculable damage to our company's reputation. We decided that, within reason, we'd undertake whatever actions would be necessary to get back to business and end these harmful distractions. Personally, I couldn't wait to regain control over our company's future, not to mention my life—the weeks of attacks and uncertainty had worn me out.

The settlement negotiations proved tedious. Each of the ten major firms involved had its own agenda, and working toward a common solution with multiple regulators slowed the process. The traditional regulatory agencies like the SEC or the National Association of Securities Dealers never got used to the prominent role played by the New York attorney general, and he seemed to control the agenda. Throughout the negotiations, he refused to waver on three demands: that research should be separated from investment banking; that securities firms should provide independent research; and that the Street should pay substantial monetary penalties. When it came to Citigroup, Spitzer argued that we should pay an especially large penalty.

I thought that idea seemed patently unfair since Citigroup never had been the worst offender. Unfortunately, when the regulatory needle pointed our way, it managed to stick—our having faced the most adverse publicity meant we couldn't extract ourselves from paying an outsized fine. While Citigroup legally did not admit any wrongdoing, the regulators insisted that I issue an apology for Citigroup's actions.* That wasn't a problem—by now, I had expressed remorse to our firm's clients more than once. In the end, we agreed to pay a $300 million fine and provide $100 million more for independent research for Smith Barney's clients.

I was traveling in Moscow when I received word that our negotiators were closing in on the settlement. For the first time in months, I began to feel better. I had been given a bottle of Russian vodka when I checked into my hotel and began wondering how it tasted. I had adhered for five months to my "Spitzer Diet" and fulfilled my self-made promise to avoid martinis and fattening foods while the regulatory investigation remained open. Now the encouraging news from New

---

*The formal apology was issued in April 2003 upon the finalization of the regulatory settlement and included me saying, "Certain of our activities did not reflect the way we believe business should be done. That should never have been the case, and I am sorry for that." In the statement, I also pledged that all senior Citigroup executives—including myself—would not communicate with our analysts about the companies under their research coverage.

York told me it would be okay, and I took a sip to celebrate our approaching deal.

A day later, I reached Paris and received a call from my colleagues in New York at 5:00 A.M. local time announcing the deal had been signed. That afternoon, Chuck phoned, and we watched a live feed of the press conference announcing the global settlements. During the question period, a reporter asked Spitzer about me, and the attorney general unequivocally responded that there would be no charges because I had not acted wrongfully. Hearing those words, I decided the time for a martini had arrived at last. It proved the tastiest one I had enjoyed in a very long time!

The sense of relief was terrific, but I'm a worrier by nature and recognized that I shouldn't count my chickens too soon. The December 20 settlement announcement represented an agreement only in principle, and the parties needed several more weeks to put everything in writing. I also learned that the NASD had come close to scuttling the deal at the eleventh hour since its staff was unhappy with Spitzer's timeline for announcing the deal. Anything which implied hesitation on the part of the regulators made me nervous since I only wanted to be sure that we had a done deal that would allow us to get back to work without distractions.

I typically bounce back from adversity and anticipated refocusing on the future. Still, I felt wounded in the wake of the settlement. Though I had gotten through this oppressive ordeal, the fact that my name had been sullied hurt deeply. Spitzer allowed my attorneys to include in the public record our white paper which rebutted in detail the aspersions cast my way during the regulatory investigation. Sadly, the public mostly overlooked the document. Joanie, too, had mixed emotions over the settlement, feeling that it ignored the damage unfairly inflicted on my reputation.

Nonetheless, I had to get on with my life and told Joanie that the settlement was the price we had to pay in order to move forward.

At Citigroup's first business heads meeting following the settlement, I repeated my words of regret once more. With the benefit of hindsight, I told my colleagues that I wished I could have foreseen the shifts in regulatory emphasis and changed our corporate practices earlier. I rued not having been more attuned to how the long-running bull market had weakened the Street's appreciation of conflicts. And I commented that I wished I had never met Jack Grubman! Not one to dwell on the past, I stressed that we now needed to put the difficult days behind us, refocus on the future, and lead by example. We had instituted many cutting-edge governance reforms well in advance of the settlement and now had to demonstrate Citigroup's commitment to these changes.

The overriding lesson from this entire experience came in teaching us that reputation risk holds importance equal to other forms of business risk. While we couldn't quantify the hit to our company's reputation, Citigroup's stock in January 2003 stood around $35 per share and had fallen by 30 percent over the prior twelve months. By every measure, it had lost the premium it had enjoyed in the days before the regulatory issues.

The regulators and the public held Citigroup to a high standard subsequent to the settlement—for better or worse, its size and scope meant that our company no longer could avoid the limelight and that we continually had to demonstrate industry best behavior. Our company established business practices committees at the corporate level and within each major business unit to guard against significant conflicts and to ensure that Citigroup would seek to advance the interests of its clients in the future, even at the risk of losing revenues.

Although I had apologized, our actions were far from the worst on the Street. It's important to recognize that other entities bore a share of responsibility for the bull market's excesses. Corporate America often subverted the benefits of awarding options to motivate key employees. The advancing bull market encouraged many companies to grant ridiculous numbers of options relative to total shares outstanding which frequently promoted shortsighted decisions. Citigroup had embraced options grants relatively early, but we always kept the awards in check. Wall Street analysts and investment bankers similarly lost perspective and embraced all sorts of novel valuation metrics, which seem ludicrous in hindsight. Somehow the number of Web site hits or earnings before interest and depreciation costs meant more than good old-fashioned cash flow.

I fault others as well. The legal profession should have thought twice before blessing structures that many companies used under the name of "financial engineering." I always assumed one could rely on legal opinions and took as an article of faith that the seal of approval couldn't be bought. Many prominent law firms apparently didn't understand—or perhaps ignored—the accounting underpinning their work.

The accountants and the regulators also bear responsibility. I recognize that it's hard for anyone to identify a well-conceived fraud, yet some of the wrongdoing that took place in corporate America involved enormous schemes that occurred over a long period of time. The regulators came in with a vengeance only *after* problems had surfaced.

Finally, the media deserves its own share of blame—it added to the hype on the market's way up in equal measure to the way it fed the panic on the way down. The media's actions weren't that different relative to earlier markets, but the ubiquity of news on television and over the Internet added to the frenzy unlike ever before.

Though weakness in corporate governance merits its own share of the blame, it's notable how the reverberations following the market crash led to profound changes. Corporate boards now typically hold longer and more substantive meetings. Lead directorships that serve as a conduit between the board and investors have become far more common. Interlocking directorships virtually have ceased, and new stock exchange rules require listed companies to have an overwhelming number of independent directors.

Meanwhile, the Sarbanes-Oxley legislation has broadened disclosure and fostered more financial transparency even as it has raised issues concerning the cost of compliance. The requirement that corporate CEOs and CFOs certify financial results has meant stepped-up reliance on internal staff and third-party accountants and lawyers to first vet results and, in effect, has revitalized the traditional corporate gatekeepers.

The securities industry, of course, has undergone profound changes of its own. The settlement required the Street to provide independent third-party research and to formally wall off research analysts from investment banking. Research departments have been required to monitor the accuracy of their ratings and maintain extra compliance staff to oversee analyst independence. Meanwhile, the industry has been forced to examine the potential risk of conflicts when distributing proprietary product.

A postmortem on the regulatory events of 2002 wouldn't be complete without some additional comments on my own management style. A number of friends and colleagues have since asked whether I delegated too much and whether my approach to management somehow added to Citigroup's issues. The premise, however, seems unfair. Running a company the size of Citigroup, I had to manage through people. It's impossible to know everything in an organization of nearly 300,000 people, and if I hadn't given authority to my managers, our company never would have attracted quality senior executives. Even so, I regret that I didn't probe my executives more and question our practices with added intensity. Top-notch execution, after all, was what I had built my reputation on.

While the global research settlement allowed everyone to get back to work, the challenge of restoring lost credibility loomed large. We initiated our business practice reforms in part to address our customers' concerns, but that didn't console the large number of our individual investor clients who had lost money during the bear market. My friends in our brokerage offices didn't shy away from reminding me of the difficulties they now faced with their clients. From my days as a broker, I knew firsthand how hard it could be to see your clients lose money.

I felt for my colleagues. Worried about the wounds that had been inflicted on our retail franchise, I decided to go on the road with Sallie Krawcheck and see as many brokers as possible. Ostensibly, I wanted to introduce Sallie, who had been in her job as head of our Private Client business for only three months; in reality, though, I yearned to connect with the people with whom I always shared a special bond. Getting in front of the field force always gave me an emotional lift.

Sallie and I hit three cities a day, and over the course of a couple of weeks, we met with nearly a third of our field force. While the meetings weren't always easy, they still were energizing. Nearly everywhere, our brokers contended with upset clients and claims that Smith Barney employees were dishonest. Knowing the truth—that these were hardworking, serious people—I felt terrible about the burden imposed on them. Fortunately, I also saw plenty of relationships which remained strong despite the raw feelings.

Drawing on my personal experiences in earlier bear markets, I did my best to buoy spirits. I told our sales force, "It's best to be honest and not to be afraid to talk to clients during the tough times. Hiding only will get you into more trouble." We were coming through our first serious bear market in eighteen years. While many had forgotten how it felt to lose money, I reassured them that I had been through similar periods before and that the brokers would come through okay so long as they stayed close to their clients.

My colleagues and I also had to work at rebuilding credibility with those institutions which invested in Citigroup's securities. We took a large charge to our earnings in the fourth quarter of 2002 to cover the costs of the settlement and to provide sizable reserves for possible credit losses. In the weeks that followed, investors questioned whether we had set aside enough to insulate our earnings from potential litigation. After all, the analogy to the tobacco industry and its open-ended litigation still hung in the air.

Investors asked, too, whether Citigroup's unique size and scope undermined management's ability to control the business. We possessed few means of countering these concerns in the short run and focused instead on how well Citigroup had performed during the prior year despite the turmoil. We realized confidence would rebuild slowly and that we had to remind investors constantly about the positives.

In fact, Citigroup performed surprisingly well during 2002. Our earnings had more than doubled from 1998 when we first created Citigroup and hit $15 billion, a record despite over $2 billion in unusual year-end charges. Fortunately, the regulatory issues hadn't seriously affected our large Consumer Business where earnings surged over 20 percent during the year. Our large business outside the United States continued to perform strongly as well. Despite what many New Yorkers may have thought, the sun did not rise and set based on what happened in the stock market!

During the early weeks of 2003, I began to grow more hopeful that our earnings would continue to grow nicely. We were benefiting from integrating Banamex and a savings and loan acquisition we had made recently in California; company-wide costs remained tightly controlled; and revenues were reviving along with business and consumer confidence. I didn't like that our stock's valuation continued to lag; however, I believed that issue would take care of itself so long as we could keep achieving solid results.

While Citigroup's performance looked good, the personal scars from the events of the prior year remained fresh. That spring, I received a call from Dick Grasso, the chairman of the New York Stock Exchange, in which he invited me to join the exchange's board of directors. The offer appealed to me, and I reasoned that an NYSE board appointment would counter the negative news stories about me which were then becoming increasingly regular.

To my dismay, the NYSE chairman assured me incorrectly that he had run my name in front of all the appropriate regulators ahead of time. Taking him at his word, I accepted the offer. When news of the nomination broke, however, Eliot Spitzer publicly scolded Grasso. I felt awful. What I had hoped would be an expression of confidence turned into yet one more embarrassment. I couldn't believe Spitzer stood in my path once again and so avidly took exception to my credentials. Wouldn't this nightmare go away?

I quickly decided that this battle wasn't worth fighting. I just had been renominated for a second term on the board of the New York Federal Reserve Bank and rationalized that this appointment meant just as much for my reputation. I told Grasso that I'd withdraw my name so long as he would issue a statement and make clear that the board seat was completely his idea. Dick Grasso faced controversy of his own later that year as Attorney General Spitzer questioned the basis of his lucrative compensation package and forced his resignation. Watching those later developments, I felt relieved that the board nomination hadn't come through after all.

The NYSE drama nearly coincided with my seventieth birthday in March 2003. Seventy seemed like a big number and forced me to consider seriously how I should spend the rest of my life. I had created the greatest financial services company in the world. I was financially independent. I had a wife I loved, supportive children, and wonderful grandkids. All these blessings led to one question: Why did I have to continue working so hard? I figured I had fifteen to twenty additional years to accomplish something more in my life, and I began to think seriously about my outside philanthropic interests and how I might step up my leadership in these institutions without the day-to-day burdens of running Citigroup. I felt excited about the challenges of globalizing the Weill Cornell Medical College, making Carnegie Hall a leader in music education, and positioning the National Academy Foundation as a model for high school education reform. If not now, when?

That March, Joanie orchestrated a wonderful birthday celebration at Carnegie Hall along with the institution's development director, Jay Golan. Jay came up with the idea to link the celebration to an effort to raise money for a music education endowment. My fellow board members and I wanted to take our music education program global and planned for new technology to assist distance learning and to work interactively with audiences around the world. Jay had announced that we'd need to raise $50 million to support the effort and proposed that we should set that figure as our fund-raising goal for my birthday celebration. "Jeez," I said, "that's a hell of a lot of money to go for in one night." Nevertheless, I gave him the green light. Given the great importance Joanie and I attached to the initiative, we announced that we'd match what others pledged.

Joanie worked hard planning that evening, and more than seven hundred people attended the gala. Emceed by Walter Cronkite, the program began with a video on my life and then segued into Carnegie Hall's music education program and the importance I attached to it. It showed how we'd create a global classroom and bring the immediacy of the concert hall even to remote areas. Sitting between former president Clinton and New York mayor Bloomberg, I beamed while my friends Yo-Yo Ma and Manny Ax performed in my honor.

Afterward, Governor Pataki, Senator Schumer, and Mayor Bloomberg offered words of tribute before President Clinton rose to speak. The president thanked me for showing that democratic capitalism stood as the best system in the world and for demonstrating America's economic system has the capacity to ensure that the less fortunate are not left behind. Finally, Joanie and Jessica and Marc offered terrific toasts of their own, and my granddaughter Laurel sang "Happy Birthday." The evening ended with a group of fifty of my close friends serenading me with a tongue-in-cheek retrospective on my life sung to the overture from *Oklahoma!*

We surpassed our goal and raised $60 million that evening (half from the attendees and half from our matching gift), a record for a single evening for any philanthropic cause. I felt proud that our personal contribution ranked as Carnegie Hall's largest ever, even surpassing Andrew Carnegie's original endowment.

That evening made a deep impact on me as it proved that I still commanded others' respect. Following the tribulations of the prior year dealing with Spitzer, I had wondered whether my reputation would remain indelibly tarnished; now I saw otherwise. That so many prominent people came to speak in my honor without embarrassment meant a great deal and gave me a boost of optimism that I had missed for so long. More broadly, I realized that I might now think about retiring on a high note, and the evening galvanized me to plan seriously for my succession.

———————

To understand the genesis of my retirement planning, it's necessary to appreciate the events that followed John Reed's departure in early 2000. At the time, Citigroup's directors established a succession committee composed of four members. I felt strongly then that we should avoid fixing a timetable for my stepping aside, and the board agreed not to push the process for a year so that our company might settle down. The original plan called for a succession announcement within two years of Reed's departure. Over a number of months, I discussed a number of potential inside candidates with the succession committee, though I didn't feel a lot of pressure to come to a decision. Around the end of 2001, however, I began to take the issue more seriously.

With three years under our belt, I realized that Citigroup had finally meshed. Frank Thomas, our longest serving and widely respected director, who served on the succession committee, also reminded me that the board took the original timetable seriously. In his typically genteel and subtle way, Frank nudged me to take control of the succession challenge. We had a lot of talented executives within Citigroup and moved quickly to identify the right candidates. In early 2002, my top choices were Mike Carpenter and Bob Willumstad, who ran our two largest businesses. Yet neither executive bowled over the succession committee.

We also considered Deryck Maughan and Tom Jones, the respective heads of our International and Asset Management businesses, although neither idea advanced far. The committee also mentioned frequently the notion of bringing in an outsider, but I steadfastly opposed that scenario and did my best to shoot it down. I thought it would be a sign of failure to go outside Citigroup. Given that we led in virtually all of our businesses, it seemed unfathomable that we didn't have the industry's best executives already within our organization.

I worried, too, that if we were to bring in an outsider, we'd risk losing a lot of our best people. Most of my executives had grown rich over the years and would have little reason to remain if they weren't happy with the outcome. I repeatedly cited the example of General Electric and how I felt that company had mishandled the succession of its popular CEO, Jack Welch. In the wake of GE's succession announcement, two of the company's top leaders left for greener pastures. That was the last scenario I wanted for Citigroup.

Still, the idea of looking for an outsider never completely went away. At one point, someone proposed recruiting Dick Kovacevich, the successful CEO of Wells Fargo and a former Citicorp retail banker. I rushed to point out that Bob Willumstad already ran a business larger and more successful than the retail-oriented Wells Fargo.

Of more concern, I sensed from several directors that Jamie Dimon may have put out feelers about possibly returning. Jamie had become CEO of the sprawling Midwestern retail bank Bank One, and some directors may have felt we might successfully recruit Jamie either alone or via a merger with Bank One. I adamantly opposed considering Jamie, though, and reminded the succession committee that he had long ago burned his bridges. The idea never got off the ground seriously as far as I know.

Once we got past the global settlement at the end of 2002, I was ready to push the process forward. I had grown tired of the day-to-day grind well before the regulatory issues arose and now felt especially ready to recast my life. While I used to love delving into our businesses, I now lacked the same zeal to stay on top of everything in the company. Somehow, learning about derivatives and structured products didn't offer a real sense of excitement, while the new governance rules mandated by Sarbanes-Oxley made it seem likely that bureaucratic needs would trump the fun of the business. I couldn't imagine approaching my job halfheartedly—that was never part of my nature.

I hoped that revived earnings momentum and stock price performance would give me the means to announce my retirement on a high note once I could gain some distance from the regulatory settlement. With the approach of my seventieth birthday, Citigroup's stock price had returned to levels seen before the start of the regulatory probes. I also felt good about our board and appreciated that my directors had stood with me throughout the regulatory ordeal. The time for decision had come, and I threw myself into working with the succession committee to devise a suitable plan.

Unfortunately, we still didn't have an obvious solution, and some important changes had taken place over recent months. Notably, Mike Carpenter's reassignment pulled him from contention while Chuck Prince's star soared thanks to his outstanding performance throughout the pressure-filled year. He had proven himself a quick study in running the Global Corporate Investment Bank and had earned the respect of his troops.

In the first few weeks of 2003, the succession committee and the full board continued to think through our succession options. Unfortunately, *The Wall Street Journal* complicated the task when it ran a story in early March detailing the board's discussions. The article mentioned specific people under consideration and even noted that some directors favored bringing back Jamie Dimon. The story evidently arose from a board-level leak, and I was incensed that something so sensitive could be put out for public consumption. Of course, the report unnerved Citigroup's senior executives and forced most to question how they might fit into a succession process which suddenly appeared quite active.

I only wanted a period of peace and stability after all we had experienced with the regulators, and the *Journal* story created another big headache which I didn't need. In an effort to calm everyone's nerves, I convened my management group and told my colleagues that, with the concurrence of the board, I planned to stay on for another two years and that no member of my senior team had yet been ruled out of the succession discussions. Our public relations department intentionally leaked my comments to the press in order to dampen the damaging external speculation that I might soon exit.

Our deliberations over my successor heated up during the spring of 2003, and we formally narrowed the field to Chuck Prince and Bob Willumstad. Both had distinctive strengths. Bob knew our Consumer Business inside and out and made sure this engine of Citigroup's growth never missed a beat. Tall, calm, and intelligent, his quiet confidence motivated his troops. Chuck, meanwhile, understood my thought process like no one else and had gained a broader perspective on our company having worked closely with me on company-wide issues for years. He enjoyed excellent relationships with our regulators and a keen appreciation for what the new regulatory era entailed. He was also a fast learner.

In many respects, Chuck's and Bob's strengths and weaknesses complemented one another. Bob had proven himself as a quality manager and operator over many years and knew the Consumer Business thoroughly, but he suffered from lack of exposure to Citigroup's full array of businesses. Chuck, on the other hand, enjoyed a full perspective on our company but had actually run a business for only several months. If I really wanted to retire, I needed to find a solution which would include both executives. At one point, I raised the notion of a co-CEO structure, though the succession committee shot down that idea in a nanosecond. This board would never accept co-heads again after watching John Reed and me go at one another.

Toward the end of the second quarter, I realized the time had come to choose and settled on Chuck as my successor. He had rapidly mastered the complexities of the Global Corporate Investment Bank, had been by my side all through our debilitating issues with the regulators, and had demonstrated his loyalty and intelligence ever since we had first met. As our general counsel for many years, Chuck also had been involved in most of our company's important decisions. These were strong attributes which tipped the balance in his favor.

To make the plan work, however, I needed to convince Bob to stay on as president and work closely with his longtime colleague. I also conceived the idea that I'd retain my role as chairman of the board for a couple of years. I was afraid of jumping headfirst into retirement and came up with the idea of remaining as chairman as a security blanket of sorts to help me ease into the next stage of my life. I reasoned, too, that many investors and employees would feel reassured that I wasn't making an overly hasty exit.

I sounded out the succession committee and received a favorable response. Even so, I wasn't ready quite yet to act on the plan. Instead, I told the committee that I wanted to mull over the idea during my June vacation. Heading off that summer, Joanie and I first made a stop in Berlin where Citigroup's local country head had arranged for me to meet with Chancellor Gerhard Schroeder. I also had scheduled a dinner with Deutsche Bank chairman Josef Ackermann, at his request. During that dinner, Ackermann stunned me by proposing a merger between his bank and Citigroup saying it would be good for Germany as well as our companies. Getting past the surprise, I immediately warmed to the idea, thinking that it would put our Global Corporate Investment Bank so far in the lead competitively that no one would be able to touch us.

Undoubtedly, a combination would offer massive cost savings and would immediately add to our earnings per share. Diversifying into euro-denominated assets appeared a good idea, and I sensed that Deutsche Bank's valuation remained exceptionally depressed following the bursting of the stock market bubble. Encouraging Ackermann, I suggested that Citigroup might be willing to move its European headquarters from London to Frankfurt, and we agreed to get our executives together to discuss the idea in more detail.

That same night, I had a very warm first meeting with Chancellor Schroeder in his official residence. We immediately took a liking to one another and stayed up late drinking a magnum of the German leader's favorite wine, a terrific French Bordeaux. I'm not sure why we hit it off so well. Perhaps our shared modest beginnings and interest in building civic institutions drew us together. By the end of the evening, I couldn't help but think that we might get his blessing should we get to the point of wanting to merge with Deutsche Bank.

After the fascinating evening in Berlin, Joanie and I went on to our vacation in the South of France where we talked at length about my retirement plans. Although merging with Deutsche Bank played to my appetite for large value-additive deals, I recognized that there would always be "just one more deal" and that I'd never retire if I gave in to that old "urge to merge."

Joanie had mixed emotions about the retirement decision yet, on balance, she liked that I'd have more time to spend with her and our family. After all, for forty-three years, she had shared me with the other love of my life, my company. By the end of our trip, I decided to plow ahead with my retirement decision. Of course, when I get a taste of a deal like Deutsche Bank, I don't let go so easily, and I planned to push Chuck and Bob to follow through on the idea.*

When I returned home, I relayed my decision to the succession committee and received these directors' blessing. I then called Chuck and invited him up to my home in the Adirondacks on the coming Saturday. That weekend coincided with July Fourth, and Chuck balked

---

*Citigroup subsequently discussed a merger with Deutsche Bank in early 2004 after my retirement as CEO. Following two days of talks in Armonk, our companies agreed that it would be worthwhile to meet again once Ackermann had consulted with his supervisory board. However, news of the talks subsequently leaked and Ackermann felt compelled to back off.

since he had planned to spend the holiday in Nantucket with his fiancée, Peggy. I wouldn't let him off the hook and countered that it was important to see him for a couple of hours and that I'd send a plane to get him back and forth so that he wouldn't be away longer than necessary.

That Saturday, I picked up Chuck at the Adirondack regional airport and drove him back to our home. During the ten-minute ride, Chuck evidently assumed I had summoned him to convey the news of a new merger, and he seemed concerned that I'd pull him out of running the Global Corporate Investment Bank. I cut him off by saying, "That's not why I wanted you here." I said nothing more. Evidently mystified, Chuck went quiet.

Once at the house, we had a quick lunch, during which I continued to keep Chuck in suspense. Finally, we moved outside to the terrace overlooking the lake, and I carefully worked up to my proposal. Chuck had no idea of what I was about to offer, and I wondered how he'd respond. For a long time, he had muttered something about leaving with me upon my retirement, and I worried he might stick to that plan. After all, he had just become engaged and was in love. If he turned me down, my careful planning would have been tossed to the wind.

I slowly got to the point. "I've been thinking a long time about the succession process. Things are going good enough now that I'd like to speak to the board at its July meeting. I've made up my mind and have gone over this with the succession committee and have their support." Pausing briefly, I then delivered the punch line: "Chuck, I'd like you to be my successor!"

The only other time I had seen Chuck's face turn so white followed a ride on a bobsled during one of our winter planning meetings in the Adirondacks. I thought he'd fall out of his chair—he obviously had never dreamed that I might promote him as my successor. He had come to my home convinced I wanted to talk about a merger, and instead I was offering him the job of a lifetime.

He sat for a minute in stunned silence. Though I waited so that he might collect his thoughts, he just sat still wearing a quizzically dazed expression. Finally, I couldn't hold back any longer. "How do you feel about what I'm saying?" I asked. I had hoped Chuck would jump at the opportunity, yet he looked hesitant. Finally, he announced that he wanted to discuss the job with Peggy. Moving inside, he tried to contact his fiancée over the phone but failed to reach her. I suppose the shock had begun to wear off by the time he returned because we soon delved into a discussion of my expectations.

I explained why I wanted to step aside now and told him up front that it would be critical to partner closely with Bob Willumstad. I also stressed that I planned to stay on as chairman until the 2006 annual meeting. "You should stay on longer. We can forget the normal-retirement-age stuff," Chuck said. As on many occasions in the past, Chuck seemed solicitous of my feelings. I responded, however, that I wouldn't go too far and that I'd work with him to ease the transition.

Chuck's excitement finally became apparent. Joanie joined in after a while and offered her own encouragement. By the time he left late that afternoon, Chuck was ready to sign on provided that his fiancée concurred. A phone call that evening sealed the deal.

I felt relieved by Chuck's acceptance, though I remained nervous about how Bob Willumstad would take the news. That Monday, I approached Bob at our weekly 8:00 A.M. business heads meeting and asked to speak with him immediately after the session. He mentioned that he had another commitment, and I ended up having to bide my time until early that afternoon. Telling Bob would be altogether different from communicating with Chuck since Bob surely would feel disappointed not getting the top job after serving more than a year as Citigroup's president.

I always placed a premium on teamwork and loyalty and worried that Bob might leave abruptly in a fit of emotion. I couldn't help but consider, too, that we might suffer other departures were he to bail out. When we finally sat down together, I didn't beat around the bush and came straight out with the succession plan. Bob sat in silence while I stressed the need for a healthy partnership. "You're a very good operator, and Chuck needs a lot of help," I said. "You and Chuck have been partners for a long time, and you'll work well together," I concluded. Bob took in my message and said that he wanted to sleep on what I had said.

The next morning, we spoke again, and my colleague commented that he felt more hurt than he had expected. He told me how much he would have liked the top job and felt that it looked bad since he had served as president for more than a year. It wasn't typical for Bob to complain, and I realized that his words didn't include an acceptance. Unsure how to respond, I proposed that he and Chuck meet for dinner that evening to discuss how they would work together and to see if they could make each other comfortable. As soon as Bob walked out of my office, I called Chuck and stressed that he should do his utmost to make Bob happy.

The two met that evening, and Chuck did his best to reach out. By Wednesday morning, I really began to get nervous since our board meeting loomed little more than a week away. Bob came to my office once more and told me that he still had reservations about how the announcement would appear. "If we're to be partners, we should be treated equally in every way—we should be paid equally; we should both be on the board; and we should enjoy the same perks." I reassured him that I'd promptly consult with the succession committee and in fact soon returned with an arrangement that met his needs. To my relief, Bob accepted his new assignment.

Our board met the following week, and the succession committee presented the plan to the other directors. The board discussed my idea to remain as chairman at some length. Several directors warned that it wouldn't be good for me or the company to remain and suggested I'd have difficulty staying out of my successor's way. I understood their point, though I asserted that my circumstance was unusual and that I needed time to fully disengage. To my relief, the board signed off on my continuing role and approved the succession plan.

Shortly after the board meeting, I conveyed the decision to the heads of each of Citigroup's businesses. Many expressed puzzlement over why I had moved so fast following the prior year's disruption, but to me, the Spitzer episode was well behind us, and our strong financial performance made this as good a time as any to move on. I believed, too, that we had come up with an elegant solution to our succession challenge—in my book, any leadership change that could be pulled off without a resulting exit of talented managers represented a significant success.

On July 16, I announced the changes in our executive lineup before a group of employees and indicated I'd step down as CEO by the end of the year. We broadcast the session to investors, and taped the meeting for distribution to our offices around the world. We made the announcement a couple of days after we had reported strong second quarter earnings and just after publicizing the acquisition of Sears' credit card business.

Taking my lead from those news items, I declared, "We're never asleep. We're always doing something . . . It wasn't enough to buy a credit card operation and report great earnings. No, I'm here today to announce a new management plan." Before moving to the meeting's real purpose, I stressed how we had the best management and competitive position in the financial services industry and expressed pride in how we had led the industry through the difficult regulatory period the year before. Slowing my delivery, I chose my next words carefully, "I always wanted to do this in a way where no one would feel they had to quit . . . I also like to surprise people . . . so here goes . . . Chuck Prince will be our new CEO . . ."

I suddenly welled up and had to pause. "For good or bad, I'm an emotional person," I finally continued and went on with the rest of the announcement.

I was relieved to get those words off my chest. Lightening the mood, I joked that Chuck and Bob had better not "screw up" or else I'd be all over them. We then moved on to field questions. Most of the questioners wondered whether our priorities would change, and Chuck and Bob assured everyone that we'd remain on course. At one point, Chuck suggested that he'd have difficulty not seeing me every day. I interjected playfully, "Chuck, there's always a fax machine . . . and, by the way, why do you think I won't still check in every day?" Finally, the meeting drew to a close, and the group offered a standing ovation.

I simply replied, "Bye, everybody," and blew a kiss.

Although I had planned to remain as CEO until the end of 2003, I realized quickly that I had become a lame duck. Meanwhile, Citigroup was doing well financially, and I was happy about how seamlessly the initial phase of the transition had gone. If anything, I reasoned we'd all be better off if I were to disengage prior to the year-end budget and compensation cycle. I typically like to move ahead right away once I make a decision. Accordingly, I changed my time horizon and told the board in mid-September that I wanted to accelerate my CEO retirement to the end of that month.

I felt numb after fixing my official retirement date—in July, the effective date seemed reasonably far in the future; now, it loomed only two weeks off. In late September, I traveled to the Breakers Resort in Palm Beach, Florida, for Smith Barney's annual Directors Council meeting of top producers. Spending time with my broker friends always offered an emotional boost, and I needed one more than ever. On this occasion, though, I couldn't help but feel sad thinking the event might be my last.

When I arrived, it looked as though every eligible broker had decided to attend—the place was packed. People went out of their way to shake my hand, and many pleaded with me not to stop coming to these meetings. During my comments before the crowd, I choked up and cried a bit as I described the great ride on which my career had taken me and noted that this meeting would be my last hurrah. It hit me that I was ending where I had begun: among a bunch of friends who happened to be brokers.

I felt awkward and disoriented during the first few weeks of not being CEO. Almost immediately, Chuck decided that it would be best to put some space between his top executives and me, and he moved his team to the floor below mine. Having everyone move off my floor and being left alone with limited interaction was difficult since I always had managed by walking the floor and dropping in unannounced on my executives. Now, I didn't feel comfortable walking downstairs and interfering at will. I continued to come into the office four days a week, but it was hard getting used to my new pace after having worked so hard for so long. Still, I managed to get over the initial discomfort. I kept busy with my philanthropic involvements, and Chuck and Bob volunteered to brief me each Wednesday over lunch.

For the next six months or so, I felt relatively good. Joanie and I spent a lot of time on our new boat, a 150-foot Italian beauty, and we enjoyed entertaining friends and vacationing with our kids and grandchildren. I relished not having to worry about the business collapsing behind me and slept easy on Sunday nights no longer having to plan for the week ahead. I enjoyed the freedom to relax and read. For fifty years, I hadn't experienced these pleasures. At the same time, I delved into my favorite not-for-profit institutions.

I became more excited than ever about each of these organizations. At Weill Cornell, we had made important strides in advancing medical science and working on future health care delivery. I was thrilled by what we had accomplished promoting education around the world especially in places like Qatar and Tanzania.

In Doha, we established the first American medical school outside the United States in cooperation with Qatar's emir and sheika. The school would graduate over fifty students each year from across the Middle East, Africa, and Asia all under Cornell University's rigorous academic standards. Opening the school in the Middle East and in the shadow of the Iraq War was gratifying since we were doing one of the only positive things in the region at a very complex and discouraging time.

In 2004, we focused on Tanzania owing to my acquaintance with a dedicated Catholic missionary named Father Peter LeJacq. An alumnus of our medical school, the priest had devoted his life to improving the quality of life in the East African country. Accompanied by an entourage from Weill Cornell and Citigroup's foundation, Joanie and I traveled to Tanzania to explore a cooperative venture with a hospital in the nation's second largest city. We had been briefed ahead of time, but we were still overwhelmed by Tanzania's health care system. For two decades, life expectancy had been in sharp decline.

As we drove to the hospital, we passed large numbers of attractive uniformed children walking barefoot to school. Joanie lamented how so many of these kids wouldn't enjoy the full life they deserved. The abysmal mortality trend illustrated the enormity of the crisis in health care facing much of the world's population. Thanks to Father LeJacq's introduction, Weill Cornell (supported in part by the Citigroup Foundation) agreed to educate doctors and committed itself to advance medical care in the country.

Closer to home, Weill Cornell strived to become the leader in advancing medical care and clinical research in the United States. Our institution moved fast when Baylor and Methodist hospitals in Texas went through a divorce, and we arranged for a cooperative joint venture so that Weill Cornell could provide top-quality medical education and treatment on a national scale. Having served for more than a decade as chairman of the Board of Overseers, I have loved working with terrific professionals and donors to advance medical research and clinical care. The experience has been among the most gratifying of my life.

Empowering people through education has represented the unifying theme behind the philanthropic institutions with which Joanie and I have been involved. Carnegie Hall has given me a passion for music, but I've been most excited about its music education programs. Since creating the music education endowment on my seventieth birthday, I've been very involved seeing this venture through. I consider music a universal language that can bridge cultural divides and bring the world closer together. In May 2005, for instance, we hosted cultural directors from four Arab countries to show them what Carnegie Hall has to offer and to illustrate how they might improve the management of their institutions.

Similarly, the National Academy Foundation has played an important role in pioneering better models for education. Since my retirement, I've concentrated on leveraging NAF's historical focus on small learning communities and the development of mentoring relationships so that NAF might become a model in the reform of the high school education system. The current high school education program typically still resembles the approach devised when the United States had a largely agrarian economy when high dropout rates for students were not seen as a huge problem. Unlike those days, however, jobs for unskilled labor today are far from plentiful. We need to equip our youth with education that matches our modern economy so that these kids can face productive lives. I hope that NAF can fill that gap.

While all three of these institutions have imparted excitement and a sense of purpose to my life in retirement, I've also enjoyed opportunities to work with foreign governments and leaders. It's important to have good relationships between the private and public sectors, and I've surprised myself by how easily I've been able to strike up relationships with influential statesmen. During 2005, for instance, I established a rapport with Russian president Vladimir Putin, a tough individual but someone with whom the West must remain engaged. I offered to arrange for ten U.S. corporate CEOs to meet with him so that the group could consider investment opportunities in his country, a proposal which the Russian leader gladly accepted. My relationships with Chancellor Schröeder and political leaders in France and Turkey also led to opportunities for Citigroup.

Following my retirement, I felt good about the succession—how it had been handled so smoothly and without management turnover. Still, it was emotionally difficult on occasion to find myself consulted less often by Chuck and Bob as time wore on. I tried not to interfere and understood that the succession would only work if I acted like a "grown-up" and let them run the company.

During 2004, Chuck had to deal with issues relating to Citigroup's civil litigation with WorldCom investors and several other matters which impacted the company's reputation. As he considered settling Citigroup's WorldCom-related litigation, Chuck had to decide if he was prepared to bolster legal reserves and accept a huge $5 billion after-tax charge. The settlement terms were difficult for me initially since the amount seemed so large and no one in the company believed we committed fraud. Nonetheless, I realized that it was important to get this matter behind the company and worried that Citigroup might face unacceptable financial costs if it were to fight the case and somehow lose. On this occasion, I violated my rule of not interfering and urged Chuck to take the settlement. Chuck made the right decision. Other banks held out for a while before finally capitulating and had to accept more onerous settlement terms.

In July 2005, Bob Willumstad decided to leave the company to seek a CEO position elsewhere. Expense pressures had been rising for a number of months which may have injected some friction into the relationship between Chuck and Bob. It saddened me that my protégés hadn't found a longer-lasting formula to work together. Our Consumer Bank head, Marge Magner, soon chose to retire as well given her close relationship with Bob. Chuck consulted me on these executive changes, and I offered him my support.

I had pinned a lot on delivering a smooth succession. Despite the turnover, I rationalized that the handoff had still been remarkably successful for a large company. I appreciated that Bob had stayed for as long as he had.

Around the same time, I devised the idea of starting a new private equity business and giving up my chairman role several months early to pursue the new endeavor. I wrestled with the idea that getting back to steering a business might be energizing and therapeutic. I didn't want to give up entirely on retirement, though I worried that my brain might turn to mush if I didn't find a way to be more engaged in some sort of business activity.

Starting a new private equity business would have been complementary to my relationship with Citigroup since I planned to seek out the company and its clients as potential investors and since Citigroup would have benefited from advising on deals my new firm might pursue. I worked on my idea with Chuck and several directors over a few months during the spring and early summer of 2005 and received positive feedback. Indeed, Chuck encouraged me to take my idea to the full board at its regular July meeting.

To my chagrin, the talks hit a snag as the board expressed unease with the way my proposed venture might relate to the noncompete clause which had been included in my employment contract. The board suggested that I renegotiate my full contract as a condition for dropping the noncompete issue. I considered the turn of events unfortunate since I certainly never had any intention of competing with the company I had founded. Rather than make an issue, I decided to drop the matter. Sadly, though, news of my discussions with the board leaked, and the press badly distorted my intentions.

The aborted private equity venture lowered my spirits and reminded me how tough it was to adapt to my new circumstances. I had hoped starting a new business would give me opportunities to learn new things and would satisfy my competitive urge. The board's position, however, forced me to look for some other way to replace the things I missed most about running a business.

Getting used to retired life remains a work in process, and I've even consulted a psychiatrist noted for working with retired business executives to help me adjust. Taking my "shrink's" advice, I am determined not to dwell on my frustrations. After all, I've almost always rationalized away my disappointments, confident that setbacks usually don't last for long and that they typically set the stage for better opportunities. I like to focus on the good things in any circumstance, and I remain especially proud of the manner in which I handled my retirement and succession.

I faced up to the fact that I no longer had the energy to devote 110 percent to the business and that it wouldn't be right to the company or our shareholders if I gave anything less. Having recognized this reality, I worked hard to ensure a smooth succession in which our company avoided a winners-and-losers mind-set and an immediate loss of valuable managerial talent. My retirement decision and the way I carried it out were consistent with the value I always placed on maintaining a high-performance culture driven by teamwork. I hope this philosophy and the way I handled my succession will provide a lesson for other business leaders.

Obviously, I need to get past the initial ups and downs of my retirement and find the right balance for my life. I have opportunities to delve further into my favorite philanthropic and civic institutions which can play important leadership roles in their respective areas. However, I'm not yet sure if these not-for-profit organizations can fully make up for the absence of a for-profit business in my life. Only time will tell.

Regardless of the difficulty disengaging from an active role at Citigroup, I'll always look to the company as my baby and will root enthusiastically for its success. Chuck is a dear friend who has clearly been growing into the job as CEO. He will prove to be an effective leader of a company whose capacity for greatness, I hope, will stand as our lasting legacy.

20

Live and Learn

generally don't like to dwell on the past. You can't do anything about things that took place long ago, and the future is much more exciting. Rethinking my life and career as I've worked on this book, therefore, has represented a change of pace. Reflecting on events that have taken place over the years has turned out to be surprisingly eye-opening, and I've been able to crystallize and put into words many business and life lessons that may help others.

In this final chapter, I take stock of where the financial services industry and Citigroup may be headed, and I zero in on some of my most compelling life lessons. I've learned a great deal about how to manage and acquire effectively. But beyond the insights strictly related to business, one of my most important lessons relates to the importance of giving back and setting an example for others in supporting philanthropic and civic institutions.

Let me begin by offering my vision for financial services and Citigroup. I'm extremely upbeat regarding the prospects for the financial services industry and see the business continuing as one of the great growth areas in the global economy along with technology, telecommunications, and health care. Financial companies make it possible for the manufacturing of goods and services to migrate to the lowest-cost regions of the world and therefore can play an important role in making the world a better place. The shifting of production to low-cost regions helps create jobs and income, which in turn spurs the creation of middle-class societies. The newly empowered consumers can then buy products or services produced elsewhere, including the developed world. While some may charge that capitalists exploit the system, I believe economic efficiency has the power to help developing and mature countries alike.

Since the fall of the Berlin Wall, much of the world has embraced capitalism, and global trading and capital flows have skyrocketed. The benefit to financial companies has been enormous as banks and other intermediaries have seen strong demand from clients for financing and advice. Assuming the global economy continues to expand, financial companies will continue to play an important role in educating and helping individuals and entrepreneurs who save and invest in their communities.

I'd caution, however, that people shouldn't assume that continued prosperity is guaranteed. Anything which threatens the world from coming closer together challenges future progress. Accordingly, civilized societies have to defeat the scourge of terrorism. Though this may take time, I'm hopeful that terror can be controlled and eventually beaten. On a more practical level, I'm not sure my bullishness on the prospects for the financial services business will filter down to every company. Relatively few financial companies have sufficient competitive strengths to pursue growth abroad. Meanwhile, excess capacity will keep driving down margins and distinguish only those companies that possess strong consolidation skills and powerful brand positioning.

I expect industry consolidation—already a hot topic for a long time—will continue as one of the key forces impacting the financial services industry. A lot of companies remain too small to afford the rising cost of new technologies or to adequately absorb earnings volatility. In order to battle these challenges and to tap into global opportunities, many companies which currently operate in just one segment may need to join with other types of companies to build bigger and broader enterprises much the same way we did at Citigroup.

Some of the most visible moves to broaden business models probably will come from the securities industry. I assume that companies like Merrill Lynch, Morgan Stanley, and Lehman Brothers one day will link up with commercial banks. I don't suggest that a stand-alone securities industry will disappear (for instance, Goldman Sachs seems intent on sticking with a narrow strategy), but I suspect that there will be less room for niche-oriented strategies among securities firms and other industry participants.

Of the various financial services segments, only property and casualty insurers seem in a poor position to broaden their businesses. The litigious U.S. legal system has saddled many of these firms with large legal liabilities (such as those related to asbestos) that have depressed share valuations and created lingering risks to balance sheets. These issues have made it nearly impossible for many of these companies to diversify in a shareholder-friendly manner.

Regulation, too, will remain a hot topic. In clamping down in the wake of the 2000–2003 bear market, regulators imposed new disciplines on financial companies. Though the stringency was justified in many instances, recent regulatory rules have restricted the industry's short-term profit growth. One probably could have anticipated the regulatory tightening that occurred after the excesses of the 1990s. Tougher regulation has followed bear markets for decades. The greatest bull market in U.S. history, which ran from 1982 to 2000, generated a lot of laxity in corporate behavior that needed to be addressed. Thus, the excesses of the bull market had to be replaced by a regulatory climate tough enough to instill renewed corporate discipline.

The regulatory cycle probably has gone too far, yet I'm confident that the system will return to balance. The Sarbanes-Oxley law that set new rules for corporate governance changed the tone in corporate America and helped rebuild investor trust after the damaging frauds that came to light, such as those related to WorldCom and Enron. The law served to remind corporate executives about the dangers of putting their firms' reputations at risk and explicitly made executives liable in the event that their companies' financial disclosures misled investors. The cost for companies to administer the new regulatory rules has been burdensome, and I expect Congress and the regulators gradually will modify some of the more onerous provisions.

Consolidation and regulation certainly stand as two of the most important forces impacting the financial services business; however, in my mind, globalization will remain the preeminent challenge for decades to come. The track record for financial companies going global has been mixed at best. During the 1980s, the large commercial banks pushed forward too aggressively and were compelled to surrender their global aspirations in the face of staggering losses when lesser developed countries defaulted on their debts. That issue subsequently faded in the 1990s, though relatively few commercial banks got back into the international business seriously.

In the United States, for instance, only Bank of America and J. P. Morgan, in addition to Citigroup, seem interested in a comprehensive global strategy. The rest of the industry has pursued a U.S.-centric approach. There are a few globally minded banks elsewhere, such as HSBC and UBS, but here, too, few companies have looked beyond their home or regional markets.

In contrast to the commercial banks, the investment banks have responded to the global challenge better, though within the confines of their focused business models. These firms now understand that their clients want them to provide more commercial bank services, particularly credit, in addition to advice and underwriting. That's a big reason why I think it's inevitable that many of the securities firms will be drawn into combinations with commercial banks.

Thinking about the competitive landscape, I feel very good about Citigroup's position. In the mid-1990s, our company was behind the curve in its global positioning; still, we faced up to that challenge and built the preeminent global financial services company. We learned what may be the most important lesson in how to grow successfully on a global basis: that a company needs strong partners in faraway markets who understand the local culture and business climate. Citigroup has built its global franchise around local staff in more than one hundred countries while instituting incentives and controls centrally. As other companies dither, Citigroup has gained valuable experience and has extended its leadership and competitive edge.

Citigroup's Emerging Markets franchise in particular should drive Citigroup's earnings for years and continues to set our company apart from competitors. In most developed countries, the share of the economy that relates to financial services typically exceeds 20 percent, yet in developing countries, this proportion lags sharply. As these emerging economies grow and become more stable, history suggests that growth in the financial sector should outstrip the economy at large.

At present, Citigroup operates with local market shares of only 2–4 percent in most of its Emerging Markets franchise. The company has only begun to focus on moving these shares higher. If it plays its cards right, Citigroup should see impressive growth from a combination of market and share expansion. While the Emerging Markets franchise currently generates nearly 30 percent of Citigroup's earnings, I expect it will grow many times faster than the company's businesses in the developed world. Opportunities in Asia and Eastern Europe remain especially attractive. There may well be bumps along the way, yet Citigroup's heft and diversification should give it the staying power to capture the enormous potential for its shareholders.

Beyond its global dimension, Citigroup is differentiated in other ways. Its management has operated for a long time as a team and knows what it takes to manage for efficiency and disciplined execution. The culture of equity ownership has been honed over many years and encourages executives to think like shareholders and put long-term performance over expediency.

I always insisted that our company build a base of recurring earnings before it engages in relatively more volatile businesses, and Citigroup now enjoys a healthy core earnings stream that should give the company a leg up in following through on strategic initiatives. Citigroup also has assembled the most diverse distribution network of any financial services organization. Most important, the company's results since its founding speak the loudest regarding its differentiation: Earnings now top $20 billion annually and have risen more than threefold in only seven years while strong returns on shareholder equity consistently have exceeded 20 percent. In terms of its scale and scope as well as its overall profits, Citigroup remains unmatched.

I hope that one of my legacies will be that I instilled an open attitude toward change and a spirit where Citigroup's leadership will think creatively about how to build shareholder value and grow the company. Chuck Prince, for one, appears to understand that Citigroup can't operate with fixed ideas regarding acquisitions or what constitutes an appropriate business mix. Undoubtedly, acquisitions will not play the same role in the company's future growth as in the past—Citigroup simply has become too big for any one deal to have an outsized impact on performance. Rather, the company now has to seize on its unique positioning and deliver most of its growth organically. That means Citigroup will have to keep innovating and look for nontraditional ways to grow.

Beyond rethinking acquisitions, Citigroup recently made a couple of high-profile divestitures by selling its Asset Management and Life Insurance businesses. When the company announced each exit, some observers were quick to suggest that I was unhappy with these moves and that the sales meant the end of the diversified financial services model that I spent much of my career championing.

These speculations have been flat-out wrong. What these people miss is that Citigroup only has gotten out of the *manufacturing* of these products. The company remains in these businesses, though now only as a distributor. I've supported these decisions and hope that by divesting the manufacturing piece, Citigroup freed capital to reallocate to higher-return activities, enhance its distribution, and minimize the risk of conflict. These actions help the company serve its customers better.

Chuck will need to zero in on growth and focus on getting the right people in place to take the company forward and grow shareholder value. With Bob Willumstad's retirement, Chuck has assumed direct and full responsibility for managing Citigroup's businesses. I believe my successor has internalized the management values which I stressed over the last twenty years and that he has learned even more about how to run a large company during his first two years as CEO. He's smart and has the support of a lot of good people. The more he succeeds, the more his self-confidence will grow.

Chuck will also have to manage another challenge: determining the right balance between centralization and local autonomy. This issue is tough and ongoing for Citigroup. To make the most of its global franchise, Citigroup needs strong and responsible local leaders since it's impossible to run most businesses from thousands of miles away. Still, the company must promote internal interaction to get successful products accepted and leveraged elsewhere rather than re-create the wheel in every local market. Getting this balance right remains an important work in process and probably will remain that way indefinitely. Ultimately, Chuck and his successors will be evaluated on how well they focus and manage an organization that spans different products, distribution systems, and geographies. Some may argue the task at hand is daunting, but I'm convinced that capable management can bring it all together.

It's relatively easy to advise Chuck on Citigroup-related issues, yet having worked for nearly fifty years, I've learned many lessons that may help other business leaders just as much. There's no single approach to management that's suitable for everyone. Still, it's vital for business people to be comfortable in their own skin, meaning they should recognize and play to their strengths.

Trying to imitate others usually doesn't work. I never could have imitated General Electric's Jack Welch or vice versa—had we tried, we both would have been failures. It's important to get others to play your game the same way successful sports teams do. I learned this lesson during the few years I spent at American Express in the 1980s. I found myself in an alien corporate culture where my style of management clashed irreconcilably with the corporation's norm and where I never gained the wherewithal to influence the company's course. It's no fun when you lose control of your situation.

It's also indispensable to develop healthy instincts by being well informed. Effective leaders understand their businesses and their competitors inside out, and they have the capacity to seize opportunities faster than others. I always read voraciously and constantly probed others for information on how we might run our company better or to learn about parts of the business I didn't understand. I consistently sought to develop relationships with others in the industry, ties which frequently led to lucrative deals—I met Gerry Tsai fifteen years before I bought Primerica; I knew Harvey Golub and Ed Budd for a decade before buying Shearson and Travelers respectively; and I made John Reed's acquaintance twenty-five years before proposing the deal to create Citigroup. I managed by walking the halls and interacting with employees, asking questions all the while.

More than just providing me with an education, the interaction helped me size up people—I could distinguish impressive executives from those who might try to snow me. Taking the time to get to know how operations worked also proved invaluable. The back office represented the guts of our company and stood behind our competitive edge since we relied so heavily on effectively leveraging cost advantages, integrating acquisitions, and cross-selling products. Understanding the mechanics of how the back office worked taught me the virtue of looking for practical, commonsense answers to problems. I always had a view of where the train was going but knew that it had to stay on the tracks in order to get there.

Good instinct alone doesn't necessarily translate into success, although combining the attribute with skill in getting others to follow represents a powerful combination. Over the years, my colleagues and I worked hard to develop a cohesive team and an effective style of management. I always insisted on informality in how my executives and I interacted and strove to build personal relationships. I was lucky that Joanie took an interest in supporting me on this and that she was willing to participate in company events. She helped me set the right tone, and our interest in our people was sincere. It's hard to create a personal culture if you're not genuine about it. We built a down-home culture that involved our employees' spouses since we felt it was important for our staff to have supportive partners at home who understood what their husbands or wives were striving for at work.

I also pushed for our employees to own an equity stake in the company and insisted that our top executives hold the vast bulk of their ownership interests so long as they worked for the company. The informality and the equity ownership culture provided powerful incentives for everyone to work together and drive for operational excellence and the long-term success of our company.

Moving contrary to the crowd also helps enormously in business. I built my reputation as a smart acquirer in the 1970s on the back of weakened competitors in which I saw inherent value. At the time, most of our competitors had become very shortsighted. Similarly, I saw opportunity later in Primerica and Travelers, companies which others were afraid to touch. I always tried to anticipate the industry's future direction in order to be alert to opportunities before others were. Taken together, healthy instincts, a contrarian bent, the capacity to act swiftly, and a strong and cohesive team all represent a potent combination that any business leader should take to heart.

At the same time, my colleagues and I made great efforts to contain our operating risks. Outsiders may have seen us taking gambles in aggressively acquiring and adding to our business, but we took care to manage our day-to-day operations in a conservative manner. Indeed, we often were *too* conservative. I always insisted that we maintain a steady base of recurring earnings and made sure we didn't use our balance sheet excessively to support proprietary risks. Moreover, we prioritized having a low-cost structure and strong capital position in order to preserve our flexibility during times of industry stress. We never were in a position in which we felt we had to stretch in order to grow at an acceptable pace. Effective management-reporting tools gave us real-time information on each business's key drivers. Keeping tabs on revenues daily helped identify anomalies early.

Of course, being human, people make mistakes. When things go wrong, it's crucial to surface the errors in judgment, correct the mistakes, and move on. I've seen many CEOs get tripped up because they cling to a fixed vision of the future. It's okay to have views on where one's business may be headed, yet effective leaders know how to read when the environment or rules begin to change. I've always lived by the adage "Rationalize what you want, but don't fool yourself." It's also helpful not to get caught up in past mistakes or failures. By nature, I'm good at explaining away setbacks and have convinced myself that better events inevitably follow disappointments. Whatever my other personality flaws, this trait gave me the resiliency to keep pushing our company forward.

I have other recommendations on how to acquire effectively. Undoubtedly, an acquisition should offer one of three things: 1) it should consolidate a company's existing businesses and generate savings and efficiencies; 2) it should add products and diversity and thereby enhance the value offered to customers; and/or 3) it should add management talent. In negotiations, it's wise to avoid pushing for the absolute cheapest deal. It is better that the seller feels good about the transaction. When you develop a reputation as a fair buyer, it raises the odds that others will take you seriously as a potential acquirer.

Similarly, effective businesspeople get to know their competitors so that if the time comes to discuss an acquisition, they understand what makes the seller tick. For instance, when I negotiated with John Reed, I understood that I had to offer a merger of equals and a co-CEO role. John initially suggested that he'd have no difficulty working for me; however, I suspected he didn't mean what he said and instead was testing my intentions. Had I not known my interlocutor that well, it's possible that the merger which created Citigroup never would have occurred.

While it's important not to push for the absolute lowest-cost deal, I still believe an acquisitive company does best when it enters negotiations from a position of strength. Over the years, our company maintained a strong balance sheet, a depth of management, and a reputation for excellence in integrating acquisitions. These assets, along with a premium stock market valuation, routinely contributed to our wherewithal to strike value-additive deals. In addition, we avoided taking on excessive leverage so that we knew that we would survive to fight another day in the event that we made a mistake in evaluating a new partner or if economic conditions worsened unexpectedly. I also worked hard to make sure our people accepted the management that came from companies we acquired and stressed that we needed to treat the other side with respect rather than as losers. When a buyer treats the seller's team as inferior, it typically guarantees problems.

I'd qualify my advice to embrace another company's management—at least at the highest levels, it applies best in acquisitions. Ironically, the strategy didn't work so well in our merger of equals with Citicorp. It took us the better part of four years to sort out our management structure and to realize fully the weaknesses of some of Citicorp's top executives. Maybe I was blinded by the opportunity in that deal, but I learned the hard way the difficulty of bringing two organizations together when there are sharp distinctions in management style and talent. I don't regret the merger for a moment; however, pursuing a merger of equals is not a strategy I'd broadly recommend for other companies.

It's also vital that management—and especially the CEO—concentrate on the nuts and bolts of the back office and other operational details to ensure an effective integration. Often an acquired company comes with marginal businesses which if not actively managed can pose out-sized risks. In the late 1980s, Commercial Credit and Primerica brought with them poorly positioned auto lending and insurance businesses which could have hurt us had we not moved to exit these areas quickly.

On the other hand, I made a serious blunder after buying Associates First Capital in 2000. In that instance, I let my guard down and didn't assign clear accountability for Associates' weak commercial finance and leasing business. That acquisition cost us in other ways, and it bothers me that our company might have avoided more than $1 billion in losses had I followed my own advice.

Finally, acquisitions demand a high degree of financial discipline in order to build value for shareholders. It's important that a deal offer the likelihood of a strong earnings kick, and the management of the acquiring company must be convinced that it will be tapping into an operation with compelling revenue growth. I typically insisted that the return on equity from an acquisition not dilute our corporate rate of return. This requirement held our company to a tough standard compared to what finance textbooks might allow. In fact, conventional wisdom suggests it's acceptable to proceed with an investment when the incremental rate of return exceeds the corporate cost of capital—

for us, the rule would have meant a far less exacting standard than the criteria we used.

I always reasoned that investors measured our performance based on our reported results, which under accepted accounting rules only showed return on equity and not internal rate of return estimates. Since we typically reported equity returns in excess of 20 percent, I felt that was the standard on which investors would judge us and insisted that all of our acquisitions exceed that threshold. By sticking with this conservative approach, we weeded out many marginal deals and reduced our risks considerably.

Over the years, we were fortunate to find many compelling acquisition opportunities. Buying back Shearson from American Express in 1993 and taking over Travelers at nearly the same time were particularly gratifying. Getting Shearson back represented one of the real highlights of my career—not only did I win back the company I had founded, but we did the acquisition on extraordinarily favorable terms, a fact immediately appreciated by investors. Travelers, meanwhile, gave us a phenomenal brand and a terrific return on our investment. Both of these acquisitions played a key role in transforming our company from a ragtag operation into the ranks of America's most widely known and respected companies. Of course, the merger with Citicorp took that position and propelled us to a new level, putting us out in front of the entire financial services industry and making us a global leader in a single stroke. It goes without saying that the creation of Citigroup represented the business thrill of a lifetime.

I'm fortunate to have enjoyed a fulfilling career in which I was able to build a lot of value for our company's shareholders and to have the capacity to grow both personally and professionally. Somewhere along the way, however, I realized that all my business-related accomplishments would feel hollow if I didn't find a way to contribute my time, energy, experience, and financial resources to help others. I am proud of my business-related achievements, yet I feel my life experience also can teach others valuable lessons in how to engage in philanthropy and work toward a better society.

I'm the first to admit that my philanthropic involvement began almost as an accident and even then initially for self-serving reasons. In the late 1970s, the securities industry in New York faced a shortage of manpower to staff its back office functions. Working closely with the New York City schools superintendent, I devised the idea of creating an organization that would build a curriculum and mentoring system to engage public high school students in careers in the financial services industry. That was the birth of the National Academy Foundation, an organization which has now flourished for more than twenty-five years. NAF opened my eyes to how business could partner with public institutions in order to devise practical solutions to community problems.

In fact, the trends in U.S. secondary education are startling when one scratches the surface. Sadly, the high school drop-out rate exceeds 50 percent for inner-city youth and approximates 30 percent for the U.S. high school population at large. Through my leadership of NAF, I've come to understand that the education system in America reflects an approach devised in the nineteenth century when the United States was geared to an agrarian and industrial economy. One hundred years ago, unskilled jobs were in abundance. Today, of course, that has changed. The information economy requires skilled employees. Unfortunately, public high schools have not been responsive and in general fail to offer practical job-oriented training for those students unable or unwilling to go on with their studies.

NAF has been ahead of its time and fortunately may offer part of the solution. Through its finance, travel and tourism, and information technology academies (and formative programs in health care and engineering), NAF has developed effective technical education programs—delivered via small learning communities—for over fifty thousand students in more than six hundred schools. In addition, NAF has built a network of over two thousand businesses which hire and mentor students. Its graduation rate tops 90 percent. NAF has perfected its model for roughly twenty-five years and has proved that it is a concept worthy of investment and expansion.

My involvement with NAF helped me see that business leaders have a special obligation to become seriously involved in community activities.

Picking one's spots in the philanthropic world should be a personal matter; however, I'd recommend some principles for how business leaders might become engaged. First, it's important to make long-term commitments and accordingly select causes where one's passion will last. Second, one should look for organizations that can benefit from one's business expertise or relationships. Business executives typically excel at setting a vision and getting others to follow; therefore, institutions that are open to change in direction may be particularly fertile ground for involvement. Third, the person who runs the organization should be one who inspires confidence and who is open to strong cooperative partnerships with active board members. Finally, I believe it's essential to concentrate one's efforts on a manageable set of activities in order to maximize impact. Many people make the mistake of spreading themselves too thin in their philanthropic or civic involvements—usually, both they and their chosen institutions suffer as a result.

Marrying my business skills to the philanthropic organizations with which I've chosen to become involved has given me immense satisfaction. I've always been a grinder. I stay at something until I see results. After years of commitment to Carnegie Hall, Weill Cornell Medical College, and the National Academy Foundation, I feel I've made an important impact on each of these institutions. Perhaps one of the things that motivated me was my insight early on that the business and philanthropic worlds offer similar means of leading people and promoting advances in society.

On one occasion years ago, Judy Arron—then the executive director of Carnegie Hall—insisted that I sit in the middle of an orchestral teaching workshop led by the conductor Georg Solti. I literally sat among a group of music teachers who came together for the workshop and I watched the maestro teach the group to work together. Within the span of forty-five minutes, he took a disparate bunch of people and transformed them into a cohesive entity. That experience left a mark on me. It showed that leadership in music is no different than in business—it's all about getting people to work together to become a team.

Later, I met other amazing musicians—people like Yo-Yo Ma and Valery Gergiev—who similarly have a great capacity to educate others and bring people closer together. All my philanthropic involvements—not just Carnegie Hall—have led me to people who change people's lives for the better.

The sense of accomplishment and the relationships spurred me on. When I first became involved with Carnegie Hall in the early 1980s, the institution had an inward-looking board. It included some very bright people but didn't accomplish much. It typically operated with an annual deficit which the board would be called upon to make up. There was little outreach to the community, and Carnegie Hall always seemed to operate on the financial brink. The institution had a great history, but its brand was tired. When Isaac Stern, Carnegie Hall's driving force, began to campaign for the renovation of the physical infrastructure, there was no natural constituency to call upon for funding. In those years, the great music institution was crying out for a new vision with which to revitalize itself.

Appointed first to chair the capital campaign and later to head the board, I set out to overhaul Carnegie Hall's financial condition and, in doing so, had the chance to materially recast the institution's mission, operating procedures, and board. Between 1991 and 2005, we raised the endowment from a paltry $2 million to over $250 million even after spending more than $120 million on infrastructure improvements. Many of the major donors came to Carnegie Hall via my relationships. We now generate more than $75 million in revenues annually (a six-fold increase from twenty years earlier) and consistently operate with an annual surplus.

Having put the financial house in order, we've dramatically increased Carnegie Hall's performances, educational programs, and community outreach. We've made Carnegie Hall young and vital again. We're now breaking new ground experimenting with ways to make orchestral music relevant to modern audiences and also to pioneer distance learning on a global basis. Carnegie Hall's progress has come over a long period of time and has been propelled by a great many inspired professionals, but I'm not sure the advances would have been possible had we not addressed the institution's administrative issues up front.

The Weill Cornell Medical College offers a similar story. When I joined it in the mid-1980s, the Board of Overseers lacked authority. Instead, the university's trustees made most major decisions. It was a bad way to attract people. The medical school never had a capital campaign and lacked a formal fund-raising effort. There was no consistency in leadership as the school's dean turned over every three years on average. No institution could accomplish anything with turnover like that. The college and the affiliated hospital constantly battled one another as well. In short, the administration was in disarray, and the college seemed hopelessly stuck in place and far from a leadership position.

Once again, along with the contributions of many committed individuals, I helped turn the institution around. We strengthened the board and brought in many new people with impressive credentials. In 1996, after I became the chairman of the Board of Overseers, we hired a respected new dean, Tony Gotto, and made sure to empower him. In contrast to past turnover, Weill Cornell now benefits from consistent strong leadership. With new professionalism injected into the board and management, we've repaired the issues that historically plagued the hospital–medical college relationship.

Over a decade, Weill Cornell has raised over $1 billion for its capital campaign to support research, teaching, and clinical services, and the school is about to kick off a new $1.5 billion campaign to further advance research. Weill Cornell also has done a better job of working with other academic departments at Cornell University, for example pioneering research in medical nanotechnology and bioscience. Thanks to its innovative expansion in Qatar, where Weill Cornell has opened the first fully accredited American medical school outside the United States, our school has begun to globalize and has pushed into a region of the world that desperately needs to better educate its youth.

Putting Weill Cornell onto a path where it will become one of the world's top medical colleges and where it can influence the lives of potentially millions of people has been a wonderful experience. Once more, the skills that I honed in business, those of bringing people together and instilling a disciplined culture for planning and financial management, have proven relevant, and I'm proud of my impact.

The satisfaction I've felt from all my involvements in the not-for-profit world has often rivaled the highs I've experienced in business. Indeed, my excitement and sense of accomplishment have only grown over time. I'm also lucky to have married someone who has helped me appreciate the rewards of helping and empowering others and who has supported me in my philanthropic endeavors every bit as much as in other parts of my life. In her own right, Joanie has helped many others through her leadership in a variety of organizations including most recently her chairmanship of Alvin Ailey and Paul Smith's College. Joanie and I take our philanthropic commitments seriously and reinforce one another's efforts. I hope our experience will encourage others to give of themselves and make a difference.

Over the years, many have wondered what has driven my energy and intensity. However, I never allowed myself the luxury of slowing down long enough to engage in much self-analysis. With more time on my hands now that I've retired, though, probing that part of my personality perhaps is worth a try. I always loved what I did for a living, and I always had a drive to do better. I found the financial markets exciting and loved waking up early each morning in order to read the newspapers and see what was happening so that I might figure out ways to build my business. My competitive instincts evolved over time. As an eight-year-old, I experienced my first taste of winning when I had my first successful paper delivery route. My high school days at military school played a more important role as the experience molded my self-confidence and demonstrated that I could excel if I approached life with discipline. My success with competitive tennis drove the point home. Joanie also played an important role in encouraging me to work hard and with discipline. As newlyweds, she reminded me to call my clients so that I'd make enough money to feed our kids.

Somehow, no matter how successful I became, I never saw a stopping point. I was always able to take risks to get to the next level. With each accomplishment, I realized that people responded well to intelligent risk taking, and that spurred me on all the more. I suppose, too, that there's an element of going to excess in a lot of the things I do. I enjoy fine food, great wine, and beautiful surroundings. I don't seek to be ostentatious, but I love quality things.

That eagerness for the best showed itself early in my career when I talked about building a great company that would stand the test of time even as I started out with my first small partnership. Later, that same passion revealed itself each time I made an important acquisition and especially when we merged with companies with great brands such as Travelers and Citicorp. Some have suggested that I was driven by insecurity. However, other than feeling nervous just before each large deal, I rarely felt my self-confidence diminish.

When all is said and done, I attribute a great deal of my drive to the luck I experienced time and again during my life. From marrying Joanie, to beating the odds and turning a tiny partnership into a force in the securities industry, to having a shot at a second career which culminated in the creation of the greatest financial services company in the world, I've had more than my fair share of good fortune. People often ask: "What would you do differently if you had your life to live over?"

In truth, the answer is simple. If I had my life to do over, I wouldn't change a thing. For all its ups and downs, my life couldn't have been any better. I pinch myself every day to make sure it's not a dream!

MY LIFE WITH SANDY
A Conversation with Joan Weill

THE EARLY YEARS

What was it about Sandy that first attracted you?

I met Sandy in 1954. His aunt knew my father from our old neighborhood in Brooklyn and fixed us up on a blind date. When Sandy first called, I had other plans and suggested he go out with a friend of mine instead. Of course, he said there was no way he was going to have a blind date set up through a blind date, and we picked another day to go out, which turned out to be April Fool's Day. My family and I then lived in Woodmere, having recently moved back to the New York area after living in California for several years.

My first impression of Sandy was that he looked short. Having grown up on the West Coast, my dream was to return there and marry a tall, blond-haired, blue-eyed guy who knew how to dance. Instead, here was this five-foot-nine-inch guy with dark hair and green eyes—and I later learned that he couldn't dance. He was good-looking, but he wasn't exactly my image. Still, we hit it off. Sandy was shy but had a cute sense of humor. For our first date, he took me for a drink, and we spent the whole night talking. He was easy to talk to. I didn't get home until three o'clock in the morning. Since I was only nineteen, my father was ready to kill me.

We fell madly in love that spring and summer.

Sandy was not aggressive at all, and I soon wondered where our relationship was heading. Finally, *I proposed to him*. We were at his parents' house in Peekskill and were watching *Gone With the Wind*. I turned to him and said, "Don't you think we should get married?" Caught off guard, Sandy seemed unsure how to respond. Finally, mimicking Rhett Butler, he blurted, "Frankly, my dear, I don't give a damn!" In truth, he *did* "give a damn," and we agreed to get married. We became engaged officially in September and married the following June.

What was it like as a young couple?

At first, it was hell! We had very little money and had to ask our parents for help. Sandy's father had left his mother. We didn't want her to be alone, so we moved into her home on weekdays—it was conveniently located near Brooklyn College where I was still going to school. On weekends, we'd switch to my parents' house.

My mother and father didn't approve of Sandy. When we got married, he didn't have a job and lacked direction. He hadn't graduated on time, and his father had walked out on his mother. My parents kept reminding me that "the apple doesn't fall far from the tree" and told me, "You can come home anytime you want." It was anything but reassuring.

Sandy obviously didn't react well to the comments, and there was constant tension. I soon became pregnant, and the impending responsibility made the pressure all the more intense. When I was in my ninth month, Sandy couldn't take our living situation anymore and declared, "You know, either we find an apartment of our own or we're not going to make it." Hearing that, I went out and found us a place of our own to live.

We may have gotten out from under our parents' roof, but that didn't eliminate the stress. I kept saying that we couldn't afford our apartment, but Sandy simply replied, "Look, we'll stretch and we'll do it." He always aimed a little higher than what we could actually afford. With little choice, we stretched. By now, Sandy had gotten a job as a runner at Bear Stearns, and I was teaching third grade two days a week at a public school in a tough section of Brooklyn and finishing my degree at the same time. Still, we were living hand to mouth. Sandy approached his father and mine for help—he had no problem asking for money. They gave us something for all of two weeks before they said they couldn't afford it any longer. He saw that many of our new neighbors were supported by wealthy parents and resented the disparity.

How did Sandy develop his drive to succeed? Was it apparent from the start of your marriage?

His drive came gradually. Remember, Sandy had planned to join the air force when we married. His entry into the securities business and our challenging living situation, however, changed everything. The first sign that he could push himself came with the decision to take that apartment. Sandy knew he had to make enough money to cover our $125 rent.

Even though Sandy soon became a salesman, he didn't flourish right away at Bear Stearns. He first lost money for many of my parents' friends; then he did the same for some family members. It was hard for him. He wanted to draw inward, and I had to encourage him to call his clients. He was shy about that sort of thing. On the other hand, nobody cared more than he did. He used to stay up nights worrying about his clients, and he developed very close relationships with a few of them. Once, one was in an automobile accident. Before phoning the doctor, this woman called Sandy for advice. He proved he could develop that sort of close relationship with people.

Some people have asked me over the years, "Did you know when you married him that he was going to be a success?" I never even thought about that. I married him because I *loved* him . . . you know, for who he was. Had Sandy joined the air force, he would have made $6,000 a year—at the time, I thought that would be fine.

It was a big leap for Sandy to leave the relative safety of working for others and go into business for himself. How did he make that decision?

Arthur Carter had a lot to do with that. We were neighbors, and Arthur and his wife became our best friends. We were extremely close.

Arthur's first wife came from a very wealthy family. They had a very different lifestyle than we did, but that had little bearing on our friendship. Sandy looked up to Arthur and admired his active mind, his strong personality, and his discipline. I think Sandy also felt some need to prove himself to Arthur. The two of them jointly came up with the idea of starting their company—Sandy probably never would have taken the step on his own.

When the two decided to go into business together, I didn't think twice about it. Sandy had developed plenty of ambition by then. Arthur's father-in-law was supposed to put quite a bit of money into the new firm. When he backed out, we scrambled to raise the funds. Sandy's mother ended up contributing virtually her entire divorce settlement of $50,000. We also invested our meager savings except for $1,000 or so just in case the kids got sick. Even though we were taking a risk, I figured everything was going to be fine. Maybe that was just plain dopey, but I had confidence in my husband and just felt we'd come out okay.

COMING INTO YOUR OWN AS A COUPLE

Jumping ahead, what was your life like during the 1960s as the business expanded?

Apart from recalling that Sandy was always busy at work, most of my memories of the 1960s are of our home life. The best part of that period was having children—Marc was born in 1956 and Jessica in 1959. We also bought our first house in '62. It was new and sited on two acres. We had to get a mortgage to cover most of the $55,000 cost. When Sandy started the business, my father didn't feel comfortable lending him money; however, on this occasion, he helped with the down payment. I was thrilled to finally have a house of our own.

Soon after we moved, the market crashed. It seemed really bad. We had just bought this house on a lot of property and now had to worry if we could still afford it. As with our first apartment, it felt like we had reached beyond our means. This was pure Sandy. He always wanted to have the best. If he couldn't buy a cashmere sweater, then he wouldn't buy a sweater at all. It wasn't about quantity; he just wanted—for whatever reason—to have the best. To save money, we did our own landscaping. With the market in the doldrums, things got quiet at Sandy's office, and he suddenly had more time to spend at home. We bought all these bushes, and late at night after the kids had gone to bed, we would go outside and plant by the light of our car's headlights.

In 1963, I fell off a chair lift while skiing and severely injured my back. My life suddenly got very difficult. The doctors misdiagnosed my injury and made light of my condition. But I knew it was something more severe. I kept saying, "Something's not right. I'm not walking . . . my leg hurts terribly . . . something's wrong." Finally, after weeks of being in traction in the hospital, the doctors recommended that I have a spinal fusion. That was a nightmare. I was stuck in the hospital even longer and was in so much pain. I felt horrible that I couldn't be home for Marc and Jessica, who were still very young. I stopped eating, and my weight dropped to only eighty-five pounds. Finally, I was sent home because I was starving to death—I guess the doctors reasoned I'd have more will to eat if I was home and in familiar surroundings. Though I slowly regained my strength, I was in a body cast for a long time. It was like living in a tin can. It was absolutely terrible.

The accident turned our home life upside down. Sandy is not good at dealing with illness because it's something he can't fix. He gets frustrated and angry when he's not in control. He also put a lot of pressure on himself to succeed and provide for our family by then. Because Sandy was always at work, I became very angry myself. I thought he could have done more to be at home and help with our children. Also, our relationship with my parents remained ambivalent, and that added to the tension. They were not very supportive of what he was doing and questioned whether he had a real profession. I felt stuck between my parents and my husband.

We often had a lot of tension in our house in those years, and I was no shrinking violet. I knew how to throw a temper tantrum to get Sandy's attention. As in any marriage, we had our ups and downs, though I never doubted that we would be okay. Looking back, I only regret that I did not channel my anger better and in a positive way explain to Marc and Jessica why their father wasn't home. To this day, Marc holds it against Sandy.

On a brighter note, Sandy shared what was going on with business. *Always*. This is something that was helpful to our relationship. Early in my life, I had decided that I would have to be part of whatever my husband did for a living. I wanted to know because my father—as many in his generation—didn't share that side of his life much. It bothered me that my mother would be given money every day to go shopping and that she had no idea about the family's finances. I never wanted to be kept in the dark. While Sandy and I forged a different sort of relationship, sometimes he'd share too much. When the stock market went through a rough patch, he'd come home and tell us to turn off the lights to save money. That sort of sharing wasn't always helpful.

How did you and Sandy deal with his initial success and the first trappings of material wealth?

In the early 1970s, we moved into this fancy apartment building on Fifth Avenue. Sandy really wanted that apartment. It showed his accomplishments. On the other hand, I felt uncomfortable—it was so stuffy. On moving day, I was in the basement when one of the fancy tenants came down and asked, "Are you Mrs. Weill?" Embarrassed from wearing a bandanna and sloppy clothes, I quickly responded, "Oh, no. *Madam* is upstairs." I never felt like we belonged in that building. I hated it.

When the market turned bad and we had to sell, Sandy was very unhappy. It was a step backward. Still, Sandy didn't dwell on it and was reassuring, saying, "We'll be fine." I was happy to leave that apartment. It was too much.

How did your life change after your children reached adulthood?

Sandy was usually demanding of my time and constantly asked me to participate in company events. When Jessica and Marc were teenagers, it caused a great deal of difficulty because it wasn't easy to leave them alone all the time. I was frequently torn.

After they left home, I felt something different. The feminist movement was in full bloom, and all my friends were back at school or pursuing interests of their own. They kept calling me an appendage since I followed Sandy on his business trips. While I enjoyed interacting with Sandy's employees, I realized that I needed to go someplace where I could be myself and not just be known as Sandy's wife. I decided to go back to school. I enrolled in the New School and took courses in social work and also went to work at Bellevue Hospital in the psychiatric ward. It was very good for me.

AMERICAN EXPRESS AND ITS AFTERMATH

Explain how Sandy failed to anticipate the problems he'd ultimately face when he agreed to sell Shearson to American Express.

The idea of selling to American Express was very exciting. Suddenly, we had the opportunity to join a well-known company with operations all over the world. It seemed like it would be a positive and eye-opening experience for both of us. When you really desire something, you see want you want and block out the rest—we really believed it would be great.

Sandy asked me to come to his office so we might meet together with Jim Robinson. He was very good about asking for my opinion before he'd plunge into important deals. On this occasion, Sandy asked if I trusted Jim Robinson. It was an unusual question, yet this was the first time in more than twenty years that Sandy would be working for someone else. I knew that whatever I'd say didn't really matter since Sandy intended to do this deal anyway. I wasn't going to say no. Besides, I thought everything would work out okay.

As soon as the deal closed, I began to see that American Express had a very different culture. I will never forget the first day when we had merged. Bettye Robinson arranged a luncheon for the ladies and had cars to take everyone. Everything was very formal down to the pecking order of who had to ride with whom. The formality turned out to be constant and very much at odds with the casual style Sandy and I had always maintained. Though it was uncomfortable, we initially looked the other way and tried not to focus on the negatives.

So what awoke both of you to the reality that American Express wasn't all you had hoped for?

It took Sandy a while to realize he had no authority. Everything had to go through Jim Robinson or the board. He soon felt ineffective. It was the first time he was really unhappy, and Sandy has *always* been happy in his job. I found it hard to give constructive advice since I was only hearing things from Sandy's viewpoint. I tried to get Sandy to look at things from a different perspective. That seemed the responsible tack to take. "Look at it from Jim Robinson's point of view. Are you being obnoxious?" I asked. After a while, though, I could see that the situation wasn't improving and that Sandy was deeply unhappy. I suggested that this was a quality-of-life issue and that he should do what would make him happy.

It was traumatic and stressful for Sandy to leave American Express, but it was the right thing to do. We both felt fortunate that we didn't have any financial worries. Sandy was young, and I felt confident that he'd find something else to do.

How did Sandy feel about Jim Robinson after the fact?

From the start, Sandy and Jim were very different. Shortly after the merger, Jim's first wife had a brain aneurysm and was rushed to the hospital in the middle of the night. Jim didn't know where to turn and called us immediately. We rushed to be with him—it was five o'clock in the morning. We entered the hospital completely bedraggled having just thrown on some clothes. In contrast, Jim was perfectly immaculate. He wore a sports jacket and a tie. Looking at Sandy and Jim at that moment showed the difference between them. Jim was always restrained and needed to behave in a very structured way while Sandy was much more emotional and ready to act.

Sandy was displeased with Jim when he resigned from American Express, but he eventually got over it. In fact, Sandy likes Jim now. A lot of the credit for the turnaround goes to Jim. He kept up the relationship after Sandy left and acted like a gentleman, even after he later lost his own job as the company's CEO. In a lot of ways, Jim had to appreciate the way Sandy approached business, especially his decisiveness.

How hard was it for you and Sandy in the year after his resignation from American Express?

At first, it was difficult as Sandy's whole identity centered on what he did for a living. He was afraid people would stop calling now that he was no longer associated with a large company. There wasn't much to do in the office, but he still insisted on going in every day. He probably drove Jamie Dimon crazy. When I'd suggest going on vacation or doing something around town such as taking in a movie, he usually refused, afraid that he might miss an important call. He wanted to be ready in case an opportunity might strike. Part of it, too, was his work ethic. At fifty-two, he wasn't ready to stop working.

Before long, the BankAmerica thing came up. I was really scared about that—I did not want to move to San Francisco. It would have been too disruptive, and I didn't want to leave our children. Sandy was eager to pursue something which might be professionally attractive, and I couldn't see how to stop him from at least exploring the opportunity. While I didn't want to move, I felt conflicted. I missed not being involved in a company. Also, I had begun working with Citymeals-on-Wheels by then (the opportunity having come to me because of Sandy's position at American Express)—the experience opened my eyes to the good things I could accomplish in the not-for-profit world, especially with the credibility lent by being part of a large company.

FROM COMMERCIAL CREDIT TO CITIGROUP

Sandy soon found Commercial Credit and was off on his second career. What did he learn from his years running Shearson and later working at American Express which helped him succeed in building Commercial Credit into Citigroup?

After American Express, he knew that he never wanted to work for anybody again. That was a big thing. Still, that experience taught him to deal with corporate-level people a lot better, especially with a board of directors. He also had become much more outgoing and confident over the years.

Sandy had a great relationship with his employees. When we were getting ready to move into the World Trade Center, I went to look at the new offices with Peter Cohen and Sandy. As we walked in, the guy who headed the printing department came over to greet us. Sandy noted that he seemed to be at work awfully early, to which he responded, "Well, I worked all night to get the printing shop set up. Would you like to see it?" Peter immediately turned him down saying he had to get to his office. Sandy, though, told the employee, "I would love to see it." Later, Sandy commented, "The guy worked all night. How could you not go in and see it." He always had a good instinct that way. Sandy has never forgotten that business is all about people.

Sandy pursued so many deals leading up to merging with Citicorp. Not including that one, which stood out for you?

The deals came one after another. It was boom, boom, boom. Sandy usually negotiated at our house. It was always fascinating to watch the group dynamics. Buying Travelers was especially fulfilling. It was interesting to watch Sandy go in as an investor and then convince Ed Budd to sell the entire company. That merger broadcast that Sandy was back in the big leagues.

Then there was Shearson. Buying it back from American Express felt so good. Of all of Sandy's deals, this one was the most meaningful for me. Shearson's employees were like family. I missed them. Many of us had grown up together. We would see them once or twice each year at all the conventions, and I'd correspond with some in between. It was just a matter of being back with my extended family. Forget the business side of it.

During the 1990s, one business success seemed to follow the next. What was it like for you during that seemingly heady time?

Nothing is perfect. We had a few personal problems in that era. For instance, I had an issue with this psychiatrist whom I had been seeing. He ended up trading on information I told him about Sandy's dealings with

BankAmerica. He was someone in whom I had placed my trust, and we ended up suing him—the entire experience was traumatic. My point is that things had a way of evening out. We had all this success, but we also quietly had a lot of demands on us. It was not a perfect period.

Merging with Citicorp and creating Citigroup must have been thrilling. What stands out most for you?

It meant everything to Sandy. He finally put together the best company in the world, something he always wanted. Once again, he renamed the company to reflect its enhanced scope and stature. You know, the only time Sandy didn't change his name was when he married me!

I couldn't help but share Sandy's excitement. Yet Citigroup was different from all of the earlier deals mainly because of its size. The challenge to meet and get to know the people was much greater. It was the opposite of winning back Shearson where we seemed to know nearly everyone. It was so big.

Before Citigroup, our company felt family-like and easier to understand. Now, I had to take in little portions at a time in order to digest things and feel comfortable. Nonetheless, traveling around the world meeting with Citigroup employees proved especially interesting. These trips allowed us to meet with smaller groups. I would visit with employees and their spouses, and enjoyed hearing them tell me about the areas of the company in which they worked, the challenges they faced in their respective countries, and the social service organizations in which they were involved. And, of course, it was exciting to travel to all sorts of exotic places.

DEALING WITH ADVERSITY

For Sandy, the euphoria of creating Citigroup didn't last long. How did you and Sandy face up to the difficulty of getting along with John Reed?

John intellectualized everything. He never showed much warmth or emotion. He was the opposite of Sandy in every way. His wife gave me the greatest example of the difference between the two. I was having hip problems, and she said, "Here's what separates John from Sandy. John would go to the library and research everything there is to know about hips. Sandy would find the best hip doctor and send you to him to get cured."

Right after the merger, it was the mutual admiration society. John and Sandy sought the opinion of the other on everything. However, the personality differences, the slowness in making decisions, and the pressures from restless colleagues soon got in the way. When Bob Lipp began saying, "I can't function this way anymore," it became very difficult. Sandy is not a particularly moody person, but you could see him trying to figure out what to do. As he usually does when he's under stress, he gained weight.

Finally, the pressures came to a head. That day of the climactic board meeting was one of the worst days of my life. I went to the movies but have no recollection of what I saw. I just couldn't stay home. It was a terrible, terrible Sunday. What made it so bad was that Sandy deserved to win the company. While he didn't need the job financially, I felt he needed it for his emotional well-being. His entire persona was wrapped up in the company; it was the culmination of everything he had dreamed.

I worried he might lose it all. If he had, it would have been for all the wrong reasons. John Reed was quite a fighter, and Sandy didn't know how to play the games that some people play. That's what troubled me more than anything. There were some old-line board members who were very much in favor of John Reed. They made me very nervous.

When it was all over, we were relieved and exhausted. Sandy came home, and I made a roast chicken. After every stressful experience, I always made my famous roast chicken.

A couple of years later, Sandy had another tough experience dealing with Eliot Spitzer. How did you feel during that situation?

This was another terrible time which fed Sandy's fear that he might lose everything. In fact, it was worse since it undermined his reputation.

I don't think it's possible for others to appreciate the frustration we felt sitting and watching this happen. I had to witness my husband be absolutely torn apart, and I couldn't do anything about it. I wanted to go to the newspapers, but the lawyers and others wouldn't let me. I was furious when Sandy brought home the transcripts of Jack Grubman's correspondence. His conversations with his girlfriend were disgusting, and showed that he was inventing the story to make Sandy look bad in order to impress her. Everyone in the attorney general's office had to know that. Worse, someone leaked it to a reporter named Charles Gasparino at *The Wall Street Journal*. The newspaper had a field day impugning Sandy's reputation but never reported the context behind the claims.

Somehow, Sandy managed to get through this harsh period. After the initial surprise, he put his head down and focused on finding a solution. Despite the stress, he lost a lot of weight—about thirty pounds. In truth, his doctor said something which scared the daylights out of him. Whatever the true motivation, Sandy turned his diet into a positive. It became a challenge, and Sandy is competitive that way. "I'm getting into my Spitzer fighting weight," he'd joke.

When the crisis ended, Sandy moved on his succession. He did not want people to feel that he was leaving because of Spitzer—that's why he waited several months after the settlement. We knew some people were going to blame it on Spitzer anyway, but that's not what happened. He had been thinking about retiring for a while, and turning seventy focused him on the fact that he didn't want the responsibility anymore.

SANDY AND HIS PROTÉGÉS

Talk about Sandy's protégés, Peter Cohen and Jamie Dimon. How would you compare and contrast Sandy's relationship with each?

Sandy had a mentoring-related issue with both Peter and Jamie. He gave a lot of responsibility to each at an early age. The problem was that Sandy was too young to step aside. So in both instances, the mentoree couldn't get past the mentor. That proved a huge problem for these very intelligent aggressive young men. And there came a point of psychological conflict. It isn't just that they wanted more responsibility. They also wanted the recognition that they felt they deserved. They had grown up and wanted space of their own. Unfortunately, they didn't know how to separate.

Sandy has a strong personality, and things always revolved around him. That didn't help matters. Yet it's also important to understand that Sandy never wanted to be surrounded by yes-men. He liked that Peter and Jamie would challenge him and never minded a well-reasoned argument. By tolerating dissent, Sandy may have disproportionately raised their sense of self-worth.

What could Sandy have done differently to have better managed his relationships with Peter and Jamie?

With Peter, the politics of American Express got in the way. Some people handle that sort of thing better than others. Jim Robinson seemed to pursue a divide-and-conquer strategy, and influenced Peter to sacrifice his loyalty to Sandy. Meanwhile, Peter and his wife got enamored with a certain lifestyle, which added to the problem. You can't change people's personalities, and I'm not sure Sandy could have done anything else to reach a different outcome.

Sandy's decision to give up responsibility for Shearson was a huge mistake. It was a green light for Peter to undermine him. This was the one time I told him I disagreed with a business decision that he made. I was very upset that he had chosen to give up his power base. I didn't trust Peter at that point. Sandy, though, felt it was something he had to do if he were to be made president of American Express.

Jamie was a very different story. We were close friends with his parents, having first met at a Shearson convention—Jamie's father, Ted, worked in the company as a broker. Jamie's mother, Themis, and I went to the New School together and became best friends. Our fondness for one another soon extended to our families. We frequently had dinners together with all the kids. Jessica, Marc, and Jamie were very close. Jamie started working with Sandy right out of school, and the two were inseparable for many years. Sadly, the relationship went off course. It wasn't all Sandy's fault, or Jamie's either. It's hard to pull out all the threads of what went wrong. It was a combination of circumstances including the fact that the company was getting bigger. Having Marc and Jessica working in the company didn't help matters, and Jamie's growing confidence was an ongoing issue. There's a reason why people like Frank Zarb and Bob Greenhill left the company. They all complained about Jamie being headstrong. Friends kept reminding Sandy that he had promoted Jamie too quickly and raised his expectations.

As their relationship deteriorated, Sandy tried to face the problem. He and I both had long heartfelt conversations with Jamie and his wife to try to address the issues. Unfortunately, it was too little, too late. Sandy should have confronted Jamie sooner.

How important was Jamie's treatment of Jessica in explaining why the relationship between Sandy and Jamie fell apart?

Sandy's big issue was that Jamie was not sharing information with him. He kept telling me that Jamie was driving him crazy by not being open. Jamie certainly didn't help matters with the way he treated Jessica, but Sandy would say the problem in their relationship predated the events which impacted Jessica. Even so, Sandy felt deeply conflicted when the problems arose. He needed to separate out being a father and look at things as CEO.

People may not realize how difficult that was for Sandy. He understood that he was CEO of a public company and that he had to place the company's interests first. That was a terrible position to be in because he was also a father who loved his daughter very much and was distressed by the way Jamie treated Jessica. What's more, Jessica did an outstanding job at the company and was well liked.

SANDY'S STRENGTHS AND WEAKNESSES

What personality traits do you think differentiate Sandy from other businesspeople and best explain his success?

Sandy is vulnerable, but he hides it well. Unfortunately, people usually don't understand this side of him. Early in his career, he would stay up all night worrying that he was going to lose money for his clients. He's also very loyal. For instance, when he had to tell Mike Carpenter that he wouldn't be running Smith Barney anymore, he tortured himself over how he'd convey the news. I think all of his worrying caught up with him and that's why he got tired of being CEO.

Some people have tried to play up Sandy's insecurities. I think that point of view has been overdone, but he and I both share some sense that we can't take our good fortune for granted. Sandy occasionally spoke about his wish to become part of the establishment. If you are the most secure person in the world, you probably don't need that sort of affirmation. Don't forget, though, that it was sort of a fluke the way he started in business and that he got into the business at all since he had absolutely the wrong background for it.

There are other traits that explain his success. He's very smart, and being intelligent certainly helps in any business. He has always had a good feel or intuition for what's happening in the world and how events might affect the business. He can integrate a lot of information very well, and he's incredibly observant. I call him a "pragmatic dreamer." In other words, he focuses on the big picture and dreams big but in a very practical way. Lastly, his relationships and the way he relates to people represent important strengths. His employees loved him. They can laugh and say he yelled too much, but they loved him because they knew he was warm and that he listened.

What are his negatives?

He's self-centered and controlling. He also can be a real pain in the neck. There are two sides to every coin. He's a very demanding person, yet he expects of himself what he asks from others. Just look at the way he worked hard, had endless numbers of meetings, traveled constantly, and spent nearly every weekend thinking about the business. When he worked on a deal, he'd be at it twenty-four hours a day. He'd stay up with the lawyers until three in the morning. He'd do whatever was necessary to make the business a success.

Sometimes he'd stay loyal for too long. He has tended to fall in love with certain colleagues, but sometimes he wouldn't fall *out of love* fast enough. I once asked Sandy what he thought was his biggest fault.

"Sometimes I'm loyal to the point where it's a mistake," he said. In those instances and on other occasions, he had trouble confronting people and delivering bad news.

GIVING BACK

Explain what you look for before supporting a philanthropic institution. In other words, how do you pick your spots and how do you make a difference?

I love the challenge of building up an organization and making its value more widely known. Citymeals-on-Wheels was the first organization in which I became seriously involved. In the early 1980s, it was barely a year old, and because of that, I felt I could make a difference. I was close to my grandfather growing up, and that's probably why I've always felt good about helping elderly people. Also, my father was alive when I was involved with Citymeals. Although he didn't have a lot of money, he gave me a lot of good ideas and taught the importance of giving back.

I later became involved with another social service organization called Women in Need, which helps battered and abused women, while Sandy concentrated on the National Academy, Carnegie Hall, and Cornell's medical college. Sandy used to joke, "You cover the streets, and I cover culture."

Several years ago, I was introduced to Alvin Ailey and immediately fell in love with the organization. It brought all my interests together, particularly my love of dance and my commitment to social services work. I saw Judith Jamison (now Ailey's artistic director) dance when I was a kid and admired her grace and artistry. Apart from its performance calendar, Ailey runs a camp for inner-city children and does wonderful outreach to the community and to public schools. I jumped at the invitation to join Ailey's board, and Judith and I soon became close friends. After six years, I was asked to chair the board of trustees. That scared me initially since I wasn't sure I'd be up to the task, but many people reassured me. It's proven one of the great experiences of my life and has since inspired me to take on additional leadership roles at Paul Smith's College and the White Nights Foundation of America.

Sandy, in particular, encouraged me. I've learned from him that you have to have a can-do attitude and persevere. It's also critical to line up funding if an organization is serious about accomplishing anything. When Sandy and I choose an organization, we become deeply involved and enjoy rolling up our sleeves so that we might offer more than just financial support. If we are going to ask friends for contributions, we need to be one hundred percent committed ourselves and be sure that the money is going to the right place and being used appropriately.

There's an important lesson here. You can't do any not-for-profit work unless you have a passion for it. I've been on boards in a more passive capacity and often thought, "What am I doing here?" You have to like the people that you work with, and your heart has to be in it. Once you have that on your side, the experience can be wonderful.

LESSONS FOR THE CORPORATE SPOUSE

How did you influence the corporate culture which took hold in the business over the years?

Almost from the start, we had a way of integrating spouses. It was Sandy's idea. When he hired people, he wanted to meet the "other half." The company originally was very small, and everyone had a lot to do with one another. The senior people in the company weren't just colleagues; they were our friends. Sandy liked the idea that one's spouse should know about the business and what his or her partner was dealing with at work. He argued that the more support one had at home the more it helped one's performance in the office.

We soon had a lot of spouses coming to the conventions we held for our brokers. In those early years, I resented that the company would send the wives off to a "spouses' program" where someone would talk about how to color your hair right or something silly like that. That's when we came up with the idea of a different sort of spouse breakfast where Sandy would talk seriously about trends in the business and then answer questions. The format respected everyone's intelligence, and that session soon became a big hit at each conference.

When we merged with both American Express and Citicorp, these companies didn't routinely include spouses in company meetings. Even worse, American Express would hold meetings over holiday weekends without including wives. Sandy immediately forced a change in that culture. We both worked hard to make these events more personal. It wasn't hard, and the spouses were so appreciative. With Citigroup, we made a point to meet with small groups of employees and their husbands and wives. As we traveled more, I especially enjoyed meeting our new colleagues and their spouses. It made a large company feel much more manageable.

Is there a lesson that spouses of other business leaders can learn from your experience?

Yes, there's a very important lesson. It's that there is a thin line that you can't go over when you are the spouse of a CEO. There is only one boss, and the spouse is not part of that job. I've seen a lot of people in business make this mistake. I never wanted to be in that position. That's why I didn't like it when people suggested that I "interview people" for Sandy. I didn't do that, and I didn't make the business decisions. Rather, I saw myself as a sounding board for my husband with the wherewithal to argue the other side of an issue if he wanted that. In any company, there's only one CEO, and any spouse who forgets that will get into big trouble.

It's also important not to let success go to your head and to keep a sense of humor and balance. While Sandy and I have enjoyed good fortune, I've always felt a sense of vulnerability that it could all suddenly disappear. I've always enjoyed interacting with people and don't believe in allowing one's social standing to determine one's friendships.

Sandy made plenty of tough decisions over his career. Were there certain ones in which you were especially involved?

I don't think you can boil it down to specific things so easily. It was more important that I was there and able to observe events and people enough to have some knowledge of who or what he was talking about. As I said, Sandy and I were careful that I shouldn't interfere with how decisions were made. I saw my role as bringing him some rational thinking when he was upset over something or needed extra advice.

There was one big decision, though, in which I was very involved: when Sandy decided it was time to pick his successor and announce his retirement. That was *major*. This was one of his most important decisions ever, and we discussed it a lot.

How hard was the decision to retire? What's it like living with Sandy now that he's retired?

I'm still trying to help him with this retirement thing. It's an ongoing process. I'm concerned about what he'll feel when he gives up being chairman. That's symbolic and very important because he will no longer have as close a connection to the company. I'm really worried about that. I've been spending a lot of time trying to talk Sandy through this so that when it happens it won't be a complete shock.

I think he would feel more upbeat if the company was consistently doing better. Some things there have been driving him crazy. I keep reminding him that it's a different era.

Sandy has recently started to see a professional to help him deal with all this change in his life. He says seeing a psychiatrist is making him "a better person." It's the funniest thing he's ever done. I hope the therapist will help. I'm counting on him! Sandy keeps saying to me, "I want *you* to go. I have nothing more to talk about." To his disappointment, though, I tell him, "No, I'm not going. This is all yours." It's probably a good thing for him. He worked all his life, and all of a sudden, everything has changed. As with so many other occasions, this is proving to be one more big drama. With Sandy, there's never a dull moment!

Appendix

MY FIRST ACT

Key Events: From Starting My Business through My Years at American Express

May 1960	Carter, Berlind, Patoma & Weill opens with an initial investment of $250,000 and annualized revenues of $400,000. Initial focus: retail securities and investment banking
1963–64	Entered the institutional securities business
1967	Our first acquisition: Bernstein-Macaulay; with the deal, we entered the asset management business
September 1968	Arthur Carter resigned; name changed to Cogan, Berlind, Weill & Levitt
1969	Established our own back office
September 1970	Acquired Hayden Stone assets and adopted CBWL–Hayden Stone name

September 1971	Initial Public Offering of CBWL–Hayden Stone; raised $12.5 million; initial public market value: $30 million
1971	Revenues reached $45 million and net income exceeded $3 million
August 1973	Acquired H. Hentz & Company, which doubled the number of our offices and increased revenues by 50%; I became CEO
May 1974	Acquired Shearson Hamill for $343 million in stock plus warrants; revenues more than doubled to $150 million; retail network topped 1,500 brokers; name changed to Shearson Hayden Stone
May 1975	"May Day": We came through commission deregulation relatively unscathed
August 1977	Acquired Faulkner Dawkins in order to boost our institutional business
May 1979	Acquired Loeb Rhoades Hornblower & Company for $85 million; the transaction brought 160 offices and 1,800 brokers, doubling our size
November 1979	Name changed to Shearson Loeb Rhoades
1980	Revenues topped $650 million and profits reached a record $55 million, surging more than fivefold in two years
April 1981	Sold Shearson Loeb Rhoades to American Express; transaction value approximated $1 billion (a healthy return on our initial $250,000 investment!)
January 1983	I became president of American Express
1983–85	I was increasingly disillusioned by my lack of authority
June 1985	I resigned from American Express

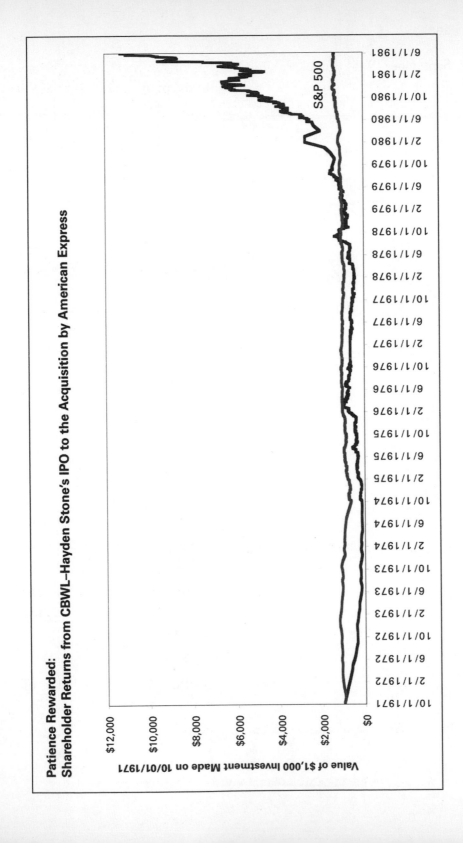

Patience Rewarded:
Shareholder Returns from CBWL–Hayden Stone's IPO to the Acquisition by American Express

Value of $1,000 Investment Made on 10/01/1971

S&P 500

$0
$2,000
$4,000
$6,000
$8,000
$10,000
$12,000

10/1/1971
2/1/1972
6/1/1972
10/1/1972
2/1/1973
6/1/1973
10/1/1973
2/1/1974
6/1/1974
10/1/1974
2/1/1975
6/1/1975
10/1/1975
2/1/1976
6/1/1976
10/1/1976
2/1/1977
6/1/1977
10/1/1977
2/1/1978
6/1/1978
10/1/1978
2/1/1979
6/1/1979
10/1/1979
2/1/1980
6/1/1980
10/1/1980
2/1/1981
6/1/1981

THE EVOLUTION OF CITIGROUP

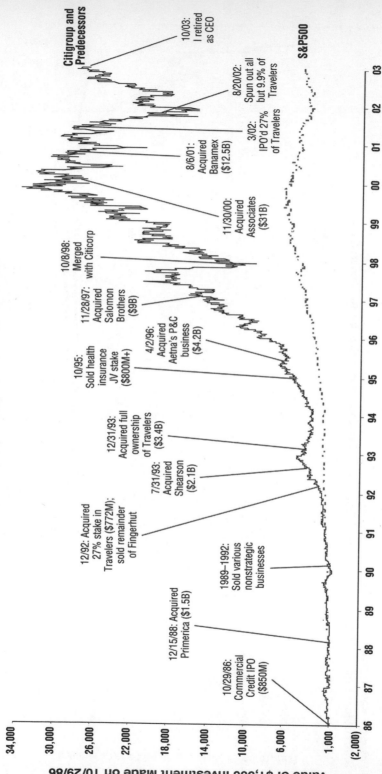

Value of $1,000 Investment Made on 10/29/86

Citigroup and Predecessors

S&P500

10/29/86: Commercial Credit IPO ($850M)

12/15/88: Acquired Primerica ($1.5B)

1989–1992: Sold various nonstrategic businesses

12/92: Acquired 27% stake in Travelers ($772M); sold remainder of Fingerhut

7/31/93: Acquired Shearson ($2.1B)

12/31/93: Acquired full ownership of Travelers ($3.4B)

10/95: Sold health insurance JV stake ($800M+)

4/2/96: Acquired Aetna's P&C business ($4.2B)

11/28/97: Acquired Salomon Brothers ($9B)

10/8/98: Merged with Citicorp

11/30/00: Acquired Associates ($31B)

8/6/01: Acquired Banamex ($12.5B)

3/02: IPO'd 27% of Travelers

8/20/02: Spun out all but 9.9% of Travelers

10/03: I retired as CEO

	86	87	88	89	90	91	92	93	94	95	96	97	98	99	00	01	02	03
Market Value ($ Bil)†	1,058	943	2,088	3,153	2,476	4,277	5,369	12,719	10,248	19,806	28,933	61,696	112,199	187,537	256,435	259,906	180,901	250,318
Assets ($ Bil)*	4.8	4.3	14.4	18.0	19.7	21.6	23.4	101.4	115.3	114.5	151.1	386.6	668.6	716.9	902.2	1,051.5	1,097.2	1,264.0
Revenues ($ Bil)*	1.0	0.9	1.0	5.7	6.2	6.6	5.1	6.8	18.5	16.6	21.3	37.6	76.4	82.0	111.8	112.0	71.3	77.4
Net Income ($ Mil)*	45.9	23.7	161.8	289	373	479	728	916	1,326	1,834	2,331	3,104	5,807	9,867	13,519	14,126	15,276	17,853
EPS†	0.07	0.05	0.14	0.22	0.29	0.37	0.55	0.47	0.70	0.97	1.22	1.36	1.29	2.20	2.69	2.74	2.97	3.46

Businesses Added

86
- Consumer finance
- Specialty finance

88
- Securities brokerage
- Investment banking
- Life insurance
- Asset management & mutual funds
- P&C insurance

93
- Retail securities (bolstered)
- Investment banking (bolstered)
- Mutual funds (bolstered)
- Full range of personal & commercial insurance
- Proprietary investments

96
- P&C business (bolstered)

97
- Int'l corporate finance
- Prop. trading
- Inv. banking (bolstered)
- Inst. securities (bolstered)

98
- Global corporate lending
- Global payments & securities services
- Int'l consumer
- Branch banking
- Mortgage banking
- Credit cards (bolstered)
- Asset mgmt (bolstered)
- Proprietary investments (bolstered)
- Global fixed income/derivatives (bolstered)

00
- Int'l consumer finance

01
- Mexican franchise (bolstered)

*Except for EPS, financial results are as originally reported.
†Split adjusted.

Taking stock of the creation of Citigroup: Each of our major deals improved our brand and the value we created for our shareholders. (Courtesy of Citigroup company archives)

Acknowledgments

More than seventy years is a long time to remember, but thankfully many friends and colleagues (the latter are usually my friends, too!) shared their memories and thereby helped me recall the major events of my life. I would like to thank everyone who took time out of their busy lives to help bring this book to life.

This book was researched in stages, so let me divide my thanks similarly into a few parts. Beginning with my childhood and adolescence, I first have to thank my sister, Helen Saffer, who shared many memories of our years growing up together and of our immediate and extended family. I also appreciate the help of Stu Fendler and Lenny Zucker, respectively my old roommates from military school and Cornell.

I am indebted to a far longer list of people who helped jog my memory on the years from 1960 to 1981, the period in which I launched my first partnership, built it into an industry power, and sold it to American Express. My relationship with my original partners, Arthur Carter, Roger Berlind, and Arthur Levitt, was always spirited, and I'm thankful that each spoke freely about our years building our company together. I also appreciate the help we received from: Peter Cohen, Wick Simmons, Duke Chapman, Herb Khaner, Bob Biggar, Harvey Krueger, Fred Joseph, Don Shagrin, Billy Mathis, George Murray, Clarence Jones, Mark Kaplan, Tony Fedele, and Barbara Kullen.

My years at American Express and the months that followed provided some of my most difficult memories given my frustrations during much of this period. I'm usually good about blocking out less than favorable events, so the recollections of many friends and colleagues in this period were especially helpful. I wish to thank Jim Robinson, John Burns, George Sheinberg, Howard Clark Jr., Allison McElvery, Warren Hellman, and—once more—Peter Cohen.

Between 1986 and 2003, I had the good fortune to take a sleepy finance company in Baltimore named Commercial Credit and transform it into the world's leading financial services powerhouse, Citigroup. These years were particularly busy ones, and I relied on an especially long list of people to help me refocus on the events of those years. Of course, I must first recognize those with whom I shared an especially close and long-standing relationship: Chuck Prince, Bob Lipp, Marge Magner, Bob Willumstad, Marty Lipton, and Gershon Kekst. These individuals and I rode the rapids together over many years and through many challenges and successes—their stories were especially fun to hear as we worked on this book.

I also thank Tom Maheras, Deryck Maughan, Mike Carpenter, Todd Thomson, Jay Fishman, Barbara Yastine, Jim Calvano, Heidi Miller, Don Cooper, Charlie Scharff, Jay Mandelbaum, Ed Budd, Steve Kittenplan, Michael Klein, Rick Roesch, Sheri Ptashek, John Reed, Mike Masin, Andy Pearson, Charlie Long, Victor Menezes, Bob Rubin, Paul Collins, Dick Parsons, Frank Thomas, Reuben Mark, Bill Campbell, Jack Morris, Jane Sherburne, Stephanie Mudick, Michael Schlein, Joan Guggenheimer, Lewis Liman, Sallie Krawcheck, Larry Pedowitz, Mark Pomerantz, Robert Volland, John Fowler, Pete Dawkins, and Bill Pike.

In the part of my life which I have spent in the philanthropic world, there are still others to thank: Klaus Jacobs, Hollis Hedrick, Dick Debs, and Jay Golan of Carnegie Hall; John Farrandino and Eugene Ludwig from the National Academy Foundation; and Tony Gotto and Hunter Rawlings of Cornell. I also thank Sharon Luckman, who helped Judah understand my wife's impact on Alvin Ailey.

Categorizing one's thanks is impossible in many instances since I have shared particularly long-lasting friendships with a great number of people. In this vein, I'd like to thank President Gerald Ford, Bobby Druskin, Jeff Lane, Mary McDermott, Mike Panitch, Harvey Golub, Frank Zarb, Joe Plumeri, Jamie Dimon, and Bob Greenhill for digging deep and recalling stories that spanned many years.

Key members of my office staff, too, have been indispensable and consistently supportive for a very long time. I especially thank my loyal and hard-working administrative assistant, Connie Garone, as well as Corny Leo and Ann-Marie Vizzini.

My two closest friends, Kenny Bialkin and Arthur Zankel, deserve special mention. I had the great fortune to meet each of these exceptional individuals early in my professional life, and they stood by me as the years turned into decades. Kenny's incisive legal observations and advice were the best any executive could have hoped for and nearly always came at just the right time. Arthur, meanwhile, had one of the sharpest business minds of anyone I've ever met and helped me enormously on a wide variety of issues. His untimely death in 2005 shook me deeply, and it's hard to believe he's really gone. I'm grateful to have benefited from his input on this book prior to his death. Good businesspeople need able advisors, and Kenny and Arthur were simply the best.

I save the most important thanks for last: the appreciation I owe to my family. Marc and Jessica readily offered their comments as the book took shape and helped Judah understand many of the nuances of my character and family life. Meanwhile, my grandchildren, Tommy, David, Laurel, and Matt, light up my life and gave me extra inspiration as I considered my life's accomplishments and legacy.

It is my wife, Joanie, however, whom I can never thank enough. Far beyond her help with this book, I owe to her nearly everything of importance which I have achieved in my life. Joanie has stood by me through thick and thin. All my successes over the years tasted sweeter because she was at my side, while the setbacks somehow didn't seem so bad with her there to console me. Being married for more than fifty years has taught me the essential importance of teamwork and commitment. Life is great when you have the perfect partner.

From Judah . . .

Writing this book proved to be the experience of a lifetime. It brought me in contact with many fascinating people; it was fun; and it taught me a great deal about the business world, the financial services industry, and what it takes to be a great business leader. I add my thanks to the people cited by Sandy for helping make this an experience I'll always treasure. I also single out Joan and thank her especially for her warm personality, her gracious hospitality, and her enduring patience. And of course, I thank Sandy for not taking no for an answer and for stubbornly insisting that I was the one to help him tell his story.

Sandy and I also recognize that this book might never have been written were it not for our agent, David Black, and Larry Kirshbaum, former chairman of Time Warner Book Group. David repeatedly demonstrated tenacity, creativity, and discipline befitting a great agent. Larry's passion for this book shone forth from the moment we met, and he spent countless hours advising on the manuscript.

We also express our gratitude to Salli Schwartz, who worked diligently as our research assistant and who took considerable time away from her business school studies to refresh our memories regarding a slew of historical market-related events.

Finally, I have a few words for my loving family. Michele: You are my life and the source of all my inspiration. Thank you for believing in me and for reading, rereading, and giving editorial advice on chapters from early in the morning to late at night. I also thank my kids for putting up with me during my many nights working in my office. Liana, Elias, and Sofia: You are full of spirit; you energize me; and you make my life wonderful!

Index